The COLLECTOR'S Anthology

Globe Book Company, Inc.
New York / Cleveland / Toronto

The COLLECTOR'S Anthology

Robert R. Potter
Ruth D. McCubbrey

Robert R. Potter received his B.S. from the Columbia University School of General Studies and his M.A. and Ed.D. from Teachers College, Columbia University.

Dr. Potter has been a teacher of English in the New York City School System, a research associate for Project English at Hunter College, and a teacher of English at the Litchfield (Conn.) High School. He has held professorships at the State University of New York and at the University of Connecticut.

Dr. Potter is the author of Globe's *Myths and Folktales Around the World, The Reading Road to Writing, Making Sense, A Better Reading Workshop, Writing Sense, Writing a Research Paper, Language Workshop, Tales of Mystery and the Unknown, The Reader's Anthology, The American Anthology,* and the co-author of *The World Anthology.*

Ruth McCubbrey received her B.A. in English from the University of Washington and her M.A. in English Literature from Dominican College of San Rafael, California.

Ms. McCubbrey has been teaching English and critical thinking at Tamalpais High School in Mill Valley for the past 20 years. She is on the Board of Directors of the International Society for General Semantics. Ms. McCubbrey has led workshops for high school and college teachers in the field of general semantics and critical thinking, and she has been involved in the Bay Area Writing Project.

Ms. McCubbrey has had articles published in *Classroom Exercises in General Semantics* and in *Et Cetera,* the general semantics journal.

Consultants

Ronald L. Gearring, Teacher of English Evanston Township High School, Evanston, Illinois

Ruth E. Joseph, Teacher of English New Rochelle City School District, New Rochelle, New York

John S. Simmons, Professor of English Education and Reading Florida State University, Tallahassee, Florida, and Chairman, International Assembly on Teaching of English, NCTE

Editor: Carol Callahan
Photo Editor: Adelaide Garvin Ungerland
Cover Design: Bass and Goldman Associates
Text Design: Celine Brandes

Acknowledgments and credits appear on pages 400–403.

ISBN: 0-87065-302-4

CONTENTS

UNIT 1:   GETTING THE PICTURE

UNIT 2: DISCOVERING DIFFERENCES

UNIT 3: CHANGE

U N I T 4:   SOME MATTERS OF JUDGMENT

UNIT 5: MENTAL MAGIC

SKILL DEVELOPMENT

INTRODUCTION

At first glance, the title of this book may seem repetitive since any anthology is a collection of readings. The word *anthology* means "collection." Think carefully about the word *collector's*, though. A collector searches, finds, judges, compares, and finally keeps only the very best. That's what this book offers you: the very best.

This anthology contains both classical literature that has stood the test of time and selections by modern writers. It offers questions that test comprehension and recall. It challenges you with writing opportunities that will increase your powers of inquiry and your clarity of expression. It also focuses on critical reading and thinking. Instead of learning to read, you'll find you're reading to learn.

What is critical reading? It is critical thinking applied to written material. When you read critically, you go beyond understanding and recall of what is on the printed page. You *do* something with the written material. You *apply* your new knowledge to fields outside the book. You *analyze* characters' reactions and behavior. You *evaluate* your own opinions and judgments to determine whether they are sound or shaky. Finally, you *utilize* insights gained from the reading to take a look at your own life.

About 200 years ago, the English poet William Blake wrote:

> The fool sees not the same tree
> that the wise man sees

Think critically about that. *Apply* Blake's statement to something you've observed recently. *Analyze* the reasons for different reactions to a tree or to anything else. *Evaluate* the advantages of each reaction. *Utilize* Blake's insight to consider how you might see the tree—or the story, or the poem. For just as no two people see the "same" tree, no two readers read the "same" story or poem. Literature is your experience with what you read.

As you read the pages that follow, try to become a collector yourself. In other words, *search, find, judge,* and *compare—apply, analyze, evaluate,* and *utilize*—and keep only the very best!

U N I T · 1

GETTING THE PICTURE

Oh, now I get the picture!

So that's how it is!

Wow, was I caught off base!

I'll never trust first impressions again!

People make statements like these every day—you probably say similar things yourself. You think you understand something, but then the true picture pops into your mind. First impressions fade as reality comes into focus. You shake your head in wonder: "I was blind, but now I see."

Through literature, you can respond to the feelings and actions—and to the virtures and vices—of story characters as they cope with the world in the story. For example, in this unit you'll read about characters whose hopes, opinions, fears, and selfish desires make them incapable of "getting the picture." In Chaucer's famous "Pardoner's Tale," for instance, the demon Greed blinds the characters to true pictures of one another—with fatal results.

Of course, reading about the characters' lives will also encourage you to think about your own life. Get into the picture yourself by reading the first selection now.

CEMETERY PATH

by Leonard Q. Ross

▶ It was a dark and stormy night . . .

Ivan was a timid little man—so timid that the villagers called him "Pigeon" or mocked him with the title "Ivan the Terrible." Every night Ivan stopped in at the saloon on the edge of the village cemetery. Ivan never crossed the cemetery to get to his lonely shack on the other side. The path through the cemetery would save him many minutes, but Ivan had never taken it—not even in the full light of the moon.

Late one winter's night, when a bitter wind and snow beat against the village saloon, the customers took up their familiar mockery of Ivan. His mild protests only fed their taunts, and they laughed when a young Cossack lieutenant flung a challenge at their quarry. "You are a pigeon, Ivan. A rabbit. A coward. You'll walk all around the cemetery in this dreadful cold, to get home, but you dare not cross the cemetery."

Ivan murmured, "The cemetery—it is nothing to cross, Lieutenant. I am not afraid. The cemetery is nothing but earth."

The lieutenant cried, "A challenge, then! Cross the cemetery tonight, Ivan, now, and I'll give you five gold rubles—five gold rubles!"

Perhaps it was the vodka. Perhaps it was the temptation of the five gold rubles. No one ever knew why Ivan, moistening his lips, blurted: "All right, Lieutenant, I'll cross the cemetery!"

As the saloon echoed with the villagers' derision and disbelief, the lieutenant winked to the others and unbuckled his saber. "Here, Ivan. Prove yourself. When you get to the very center of the cemetery, in front of the biggest tomb, stick my saber into the ground! In the morning we shall go there. And if the saber is in the ground— five gold rubles to you!"

Slowly Ivan took the saber. The villagers drank a toast: "To Ivan the Hero! Ivan the Terrible!" They roared with laughter.

The wind howled around Ivan as he closed the door of the

- **taunt** (TAWNT) jeer at; insult; challenge in a rude way
- Cossack (KOS ak) **one of a group of horsemen in precommunist Russia**
- quarry (KWOR ee) **hunted or attacked creature**
- **ruble** (ROO bul) **unit of Russian money**
- derision (dih RIZH un) **scorn; mockery; rude laughter**

saloon behind him. The cold was as sharp as a butcher's knife. He buttoned his long coat and crossed the dirt road. He could hear the lieutenant's voice, louder than the rest, calling after him, "Five rubles, little pigeon! Five rubles—if you live!"

Ivan strode to the cemetery gates, and hesitated, and pushed the gate open.

He walked fast. "Earth, it's just earth . . . like any other earth." But the darkness was a massive dread. "Five gold rubles. . . ." The wind was savage, and the saber was like ice in his hands. Ivan shivered under the long, thick coat and broke into a limping run.

He recognized the large tomb. No one could miss that huge edifice. Ivan must have sobbed—but that was drowned in the wind. And Ivan kneeled, cold and terrified, and in a frenzy of fear drove the saber into the hard ground. It was hard to do, but he beat it down into the hard earth with his fist, down to the very hilt. It was done! The cemetery . . . the challenge . . . five rubles . . . five gold rubles!

Ivan started to rise from his knees. But he could not move. Something was holding him! He strained to rise again. But something gripped him in an unyielding, implacable hold. Ivan swore and tugged and lurched and pulled—gasping in his panic, sweating despite the knife-edged cold, shaken by fear. But something held Ivan.

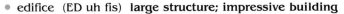

- edifice (ED uh fis) **large structure; impressive building**
- frenzy (FREN zee) **great excitement**
- implacable (im PLAK uh bul) **merciless; relentless**

3

He cried out in terror and strained against the unseen imprisonment, and he tried to rise, using all his strength. But he could not rise.

They found Ivan, the next morning, on the ground right in front of the great tomb that was in the very center of the cemetery. His face was not that of a frozen man, but of a man slain by some nameless horror. And the lieutenant's saber was in the ground where Ivan had pounded it—through the dragging folds of his long and shabby coat.

ALL THINGS CONSIDERED

1. At the beginning of the story, Ivan is used to (a) being teased. (b) crossing the cemetery. (c) performing brave deeds.
2. One of the reasons Ivan accepts the lieutenant's challenge is (a) his patriotism. (b) his sense of humor. (c) the five gold rubles.
3. As a challenge, Ivan is told to stick a saber (a) in front of the biggest cemetery tomb. (b) near the cemetery exit. (c) in the ground anywhere in the cemetery.
4. Near the end of the story, Ivan (a) panics and runs. (b) does just what the lieutenant had requested. (c) finds the lieutenant's challenge impossible.
5. Ivan is actually killed by (a) the saber. (b) his own terror. (c) the lieutenant.

THINKING IT THROUGH

1. If you can name the country in which the story happens, you are making an **inference** (a guess based on the available evidence). What is the country? Why do you think so?
2. Now make another inference: Approximately when does the story take place? Today? A hundred years ago? Explain the reasons for your guess or inference.
3. The **setting** of a story includes the *place,* the *time,* and certain *natural events,* such as the weather. You have already inferred the place and time. (a) What natural events are mentioned in the story? (b) How do they make the story more believable and add to the horror?
4. Stories that end in a tragic death are usually sad. Yet this one is not sad—in fact many readers smile as they read the last sentence. Try to explain why.

Critical Thinking

Maps and Territories

In real life, you use maps to try to picture places, or territories. The maps, if they are accurate, show the relationship of places to one another. For example, a good road map ought to indicate how many miles it is from one place to another and show their locations. Maps represent the territories—they are *not* the territories themselves.

People's thinking can be compared to maps and territories. **Mental maps** include people's impressions and thoughts about the world around them, other people, and themselves. The **territories** include what the world *really* is and what the people are *really* like. People can only interpret what they see, feel, read about, and hear from others. But the mind plays tricks on people. Sometimes people confuse their mental maps with the real world!

Writers use this idea of maps and territories to develop story characters.

Some characters have faulty mental maps. For example, Ivan has an incorrect impression of his situation after he sticks the saber into the ground.

Here are four events from "Cemetery Path." Put yourself in the place of the character(s) mentioned. Answer each question about the mental map.

1. The villagers share a common mental map of Ivan. Tell how they "see" him.
2. What kind of map does Ivan seem to have of himself when he says, "I am not afraid"?
3. What map is the young Cossack lieutenant trying to pass along when he winks at the other customers and gives Ivan the saber?
4. When Ivan says to himself, "Earth, it's just earth . . . like any other earth," what map is he trying to create in his mind?

Composition

1. "Ivan has an incorrect impression of his situation after he sticks the saber into the ground." In a few sentences, explain this statement in terms of Ivan's maps (his impressions) and territories (the real situation).

2. Everyone has made mistakes caused by faulty mental maps. For instance, a man was driving down a country road on a snowy night. Far ahead, the lights of a "car" appeared. The "car" seemed to race toward him at a terrific speed. Panic stricken, the man jammed on his brakes and skidded into a ditch. Soon all was explained. The man's mental map of a "car" was actually two snowmobiles, side by side. The man had interpreted their two lights drifting apart as rapid forward speed.

   Think of a time when a faulty mental map of a situation got you into trouble. Explain in detail.

LONG WALK TO FOREVER

by Kurt Vonnegut, Jr.

▶ Catharine looked into Newt's eyes, and she realized how wrong she'd been. It's hard to hide your mental maps from someone else—especially from someone you love.

They had grown up next door to each other, on the fringe of a city, near fields and woods and orchards, within sight of a lovely bell tower that belonged to a school for the blind.

Now they were twenty, had not seen each other for nearly a year. There had always been playful, comfortable warmth between them, but never any talk of love.

His name was Newt. Her name was Catharine. In the early afternoon, Newt knocked on Catharine's front door.

Catharine came to the door. She was carrying a fat, glossy magazine she had been reading. The magazine was devoted entirely to brides. "Newt!" she said. She was surprised to see him.

6

"Could you come for a walk?" he said. He was a shy person, even with Catharine. He covered his shyness by speaking absently, as though what really concerned him were far away—as though he were a secret agent pausing briefly on a mission between beautiful, distant, and sinister points. This manner of speaking had always been Newt's style, even in matters that concerned him desperately.

"A walk?" said Catharine.

"One foot in front of the other," said Newt, "through leaves, over bridges——"

"I had no idea you were in town," she said.

"Just this minute got in," he said.

"Still in the Army, I see," she said.

"Seven more months to go," he said. He was a private first class in the Artillery. His uniform was rumpled. His shoes were dusty. He needed a shave. He held out his hand for the magazine. "Let's see the pretty book," he said.

She gave it to him. "I'm getting married, Newt," she said.

"I know," he said. "Let's go for a walk."

"I'm awfully busy, Newt," she said. "The wedding is only a week away."

"If we go for a walk," he said, "it will make you rosy. It will make you a rosy bride." He turned the pages of the magazine. "A rosy bride like her—like her—like her," he said, showing her rosy brides.

Catharine turned rosy, thinking about rosy brides.

"That will be my present to Henry Stewart Chasens," said Newt. "By taking you for a walk, I'll be giving him a rosy bride."

"You know his name?" said Catharine.

"Mother wrote," he said. "From Pittsburgh?"

"Yes," she said. "You'd like him."

"Maybe," he said.

"Can—can you come to the wedding, Newt?" she said.

"That I doubt," he said.

"Your furlough isn't for long enough?" she said.

"Furlough?" said Newt. He was studying a two-page ad for flat silver. "I'm not on furlough," he said.

"Oh?" she said.

"I'm what they call A.W.O.L.," said Newt.

"Oh, Newt! You're not!" she said.

"Sure I am," he said, still looking at the magazine.

"Why, Newt?" she said.

"I had to find out what your silver pattern is," he said. He read names of silver patterns from the magazine. "Albemarle? Heather?"

- flat silver—flatware: silver spoons, forks, knives, etc.
- A.W.O.L.—(*often pronounced* AY wawl) Absent Without Official Leave from a military unit

he said. "Legend? Rambler Rose?" He looked up, smiled. "I plan to give you and your husband a spoon," he said.

"Newt, Newt—tell me really," she said.

"I want to go for a walk," he said.

She wrung her hands in sisterly anguish. "Oh, Newt—you're fooling me about being A.W.O.L.," she said.

Newt imitated a police siren softly, raised his eyebrows.

"Where—where from?" she said.

"Fort Bragg," he said.

"North Carolina?" she said.

"That's right," he said. "Near Fayetteville—where Scarlet O'Hara went to school."

"How did you get here, Newt?" she said.

He raised his thumb, jerked it in a hitchhike gesture. "Two days," he said.

"Does your mother know?" she said.

"I didn't come to see my mother," he told her.

"Who did you come to see?" she said.

"You," he said.

"Why me?" she said.

"Because I love you," he said. "Now can we take a walk?" he said. "One foot in front of the other—through leaves, over bridges——"

They were taking the walk now, were in a woods with a brown-leaf floor.

Catharine was angry and rattled, close to tears. "Newt," she said, "this is absolutely crazy."

"How so?" said Newt.

"What a crazy time to tell me you love me," she said. "You never talked that way before." She stopped walking.

"Let's keep walking," he said.

"No," she said. "So far, no farther. I shouldn't have come out with you at all," she said.

"You did," he said.

"To get you out of the house," she said. "If somebody walked in and heard you talking to me that way, a week before the wedding——"

"What would they think?" he said.

"They'd think you were crazy," she said.

"Why?" he said.

Catharine took a deep breath, made a speech. "Let me say that I'm deeply honored by this crazy thing you've done," she said. "I can't believe you're really A.W.O.L., but maybe you are. I can't believe you really love me, but maybe you do. But——"

● **anguish** (ANG gwish) distress; agony

"I do," said Newt.

"Well, I'm deeply honored," said Catharine, "and I'm very fond of you as a friend, Newt, extremely fond—but it's just too late." She took a step away from him. "You've never even kissed me," she said, and she protected herself with her hands. "I don't mean you should do it now. I just mean this is all so unexpected. I haven't got the remotest idea of how to respond."

"Just walk some more," he said. "Have a nice time."

They started walking again.

"How did you expect me to react?" she said.

"How would I know what to expect?" he said. "I've never done anything like this before."

"Did you think I would throw myself into your arms?" she said.

"Maybe," he said.

"I'm sorry to disappoint you," she said.

"I'm not disappointed," he said. "I wasn't counting on it. This is very nice, just walking."

Catharine stopped again. "You know what happens next?" she said.

"Nope," he said.

"We shake hands," she said. "We shake hands and part friends," she said. "That's what happens next."

Newt nodded. "All right," he said. "Remember me from time to time. Remember how much I loved you."

Involuntarily, Catharine burst into tears. She turned her back to Newt, looked into the infinite colonnade of the woods.

"What does that mean?" said Newt.

"Rage!" said Catharine. She clenched her hands. "You have no right——"

"I had to find out," he said.

"If I'd loved you," she said, "I would have let you know before now."

"You would?" he said.

"Yes," she said. She faced him, looked up at him, her face quite red. "You would have known," she said.

"How?" he said.

"You would have seen it," she said. "Women aren't very clever at hiding it."

Newt looked closely at Catharine's face now. To her consternation, she realized that what she had said was true, that a woman couldn't hide love.

Newt was seeing love now.

- **remotest** (ri MOHT est) **slightest; faintest**
- **colonnade** (kol uh NAYD) **rows of columns or trees**
- **consternation** (kon stur NAY shun) **amazement; dismay**

And he did what he had to do. He kissed her.

"You're hell to get along with!" she said when Newt let her go.

"I am?" said Newt.

"You shouldn't have done that," she said.

"You didn't like it?" he said.

"What did you expect," she said—"wild, abandoned passion?"

"I keep telling you," he said, "I never know what's going to happen next."

"We say good-by," she said.

He frowned slightly. "All right," he said.

She made another speech. "I'm not sorry we kissed," she said. "That was sweet. We should have kissed, we've been so close. I'll always remember you, Newt, and good luck."

"You too," he said.

"Thank you, Newt," she said.

"Thirty days," he said.

"What?" she said.

"Thirty days in the stockade," he said—"that's what one kiss will cost me."

"I—I'm sorry," she said, "but I didn't ask you to go A.W.O.L."

"I know," he said.

"You certainly don't deserve any hero's reward for doing something as foolish as that," she said.

"Must be nice to be a hero," said Newt. "Is Henry Stewart Chasens a hero?"

"He might be, if he got the chance," said Catharine. She noted uneasily that they had begun to walk again. The farewell had been forgotten.

"You really love him?" he said.

"Certainly I love him!" she said hotly. "I wouldn't marry him if I didn't love him!"

"What's good about him?" said Newt.

"Honestly!" she cried, stopping again. "Do you have any idea how offensive you're being? Many, many, many things are good about Henry! Yes," she said, "and many, many, many things are probably bad too. But that isn't any of your business. I love Henry, and I don't have to argue his merits with you!"

"Sorry," said Newt.

"Honestly!" said Catharine.

Newt kissed her again. He kissed her again because she wanted him to.

They were now in a large orchard.

"How did we get so far from home, Newt?" said Catharine.

"One foot in front of the other—through leaves, over bridges," said Newt.

● stockade (stok AYD) **military jail**

"They add up—the steps," she said.

Bells rang in the tower of the school for the blind nearby.

"School for the blind," said Newt.

"School for the blind," said Catharine. She shook her head in drowsy wonder. "I've got to go back now," she said.

"Say good-by," said Newt.

"Every time I do," said Catharine, "I seem to get kissed."

Newt sat down on the close-cropped grass under an apple tree. "Sit down," he said.

"No," she said.

"I won't touch you," he said.

"I don't believe you," she said.

She sat down under another tree, twenty feet away from him. She closed her eyes.

"Dream of Henry Stewart Chasens," he said.

"What?" she said.

"Dream of your wonderful husband-to-be," he said.

"All right, I will," she said. She closed her eyes tighter, caught glimpses of her husband-to-be.

Newt yawned.

The bees were humming in the trees, and Catharine almost fell asleep. When she opened her eyes she saw that Newt really was asleep.

He began to snore softly.

Catharine let Newt sleep for an hour, and while he slept she adored him with all her heart.

The shadows of the apple trees grew to the east. The bells in the tower of the school for the blind rang again.

"*Chick-a-dee-dee-dee,*" went a chickadee.

Somewhere far away an automobile starter nagged and failed, nagged and failed, fell still.

Catharine came out from under her tree, knelt by Newt.

"Newt?" she said.

"H'm?" he said. He opened his eyes.

"Late," she said.

"Hello, Catharine," he said.

"Hello, Newt," she said.

"I love you," he said.

"I know," she said.

"Too late," he said.

"Too late," she said.

He stood, stretched groaningly. "A very nice walk," he said.

"I thought so," she said.

"Part company here?" he said.

"Where will you go?" she said.

"Hitch into town, turn myself in," he said.

"Good luck," she said.

"You, too," he said. "Marry me, Catharine?"

"No," she said.

He smiled, stared at her hard for a moment, then walked away quickly.

Catharine watched him grow smaller in the long perspective of shadows and trees, knew that if he stopped and turned now, if he called to her, she would run to him. She would have no choice.

Newt did stop. He did turn. He did call. "Catharine," he called.

She ran to him, put her arms around him, could not speak.

• **perspective** (pur SPEK tiv) **view from a distance**

ALL THINGS CONSIDERED ⎯⎯⎯⎯⎯⎯⎯⎯⎯⎯⎯⎯⎯⎯⎯⎯

1. The best proof of Newt's love for Catharine is that he (a) wants to know her silver pattern for a gift. (b) has gone A.W.O.L. to see her. (c) often speaks poetically: ". . . through leaves, over bridges."

2. During the story, Newt stops speaking absently and starts speaking (a) directly. (b) angrily. (c) jokingly.

3. It becomes clear that Catharine (a) never loved Henry Stewart Chasens. (b) has lied to others about her love all along. (c) doesn't love Henry as much as she loves Newt.

4. Catharine's true feelings are revealed when she (a) says her last word, "No." (b) watches Newt while he sleeps. (c) invites Newt to her wedding.

5. The very end of the story depends on (a) Newt's decision. (b) pure chance. (c) Catharine's decision.

THINKING IT THROUGH ⎯⎯⎯⎯⎯⎯⎯⎯⎯⎯⎯⎯⎯⎯⎯⎯⎯

1. Review the events that bring Newt to Catharine's front door. From your knowledge of human behavior, does his sudden appearance seem normal? Explain.

2. From the initial word of the story to the final word, whose mental map of the other changes the most? Explain.

3. It's not usual in a love story for one of the characters to sleep through a substantial portion of the time period covered. How is Newt's sleep significant in more than one way?

4. At one point, Catharine says, "Women aren't very clever at hiding it [love]" (page 9). What does she realize immediately after saying this?

5. As they settle down under separate trees, Catharine closes her eyes and catches "glimpses of her husband-to-be." (a) Whom do you think she is seeing? (b) Does your opinion now differ from when you first read the words? If so, why?

6. Here's a good example of the author's skill. What are the two last spoken words in the story? Compare the spoken words with the action that takes place at that time.

Bonus question: Early in the story, Newt unexpectedly and rather awkwardly mentions Scarlet O'Hara. If you recognize this name, you may also recognize the connection with the story. Tell what it is.

Critical Thinking

Fact and Opinion

A **fact** is something known to be true. Most facts can be checked and proved by examining something in the world around you. Fact language is territory language.

An **opinion** is what you think or believe about something. Opinions exist in your mind, and may or may not be based on facts. Opinions are part of your mental maps.

You live in a rather confusing world. Your mental maps of that world contain both facts and opinions—and it is important to keep the difference clear.

In literature, facts and opinions play a part in the following ways:

A. The author wants the reader to accept certain "story facts" as true.

B. The characters themselves deal with their own opinions as well as with facts.

C. The reader forms opinions and relates them to the story.

Label each of the sentences below as **SF** (story fact), **CO** (character's opinion), or **RO** (reader's opinion).

1. Newt and Catharine should have been described so that the reader could really *see* them.

2. The story takes place near a school for the blind.

3. Catharine is certainly the kind of girl worth going A.W.O.L. for.

4. There is an underlying meaning in the bells ringing in the school for the blind.

5. Henry Stewart Chasens should not be disappointed or betrayed.

6. Catharine is speechless at the end of the story.

Composition

1. After finishing a story, the reader usually has an opinion about it. What is your opinion of the story "Long Walk to Forever"? State that opinion in a complete sentence. Then state at least two facts upon which your opinion is based.

2. Catharine's experience in handling her feelings is believable for many readers because similar situations in real life happen often. Have you ever thought you felt one way for a good reason, only to have your real feelings come out for a better reason? Choose one such experience you are willing to share with others. In a paragraph, explain the details and tell how you felt afterwards.

THE BOG TURTLE

by Martha Scheiner

I had always disliked your face
until a picture of you appeared
in the local papers with a caption
saying you had found a bog turtle
5 a very rare and gemlike turtle,
which hides shyly in the marsh,
    feeding on slugs
        and bugs.

I could have loved you then
10 standing in the sunfield
with skinny hands,
looking down at your turtle
with a long madonna smile
which smoothed away all that was not
15 beautiful in you, and so for
that instant
    you were rare,
        you too.

WAYS OF KNOWING*

1. How had the speaker previously thought of the person described? How has the speaker's impression of the person changed?
2. In which case does the word *rare* say more: in line 5 or in line 17? Explain.

- **bog** (BOG) swamp; marsh
- **caption** (KAP shun) title or explanation of a picture
- madonna (muh DON uh) Italian for "my lady" (capitalized: the Virgin Mary)

*"A poem is a way of knowing."—John Hall Wheelock

WHILE THE AUTO WAITS

by O. Henry

▶ First impressions . . . are they always correct? Of course not. Follow the mental maps of the two characters in this story as they lead toward a double surprise. The setting is New York City in the year 1903.

Promptly at the beginning of twilight, the girl in gray came again to that quiet corner of that quiet, small park. She sat upon a bench and read a book, for there was yet to come a half hour in which print could be seen.

To repeat: Her dress was gray—and plain. A large-meshed veil covered her turban hat and a face that shone through it with a calm and unconscious beauty. She had come there at the same hour on the previous day, and on the day before that. And there was one person who knew it.

The young man who knew it hovered near. His attention was rewarded, for, in turning a page, her book slipped from her fingers and fell to the ground.

The young man pounced upon it. He returned it to its owner with the kind of manner that seems to flourish in parks and public places—a compound of courtesy and hope, mixed with respect for the police officer on the beat. In a pleasant voice, he risked a remark on the weather. Then he stood quite still for a moment, awaiting his fate.

The girl looked him over leisurely—at his ordinary, neat clothing, at features that revealed nothing particular in the way of expression.

"You may sit down if you like," she said, in a clear, controlled voice. "Really, I would like you to do so. The light is too bad for reading. I would prefer to talk."

The servant of Luck slid upon the seat by her side.

"Do you know," he said, speaking the words with which park chairmen open their meetings, "that you are quite the prettiest girl I've seen in a long time? I had my eye on you yesterday. Didn't know somebody was bowled over by those beautiful blinkers of yours, did you, honeysuckle?"

"Whoever you are," said the girl, in icy tones, "you must remember that I am a lady. I'll excuse the remark you just made because the mistake was, doubtless, a natural one—in your circle. I asked you to sit down. But if the invitation must make me your 'honeysuckle,' forget it."

"I earnestly beg your pardon," pleaded the young man. He looked truly sorry. "It was my fault, you know. I mean,

---

- large-meshed (MESHT) **having large open spaces, as in a net or veil**
- hover (HUV ur) **stay nearby**

there are girls in parks, you know—that is, of course, you don't know, but——"

"Abandon the subject, if you please," she cut in. "Of course I know. Now, tell me about these people passing along the paths. Where are they going? Why do they hurry so? Are they happy? To tell the truth, I come here to sit because here, only, can I be near the great, common, throbbing heart of humanity. Most of my life is lived where its beats are never felt. Can you surmise why I spoke to you, Mr. ——?"

"Parkenstacker," supplied the young man. Then he looked eager and hopeful.

"No, not *my* name," said the girl. She held up a slender finger and smiled slightly. "You would recognize it immediately. It's impossible to keep the name out of the papers. Or even my picture. This veil and this hat of my maid furnish me with a kind of disguise." She chuckled. "You should have seen the chauffeur stare at it. I spoke to you, Mr. Stackenpot——"

"Parkenstacker," corrected the young man, modestly.

"——Mr. Parkenstacker, because I wanted to talk, for once, with a common man—one unspoiled by wealth and supposed social superiority. Oh! you cannot know how tired I am of it—money, money, money. And of the men who surround me, dancing like little puppets all cut from the same pattern. I am sick of jewels, of travel, of society, of luxuries of all kinds."

"I always had the idea," said the young man, with a pause, "that money must be a pretty good thing."

"But when you have so many millions that——!" She continued the sentence with a gesture of despair. "It's the

• **surmise** (sur MYZ) guess; suspect

monotony of it. Drives, dinners, theaters, parties—sometimes the very tinkle of ice in my champagne glass nearly drives me mad."

Mr. Parkenstacker looked interested.

"I've always liked," he said, "to read and hear about the ways of wealthy people. But I like to have my information accurate. You know, I've always thought that champagne is cooled in the bottle, not by placing ice in the glass."

The girl gave a musical laugh of genuine amusement.

"You should learn," she explained, in a patient tone, "that we wealthy people depend for our fun upon departure from precedent. Just now it's the fad to put ice in the glass. The idea began when the Prince of Tartary dined at the Waldorf. It will soon give way to some other whim. Just this week, at a dinner party on Madison Avenue, a green leather glove was laid by each plate, to be used while eating olives."

"I see," admitted the young man, humbly. "These special habits of the inner circle never get known by the common public."

"Sometimes," continued the girl, accepting his confession of error with a slight bow, "I have thought that if I ever should love a man, he might be a worker. Just a kind, honest, uncomplicated common man. But, doubtless, the claims of wealth will prove stronger than my wishes. Just now I'm fighting off two. One is a German grand duke. I think he has, or has had, a wife somewhere, driven mad by his drinking and cruelty. The other is an English marquis. Oh, what is it that makes me tell you all these things, Mr. Packenstacker?"

"Parkenstacker," breathed the young man. "You cannot know how much I appreciate your confidences."

The girl gave him a calm, impersonal look, in keeping with their difference in social standing.

"What is your line of business, Mr. Parkenstacker?" she asked.

"A very humble one. But I hope to rise in the world. Were you really in earnest when you said that you could love a man of lowly position?"

"Indeed I was. But I said 'might.' Remember the grand duke and the marquis." She lifted her chin. "But if the man were what I wanted him to be, no job he could have would be too humble."

"I work," declared Mr. Parkenstacker, "in a restaurant."

The girl shrank slightly.

"Not as a waiter?" she said, a little concerned. "Hard labor is noble, but— personal service, you know—valets and——"

"I'm not a waiter. I'm cashier in"—on the opposite side of the park was a brilliant electric sign, RESTAURANT—"in that restaurant you see there."

The girl glanced at the small watch set in a bracelet of rich design. Then she rose, hurriedly.

"Why are you not at work?" she asked.

"I'm on the night shift," said the young man. "It's still an hour before my turn begins. May I hope to see you again?"

"I do not know. Perhaps. But the whim to come here might not seize me again. I must go quickly now. There is a dinner, and a box at the play—oh! the same old round. Perhaps you noticed an

----

- **precedent** (PRES i dunt) previously set example
- marquis (MAHR kwis) nobleman ranking just below a duke
- **valet** (val AY) male servant who attends to personal needs

automobile at the upper corner of the park. One with a white body?"

"And red trim?" asked the young man, knitting his brows in thought.

"Yes. I always come in that. Pierre waits for me there. He supposes that I go shopping in the department store across the square. Imagine the kind of life in which we must fool even our chauffeurs! Good night."

"But it's dark now," said Mr. Parkenstacker, "and the park is full of all sorts of people. May I not walk——?"

"If you have the slightest regard for my wishes," said the girl, firmly, "you will do this. Remain on this bench for five minutes after I have left. I do not mean to accuse you, but you must know that expensive autos generally bear the monogram of their owner. Again, good night."

Swiftly and gracefully she moved away through the dusk. The young man watched as she reached the pavement on the park's edge, and turned up along it toward the corner where the automobile stood. Then he began to dodge and skim among the trees and bushes in a line parallel to her route, keeping her well in sight.

When she reached the corner, she turned her head to glance at the motor car. Then she passed it, continuing on across the street. From behind a convenient standing cab, the young man followed her movements closely with his eyes. Passing on down the sidewalk, she entered the restaurant with the blazing sign. It was one of those glaring places, all white paint and glass, where one can eat cheaply. The girl went through a door at the back, from which she reappeared without her hat and veil.

The cashier's desk was well to the front. A red-haired girl on the stool climbed down, glancing at the clock as she did so. The girl in gray mounted to her place.

The young man thrust his hands into his pockets and walked slowly back along the sidewalk. At the corner he lounged for a minute. Then he stepped into the automobile, reclined among the cushions, and said two words to the chauffeur:

"Club, Henri."

ALL THINGS CONSIDERED

1. The young man comes to the park (a) by accident. (b) because he's seen the girl there before. (c) to kill time before he starts work.

2. The *first* person to pretend to be someone else is the (a) girl in gray. (b) young man. (c) chauffeur.

3. Mr. Parkenstacker's suspicions about the girl are aroused when she (a) drops a book. (b) says it's too dark to read. (c) speaks of putting ice in champagne.

4. The girl certainly knows the man is being dishonest when he says (a) she is pretty. (b) his name is Parkenstacker. (c) he is a cashier at a nearby restaurant.

5. At the end, the reader can be pretty sure that the (a) girl is wealthy. (b) man is wealthy. (c) two characters will marry in the near future.

THINKING IT THROUGH

1. In your opinion, why does the girl act and speak as she does? Do you think her motive is a worthy one?

2. The story ends with not one but two trick endings. (a) What are they? (b) Which tricked you the most?

3. Some readers of the story believe that the girl really is wealthy and works in the restaurant to be near the "great, common, throbbing heart of humanity." What is your opinion of this interpretation? Explain.

4. At the end of the story, which character has the more accurate map of the entire situation? Explain.

Critical Thinking

Four Fallacies of Logic

You have just been asked to think about "While the Auto Waits" in terms of maps and territories. Clearly, the whole story is based on the inaccurate maps the characters have of each other.

The best mental maps truly relate to their territories. Good mental maps are necessary for good **logic,** or clear reasoning. When a map is incorrect, a **fallacy,** or error in reasoning, results. Here are four common fallacies of logic, or errors in reasoning.

A. Hasty generalization. A hasty generalization is a sweeping statement made on the basis of too few examples. For instance, you may have met only two or three great dancers from Chicago in your lifetime. You might now have formed this generalization: *All Chicagoans are great dancers.* This would be a hasty generalization. You are basing your belief about *all* the people in Chicago on only the two or three people you have met.

B. After the fact, therefore because of the fact. (Cause/Effect Fallacy) There is a tendency to believe that if Event A occurs before Event B, then A must have caused B. Suppose a man who suffers from arthritis hears that wearing a copper bracelet will cure arthritis. He starts wearing such a bracelet (Event A), and in a few weeks his arthritis is much better (Event B). Therefore, he concludes that the bracelet really *caused* the cure. This may be true, but is highly unlikely.

C. Emotional appeal. An emotional appeal is an argument based not on reasoning but on personal feelings. Suppose a worker appeals to the boss in this fashion: "You should raise my salary. I'm married to your cousin." Is this really a good *reason?* No, the worker is using emotional appeal— "I'm married to your cousin."—to make the boss feel guilty, and raise the salary.

D. False analogy. An analogy is a statement that two things, or two pairs, are alike in some way. There is a tendency, however, to assume that because two things or people are alike in some ways, they are alike in other ways. When this happens, a false analogy results. Suppose you and a friend are alike in many ways. You have many common interests and other people are used to seeing you together. Then one day your friend gets picked up for shoplifting while you are in the store also. By making a false analogy, the store manager might accuse you, too, even though you are innocent.

On your paper, write the following:

A. Hasty generalization

B. After the fact, therefore because of the fact

C. Emotional appeal

D. False analogy

Then match each of the items on the next page with one of the fallacies of logic you have listed. Write the number after the fallacy. If you believe that two fallacies are involved, list both, but be prepared to explain your answer.

1. A student says, "Please vote for Carmella for class president because she's my best friend and she wants to win."

2. After changing his uniform, Ted gets his first hit in 14 tries. He's sure that he got the hit because he changed his uniform.

3. Carmen speaks to the first three students she meets outside her new school. They are rude, and she decides that the students in the school are unfriendly.

4. The McAlpine twins are almost identical. Both are good at math and basketball. But teachers have always been puzzled by the fact that Dan is much better than Ed in English.

5. A candidate for president promises that if he is elected, employment will increase. He wins the election, and six months later employment picks up. Most of his supporters believe the brighter employment picture is due to the new president.

6. A commercial for a soft drink says nothing about sugar or caffeine, but simply shows a group of happy, attractive college students having the soft drink at a sensational party.

Composition

1. Without looking back, define the term *hasty generalization* in a sentence. Then give an original example of such a fallacy in logic. If possible, make your example something that really happened to you or to a person you know.

2. In "While the Auto Waits," both characters make hasty generalizations about each other. First explain the young woman's hasty generalization about the young man. Then tell about the man's hasty generalization about the young woman.

LOVE IS A FALLACY

by Max Shulman

▶ A **satire** (SA tyr) is a work of literature that pokes fun at some form of literature, some idea, or at some human weakness. Most satires have a serious purpose: to improve the reader's thinking on a certain subject. The satire that follows is a minor classic. It was written about 35 years ago, when raccoon coats—a fad during the 1920s—were making a comeback.

Cool was I and logical. Keen, calculating, acute and astute—I was all of these. My brain was as powerful as a dynamo, as precise as a chemist's scales. And—think of it!—I was only 18.

It is not often that one so young has such a giant intellect. Take, for example, Petey Bellows, my roommate at the university. Same age, same background, but dumb as an ox. A nice enough fellow, you understand, but nothing upstairs. Emotional type. Unstable. Worst of all, a faddist. Fads, I believe, are the very opposite of reason. To be swept up in every new craze that comes along, to surrender yourself just because everybody else is doing it—this, to me, is the acme of mindlessness. Not, however, to Petey.

One afternoon I found Petey lying on his bed with an expression of such distress on his face that I immediately diagnosed appendicitis. "Don't move," I said. "Don't take a laxative. I'll get a doctor."

"Raccoon," he mumbled thickly.

"Raccoon?" I said, pausing in my flight.

"I want a raccoon coat," he wailed.

I perceived that his trouble was not physical, but mental. "Why do you want a raccoon coat?"

"I should have known it," he cried, pounding his head. "I should have known they'd come back into style. Like a fool I spent all my money for textbooks, and now I can't get a raccoon coat."

"Can you mean," I said in disbelief, "that people are actually wearing raccoon coats again?"

"All the Big People are wearing them. Where've you been?"

- **fallacy** (FAL uh see) untrue idea; error in reasoning
- **astute** (uh STOOT) shrewd; clever
- **acme** (AK mee) highest point
- **perceive** (pur SEEV) become aware

"In the library," I said, naming a place not often visited by Big People.

He leaped from the bed and paced the room. "I've got to have a raccoon coat," he said passionately. "I've got to!"

"Petey, why? Look at it rationally. Raccoon coats are unsanitary. They shed. They smell bad. They weigh too much. They——"

"You don't understand," he interrupted impatiently. "It's the thing to do. I'd give anything for a raccoon coat. Anything!"

My brain, that precision instrument, slipped into high gear. "Anything?" I asked, looking at him narrowly.

"Anything," he cried in ringing tones.

I stroked my chin thoughtfully. It so happened that I knew where to get my hands on a raccoon coat. My father had had one in his college days. It lay now in a trunk in the attic back home. It also happened that Petey had something I wanted. At least he had first rights on it. I refer to his girl, Polly Espy.

I had long admired Polly Espy. Let me emphasize that my desire for this young woman was not emotional in nature. I was not one to let my heart rule my head. I wanted Polly for a practical, entirely sensible reason.

I was a freshman in law school. In a few years I would be out in practice. I was well aware of the importance of the right kind of wife in a lawyer's career. The successful lawyers I had observed were, almost without exception, married to beautiful, gracious, intelligent women. With one exception, Polly fitted these specifications perfectly.

Beautiful she was. Gracious she was. Intelligent she was not. In fact, she veered in the opposite direction. But I believed that under my guidance she would smarten up. At any rate, it was worth a try.

"Petey," I said, "are you in love with Polly Epsy?"

"I think she's a great kid," he replied, "but I don't know if you'd call it love. Why?"

"Do you," I asked, "have any kind of formal arrangement with her? I mean are you going together or anything like that?"

"No. We see each other quite a bit, but we both have other dates. Why?"

"Is there," I asked, "any other man?"

"Not that I know of. Why?"

I nodded with satisfaction. "In other words, if you were out of the picture, the field would be open. Is that right?"

"I guess so. What are you getting at?"

"Nothing, nothing," I said innocently, and took my suitcase out of the closet.

"Where you going?" asked Petey.

- **rationally** (RASH un uh lee) **reasonably; sensibly**
- veer (VEER) **head in a different direction**

"Home for the weekend." I threw a few things into the bag.

"Listen," he said, clutching my arm eagerly, "while you're home, you couldn't get some money from your old man, could you, and lend it to me so I can buy a raccoon coat?"

"I may do better than that," I said with a mysterious wink and closed my bag and left.

"Look," I said to Petey when I got back Monday morning. I threw open the suitcase and revealed the huge, hairy object that my father had worn.

Petey plunged his hands into the raccoon coat.

"Would you like it?" I asked.

"Oh, yes!" he cried, clutching the greasy pelt to him. Then a canny look came into his eyes. "What do you want for it?"

"Your girl," I said.

"Polly?" he said in a horrified whisper. "You want Polly?"

"That's right."

He flung the coat from him. "Never," he said firmly.

I shrugged. "Okay. I guess it's your business."

● **canny** (KAN ee) sly; shrewd

25

I sat down in a chair and pretended to read a book, but out of the corner of my eye I kept watching Petey. He was a torn man. First he looked at the coat. Then he turned away and set his jaw. Then he looked back at the coat, with even more longing in his face. Back and forth his head swiveled, desire waxing, resolution waning. Finally he didn't turn away at all; he just stood and stared with mad desire at the coat.

"It isn't as though I was in love with Polly," he said thickly. "Or going together or anything like that."

"That's right," I murmured.

"What's Polly to me, or me to Polly?"

"Not a thing," said I.

"It's just been a casual kick—just a few laughs, that's all."

"Try on the coat," said I.

He complied. The coat bunched high over his ears and dropped all the way down to his shoe tops. He looked like a mound of dead raccoons. "Fits fine," he said happily.

I rose from my chair. "Is it a deal?" I asked, extending my hand.

He swallowed. "It's a deal," he said and shook my hand.

I had my first date with Polly the following evening. I wanted to find out just how much work I had to do to get her mind up to the standard I required. I took her first to dinner. Then I took her to a movie, and then home. I went back to my room with a heavy heart.

I had gravely underestimated the size of my task. This girl's lack of information was terrifying. Nor would it be enough merely to supply her with information. First she had to be taught to *think*. At first I was tempted to give her back to Petey. But then I got to thinking about her physical charms and about the way she entered a room and the way she handled a knife and fork, and I decided to make an effort.

I went about it, as in all things, systematically. I gave her a course in logic. It happened that I, as a law student, was taking a course in logic myself. "Polly," I said to her when I picked her up on our next date, "tonight we are going over to the Knoll and talk."

"Oo, terrif," she replied. One thing I will say for this girl: you would go far to find another so agreeable.

We went to the Knoll, and we sat down under an old oak, and she looked at me expectantly. "What are we going to talk about?" she asked.

"Logic."

She thought this over for a minute and decided she liked it. "Magnif," she said.

- **waxing** (WAKS ing) **growing larger**
- waning (WAYN ing) **becoming smaller**
- **comply** (kum PLY) **agree; obey**

"Logic," I said, clearing my throat, "is the science of thinking. Before we can think correctly, we must first learn to recognize the common fallacies of logic. These we will take up tonight."

"Terrif!" she cried, clapping her hands delightedly.

I winced, but went bravely on. "First let us examine the fallacy called *oversimplification*."

"By all means," she urged, batting her lashes eagerly.

"Oversimplification means an argument based on an unsupported general statement. For example: Exercise is good. Therefore everybody should exercise."

"I agree," said Polly earnestly. "I mean exercise is wonderful. I mean it builds the body and everything."

"Polly," I said gently, "the argument is a fallacy. *Exercise is good* is an unsupported generalization. For instance, if you have serious heart disease, exercise can be bad, not good. Many people are ordered by their doctors *not* to exercise. You must say exercise is *usually* good, or exercise is good *for most people*. Otherwise you have committed an oversimplification. Do you see?"

"No," she confessed. "But this is magnif. Do more! Do more!"

"It will be better if you stop tugging at my sleeve," I told her, and when she stopped, I continued. "Next we take up a fallacy called *hasty generalization*. Listen carefully: You can't speak French. I can't speak French. Petey Bellows can't speak French. I must therefore conclude that nobody at the university can speak French."

"Really?" said Polly, amazed. "*Nobody?*"

● wince (WINS) **flinch; draw back**

I hid my exasperation. "Polly, it's a fallacy. The generalization is reached too hastily. There are too few instances to support such a conclusion."

"Know any more fallacies?" she asked breathlessly. "This is more fun than dancing even."

I fought off a wave of despair. I was getting nowhere with this girl, absolutely nowhere. Still, I continued. "Next comes *after the fact, therefore because of the fact.* Listen to this: Let's not take Bill on our picnic. Every time, soon after we take him with us, it rains."

"I know somebody just like that," she exclaimed. "A girl back home—Eula Becker, her name is. It never fails. Every single time we take her on a picnic—"

"Polly," I said sharply, "It's a fallacy. Eula Becker doesn't *cause* the rain. She has no connection with the rain."

She scratched her pretty, empty head. "I'm all confused," she admitted.

"Of course you are."

"Tell me some more of this stuff," she said eagerly.

I consulted my watch. "I think we'd better call it a night. I'll take you home now, and you go over all the things you've learned. We'll have another session tomorrow night."

I deposited her at the girls' dormitory, where she assured me that she had had a perfectly terrif evening, and I went glumly home to my room. Petey lay snoring in his bed, the raccoon coat huddled like a great hairy beast at his feet. For a moment I considered waking him and telling him that he could have his girl back. It seemed clear that my project was doomed to failure. The girl simply had a logic-proof head.

But then I reconsidered. I had wasted one evening; I might as well waste another. Who knew? I decided to give it one more try.

Seated under the oak the next evening I said, "Our first fallacy tonight is called *emotional appeal.*"

She quivered with delight.

"Listen closely," I said. "A man applies for a job. When the boss asks him what his qualifications are, he replies that he has a wife and six children at home, the wife is helpless, the children have nothing to eat, no clothes to wear, no shoes on their feet, there are no beds in the house, no oil in the tank, and winter is coming."

A tear rolled down each of Polly's pink cheeks. "Oh, this is awful, awful," she sobbed.

"Yes, it's awful," I agreed, "but it's no argument. The man never answered the boss's question about his qualifications. Instead he

---

- **exasperation** (ig zas puh RAY shun) anger; irritation; annoyance

appealed to the boss's sympathy. He committed the fallacy of emotional appeal. Do you understand?"

I tried to keep from screaming while she wiped her eyes. "Next," I said in a carefully controlled tone, "we will discuss *false analogy.* Here is an example: Students should be allowed to look at their textbooks during examinations. After all, surgeons have X-rays to guide them during an operation, lawyers have briefs to guide them during a trial, carpenters have blueprints to guide them when they are building a house. Why, then, shouldn't students be allowed to look at their textbooks during an examination?"

"There now," she said enthusiastically, "is the most terrif idea I've heard in years."

"Polly," I said sharply, "the argument is all wrong. Doctors, lawyers, and carpenters aren't taking a test to see how much they have learned, but students are. The situations are altogether different, and you can't make an analogy between them."

"I still think it's a good idea," said Polly.

One more chance, I decided. But just one more. There is a limit to what flesh and blood can bear. "The next fallacy is called *poisoning the well.*"

"How cute!" she gurgled.

"Two men are having a debate. The first one gets up and says, 'My opponent is a notorious liar. You can't believe a word that he is going to say.' . . . Now, Polly, think. Think hard. What's wrong?"

I watched her closely as she knit her creamy brow in concentration. Suddenly a glimmer of intelligence—the first I had seen—came into her eyes. "It's not fair," she said with indignation. "It's not a bit fair. What chance has the second man got if the first man calls him a liar before he even begins talking?"

"Right!" I cried. "One hundred percent right. It's not fair. The first man has *poisoned the well* before anybody could drink from it. He has tied his opponent up before he could even start. . . . Polly, I'm proud of you."

"Aw," she murmured, blushing with pleasure.

"You see, these things aren't so hard. All you have to do is concentrate. Think—examine—evaluate. Come now, let's review everything we have learned."

"Fire away," she said with a wave of her hand.

I began a long, patient review of all I had told her. At first everything was work, sweat, and darkness. I had no idea when I would reach the light, or even *if* I would. But I persisted. I pounded and

---

- **analogy** (uh NAL uh jee) observed likeness; relationship between things
- brief (BREEF) lawyer's summary of a court case
- **notorious** (nuh TORE ee us) widely and unfavorably known

clawed and scraped, and finally I was rewarded. I saw a chink of light. And then the chink got bigger and the sun came pouring in and all was bright.

Five long evenings this took, but it was worth it. I had taught her to think. My job was done. She was worthy of me at last. She was a fit wife for me, a proper hostess for my mansion, a suitable mother for my children.

It must not be thought that I was without love for this girl. Quite the opposite. I decided to acquaint her with my feelings at our very next meeting. The time had come to change our relationship from academic to romantic.

"Polly," I said when next we sat beneath our oak, "tonight we will not discuss fallacies."

"Aw, gee," she said, disappointed.

I favored her with a smile, "we have now spent several evenings together. We have gotten along splendidly. It is clear that we are well matched."

"Hasty generalization," said Polly brightly.

"I beg your pardon," said I.

"Hasty generalization," she repeated. "How can you say that we are well matched on the basis of only a few dates?"

I chuckled with amusement. The beautiful kid had learned her lessons well. "Polly," I said, patting her hand in a tolerant manner, "a few dates is plenty. After all, you don't have to eat a whole cake to know that it's good."

"False analogy," said Polly promptly. "I'm not a cake. I'm a girl."

I chuckled with somewhat less amusement. She had learned her lessons perhaps too well. I decided to change tactics. Obviously the best approach was a simple, strong, direct declaration of love. I paused for a moment while my massive brain chose the proper words. Then I began:

"Polly, I love you. You are the whole world to me, and the moon and the stars and the constellations of outer space. Please, say that you will go with me, for if you will not, life will be meaningless. I will languish. I will refuse my meals. I will wander the face of the earth, a shambling hollow-eyed hulk."

There, I thought, folding my arms, that ought to do it.

"Emotional appeal," said Polly.

I dashed perspiration from my brow. "Polly," I croaked, "you mustn't take all these things so literally. I mean this is just class-room stuff. You know that the things you learn in school don't have anything to do with life."

- languish (LANG gwish) **grow feeble**
- **literally** (LIT ur uh lee) **exactly as stated**

"Oversimplification," she said, wagging her finger at me playfully.

That did it. I leaped to my feet, bellowing like a bull. "Will you or will you not go with me?"

"I will not," she replied.

"Why not?" I demanded.

"Because this afternoon I promised Petey Bellows that I would go with him."

I reeled back, overcome with the infamy of it. After he promised, after he made a deal, after he shook my hand! "The rat!" I shrieked, kicking up great chunks of turf. "You can't go with him, Polly. He's a liar. He's a cheat. He's a rat."

"Poisoning the well," said Polly, "and stop shouting. I think shouting must be a fallacy too."

With an immense effort, I softened my voice. "All right," I said. "Let's look at this thing logically. How could you choose Petey Bellows over me? Look at me—a brilliant student, a tremendous intellectual, a man with an assured future. Look at Petey—a knothead, a guy who'll never know where his next meal is coming from. Can you give me one logical reason why you should go with Petey Bellows?"

"I certainly can," declared Polly. "He's got a raccoon coat."

• infamy (IN fuh mee) **disgrace; extreme wickedness**

ALL THINGS CONSIDERED

1. At the beginning, the **narrator,** or person who tells the story, wants to date Polly because he (a) feels sorry for her. (b) believes in always following his feelings. (c) thinks she might become an ideal wife for him.

2. On the first date, (a) they go to dinner and a movie. (b) Polly learns about fallacies of logic. (c) the narrator argues with Polly.

3. On the next few dates, (a) they go to dinner and see movies. (b) Polly learns about fallacies of logic. (c) the narrator argues with Polly.

4. The high point of the story comes when Polly (a) finds logic too hard and gives up. (b) falls hopelessly in love with the narrator. (c) uses the narrator's logic against him.

5. At the end of the story, the most disappointed character is undoubtedly (a) the narrator. (b) Polly. (c) Petey.

THINKING IT THROUGH

1. The introduction to the story (page 23) states that the story is a *satire,* or a criticism of some idea or human weakness. Clearly, the author makes a good deal of fun of the narrator and the narrator's ideas. What aspects of the narrator's personality and ideas does the author hold up to ridicule? Explain your answer.

2. Think about the agreement the narrator makes with Petey. In your opinion, would most of today's college students make a deal like this one? Explain your answer.

3. Think about the story in terms of maps and territories. (a) In one sentence, tell what the narrator's mental map of Polly is at the beginning and throughout most of the story. (b) In another sentence, tell what his mental map of her is at the end of the story.

4. Most stories in which the main character is defeated can be said to have an unhappy ending. Yet "Love Is a Fallacy" leaves most readers laughing. In your opinion, why can't the ending really be termed sad?

Literary Skills

The Elements of Plot

The **plot** of a story concerns not only *what* happens but also *the way* things happen—the way different scenes relate to each other so that the reader is satisfied when the story is concluded.

To begin with, a plot usually gets the reader involved quickly. The reader wonders "What will happen next?" Without a what-will-happen-next question, the reader's mind will wander, and the reader will lose interest. A well-written plot has a sequence of events and actions that progress through *conflict* and *rising action* to a *climax*. A *resolution* or a *surprise ending* may follow the climax.

Conflict and Rising Action: All plots depend on conflict and rising action. A **conflict** develops when two opposite forces meet. In many stories, the conflict is between two people or groups of people. For example, in the first part of "Love Is a Fallacy," the conflict is between the narrator and Petey. (Will the narrator get Petey's girl, or not?) The conflict then shifts to the narrator and Polly. (Will Polly learn the narrator's lessons, or not? Who will win the final argument?)

The writer creates excitement, or **rising action,** by making each plot problem or conflict more interesting than the one before it.

Climax: The **climax,** or most exciting part of the story, comes at or near the end. It acts as a turning point in the story. It is at this point that the final *major* conflict is resolved.

Resolution/Surprise Ending: Some stories, like "Love Is a Fallacy," end quickly after the climax. The story ends with a short, single sentence—a "punch line." A quick, unexpected ending is called a **surprise ending.** In other stories, a short resolution follows the climax. A **resolution** solves any unanswered *minor* questions and gives the story a "rounded out" feeling. Suppose, for example, that "Love Is a Fallacy" continued with a short scene in which the narrator and Petey discuss girls, the nature of love, and their own friendship. That section would be called a resolution.

1. Define each of these terms in your own words: *plot, conflict, rising action, climax, resolution.*

2. Name at least three major plot problems in "Love Is a Fallacy." In other words, what plot problems kept *you* interested? (Which what-will-happen-next questions entered your mind as you read the story?)

3. In your opinion, does the story contain rising action, or does it become less and less interesting as it goes along? Explain.

4. What is the climax of the story? That is, what is the issue that makes the narrator lose his patience and scream?

Composition

1. Write a letter from Polly to a friend back home describing her experiences with the law student. Follow the story plot to tell *what* happened and *the way* things happened.

2. In your opinion, has the self-centered narrator of the story learned anything about the nature of love from his experience? Will he ever realize that one person has to love another for what that person *is*, not what the person might become? Try writing a short resolution (added scene) to the story that answers these questions. You might want to begin like this:

> When I got back to the room I found Petey brushing his raccoon coat.
> I said, "What I don't know about women!"

VOCABULARY AND SKILL REVIEW

Before completing the exercises that follow, you may wish to review the **bold-faced** words on pages 2 to 33.

I. On a separate sheet of paper, write the term in each line that means the same, or nearly the same, as the term in *italics*.

1. *bog*: large animal, stool, swamp, injury on skin
2. *taunt*: insult, tight, compliment, disease
3. *comply*: refuse, explain, overcome, obey
4. *acme*: disease, dark place, highest point, scholar
5. *astute*: clever, clumsy, impossible, friendly
6. *rationally*: angrily, very slowly, reasonably, helpfully
7. *analogy*: card game, likeness, study of sound, blueprint
8. *valet*: large building, fruit, owner, manservant
9. *precedent*: example, mistake, victory, valve
10. *canny*: silly, shrewd, excited, uninterested

II. On a separate sheet of paper, write the *italicized* term that best fills the blank in each sentence.

literally	*remotest*	*notorious*
perceive	*perspective*	*caption*
fallacy	*surmise*	*exasperation*
		waxing

1. Sara immediately saw the ———— in the argument.

2. Our eyes let us ———— color, shape, and distance.

3. People who exaggerate all the time do not speak ———— .

4. A picture in a newspaper usually has a ———— under it.

5. A ———— moon is growing larger.

6. I had only the ———— idea of how to prepare an omelet.

7. With ————, the teenager searched everywhere for the mislaid car key.

8. Gary is ———— for arriving early.

9. To ———— that something is true is to make an inference.

10. We climbed a hill to get a good ———— of my uncle's farm.

III. Read this short story carefully before answering the questions that follow it.

POINT OF VIEW

by A. Averchenko

"Men are comic!" she said, smiling dreamily. Not knowing whether this indicated praise or blame, I answered noncommittally: "Quite true."

"Really. My husband's a regular Othello.* Sometimes I'm sorry I married him."

I looked helplessly at her. "Until you explain—" I began.

"Oh, I forgot that you haven't heard. About three weeks ago I was walking home with my husband through the square. I had a large black hat on, which suits me awfully well, and my cheeks were quite pink from walking. As we passed under a street light, a pale, dark-haired fellow standing nearby glanced at me and suddenly took my husband by his sleeve.

• noncommittally (non kuh MIT uh lee) **without indicating yes or no**

*Othello (oh THEL oh) famous Shakespearan character, known for his jealousy

"'Would you oblige me with a light?' he says. Alexander pulled his arm away, stooped down, and quicker than lightning banged him on the head with a brick. He fell like a log. It was awful."

"Why, what on earth made your husband get jealous all of a sudden?"

She shrugged her shoulders. "I told you men are very comic."

Bidding her farewell, I went out, and at the corner came across her husband.

"Hello, old chap," I said. "They tell me you've been breaking people's heads."

He burst out laughing: "So you've been talking to my wife. It was jolly lucky that brick came so pat into my hand. Otherwise, just think: I had about fifteen hundred rubles in my pocket, and my wife was wearing her diamond earrings."

"Do you think he wanted to rob you?"

"A man accosts you in a deserted spot, asks for a light and gets hold of your arm. What more do you want?"

Perplexed, I left him and walked on.

"There's no catching you today," I heard a voice say from behind.

I looked around and saw a friend I hadn't set eyes upon for three weeks.

"What on earth has happened to you?" I exclaimed.

He smiled faintly and asked in turn: "Do you know whether any lunatics have been at large lately? I was attacked by one three weeks ago. I left the hospital only today."

With sudden interest, I asked: "Three weeks ago! Were you sitting in the square?"

"Yes, I was. The most absurd thing. I was sitting in the square dying for a smoke. No matches! After ten minutes or so, a gentleman passes with some old hag. He was smoking. I go up to him, touch him on the sleeve and ask in my most polite manner: 'Can you oblige me with a light?' And what d'you think? The madman stoops down, picks something up, and the next moment I am lying on the ground with a broken head, unconscious. You probably read about it in the newspaper."

I looked at him, and asked earnestly: "Do you really believe you met up with a lunatic?"

"I am sure of it."

- accost (uh KOST) **approach and speak to**
- perplexed (pur PLEKST) **puzzled**

An hour afterwards I was eagerly digging in old back numbers of the local paper. At last I found what I was looking for: a short note in the accident column:

> ### UNDER THE INFLUENCE OF DRINK
>
> Yesterday morning, the keepers of the square found on a bench a young man whose papers show him to be of good family. He had evidently fallen to the ground while in a state of extreme intoxication, and had broken his head on a nearby brick. The distress of this prodigal's parents is indescribable.

1. This story is called "Point of View" for good reason. Four mental maps that more or less cover the same territory are considered. Different opinions are expressed. In your own words, retell the story from the point of view of the (a) wife, (b) husband, (c) young dark-haired man, and (d) newspaper writer.

2. What is the one plot problem that all four viewpoints try to answer?

3. How does the wife's mental map of herself differ from the young man's?

4. In your judgment, whose viewpoint probably consists mostly of *facts?* Explain.

5. Choose one person's viewpoint that you think is clearly an opinion. Explain the fallacy in reasoning that led to the incorrect opinion. You may choose to use one of the four fallacies on page 21 in your answer, but be sure to explain the fallacy in your own words.

● prodigal (PROD uh gul) **carefree, wasteful person**

► Can dreams be mental maps? Do animals dream? If so, what do they dream about? Think about these questions as you read this unusual poem.

DREAMS OF THE ANIMALS

by Margaret Atwood

Mostly the animals dream
of other animals each
according to its kind

       (though certain mice and small rodents
5   have nightmares of a huge pink
       shape with five claws descending)

:moles dream of darkness and delicate
mole smells

frogs dream of green and golden
10 frogs
sparkling like wet suns
among the lilies

red and black
striped fish, their eyes open
15 have red and black striped
dreams defence, attack, meaningful
patterns

birds dream of territories
enclosed by singing.

20 Sometimes the animals dream of evil
in the form of soap and metal
but mostly the animals dream
of other animals.

There are exceptions:

25   the silver fox in the roadside zoo
       dreams of digging out
       and of baby foxes, their necks bitten

                         the caged armadillo
                         near the train
    30   station, which runs
                         all day in figure eights
                         its piglet feet pattering,
                         no longer dreams
                         but is insane when waking;

    35   the iguana
                         in the petshop window on St. Catherine Street
                         crested, royal-eyed, ruling
                         its kingdom of water-dish and sawdust

                         dreams of sawdust.

WAYS OF KNOWING

1. (a) According to the poet, what do animals usually dream of? (b) In your opinion, how does this compare with humans and their dreams?

2. The animal dreamed of in lines 4–6 is not named directly. What might it be?

3. Lines 20 and 21 refer to evil dreams "in the form of soap and metal." What might these dreams be about?

4. In general, the animals named in lines 1–23 are in a different situation from the animals named in lines 24–39. What is this difference? How does this difference result in different dreams?

5. (a) In your opinion, which is the happiest dream in the poem? (b) Which is the saddest?

6. Some poems have regular patterns of rhythm and rhyme. Those that do not are called **free verse.** "Dreams of the Animals" is an excellent example of free verse. In your own words, tell what free verse is by referring to the poem.

7. A **simile** (SIM uh lee) is a comparison between two things that is made with a special comparing word (usually *like* or *as*). As any figure of speech, a simile is not meant to be interpreted in its literal sense or ordinary way. There is one simile in the first 15 lines of the poem. What is it?

Bonus question: Margaret Atwood chose to put a colon (:) at the beginning of line 7. Why do you think she did this?

• iguana (i GWAH nuh) **type of large lizard**
• crested (KREST id) **having a growth on top of the head**

THE TURN OF THE TIDE

by C. S. Forester

▶ This story by the popular British author C. S. Forester will keep you guessing till the very last sentence. It's a perfect little crime story about a not-quite-perfect crime.

"What always beats them in the end," said Dr. Matthews, "is how to dispose of the body. But, of course, you know that as well as I do."

"Yes," said Slade. He had, in fact, been devoting far more thought to what Dr. Matthews believed to be this accidental subject of conversation than Dr. Matthews could ever guess.

"As a matter of fact," went on Dr. Matthews, warming to the subject to which Slade had so tactfully led him, "it's a terribly knotty problem. It's so difficult, in fact, that I always wonder why anyone is fool enough to commit murder."

"All very well for you," thought Slade, but he did not allow his thoughts to alter his expression. "You don't know the sort of difficulties a man can be up against."

"I've often thought the same," he said.

"Yes," went on Dr. Matthews, "it's the body that does it, every time. To use poison calls for special facilities, which are good enough to hang you as soon as suspicion is roused. And that suspicion—

well, of course, part of my job is to detect poisoning. I don't think anyone can get away from it, nowadays.

"I quite agree with you," said Slade. He had no intention of using poison.

"Well," went on Dr. Matthews, developing his logical argument, "if you rule out poison, you rule out the chance of getting the body disposed of under the impression that the victim died a natural death. The only other way, if a man cares to stand the racket of having the body to give evidence against him, is to fake things to look like suicide. But you know, and I know, that it just can't be done. The mere fact of suicide calls for a close examination, and no one has ever been able to fix things so well as to get away with it. You're a lawyer. You've probably read a lot of reports of trials where the murderer has tried it. And you know what's happened to them."

"Yes," said Slade.

He certainly had given a great deal of consideration to the matter. It was only after long thought that he had, finally, put aside the notion of disposing of young Spalding and concealing his guilt by a sham suicide.

"That brings us to where we started, then," said Dr. Matthews. "The only other thing left is to try and conceal the body. And that's more difficult still."

"Yes," said Slade. But he had a perfect plan for disposing of the body.

"A human body," said Dr. Matthews, "is a most difficult thing to get rid of. That chap Oscar Wilde, in that book of his—*Dorian Grey*, isn't it?—gets rid of

one by the use of chemicals. Well, I'm a chemist as well as a doctor, and I wouldn't like the job."

"No?" said Slade, politely.

Dr. Matthews was not nearly as clever a man as himself, he thought.

"There's altogether too much of it," said Dr. Matthews. "It's heavy, and it's bulky, and it's bound to undergo corruption. Think of all those poor devils who've tried it. Bodies in trunks, and bodies in coal cellars, and bodies in chicken runs. You can't hide the thing, try as you will."

"Can't I? That's all you know," thought Slade, but aloud he said: "You're quite right. I've never thought about it before."

"Of course, you haven't," agreed Dr. Matthews. "Sensible people don't, unless it's an incident of their profession, as in my case.

"And yet, you know," he went on, "there's one decided advantage about getting rid of the body altogether. You're much safer, then. It's a point which ought to interest you, as a lawyer, more than me. It's rather an obscure point of law, but I fancy there are very definite rulings on it. You know what I'm referring to?"

"No, I don't," said Slade, genuinely puzzled.

"You can't have a trial for murder unless you can prove there's a victim," said Dr. Matthews. "There's got to be a corpus delicti, as you lawyers say in your horrible dog-Latin. A corpse, in other words, even if it's only a bit of one. No corpse,

---

- sham (SHAM) **fake; not genuine**
- corruption (kuh RUP shun) **decay; rottenness**
- incident (IN suh dunt) **necessary or connected part**
- **obscure** (ub SKYOOR) **not well known**
- corpus delicti (KOR pus di LIK ty) **proof of a crime; material substance such as the body of a murder victim**

41

no trial. I think that's good law, isn't it?"

"By Jove, you're right!" said Slade. "I wonder why that hadn't occurred to me before?"

No sooner were the words out of his mouth than he regretted having said them. He did his best to make his face immobile again; he was afraid lest his expression might have hinted at his pleasure in discovering another very reassuring factor in this problem of killing young Spalding. But Dr. Matthews had noticed nothing.

"Well, as I said, people only think about these things if they're incidental to their profession," he said. "The entire destruction of a body is practically impossible. But, I suppose, if a man could achieve it, he would be all right. However strong the suspicion was against him, the police couldn't get him without a corpse. There might be a story in that, Slade, if you or I were writers."

"Yes," assented Slade, and laughed harshly.

There never would be any story about the killing of young Spalding.

"Well," said Dr. Matthews, "we've had a pretty gruesome conversation, haven't we? And I seem to have done all the talking, somehow. That's the result, I suppose, Slade, of the very excellent dinner you gave me. I'd better push off now. Not that the weather is very inviting."

Nor was it. As Slade saw Dr. Matthews into his car, the rain was driving down in a real winter storm, and there was a bitter wind blowing.

"Shouldn't be surprised if this turned to snow before morning," were Dr. Matthew's last words before he drove off.

Slade was glad it was such a tempestuous night. It meant that, more certainly than ever, there would be no one out in the lanes, no one out on the sands when he disposed of young Spalding's body.

Back in his drawing room, Slade looked at the clock. There was still an hour to spare; he could spend it in making sure that his plans were all correct.

He looked up the tide tables. Yes, that was right enough. Spring tides. The lowest of low water on the sands. There was not so much luck about that; young Spalding came back on the midnight train every Wednesday night, and it was not surprising that, sooner or later, the Wednesday night would coincide with a spring tide. But it was lucky that this particular Wednesday night should be one of tempest; luckier still that low water should be at one-thirty, the best time for him.

He opened the drawing-room door and listened carefully. He could not hear a sound. Mrs. Dumbleton, his housekeeper, must have been in bed some time now. She was as deaf as a post, anyway, and would not hear his departure. Nor his return, when Spalding had been killed and disposed of.

The hands of the clock seemed to be moving very fast. He must make sure everything was correct. The plow chain and the other iron weights were already in the back seat of the car; he had put them there before old Matthews arrived to dine. He slipped on his overcoat.

From his desk, Slade took a curious little bit of apparatus: eighteen inches of strong cord, tied at each end to a six-inch

---

- **immobile** (i MOH bil) motionless
- tempestuous—(tem PES choo us) very stormy; like a tempest
- **drawing room** parlor; living room
- apparatus (ap uh RAT us) equipment; tools for a specific use

length of wood so as to make a ring. He made a last close examination to see that the knots were quite firm, and then he put it in his pocket; as he did so, he ran through, in his mind, the words—he knew them by heart—of the passage in the book about the Thugs of India, describing the method of strangulation employed by them.

He could think quite coldly about all this. Young Spalding was a busybody. A word from him, now, could bring ruin upon Slade, could send him to prison, could have him struck off the rolls.

Slade thought of other defaulting solicitors he had heard of, even one or two with whom he had come into contact professionally. He remembered his brother solicitors' remarks about them. He thought of having to beg his bread in the streets on his release from prison, of cold and misery and starvation. The shudder which shook him was succeeded by a hot wave of resentment. Never, never, would he endure it.

What right had young Spalding, who had barely been qualified two years, to condemn a gray-haired man twenty years his senior to such a fate? If nothing but death would stop him, then he deserved to die. He clenched his hand on the cord in his pocket.

A glance at the clock told him he had better be moving. He turned out the lights and tiptoed out of the house, shutting the door quietly. The bitter wind flung icy rain into his face, but he did not notice it.

He pushed the car out of the garage by hand and locked the garage doors, as a precaution against the chance that, on a night like this, someone should notice that his car was out.

He drove cautiously down the road. Of course, there was not a soul about in a quiet place like this. The few street lamps were already extinguished.

There were lights in the station as he drove over the bridge; they were awaiting there the arrival of the twelve-thirty train. Spalding would be on that. Every Wednesday he went over to his subsidiary office, sixty miles away. Slade turned into the lane a quarter of a mile beyond the station and then reversed his car so that it pointed toward the road. He put out the side lights, and settled himself to wait; his hand fumbled with the cord in his pocket.

The train was a little late. Slade had been waiting a quarter of an hour when he saw the lights of the train emerge from the cutting and come to a standstill in the station. So wild was the night that he could hear nothing of it. Then the train moved slowly out again. As soon as it was gone, the lights in the station began to go out, one by one; Hobson, the porter, was making ready to go home, his turn of duty completed.

Next, Slade's straining ears heard footsteps.

Young Spalding was striding down the road. With his head bent before the storm, he did not notice the dark mass of the motor car in the lane, and he walked past it.

Slade counted up to two hundred,

- Thugs (THUGZ) **former group of criminals in India**
- defaulting solicitor (di FAWLT ing suh LIS i tur) **An English lawyer who has misused money entrusted to his care**
- subsidiary (sub SID ee er ee) **branch; part of a larger company**

slowly, and then he switched on his lights, started the engine, and drove the car out into the road in pursuit. He saw Spalding in the light of the head lamps and drew up alongside.

"Is that Spalding?" he said, striving to make the tone of his voice as natural as possible. "I'd better give you a lift, old man, hadn't I?"

"Thanks very much," said Spalding. "This isn't the sort of night to walk two miles in."

He climbed in and shut the door. No one had seen. No one would know. Slade let in his clutch and drove slowly down the road.

"Bit of luck, seeing you," he said. "I was just on my way home from bridge at Mrs. Clay's when I saw the train come in and remembered it was Wednesday and you'd be walking home. So I thought I'd turn a bit out of my way to take you along."

"Very good of you, I'm sure," said Spalding.

"As a matter of fact," said Slade, speaking slowly and driving slowly, "it wasn't altogether disinterested. I wanted to talk business to you, as it happened."

"Rather an odd time to talk business," said Spalding. "Can't it wait till tomorrow?"

"No, it cannot," said Slade. "It's about the Lady Vere trust."

"Oh, yes. I wrote to remind you last week that you had to make delivery."

"Yes, you did. And I told you, long before that, that it would be inconvenient, with Hammond abroad."

"I don't see that," said Spalding. "I don't see that Hammond's got anything to do with it. Why can't you just hand over and have done with it? I can't do anything to straighten things up until you do."

"As I said, it would be inconvenient."

Slade brought the car to a standstill at the side of the road.

"Look here, Spalding," he said, desperately, "I've never asked a favor of you before. But now I ask you, as a favor, to forego delivery for a bit. Just for three months, Spalding."

But Slade had small hope that his request would be granted. So little hope, in fact, that he brought his left hand out of his pocket holding the piece of wood, with the loop of cord dangling from its ends. He put his arm around the back of Spalding's seat.

"No, I can't, really I can't," said Spalding. "I've got my duty to my clients to consider. I'm sorry to insist, but you're quite well aware of what my duty is."

"Yes," said Slade. "But I beg you to wait."

"I see," said Spalding, after a long pause.

"I only want three months," pressed Slade. "Just three months. I can get straight again in three months."

Spalding had known of other men who had had the same belief in their ability to get straight in three months. It was unfortunate for Slade—and for Spalding—that Slade had used those words. Spalding hardened his heart.

"No," he said. "I can't promise anything like that. I don't think it's any use continuing this discussion. Perhaps I'd better walk home from here."

He put out his hand to the latch of the door, and, as he did so, Slade jerked the loop of cord over his head. A single turn of Slade's wrist—a thin, bony, old man's wrist, but as strong as steel in that wild moment—tightened the cord about Spalding's throat. Slade swung round in his seat, getting both hands to the piece of wood, twisting madly. His breath hissed between his teeth with the effort, but Spalding never drew breath at all. He lost consciousness long before he was dead. Only Slade's grip of the cord round his throat prevented the dead body from falling forward, doubled up.

Nobody had seen, nobody would know. And what that book had stated about the method of assassination practiced by Thugs was perfectly correct.

Slade had gained, now, the time in which he could get his affairs into order. It only remained to dispose of Spalding's body, and he had planned to do that very satisfactorily. Just for a moment Slade felt as if all this were only some heated dream, some nightmare, but then he came back to reality and went on with the plan he had in mind.

He pulled the dead man's knees forward so that the corpse lay back in the seat, against the side of the car. He put the car in gear, let in his clutch, and drove rapidly down the road—much faster than when he had been arguing with Spalding. Low water was in three-quarters of an hour's time, and the sands were ten miles away.

Slade drove fast through the wild night. There was not a soul about in those lonely lanes. He knew the way by heart—he had driven repeatedly over that route recently in order to memorize it.

The car bumped down the last bit of lane, and Slade drew up on the edge of the sands.

It was pitch dark, and the bitter wind was howling about him, under the black sky. Despite the noise of the wind, he could hear the surf breaking far away, two miles away, across the level sands.

He climbed out of the driver's seat and walked round to the other door. When he opened it the dead man fell sideways, into his arms.

With an effort, Slade held him up, while he groped into the back of the car for the plow chain and the iron weights. He crammed the weights into the dead man's pockets, and he wound the chain round and round the dead man's body, tucking in the ends to make it all secure. With that mass of iron to hold it down, the body would never be found again when dropped into the sea at the lowest ebb of spring tide.

Slade tried now to lift the body in his arms, to carry it over the sands. He reeled and strained, but he was not strong enough—Slade was a man of slight figure, and past his prime. The sweat on his forehead was icy in the icy wind.

For a second, doubt overwhelmed him, lest all his plans should fail for want of bodily strength. But he forced himself into thinking clearly; he forced his frail body into obeying the commands of his brain.

He turned round, still holding the dead man upright. Stooping, he got the heavy burden on his shoulders. He drew the arms round his neck and, with effort, he got the legs up round his hips. The dead man now rode him pick-a-back. Bending nearly double, he was able to carry the heavy weight in this fashion, the arms tight round his neck, the legs tight round his waist.

He set off, staggering, down the slope of the sands toward the sound of the surf. The sands were soft beneath his feet—it was because of this softness that he had not driven the car down to the

• pick-a-back—British expression equivalent to *piggyback* in American English; riding on someone's shoulders and back

water's edge. He could afford to take no chances.

The icy wind shrieked round him all that long way. The tide was nearly two miles out. That was why Slade had chosen this place. In the depth of winter, no one would go out to the water's edge at low tide for months to come.

He staggered on over the sands, clasping the limbs of the body close about him. Desperately, he forced himself forward, not stopping to rest, for he only just had time now to reach the water's edge before the flow began. He went on and on, driving his exhausted body with fierce urgings from his frightened brain.

Then, at last, he saw it: a line of white in the darkness which indicated the water's edge. Farther out, the waves were breaking. Here, the fragments of the rollers were only just sufficient to move the surface a little.

He was going to make quite sure of things. Steadying himself, he stepped into the water, wading in farther and farther so as to be able to drop the body into comparatively deep water. He held to his resolve, staggering through the icy water, knee deep, thigh deep, until it was nearly at his waist. This was far enough. He stopped, gasping in the darkness.

He leaned over to one side, to roll the body off his back. It did not move. He pulled at its arms. They were obstinate. He could not loosen them. He shook himself, wildly. He tore at the legs round his waist. Still the thing clung to him. Wild with panic and fear, he flung himself about in a mad effort to rid himself of the burden. It clung on as though it were alive. He could not break its grip.

Then another breaker came in. It splashed about him, wetting him far above his waist. The tide had begun to turn now, and the tide on those sands comes in like a race horse.

He made another effort to cast off the load, and when it still held him fast, he lost his nerve and tried to struggle out of the sea. But it was too much for his exhausted body. The weight of the corpse and of the iron with which it was loaded overbore him. He fell.

He struggled up again in the foam-streaked, dark sea, staggered a few steps, fell again—and did not rise. The dead man's arms were round his neck, throttling him, strangling him. Rigor mortis had set in and Spalding's muscles had refused to relax.

- **resolve** (ri ZOLV) purpose; course of action decided upon
- **obstinate** (OB stuh nit) stubborn; unyielding
- rigor mortis (RIG ur MOR tis) stiffening of body after death

ALL THINGS CONSIDERED ——————————————————

1. Early in the story, Dr. Matthews explains that for a person to be tried for murder, there must be (a) two witnesses. (b) a body. (c) a clear motive.

2. When he talks to Dr. Matthews, Slade thinks that he knows more than the doctor about (a) poisons. (b) faking a suicide. (c) disposing of a corpse.

3. Slade's motive for the killing is to (a) get Spalding's money. (b) prevent Spalding from getting his job. (c) protect himself from exposure and a prison term.

4. Slade's carefully planned murder turns out to involve (a) a mistaken victim. (b) a faulty weapon. (c) his own death.

5. "The Turn of the Tide" differs from the usual murder story in that it lacks a (a) detective. (b) corpse. (c) murderer.

THINKING IT THROUGH ——————————————————

1. Think about the way the story is constructed. The first quarter concerns not the crime itself but Slade's conversation with Dr. Matthews. Why didn't the author skip all the conversation and start right in with the crime itself?

2. Turn back to page 43 and reread Slade's excuse for considering the murder. Clearly, something is wrong with Slade's logic and reasoning at this point. Exactly what is wrong?

3. Slade makes a fatal mistake because his mental map lacks one very important fact. What fact is this?

4. If the story were continued, what do you suppose might happen the next day? Will either of the bodies be discovered? Will both be discovered? If so, how? Explain the details.

5. An **allusion** (uh LOO zhun) in a story is a reference to some other work of literature or to some person, place, or event in history. "The Turn of the Tide" contains two allusions. One is to Oscar Wilde's book *The Picture of Dorian Grey*. The other is to the Thugs of India. Look up both of these in reference books and explain why they are used in the story.

48

Reading and Analyzing

Appreciating Mood and Tone

Two very useful words in the discussion of literature are *mood* and *tone*. They sometimes mean about the same thing, but it is helpful to make a slight difference clear.

The **mood** of a piece of literature is the feeling it gives the reader. For instance, some stories create a mood of fear, or even terror. A suspenseful mood makes the reader desperate to know what happens next. Other stories can make you sorrowful, thoughtful, or tender. Still others leave you joyful.

The word **tone** refers to the attitude a writer seems to have toward the subject matter. For instance, some writers pretend to be critical about the subject, but they really aren't. Others treat heavy subjects in a lighthearted way, or light subjects in a serious way. Besides critical, lighthearted, and serious, the tone can be humorous, horrified, or sarcastic. The tone can also show the writer's attitude toward the reader. You can see that the writer has many options about what tone to use.

1. Choose two words to describe the *mood* of "The Turn of the Tide." Then explain briefly what the author has done to achieve the mood.

2. *Tone* is a key consideration for a tale like "The Turn of the Tide." On one level, the story concerns a brutal murder and a horrible accidental death. Yet on another level, the story is hardly gruesome at all. Did you finish the story with tears in your eyes or a slight smile on your lips? What did you infer the author's attitude to be? Do you think it is accurate to say that the author treats a heavy subject in a rather light way? Explain your answer.

Composition

1. Suppose the author C. S. Forester were going to visit your class tomorrow. Write the one most important question you can think of to ask him about "The Turn of the Tide." Then imagine that you are Forester. Write a short paragraph in reply to your question. Make up the details. Be creative—even funny if you choose.

2. Choose one of the stories you have read in this unit. Reread it and analyze the tone the writer conveyed to you. Was the tone humorous or sad? Full of wonder, horror, or something else? In a paragraph, name the story of your choice and discuss its tone.

THE SPARROW

by Ivan Turgenev
(1818—1883)

▶ Many authors have written about the mental maps that animals may—or may not—have. On page 38, you read some poetic speculations by the Canadian writer Margaret Atwood. Here is an experience of the celebrated Russian author Ivan Turgenev.

I was returning from a day's hunting and was walking toward the house along an alley in my garden. My dog was running ahead of me.

Suddenly she slowed her pace and began to advance stealthily, as though she had caught scent of game.

I looked down the path and saw a young sparrow with a streak of yellow near its beak and a bit of puff on its head. It had fallen out of the nest. (A strong wind was swaying the birch trees.) The tiny bird sat there trying helplessly to use its barely grown wings.

My dog was stealing up to the infant sparrow when, abruptly, an old black-chested bird fell like a stone right in front of the dog's face,

---

- speculation (spek yuh LAY shun) **idea; theory; view**
- stealthily (STEL thuh lee) **in a manner to escape notice**

and with all its feathers standing on end, misshapen, uttering a desperate and pitiful chirp, it hopped once and then again in the direction of the dog's open jaw.

The bird had thrown itself in front of the dog to shield its young one, but its own small body was trembling with terror, its little voice was frenzied and hoarse, and it was numb with fright—it was sacrificing itself!

What a huge monster the dog must have seemed to the mother sparrow! Nevertheless, it could not bear to stay on its high, safe perch in the tree. A force stronger than its will to remain alive made it hurl itself to the rescue.

My Treasure, the dog, stopped still and then backed up. Evidently she, too, recognized that force. . . .

I hastened to call off the puzzled dog and went on my way, awed.

Yes, do not laugh. I was awed by that small, heroic bird—by its impulse of love.

Love, I felt more than ever, is stronger than death and the fear of death. Only through love is life sustained and nourished.

THINKING IT THROUGH

1. Do you agree with Turgenev that the mother sparrow's actions can be called "an impulse of love"? Or was it simply thoughtless instinct?
2. Think about the dog. In your opinion, was a recognition of "love" in any way a part of the dog's mental map?
3. **Fiction** is writing such as a short story or a novel that is purely made up by a writer. **Nonfiction** is about events that happened in real life. Do you think that "The Sparrow" is fiction or nonfiction? Tell why you think so.

● awed (AWD) **overcome with wonder and emotion**

Geoffrey Chaucer (1340?-1400)

Some of the travelers in *The Canterbury Tales*

Geoffrey Chaucer, often called "the father of English poetry," was born in London, the son of a successful wine merchant. At the age of 17, he became a page in a royal household. His talents were recognized at once, and he went on to spend his entire working life in government service. He served as a soldier, as a squire, and as a diplomat to France and Italy. He held such posts as customs supervisor in the port of London, royal forester, and clerk to King Richard II.

In Chaucer's time, long before the invention of the printing press, there was no career called *author* or *writer*. For Chaucer, writing was a hobby. He worked hard at it, and several of his works survive. The best known is the great classic *The Canterbury Tales*. It was begun about 1386 and was left unfinished at the poet's death.

Chaucer's plan for *The Canterbury Tales* was an ambitious one. Thirty characters, drawn from every level of society, would gather in London for a religious pilgrimage or journey to a famous sacred shrine in Canterbury. Parts of the long poem would involve these characters, from detailed descriptions of each to sudden arguments they might have. Other parts would be the tales told by the characters to pass time during the trip. The result was a rich tapestry of the medieval world— not a formal history but an inside view. To read Chaucer is to learn that in some ways human beings have changed very little over the last 600 years.

from

THE PARDONER'S TALE

by Geoffrey Chaucer

▶ Among the best of Chaucer's *Canterbury Tales* is the story told by the pardoner. In fourteenth-century England, a pardoner was a person who sold religious articles that were supposed to pardon, or excuse from punishment, some sin of the buyer. One might expect a pardoner's story to concern reward for virtue. As Chaucer and his pardoner knew, however, the punishment for vice makes for much better reading!

In Flaundres whylom was a companye
Of yonge folk, that haunteden folye;
They daunce and pleye at dees both day and night,
And ete also and drinken over her might.

(*Whoops! That's Chaucer's fourteenth-century English. Let's try a modern translation.*)

In Flanders once there was a company
Of young folk that were bent on chasing folly;
They danced and played at dice both day and night,
And also ate and drank beyond their might.

These rioters three, of whom I will now tell,
Long before the sound of morning bell,
Were sitting in a tavern, talking, drinking,
Till too much drink began to cloud their thinking:
"Let each of us now pledge to both the others
That we three are—hic, hic—the best of brothers!"
Then up they jumped and hastened from the village,
Intent on riot, merriment, or pillage.

- **vice** (VYS) **evil habit or act**
- Flanders (FLAN durz) **medieval country in Western Europe (now included in France, Belgium, and Holland)**
- rioter (RY ut ur) **one who leads a noisy, disorderly, uncontrolled life**
- pillage (PIL ij) **robbery especially in wartime**

When they had gone not fully half a mile,
Just as they were about to climb a stile,
Among some trees, there lying on the ground,
A mighty heap of golden coins they found.
The pile was huge—bushels, as they thought;
They'd have to haul it off, and not get caught.
Oh, each of them was so glad at the sight
Because the florins were so large and bright!
They sat down then beside this precious hoard;
The worst of them, he uttered the first word.
"Brothers," he said, "now hear well what I say;
My mind is clear, although I joke and play.
Fortune's given us this precious treasure
So that we may live out our lives in pleasure.
We've got to carry all this gold away,
But surely, it cannot be done by day.

- stile (STYL) **steps in or over a wall or fence**
- florin (FLOR in) **former gold coin of several countries**

This treasure must be carried off by night,
As wisely and as slyly as we might.
Therefore, I think that right now we should all
Draw lots, to see to whom the lot will fall
To run to town, and bring us bread and wine,
So that, before our labor, we may dine.
And two of us will keep close watch right here
In case some other rascals might appear."
Then they drew straws, to see whose lot would fall,
And it fell upon the youngest of them all
To make the quick trip back and forth to town.
The other two shook hands and sat back down.

Then one of them spoke thus unto the other:
"You know my friend, that you're my best-loved brother.
Let's talk about this gold, just me and you:
Why can't these coins be split between us two?"
The other answered, "Fine! Two now, not three!
But I know not just how that's going to be.
He knows the gold is right here with us two.
What shall we say to him? What shall we do?"
"It won't be hard at all," the other said.
"We'll stab him through both sides and leave him dead.
And then shall all the gold divided be,
My dearest friend, between yourself and me."

The youngest then, the one who went to town,
Let evil fancies pull him down and down.
The beauty of those florins, new and bright!
There had to be a way—some plan that might
Win *all* the gold for him that very night!
And soon it was his very clear intention
To carry out a plan I hate to mention.
He hurried on—no longer would he tarry—
And once in town found an apothecary
And asked the man for poison. "To kill rats,"
He said, "and, in my poultry yard, polecats
That raid my chicken coop most every night.
I want to kill the vermin, if I might."

- draw lots—choose by chance
- **fancy** (FAN see) **notion; thought**
- apothecary (uh POTH u ker ee) **pharmacist;   person   li-
censed to sell medicines**
- polecat (POHL kat) **European animal much like a skunk**
- vermin (VUR min) **harmful small animals or insects**

"What I have here," said the apothecary,
"Is something that is strong and very scary.
To tell the truth, there is no living creature
It will not kill. And, another feature,
A piece no bigger than a grain of wheat
Is all that poor, doomed creature has to eat."
Taking the poison, away the rascal ran
Into the next street, where he met a man
Who sold him three small jugs of rosy wine.
Alone again, he marked one jug: "That's mine!
I'll put the poison in the other two;
Then I'll return, and see what it will do!"

Why need this sermon go on any more?
For as the two had planned so well before,
Just so they killed him, just like that.
And then, upon the bloody ground they sat.
One said, "Let's have a drink, and make us merry,
And afterward we will his body bury."
And with those words, it happened that he took
A bottle with the poison. Then with a look
Of joy he drank, and passed to his good friend
The jug. Mercy! Horrors! What an end!

Thus both were poisoned for their homicide,
And thus the fiendish poisoner also died.

fiendish (FEEN dish) savagely cruel

ALL THINGS CONSIDERED

1. For modern readers, the English of Chaucer's time (see sample on page 53) is (a) hard but possible to read. (b) very easy to understand. (c) completely impossible to read.

2. The first man to die is (a) an apothecary. (b) the worst of the rioters. (c) the youngest of the three rioters.

3. The chief vice of the three rioters is their (a) dancing and drinking. (b) playing with dice. (c) willingness to kill for greed.

4. The hardest part of the story to believe is (a) that poisons were known 600 years ago. (b) the sudden and unexplained appearance of the pile of gold. (c) that the three men did not report their find to the police.

5. Chaucer's pardoner tells his tale as (a) an exercise in logical thinking. (b) a sermon with a lesson. (c) an example of the way foreigners act.

THINKING IT THROUGH

1. (a) What lie does the youngest rioter tell the apothecary? (b) Why might he think the lie is necessary?

2. In which ways were the rioters truly friends? In which ways were the rioters deceitful with one another?

3. Think about the story in terms of maps and territories. Choose any character and explain what is wrong with his mental map of the situation as the tale nears its climax.

4. Before the invention of the printing press, stories were often written and told in the manner of "The Pardoner's Tale"—as long narrative poems. A **narrative poem** tells a story. It has a rather regular pattern of rhyme and rhythm. Why might stories have been told as narrative poems before printing became common?

5. **Onomatopoeia** (on uh mat uh PEE uh) is the use of a word that imitates the natural sound associated with a certain action or a certain thing. For example, when you say the word *buzz*, you can almost hear the sound of a bee. There is a good example of onomatopoeia near the bottom of page 53. What is it?

6. The pardoner calls this tale a sermon. What lesson or moral does it convey to you?

Reading and Analyzing

Recognizing Irony

In shaping their plots, successful authors use many time-proven literary techniques. Among the most common of these techniques is the use of *irony* (EYE ruh nee).

Irony is the use of words to say something quite different from what is actually meant or appears true. For example, suppose a friend drags into school suffering from a three-day cold, a sleepless night, and a ten-block walk through a downpour. You might say, "You really look great!" If so, you would be using irony.

In the study of literature, the word *irony* has other special uses:

Irony of situation occurs when there is a striking difference between what a character expects to happen and what actually does happen. For instance,

in "Love Is a Fallacy" (page 23), the narrator's plan to remake Polly into a "logical" person who loves him fails completely. Polly uses her new understanding of logic against the narrator and announces that she'd prefer to be with someone else. Because the narrator's efforts end in the opposite result from what he hoped, the story ends in an ironic situation.

Dramatic irony goes further than irony of situation by involving the *reader's* understanding. Dramatic irony occurs when a reader knows something important that a character doesn't know. Near the end of "Love Is a Fallacy," you probably understood what Polly would do with her new knowledge of fallacies before the self-centered narrator did. If so, you enjoyed a moment or two of dramatic irony.

Composition

1. You experienced dramatic irony during your reading of "The Pardoner's Tale." In one sentence, tell what you know about the two older rioter's plan before the youngest rioter knows. In a second sentence, tell what you know about the youngest rioter's plan before his fellow rioters know.

2. Write two short paragraphs analyzing how Chaucer uses irony in "The Pardoner's Tale." Are the characters' expectations fulfilled at the end? What does the reader know and foresee as the climax approaches? Use both the terms *irony of situation* and *dramatic irony* in your paragraphs.

VOCABULARY AND SKILL REVIEW

Before completing the exercises that follow, you may wish to review the **bold-faced** words on pages 39–58.

I. 1. The *drawing room* in a nineteenth-century mansion would be the (a) living room. (b) children's activity room. (c) pantry.

2. *Educated* is to *ignorant* as *virtue* is to (a) *habit.* (b) *pleasure.* (c) *vice.*

3. An *obstinate* person is (a) overweight and slow moving. (b) stubborn and hard to persuade. (c) friendly and very generous.

4. An *obscure* part of the world would be (a) visited by few people. (b) rich in natural resources. (c) a danger to other countries.

5. Your face is most *immobile* when you are (a) eating. (b) shouting. (c) sleeping.

6. An idle *fancy* is a(n) (a) unused machine. (b) unworn piece of jewelry. (c) casual notion or thought.

7. An example of an *allusion* is (a) "as sad as a Christmas tree on a February street." (b) "'I'm . . . ,' she stammered." (c) "he hit the ball like Babe Ruth."

8. When you speak with *irony,* you usually (a) want to hurt someone's feelings. (b) say the opposite of what you really mean. (c) imitate another person's speech habits.

9. The *tone* of a work of literature is (a) the feeling it gives the reader. (b) what seems to be the author's attitude. (c) difficulty of the vocabulary.

10. If you start the new year with *resolve,* you start with (a) a determined purpose. (b) fear of the future. (c) no worries.

59

II. Read this Chinese folktale carefully before answering the questions that follow it.

THE CLOCKMAKER
AND THE TIMEKEEPER

retold by Isabelle C. Chang

There was once a clockmaker who had a shop in the center of the village. Every day a man stopped by and looked in the window, before hurrying on his way. After a year, the clockmaker hailed the man one day and asked him why he always hesitated by the window, but never entered the shop.

The man replied, "I am the timekeeper for the town, and I have to ring the church bells at exactly twelve o'clock noon. To be accurate, I always check with your clock first."

"Ah," said the clockmaker, "but I always set my clock after I hear the chimes of the church bells."

1. In Chang's original book of folktales, the story was followed by a short moral, or lesson. You can *infer* that the moral is (a) "If at first you don't succeed, try, try again." (b) "Look before you leap." (c) "The world is made up of the blind leading the blind."
2. Tell which two of the following terms best describe the *mood* of the story: *thoughtful, fearful, angry, reverential, humorous, tearful, deliriously happy.*

UNIT REVIEW

I. Match the terms in Column A with their definitions in Column B.

A	B
1. inference	**a)** exciting part of story at or near the end
2. climax	**b)** work of literature that pokes fun at some idea or human weakness
3. logic	
4. fallacy	**c)** reader's knowledge of something important that a character doesn't know
5. simile	
6. narrator	**d)** guess based on the available evidence
7. irony of situation	**e)** error in reasoning
	f) events actually happen far differently from what a character expects
8. dramatic irony	
	g) clear thinking
9. satire	**h)** storyteller
10. onomatopoeia	**i)** use of a word that imitates the natural sound
	j) comparison made with a word such as *like* or *as*

II. Comment on the cartoon below in terms of maps and territories. What mental maps do the men shown have for the word *wheel?* What does the complete territory suggest? Can you infer any "deeper meaning" from the cartoon about the way people sometimes think and behave? Explain your inference(s).

Deeper Meanings #36

Bonus questions: Here are 20 questions that require careful reading and logical thinking. Write all the answers on a sheet of paper before checking them on page 314.

1. If a doctor gave you three pills and told you to take one every half hour, how long before you would be out of pills?
2. If you went to bed at eight o'clock at night and set the alarm to get up at nine o'clock in the morning, how many hours of sleep would this permit you to have?
3. Do they have a fourth of July in England?
4. How many birthdays does the average American male have?
5. Why can't a woman living in North Carolina be buried west of the Mississippi River?
6. If you had only one match and wanted to light a lamp, an oil heater, and some kindling wood, which would you light first?
7. Some months have thirty days; some have thirty-one. How many have twenty-eight days?
8. A person builds a house with four sides—a rectangular structure with each side having a southern exposure. A big bear comes wandering by. What color is the bear?
9. How far can a dog run into the woods?
10. What four words appear on every piece of U.S. money?
11. How many players on a baseball team? How many outs in each inning?
12. If two U.S. coins total 55¢ and one is not a nickel (please keep that in mind) what are the two coins?
13. A farmer had seventeen sheep; all but nine died. How many are left?
14. Divide 30 by ½. Add 10. What is the answer?
15. Two men played five games of checkers. Each man won the same number of games. How can that be?
16. If you take two apples from three apples that are on the table, how many do you have?
17. The person who said he found a gold coin marked "40 B.C." was either lying or kidding. Why?
18. How many animals of each species did Moses take aboard the ark?
19. A woman gives a beggar 50¢. The woman is the beggar's sister, but the beggar is not the woman's brother. How come?
20. Is it legal for a man to marry his widow's sister?

SPEAKING UP

Pantomiming: Many beginning speakers report that, when speaking before a group, they get so tense that their bodies look stiff and unnatural. These speakers may not realize the importance of *body language.*

A good way to begin to relax your body is to **pantomime** or act out a short scene without speaking. In order to be effective you should act exactly as if you are doing the thing you chose to pantomime. Use very definite, detailed actions to make your pantomime understandable and enjoyable for the audience.

Choose one of the following actions to pantomime. Your pantomime need last only one to three minutes.

1. Washing an elephant
2. Trying on a new fur coat in a department store
3. Eating lunch
4. Filling an order for a customer in a fast food restaurant
5. Trying to train a new puppy
6. Reluctantly walking into the backyard and fixing a fence that has fallen down

Now try *pantomiming* (acting without using words) a scene from a selection in Unit I.

In most scenes, two or three students should work together. First of all, reread the selection you chose. Pay particular attention to the page(s) mentioned below. Plan what you will do to bring out the feelings and the actions of the character(s).

1. "Cemetery Path" (for one student—as Ivan) Pantomime the scene in which Ivan walks alone through the cemetery and then pounds the saber into the ground. End the pantomime at the terrifying moment when Ivan discovers he can't move (see page 3).
2. "The Pardoner's Tale" (for three students—as the three rioters) Pantomime the entire story (see pages 53–56).
3. "The Turn of the Tide" (for two students playing Slade and Spalding) Begin the action as Slade picks up Spalding in his car. Pantomime to the end of the story (see pages 44–47).
4. "Love Is a Fallacy" (for two students playing the narrator and his roommate, Petey) Begin as the narrator throws open his suitcase to reveal "the huge, hairy object"—the raccoon coat (see page 25). End as the two students shake hands, having made their deal (see page 26).

WRITING A NEWS STORY

Prewriting: Before writing a news story, a reporter gathers the facts. As an illustration, pretend that the events in the story "Cemetery Path" actually happened. You may choose this selection or another one from the unit. Whichever selection you choose, read it again. As you read, list the facts given in the story. Here are the first four facts that might be listed for "Cemetery Path."

- The villagers teased Ivan because he was so timid.

- Ivan had never crossed the cemetery before.

- Ivan stopped in at the saloon on the edge of the village cemetery every night.

- There was a bitter wind and it was snowing.

When you have finished, look over your list. What is the most important fact? Obviously, in this story it is the fact that Ivan died. Now go through your list and number each fact in order of importance. The most important fact should be number one, the next most important should be number two . . . all the way down to the least important fact.

Now see if you can answer the following questions. (These questions are the famous "Five W's" that news writers often try to include in the first paragraph of a story.)

- *WHO* was the main person involved? (You may wish to invent a last name if it is not given in the selection you choose.)

- *WHAT* happened? How did it happen?

- *WHEN* did it happen? (Because this is a news story, assume that the events occurred "last night.")

- *WHERE* did it happen? (Invent a name for the town, if necessary.)

- *WHY* did it happen? (For example, what events led to Ivan's death?)

Writing: To begin a news story, first write the *lead* (LEED). The lead is the first sentence of a news story. Although it is only one sentence, it gives a summary of the most important events. In your lead, summarize the most important facts. Use your answers to three of the "Five W's." For example, tell *WHO, WHAT,* and *WHEN.* Then conclude your first paragraph by writing an additional sentence. Include any other answers to the "Five W's." For example, answer the questions *WHERE* and *WHY.*

The remainder of the paragraphs in a news story give additional information. In order to be as clear as possible, news writers often give the additional facts one at a time, sentence by sentence.

Look at your organized list of facts from the story. Try to use each fact in a separate sentence, beginning with the most important fact and ending with the least important. For example, if you chose "Cemetery Path" you might mention the facts surrounding Ivan's death. You might also include further information about the bet. You may want to add other less important information such as the fact that the villagers often teased Ivan about his fearfulness, the fact that Ivan had never crossed the cemetery before, and the facts about the weather.

Revising: After writing your news story, study it carefully. Make improvements where they are needed. Use the checklist below as an aid in revising your news story. (Note: You may prefer to exchange your news story with a classmate and use the checklist to evaluate each other's news story for revision.)

1. Reread your lead. Is the information stated clearly?
2. Are answers to most of the "Five W's" included in your first paragraph?
3. Look at your other paragraphs. Does each sentence tell only one important fact? If not, rewrite any sentence with more than one fact as two or more short sentences.
4. Does the news article include one or two of the fascinating *minor* details?
5. Are adjectives, words that describe, used sparingly in your news story? Go through your story and cross out any *unnecessary* adjectives.
6. Did you use vivid, colorful verbs? Look at the action words in your story. Do they create vivid pictures, or do they seem uninteresting and stale? For example, note that in the story "Cemetery Path" Ivan *blurted* (rather than just *said*). The wind *howled* (rather than *blew*). Ivan *strode* to the cemetery gates (rather than *walked*). Make use of these vivid action verbs in your news story.
7. Consider whether or not your story will appeal to your readers. Who might read your news story? Did you write about something that will be of interest to them? Did you make your story interesting through a clear presentation with interesting details?

U N I T · 2

DISCOVERING DIFFERENCES

You are so accustomed to seeing and looking for similarities in the environment that you may forget that everything in the universe is unique. That is, every single thing in the environment is different from everything else.

"How elementary!" you may exclaim. Yet how often do you act as though all things called by the same name are exactly alike? For example, what happens when you hear the words "police officers"? Does a picture form in your head? Do you see just the uniforms—or do you see individual faces? *Some* people might say, "All police officers are just like that one who gave me a ticket!" But are they?

When you stop to think about it, it is obvious that no two things are ever *exactly* alike. Think, for example, about snowflakes. Have you ever caught snowflakes on a dark coat sleeve and really looked at their shapes? If so, you've proved for yourself the old adage that each snowflake is unique. Well, just as each snowflake is unique, so is each apple, each tree, each teenager, each police officer.

In this unit you are asked to think about *differences*. What's different about a certain "murder"? What's different about a certain runaway teenager? What differences does a man discover about his wife—a woman he thought he knew very well? You'll find unexpected answers to these questions—and more—as you read the selections that follow.

A KIND OF MURDER

by Hugh Pentecost

▶ Hugh Pentecost has written scores of full-length mystery novels about adults who commit murder. In "A Kind of Murder," the narrator and "murderer" is a teenager. As you read the story, try to determine whether or not you would have been as guilty as the narrator if you were in the same situation.

You might say this is the story of a murder—although nobody was killed. I don't know what has become of Mr. Silas Warren, but I have lived for many years with the burden on my conscience of having been responsible for the existence of a walking dead man.

I was fifteen years old during the brief span of days that I knew Mr. Silas Warren. It was toward the end of the winter term at Morgan Military Academy. Mr. Etsweiler, the chemistry and physics teacher at Morgan, had died of a heart attack one afternoon while he was help-

ing to coach the hockey team on the lake. Mr. Henry Huntingdon Hadley, the headmaster, had gone to New York to find a replacement. That replacement was Mr. Silas Warren.

I may have been one of the first people to see Mr. Warren at the Academy. I had been excused from afternoon study period because of a heavy cold, and allowed to take my books to my room to work there. I saw Mr. Warren come walking across the quadrangle toward Mr. Hadley's office, which was located on the ground floor under the hall where my room was.

● headmaster (HED mas tur) **school principal**

Mr. Warren didn't look like a man who was coming to stay long. He carried one small, flimsy suitcase spattered with travel labels. Although it was a bitter March day he wore a thin, summer-weight topcoat. He stopped beside a kind of brown lump in the snow. That brown lump was Teddy, the school dog.

Teddy was an ancient collie. They said that in the old days you could throw a stick for Teddy to retrieve until you, not he, dropped from exhaustion. Now the old, gray-muzzled dog was pretty much ignored by everyone except the chef, who fed him scraps from the dining room after the noon meal. Teddy would be at the kitchen door, promptly on time, and then find a comfortable spot to lie down. He'd stay there until someone forced him to move.

Mr. Warren stopped by Teddy, bent down, and scratched the dog's head. The old, burr-clotted tail thumped wearily in the snow. Mr. Warren straightened up and looked around. He had narrow, stooped shoulders. His eyes were pale blue, and they had a kind of frightened look in them. *He's scared,* I thought; *coming to a new place in the middle of a term, he's scared.*

I guess most of the other fellows didn't see Mr. Warren until he turned up at supper time at the head of one of the tables in the dining room. We marched into the dining room and stood behind our chairs waiting for the cadet major to give the order to be seated. The order was delayed. Mr. Henry Huntingdon Hadley, known as Old Beaver because of his snowy white beard, made an announcement.

"Mr. Warren has joined our teaching staff to fill the vacancy created by the un-fortunate demise of Mr. Etsweiler." Old Beaver had false teeth and his s's whistled musically. "I trust you will give him a cordial welcome."

"Be seated," the cadet major snapped.

We sat. Old Beaver said grace. Then we all began to talk. I was at Mr. Warren's right. He had a genial, want-to-be-liked smile.

"And your name is?" he asked me in a pleasant but flat voice.

"Pentecost, sir."

He leaned toward me. "How's that?" he asked.

"Pentecost, sir."

Sammy Callahan sat across from me on Mr. Warren's left. Sammy was a fine athlete and a terrible practical joker. I saw a gleam of interest in his eyes. As Mr. Warren turned toward him Sammy spoke in an ordinary conversational tone. "Why don't you go take a jump in the lake, sir?"

Mr. Warren smiled. "Yes, I guess you're right," he said.

Sammy grinned at me. There was no doubt about it—Mr. Warren was quite deaf!

It was a strange kind of secret Sammy and I had. We didn't really know what to do with it, but we found out that night. Old Beaver was not a man to start anyone in gradually. It would have been Mr. Etsweiler's turn to take the night study hour, so that hour was passed on to Mr. Warren.

He sat on the little platform at the head of the study hall—smiling and smiling. I think there must have been terror in his heart then. I think he may even have been praying.

Everyone seemed unusually busy studying, but we were all waiting for the

---

- demise (duh MYZ) **death**
- genial (JEE nyul) **pleasant**

test. The test always came for a new master the first time he had night study hour. There would be a minor disturbance and we'd find out promptly whether this man could maintain discipline, or not. It came after about five minutes—a loud, artificial belch.

Mr. Warren smiled and smiled. He hadn't heard it.

Belches sprang up all over the room. Then somebody threw a handful of torn paper in the air. Mr. Warren's smile froze.

"Now, now boys," he said.

More belches. More torn paper.

"Boys!" Mr. Warren cried out, like someone in pain.

Then Old Beaver appeared, his eyes glittering behind rimless spectacles. There was something I never understood about Old Beaver. Ordinarily his shoes squeaked. You could hear him coming from quite a distance away—squeak-squeak, squeak-squeak. But somehow, when he chose, he could approach as noiselessly as a cat, without any squeak at all. And there he was.

The study hall was quiet as a tomb. But the silence was frighteningly loud, and the place was littered with paper.

"There will be ten demerit marks against every student in this room," Old Beaver said in his icy voice. "I want every scrap of paper picked up instantly."

Several of us scrambled down on our hands and knees. Mr. Warren smiled at the headmaster.

"Consider the lilies of the field," Mr. Warren said. "They toil not, neither do they spin. Yet I tell you that Solomon in all his glory—"

"Silence!" Old Beaver hissed, with all the menace of a poised cobra. He turned to Mr. Warren. "I'll take the balance of this period, Mr. Warren. I suggest you go to your room and prepare yourself for tomorrow's curriculum."

● curriculum (kuh RIK yuh lum) **course of study**

I didn't have any classes with Mr. Warren the next day, but all you heard as you passed in the corridors from one class period to the next were tales of the jokes and disorders in the physics and chemistry courses. Somehow nobody thought it was wrong to take advantage of Mr. Warren.

The climax came very quickly. In the winter, if you weren't out for the hockey or winter sports teams, you had to exercise in the gym. There were the parallel bars, and the rings, and the tumbling mats. And there was boxing.

The boxing teacher was Major Durand, the military commandant. I know now that he was a sadist. Major Durand was filled with contempt for everyone but Major Durand. I saw the look on his face when Mr. Warren appeared.

Mr. Warren had been assigned to help in the gym. He was something to see—just skin and bones. He had on a pair of ordinary black socks and, I suspect, the only pair of shoes he owned— black oxfords. He'd borrowed a pair of shorts that could have been wrapped twice around his skinny waist. Above that was a much mended short-sleeved undershirt. He looked around, hopeless, amiable.

"Mr. Warren!" Major Durand said. "I'd like you to help me demonstrate. Put on these gloves if you will." He tossed a pair of boxing gloves at Mr. Warren, who stared at them stupidly. One of the boys helped him tie the laces.

"Now, Mr. Warren," Durand said. The Major danced and bobbed and weaved, and shot out his gloves in short vicious jabs at the air. "You will hold your gloves up to your face, sir. When you're ready you'll say 'Hit!'—and I shall hit you."

I'd seen Major Durand do this with a boy he didn't like. You held up the gloves and you covered your face and then, with your throat dry and aching, you said "Hit!"—and Major Durand's left or right would smash through your guard and pulverize your nose or mouth. It was sheer strength I know now, not skill.

Mr. Warren held up his gloves, and he looked like an actor in an old Mack Sennett* comedy—the absurd clothes, the sickly smile.

Durand danced in front of him. "Whenever you say, Mr. Warren. Now watch this, boys. The feint—and the jab."

"Hit!" said Mr. Warren, his voice suddenly falsetto.

Pow! Major Durand's left jab smashed through the guard of Mr. Warren's nose. There was a sudden geyser of blood.

"Again, Mr. Warren!" the Major commanded, his eyes glittering.

"I think I'd better retire to repair the damage," Mr. Warren said. His undershirt was spattered with blood and he had produced a soiled handkerchief which he held to his nose. He hurried out of the gym at a sort of shambling gallop.

That night the payoff came in study hall. Mr. Warren was called on this time to

---

- commandant (KAWM un dant) **commanding officer**
- sadist (SAY dist) **one who enjoys being cruel to others**
- contempt (kun TEMPT) **scorn; lack of respect**
- **amiable** (AY mee uh bul) **good natured and friendly**
- feint (FAYNT) **pretended attack or blow at one point when another point is really intended to be struck**
- falsetto (fawl SET oh) **artificially high male voice**

*Mack Sennett (1884–1960): producer of movie comedies

substitute for Old Beaver, who had taken over for him the night before. Sammy Callahan staged it. Suddenly handkerchiefs were waved from all parts of the room—handkerchiefs stained red. Red ink, of course.

"Hit!" somebody shouted. "Hit, hit!" Nearly all the boys were bobbing, weaving, jabbing.

Mr. Warren, pale as a ghost, cotton visibly stuffed in one nostril, stared at us like a dead man.

Then there was Old Beaver again.

Somehow the word was out at breakfast the next morning. Mr. Warren was leaving. He didn't show at the breakfast table. I felt a little squeamish about it. He hadn't been given a chance. Maybe he wasn't such a bad guy.

It was during the morning classroom period that we heard it. It was a warm day for March and the ice was breaking up on the lake. The scream was piercing and terrified. Somebody went to the window. The scream came again.

"Somebody's fallen through the ice!"

The whole school—a hundred and fifty boys and masters—hurried down to the shore of the lake. The sun was so bright that all we could see was a dark shape flopping out there, pulling itself up on the ice and then disappearing under water as the ice broke. Each time the figure rose there was a wailing scream.

Then the identification. "It's Teddy!" someone shouted.

The school dog. He'd walked out there and the ice had caved in on him. The screams were growing weaker. A couple of us made for the edge of the ice. Old Beaver and Major Durand confronted us.

"I'm sorry, boys," Old Beaver said. "It's a tragic thing to have to stand here and watch the old dog drown. But no one—no one connected with the school—is to try to get to him. I'm responsible for your safety. That's an order."

We stood there, sick with it. Old Teddy must have seen us because for a moment there seemed to be new hope in his strangled wailing.

Then I saw Mr. Warren. He was by the boathouse, his old suitcase in his hand. He looked out at the dog, and so help me there were tears in Mr. Warren's eyes. Then, very calmly, he put down his bag, took off his thin topcoat and suit jacket. He righted one of the overturned boats on the shore and pulled it to the edge of the lake.

"Mr. Warren! You heard my order!" Old Beaver shouted at him.

Mr. Warren turned to the headmaster, smiling. "You seem to forget, sir, I am no longer connected with Morgan Military Academy, and therefore not subject to your orders."

"Stop him!" Major Durand ordered.

● squeamish (SKWEE mish) **shocked; disgusted**

But before anyone could reach him, Mr. Warren had slid the flat-bottomed rowboat out onto the ice. He crept along on the ice himself, clinging to the boat, pushing it across the shiny surface toward Teddy. I heard Mr. Warren's thin, flat voice.

"Hold on, old man! I'm coming."

The ice gave way under him, but he clung to the boat and scrambled up—and on.

"Hold on, old man!"

It seemed to take forever. Just before what must have been the last, despairing shriek from the half-frozen dog, Mr. Warren reached him. How he found the strength to lift the watersoaked collie into the boat, I don't know; but he managed, and then he came back toward us, creeping along the cracking ice, pushing the boat to shore.

The chef wrapped Teddy in blankets, put him behind the stove in the kitchen, and gave him a dose of warm milk and cooking brandy. Mr. Warren was hustled to the infirmary. Did I say that when he reached the shore with Teddy the whole school cheered him?

Old Beaver, for all his tyranny, must have been a pretty decent guy. He announced that night that Mr. Warren was not leaving after all. He trusted that, after Mr. Warren's display of valor, the boys would show him the respect he deserved.

I went to see Mr. Warren in the infirmary that first evening. He looked pretty done in, but he also looked happier than I'd ever seen him.

"What you did took an awful lot of courage," I told him. "Everybody thinks it was really a swell thing to do."

Mr. Warren smiled at me—a thoughtful kind of a smile. "Courage is a matter

---

- **infirmary** (in FUR muh ree) place for the sick
- **tyranny** (TEER uh nee) unjust use of power
- **valor** (VAL ur) courage

73

of definition," he said. "It doesn't take courage to stand up and let yourself get punched in the nose, boy. It takes courage to walk away. As for Teddy— somebody had to go after him. There wasn't anyone who could but me, so courage or not, I went. You'd have gone if Mr. Hadley hadn't issued orders." He sighed. "I'm glad to get a second chance here. Very glad."

Somehow I got the notion it was a last chance—the very last chance he'd ever have.

It was a week before Mr. Warren had the night study hall again. It was a kind of test. For perhaps fifteen minutes nothing happened and then I heard Sammy give his fine, artificial belch. I looked up at Mr. Warren. He was smiling happily. He hadn't heard. A delighted giggle ran around the room.

I was on my feet. "If there's one more sound in this room I'm going after Old Beaver," I said. "And after that I'll personally take on every guy in this school if necessary, to knock sense into him!"

The room quieted. I was on the student council and I was also captain of the boxing team. The rest of the study period was continued in an orderly fashion. When it was over and we were headed for our rooms, Mr. Warren flagged me down.

"I don't know quite what was going on, Pentecost," he said, "but I gather you saved the day for me. Thank you. Thank you very much. Perhaps when the boys get to know me a little better they'll come to realize—" He made a helpless little gesture with his bony hands.

"I'm sure they will, sir," I said. "I'm sure of it."

"They're not cruel," Mr. Warren said. "It's just high spirits, I know."

Sammy Callahan was waiting for me in my room. "What are you, some kind of a do-gooder?" he said.

"Give the guy a chance," I said. "He proved he has guts when it's needed. But he's helpless there in the study hall."

Sammy gave me a sour grin. "You and he should get along fine," he said. "And you'll need to. The guys aren't going to be chummy with a do-gooder like you."

It was a week before Mr. Warren's turn to run the study hour came around again. In that time I'd found that Sammy was right. I was being given the cold shoulder. Major Durand, who must have hated Mr. Warren for stealing the heroic spotlight from him, was giving me a hard time. One of the guys I knew well came to me.

"You're making a mistake," he told me. "He's a grown man and you're just a kid. If he can't take care of himself it's not your headache."

I don't like telling the next part of it, but it happened.

When Mr. Warren's night came again, the study hall was quiet enough for a while. Then came a belch. I looked up at Mr. Warren. He was smiling. Then someone waved one of those fake bloody handkerchiefs. Then, so help me, somebody let out a baying howl—like Teddy in the lake.

Mr. Warren knew what was happening now. He looked down at me, and there was an agonizing, wordless plea for help in his eyes. I—well, I looked away. I was fifteen. I didn't want to be called a do-gooder. I didn't want to be snubbed. Mr. Warren *was* a grown man and he should have been able to take care of himself. The boys weren't cruel: they were just high spirited—hadn't Mr. Warren himself said so?

• do-gooder—someone who tries to reform bad conditions

I looked up from behind a book. Mr. Warren was standing, looking out over the room. His stooped, skinny shoulders were squared away. Two great tears ran down his pale cheeks. His last chance was played out.

Then he turned and walked out of the study hall.

No one ever saw him again. He must have gone straight to his room, thrown his meager belongings into the battered old suitcase, and taken off on foot into the night.

You see what I mean when I say it was a kind of murder?

And I was the murderer.

ALL THINGS CONSIDERED

1. Mr. Warren (a) has been teaching at Morgan Military Academy for over 20 years. (b) is hired to teach boxing. (c) is selected to replace a teacher who died suddenly.

2. Teddy is the (a) narrator's best friend. (b) school's ancient collie dog. (c) stuffed bear the narrator keeps on his bed.

3. Mr. Warren has trouble controlling the boys partly because he is (a) quite deaf. (b) too strict. (c) very ill.

4. Old Beaver gives Mr. Warren a second chance to stay because (a) his wife is Mr. Warren's cousin. (b) Mr. Warren saves Teddy's life. (c) he can't find a replacement.

5. The narrator refuses to help Mr. Warren the second time because (a) he doesn't want to be called a do-gooder. (b) Mr. Warren gave him a low grade in physics. (c) he wants Mr. Warren to leave the school.

THINKING IT THROUGH

1. "Courage is a matter of definition," he [Mr. Warren] says. "It doesn't take courage to stand up and let yourself get punched in the nose, boy. It takes courage to walk away" (page 74). Explain what Mr. Warren means by his definition of courage. Do you agree with it? Explain your answer.

2. Is the boys' behavior toward Mr. Warren different from Major Durand's? If so, how does it differ?

3. The narrator has conflicting feelings. In one way he wants to help Mr. Warren, and in another way he doesn't. (a) What are the two feelings? Try to explain *why* he feels both ways. (b) Which feeling wins at the end of the story?

4. Why does the narrator consider himself a murderer? Do you think he is responsible for Mr. Warren's "walking death"? Explain your answer.

5. What truths about human nature does the story illustrate?

Reading and Analyzing

Evaluating Character Clues

If you are to understand the main characters of a story fully, you need to make inferences, guesses based on available facts about the characters. Consider what the characters say and what they do. The clues the author gives readers through a character's actions and speeches are called **character clues.**

Keep in mind that a character may be *dynamic* or *static*. A **dynamic character** changes in some way as the story progresses. The change may be shown through the character's thoughts, words, or actions. A **static character** remains the same throughout the story.

Read the following character clues about Mr. Warren. Explain what you can infer about him from each clue.

1. He carried one small, flimsy suitcase spattered wth travel labels. Although it was a bitter March day, he wore a thin, summer-weight topcoat.

2. He [Major Durand] tossed a pair of boxing gloves at Mr. Warren, who stared at them stupidly. One of the boys helped him tie the laces.

3. He looked out at the dog, and so help me there were tears in Mr. Warren's eyes.

4. Mr. Warren turned to the headmaster, smiling. "You seem to forget, sir, I am no longer connected with Morgan Military Academy, and therefore not subject to your orders."

5. But before anyone could reach him, Mr. Warren had slid the flat-bottomed rowboat out onto the ice. He crept along on the ice himself, clinging to the boat, pushing it across the shiny surface toward Teddy. I heard Mr. Warren's thin, flat voice.

   "Hold on, old man! I'm coming!"

Composition

1. "A Kind of Murder" tells about what happens when some teenage boys play practical jokes on a teacher who has some weaknesses. In a short paragraph, express your opinion of the boys' actions in the study hall.

2. From character clues the author gives you about the narrator of the story, describe the narrator in your own words. Was he different from the other boys, or just like them? Put your ideas in a short paragraph.

▶ Robert Burns, a world-renowned Scottish poet, was also a farmer. In his poem "To a Mouse" you'll see Burns's concern for a mouse whose nest he has just plowed up. The poem's most famous line states that people and mice have something in common—but Burns goes on to say that, in one significant difference, mice are luckier than we! Read the poem and see if you think he's right.

TO A MOUSE
On Turning Her Up In Her Nest With the Plow, November, 1785

by Robert Burns (1759–1796)

Wee sleek and cowering fearful beastie,
O, what a panic's in thy breastie!
Thou need not start away so hasty,
    With scurrying scamper!
I would be loath to run and chase thee,
    Your life to tamper!

- **cowering** (KOU ur ing) crouching fearfully, shrinking from
- **loath** (LOHTH) unwilling; reluctant

I'm sure that sometimes thou may thieve;
So what? poor beastie, thou must live!
A grain or two occasionally
    'S a small request;
The rest's a blessing come to me,
    So I'll never miss it!

Thy tiny housie, too, in ruin!
Its silly walls the winds are strewin'!
And nothing, now, to build a new one,
    No foliage green!
And bleak December's winds ensuin'
    Biting and keen!

Thou saw the fields laid bare and waste,
And weary winter coming fast,
And cozy here, beneath the blast,
    Thou thought to dwell—
Till crash! the cruel plowshare passed
    Right through they cell.

That wee bit heap of leaves and stubble
Has cost thee many a weary nibble!
Now thou's turned out for all thy trouble,
    Without a home
To bear the winter's sleety dribble
    And frozen loam!

But Mousie, thou art not alone,
In proving foresight may be vain;
The best-laid schemes of mice and men
    Gang aft agley,
And leave us nought but grief and pain,
    For promised joy!

- foliage (FOH lee ij) **leaves of one or more plants**
- ensuing (in SOO ing) **taking place afterward or as a result**
- plowshare (PLOU shayr) **blade of a plow**
- loam (LOHM) **rich soil**
- gang aft agley (GANG AFT uh GLAY) **go often astray**

Still thou art blest, compared with me!
The present only toucheth thee:
But oh! I backward cast my eye,
    On prospects drear!
And forward, though I cannot see,
    I guess and fear!

WAYS OF KNOWING

1. A **stanza** is a division of a poem. Very often a new stanza signifies a change in ideas. At other times, the tone of the poem changes with a new stanza. "To a Mouse" has seven stanzas. What words in the first stanza show us how the mouse seems to feel when the plowshare turns up its nest?

2. How does the narrator feel about the mouse's stealing grain from the field (stanza two)?

3. The narrator realizes that the mouse will have a big problem in the near future. What is it? (Look at stanzas three, four, and five.)

4. Notice that there are many exclamation marks throughout the poem. (a) What do the exclamations suggest about how the narrator feels? (b) In general, how should the lines with exclamations sound if read aloud?

5. What is an example of *onomatopoeia* (see page 57) near the end of the fourth stanza?

6. In the last two of the seven stanzas the theme of the poem is stressed. The narrator sees an important similarity and an important difference between "mice and men." In your own words, what is (a) the similarity, and (b) the difference?

● drear (DREER) **gloomy**

THE FALSE GEMS

by Guy de Maupassant (1850—1893)

▶ Monsieur Lantin was completely happy with his wife. Her only faults were her love for the theater and her passion for false jewelry—or so her husband thought.

Monsieur Lantin met the young woman at a party at the house of the assistant chief of his bureau, and at first sight he fell madly in love with her.

She was the daughter of a country doctor who had died some months previously. She had come to live in Paris, with her mother, who visited her acquaintances often in hopes of making a good marriage for her daughter. The two were poor and honest, quiet and gentle.

The young girl was the perfect type of woman whom every sensible young man dreams of one day marrying. Her simple beauty had the charm of angelic shyness, and the slight smile which constantly hovered about her lips seemed the reflection of her pure and lovely heart. Everybody sang her praises; all who knew her kept saying, "The man who gets her will be lucky. No one could find a nicer girl than that."

M. Lantin, who had a decent income from his job as chief clerk in the office of the Minister of the Interior, proposed to her and was accepted.

He was completely happy with her. She governed his household so cleverly and economically that they seemed to live in luxury. She lavished affection on her husband, tenderly and playfully caressing him. Her charm was so great that, six years after he married her, M. Lantin discovered that he loved his wife even more than during the first days of their honeymoon.

There were only two points upon which he ever found fault with her: her love of the theater, and her passion for false jewelry. Her friends (she was acquainted with some officers' wives) were always bringing her tickets for the theater; whenever there was a new, sensational play, she always had a box secured, even on opening nights. And she would drag her husband with her to all these entertainments, though they bored him horribly after a day's work at the office.

● monsieur (mus YUR) the title in French, abbreviated as M., that corresponds to "mister" (Mr.) in English

After a while, M. Lantin begged his wife to go with one of her lady friends. At first she was opposed to such an arrangement, but, after much persuasion on his part, she finally consented—to her husband's great joy.

Now, with her love for the theater, came also the desire to adorn herself with jewels. Her dresses remained simple and in good taste; but she soon began to ornament her ears with huge rhinestones, which glittered and sparkled like diamonds. Around her neck she wore strings of false pearls, and on her arms bracelets of imitation gold.

Her husband, who felt shocked by her gaudy jewelry, would often say, "My dear, when one cannot afford real jewelry, one should appear adorned only with one's natural beauty and charm—these gifts are the rarest of jewels."

But she would smile sweetly and say, "What can I do? I am so fond of jewelry. It is my only weakness. We can't change our natures."

Then she would roll the pearl necklaces around her fingers, and hold up the bright gems for her husband to admire, saying, "Look! Aren't they lovely? One would swear they were real."

M. Lantin would then answer, smiling, "You have the tastes of a regular gypsy."

• **gaudy** (GAW dee) cheaply showy; tastelessly ornamented

Sometimes in the evening, when they were enjoying chatting together by the fireside, she would place on the tea table the leather box containing the "trash," as M. Lantin called it. She would examine the false gems with a passionate delight, as though they were in some way connected with a deep and secret joy. She often insisted on placing a necklace around her husband's neck, and laughing heartily would exclaim, "Oh! how funny you look!" Then she would throw herself into his arms and kiss him ardently.

One evening in winter she attended the opera, and she came home thoroughly chilled. The next day she had a bad cough. Eight days later she died of pneumonia.

M. Lantin's despair was so great that his hair turned white in one month. He wept from morning until night. His heart was torn with grief, and his mind was haunted by the memory, the smile, the voice—by every charm of his beautiful, dead wife.

Time did not ease his grief. Often during office hours, while his fellow clerks were discussing the topics of the day, his eyes would suddenly fill with tears and he would break into heart-rending sobs.

He had kept his wife's room just as she had left it, and he used to lock himself up in it every night to think about her. All the furniture, and even all her dresses, remained in the same place they had been on the last day of her life.

But life soon became hard for him. His salary, which in his wife's hands had covered all household expenses, was now no longer sufficient to supply his needs. And he wondered how she could have managed to buy such excellent wines and rare, delicious things to eat which he could not now afford at all.

He got into debt and was soon reduced to absolute poverty. One morning, finding himself without a cent in his pockets, he thought of selling something. Almost immediately it occurred to him to sell his wife's paste jewels—for he had always borne a secret grudge against the false gems. They had irritated him in the past, and the very sight of them spoiled somewhat the memory of his lost darling.

He tried a long time to make a choice among the heap of trinkets she had left behind her; for up to the very last days of her life, she had continued to make purchases, bringing home new gems almost every evening. He decided to sell the heavy necklace that she seemed to prefer and which, he thought, ought to be worth about six or seven francs, as it was really very nicely mounted for an imitation necklace.

- ardently (AR dent lee) **very warmly and eagerly**
- heart-rending (HART rend ing) **distressing; heartbreaking**
- paste (PAYST) **artificial jewel**
- franc (FRANK) **unit of French money; at that time one franc was worth approximately 20 cents**

He put it in his pocket and started out in search of a jeweler's shop. Finally he saw a place and went in, feeling a little ashamed of thus exposing his misery and of trying to sell such a worthless object.

"Sir," he said to the jeweler, "I would like to know what this is worth."

The jeweler took the necklace, examined it, weighed it, took up a magnifying glass, called his clerk, talked to him in whispers, put down the necklace on the counter, and looked at it from a distance to judge the effect.

M. Lantin, annoyed and embarrassed by all this detail, started to say, "Oh! I know it can't be worth much," when the jeweler interrupted saying, "Sir, that necklace is worth from twelve to fifteen thousand francs, but I cannot buy it unless you tell me exactly how you come to have it."

The widower opened his eyes wide and stood gaping, unable to understand. Finally he stammered, "You said? . . . Are you sure?" The other, misunderstanding the cause of M. Lantin's astonishment, replied drily, "Go elsewhere if you like and see if you can get any more for it. The very most I would give for it is fifteen thousand. Come back and see me again, if you can't do better."

M. Lantin, feeling perfectly idiotic, took his necklace and left the store. He wanted a chance to think.

Once outside on the street, he began to laugh, and he muttered to himself, "The fool! Had I only taken him at his word! That jeweler cannot tell real diamonds from paste."

A few minutes later, he entered another store in the Rue de la Paix. The moment the jeweler set eyes on the necklace, he exclaimed, "Hello! I know that necklace! It was bought here!"

M. Lantin, very nervous, asked, "What's it worth?"

"Well, I sold it for twenty thousand francs. I am willing to buy it back for eighteen thousand francs, if you can prove to me satisfactorily how you came into possession of it." This time M. Lantin was simply paralyzed with astonishment.

"But . . . but please examine it again. I always thought until now that it was . . . was false."

"What is your name, sir?" the jeweler asked.

"M. Lantin—I am employed at the office of the Minister of the Interior. I live at 16 Rue des Martyrs."

The merchant looked through his books, found the entry, and said, "That necklace was sent to Madame Lantin's address, 16 Rue des Martyrs, on July 20, 1876."

The two men looked into each other's eyes—the widower wild with surprise, the jeweler suspecting he had a thief before him. The latter broke the silence by saying, "Will you leave this necklace here for twenty-four hours? I will give you a receipt."

"Certainly," answered M. Lantin hastily. Then, putting the ticket in his pocket, he left the store.

He wandered aimlessly through the streets, his mind in a state of dreadful confusion. He tried to reason, to understand. His wife could never have bought so valuable an object as that. Never. But, then, it must have been a present! . . . A present from whom? Why was it given to her?

He stopped and stood stock-still in the middle of the street. A horrible doubt entered his mind . . . She? . . . But then all those other pieces of jewelry must have been presents also! . . . Then it seemed to him that the ground was heaving under his feet; that a tree, right in front of him, was falling toward him. He thrust out his arms instinctively, falling unconscious to the ground.

He regained consciousness again in a drug store to which some bystanders had carried him. He had them take him home, and he locked himself in his room. Until nightfall he cried without stopping. Finally, overcome with grief and fatigue, he threw himself on the bed, where he passed an uneasy, restless night.

The following morning he arose and prepared to go to the office. It was hard to have to work after such a shock. He sent a letter to his employer asking to be excused. Then he remembered he had to return to the jeweler's. The thought made him purple with shame, but he could not leave the necklace with that man. So he put on his coat and went out.

---

* instinctively (in STINK tiv lee) **without thought; automatically**

It was a lovely day; a clear blue sky smiled on the busy city below. Strollers were walking aimlessly about, their hands in their pockets.

Lantin thought, as he saw them passing, "How lucky the men are who are rich! With money a man can even shake off grief. You can go anywhere you please, travel, amuse yourself! Oh, if only I were rich!"

He suddenly discovered he was hungry, not having eaten since the night before. But his pockets were empty. He again remembered the necklace. Eighteen thousand francs! Eighteen thousand francs! What a sum!

He made his way to the Rue de la Paix, opposite the jeweler's. He began walking back and forth on the sidewalk. Twenty times he started to go in, but shame always kept him back.

Still, he was hungry—very hungry—and had not a cent. He decided quickly, ran across the street in order not to let himself have time to think over the matter, and rushed into the store.

The jeweler immediately came forward, and offered him a chair with smiling politeness. The clerks glanced at M. Lantin knowingly, with amusement in their eyes.

"I have made inquiries," said the jeweler, "and if you still wish to dispose of the gems, I am ready to pay you the price I offered."

"Certainly, sir," stammered M. Lantin.

The jeweler took from a drawer eighteen large bills, counted them, and held them out to the widower. Lantin signed a receipt and, with a trembling hand, put the money into his pocket.

Then, as he was about to leave the store, he turned to the ever-smiling merchant, and said, lowering his eyes, "I have—I have other gems that I have received from the same—from the same inheritance. Will you buy them also?"

The merchant bowed. "Why certainly, sir—certainly . . ." One of the clerks rushed out to laugh at his ease; another kept blowing his nose as hard as he could.

Lantin said gravely, "I will bring them to you." An hour later he returned with the gems.

The large diamond earrings were worth twenty thousand francs; the bracelets thirty-five thousand; the rings, sixteen thousand; a set of emeralds and sapphires, fourteen thousand; a gold chain with solitaire pendant, forty thousand—making the total value one hundred and forty-three thousand francs.

The jeweler remarked jokingly, "The person who owned these must have put all her savings into precious stones."

"Perhaps that is as good a way of saving money as any other," M. Lantin replied seriously.

- solitaire (SAHL uh tair) **a single gem (as a diamond) set alone**

That day he had lunch at Voisin's and ordered wine worth twenty francs a bottle. Then he hired a cab and made a tour of the Bois. He looked at the carriages passing with a sort of contempt, and he had a wild desire to yell out to the occupants, "I, too, am rich!—I have two hundred thousand francs!"

Suddenly he thought of his employer. He drove up to the office and entered gaily. He walked right into the superintendent's private room and said, "Sir, I have come to give you my resignation. I have just inherited three hundred thousand francs." He shook hands with his former colleagues and told them all about his plans for a new career. Then he went to dinner at the Cafe Anglais.

He seated himself beside a gentleman of aristocratic bearing. During the meal, he could not resist telling him, with an air of confidentiality, that he had just inherited a fortune of four hundred thousand francs.

For the first time in his life he was not bored at the theater, and he spent the night in wild merrymaking.

Six months afterward he married again. His second wife was the most upright of spouses, but had a terrible temper. She made his life very miserable.

- **contempt** (kun TEMPT) scorn; lack of respect
- **colleague** (CAHL eeg) associate in a profession
- aristocratic (uh ris tuh KRAT ik) upper class
- **spouse** (SPOUS) a husband or a wife

ALL THINGS CONSIDERED

1. After six years of marriage, M. Lantin is (a) sorry that he decided to get married. (b) more in love with his wife than he was on their honeymoon. (c) suspicious of his wife's activities.

2. M. Lantin dislikes his (a) mother-in-law. (b) job. (c) wife's love of imitation jewelry.

3. When M. Lantin decides to sell his wife's jewelry, he is surprised to discover that the (a) jewels he thought were fake are actually genuine. (b) jewelry was stolen. (c) jewelry is worth far less than he had hoped.

4. After visiting the second jeweler, M. Lantin wanders the streets thinking and then falls unconscious because he (a) is weak from hunger. (b) has just discovered how much the jewelry is worth. (c) realizes his wife received the jewels as presents.

5. M. Lantin's second wife (a) loves to spend money to buy jewelry. (b) has a terrible temper and makes him miserable. (c) makes him happier in marriage than he ever believed possible.

THINKING IT THROUGH

1. After his wife's death, M. Lantin finds that his salary, which once supported two people in fine style, now isn't enough for one. What might he have inferred from this fact alone?

2. At what point in the story does M. Lantin realize that his wife deceived him?

3. As he walks along a busy city street, M. Lantin wishes he were rich, for he thinks wealthy people can buy happy lives for themselves. Do you think he still believes this at the end? Explain your answer.

4. M. Lantin learns that his wife's jewelry is worth 143,000 francs. Why, do you think, does he later tell others that he has inherited much more than that?

5. Think about the story in terms of discovering differences. (a) What changes in personality or in values do you see in M. Lantin between the time he sells the first necklace and just before he marries his second wife? (b) In your opinion, what causes these changes?

6. Which descriptions in the story give you insight into "the new" M. Lantin? What are some things he says that serve as character clues?

7. Some people believe de Maupassant was a cynic—one who believes human actions are prompted by less than noble motives. Having read "The False Gems," do you believe de Maupaussant was a cynic? Explain why or why not.

Literary Skills

Characterization

Characterization refers to the methods that a writer uses to develop each character in a story. There are four main methods of characterization:

A. Direct statements made by the writer
(The young man was overjoyed.)

B. Speeches as well as thoughts of the character
("Oh boy! Oh boy! Oh boy!" he thought.)

C. Actions of the character
(He jumped up in the air and clicked his heels together.)

D. Reactions of other characters to the character
("You look extremely happy today," she remarked.)

The following passages are from "The False Gems." Identify which of the four methods listed above de Maupassant uses in each passage. (Note: 1–3 are about M. Lantin, 4–6 are about his wife.)

1. Often during office hours, while his fellow clerks were discussing the topics of the day, his eyes would suddenly fill with tears and he would break into heart-rending sobs.

2. He had kept his wife's room just as she had left it, and he used to lock himself up in it every night to think about her.

3. "How lucky the men are who are rich! With money a man can even shake off grief. You can go anywhere you please, travel, amuse yourself! Oh, if only I were rich!"

4. Her simple beauty had the charm of angelic shyness. . . .

5. "I am so fond of jewelry. It is my only weakness."

6. Everybody sang her praises; all who knew her kept saying, "The man who gets her will be lucky. No one could find a nicer girl than that."

Composition

1. Suppose you suddenly found yourself $50,000 richer. How would you spend the money? In one paragraph describe what you would do with the money. In a second paragraph, compare yourself to M. Lantin. Use these questions to guide you. Would your personality change? What similarities do you see between M. Lantin and yourself? What differences do you perceive?

2. Write a paragraph that explains the irony of situation within the story.

TOO SOON A WOMAN

by Dorothy M. Johnson

▶ At first, Pa thought Mary was just another runaway teenager.
Then he discovered an important difference.

We left the home place behind, mile by slow mile, heading for the mountains, across the prairie where the wind blew forever.

At first there were four of us with the one-horse wagon and its skimpy load. Pa and I walked, because I was a big boy of eleven. My two little sisters romped and trotted until they got tired and had to be boosted up into the wagon bed.

That was no covered Conestoga, like Pa's folks came West in, but just an old farm wagon, drawn by one weary horse, creaking and rumbling westward to the mountains, toward the little woods town where Pa thought he had an old uncle who owned a little two-bit sawmill.

Two weeks we had been moving when we picked up Mary, who had run away from somewhere that she wouldn't tell. Pa didn't want her along, but she stood up to him with no fear in her voice.

"I'd rather go with a family and look after kids," she said, "but I ain't going back. If you won't take me, I'll travel with any wagon that will."

Pa scowled at her, and her wide blue eyes stared back.

• Conestoga (kon uh STOH guh) **a large covered wagon**

"How old are you?" he demanded.

"Eighteen," she said. "There's teamsters come this way sometimes. I'd rather go with you folks. But I won't go back."

"We're prid'near out of grub," my father told her. "We're clean out of money. I got all I can handle without taking anybody else." He turned away as if he hated the sight of her. "You'll have to walk," he said.

So she went along with us and looked after the little girls, but Pa wouldn't talk to her.

On the prairie, the wind blew. But in the mountains, there was rain. When we stopped at little timber claims along the way, the homesteaders said it had rained all summer. Crops among the blackened stumps were rotted and spoiled. There was no cheer anywhere, and little hospitality. The people we talked to were past worrying. They were scared and desperate.

So was Pa. He traveled twice as far each day as the wagon, ranging through the woods with his rifle, but he never saw game. He had been depending on venison, but we never got any except as a grudging gift from the homesteaders.

He brought in a porcupine once, and that was fat meat and good. Mary roasted it in chunks over the fire, half crying with the smoke. Pa and I rigged up the tarp sheet for a shelter to keep the rain from putting the fire clean out.

The porcupine was long gone, except for some of the dried-out fat that Mary had saved, when we came to an old, empty cabin. Pa said we'd have to stop. The horse was wore out, couldn't pull anymore up those grades on the deep-rutted roads in the mountains.

At the cabin, at least there was shelter. We had a few potatoes left and some corn meal. There was a creek that probably had fish in it, if a person could catch them. Pa tried it for half a day before he gave up. To this day I don't care for fishing. I remember my father's sunken eyes in his gaunt, grim face.

He took Mary and me outside the cabin to talk. Rain dripped on us from branches overhead.

- teamsters (TEEM sturz) **drivers of teams of horses**
- **gaunt** (GAWNT) **very thin**

"I think I know where we are," he said. "I calculate to get to old John's and back in about four days. There'll be grub in the town, and they'll let me have some whether old John's still there or not."

He looked at me. "You do like she tells you," he warned. It was the first time he had admitted Mary was on earth since we picked her up two weeks before.

"You're my pardner," he said to me, "but it might be she's got more brains. You mind what she says."

He burst out with bitterness. "There ain't anything good left in the world, or people to care if you live or die. But I'll get grub in the town and come back with it."

He took a deep breath and added, "If you get too all-fired hungry, butcher the horse. It'll be better than starvin'."

He kissed the little girls good-by and plodded off through the woods with one blanket and the rifle.

The cabin was moldy and had no floor. We kept a fire going under a hole in the roof, so it was full of blinding smoke, but we had to keep the fire so as to dry out the wood.

The third night, we lost the horse. A bear scared him. We heard the racket, and Mary and I ran out, but we couldn't see anything in the pitch-dark.

In gray daylight I went looking for him, and I must have walked fifteen miles. It seemed like I had to have that horse at the cabin when Pa came or he'd whip me. I got plumb lost two or three times and thought maybe I was going to die there alone and nobody would ever know it, but I found the way back to the clearing.

That was the fourth day, and Pa didn't come. That was the day we ate up the last of the grub.

The fifth day, Mary went looking for the horse. My sisters whimpered, huddled in a quilt by the fire, because they were scared and hungry.

I never did get dried out, always having to bring in more damp wood and going out to yell to see if Mary would hear me and not get lost. But I couldn't cry like the little girls did, because I was a big boy, eleven years old.

It was near dark when there was an answer to my yelling, and Mary came into the clearing.

Mary didn't have the horse—we never saw hide nor hair of that old horse again—but she was carrying something big and white that looked like a pumpkin with no color to it.

She didn't say anything, just looked around and saw Pa wasn't there yet, at the end of the fifth day.

"What's that thing?" my sister Elizabeth demanded.

"Mushroom," Mary answered. "I bet it hefts ten pounds."

"What are you going to do with it now?" I sneered. "Play football here?"

"Eat it—maybe," she said, putting it in a corner. Her wet hair hung over her shoulders. She huddled by the fire.

My sister Sarah began to whimper again. "I'm hungry!" she kept saying.

"Mushrooms ain't good eating," I said. "They can kill you."

"Maybe," Mary answered. "Maybe they can. I don't set up to know all about everything, like some people."

"What's that mark on your shoulder?" I asked her. "You tore your dress on the brush."

● plumb (PLUM) **completely; absolutely**

"What do you think it is?" she said, her head bowed in the smoke.

"Looks like scars," I guessed.

"'Tis scars. They whipped me. Now mind your own business. I want to think."

Elizabeth whimpered. "Why don't Pa come back?"

"He's coming," Mary promised. "Can't come in the dark. Your pa'll take care of you soon's he can."

She got up and rummaged around in the grub box.

"Nothing there but empty dishes," I growled. "If there was anything, we'd know it."

Mary stood up. She was holding the can with the porcupine grease.

"I'm going to have something to eat," she said coolly. "You kids can't have any yet. And I don't want any squalling, mind."

It was a cruel thing, what she did then. She sliced that big, solid mushroom and heated grease in a pan.

The smell of it brought the little girls out of their quilt, but she told them to go back in so fierce a voice that they obeyed. They cried to break your heart.

I didn't cry. I watched, hating her.

I endured the smell of the mushroom

frying as long as I could. Then I said, "Give me some."

"Tomorrow," Mary answered. "Tomorrow, maybe. But not tonight." She turned to me with a sharp command: "Don't bother me! Just leave me be."

She knelt there by the fire and finished frying the slice of mushroom.

If I'd had Pa's rifle, I'd have been willing to kill her right then and there.

She didn't eat right away. She looked at the brown, fried slice for a while and said, "By tomorrow morning, I guess you can tell whether you want any."

The little girls stared at her as she ate. Sarah was chewing an old leather glove.

When Mary crawled into the quilts with them, they moved away as far as they could get.

I was so scared that my stomach heaved, empty as it was.

Mary didn't stay in the quilts long. She took a drink out of the water bucket and sat down by the fire and looked through the smoke at me.

She said in a low voice, "I don't know how it will be if it's poison. Just do the best you can with the girls. Because your pa will come back, you know. . . . You better go to bed. I'm going to sit up."

And so would you sit up. If it might be your last night on earth and the pain of death might seize you at any moment, you would sit up by the smoky fire, wide-awake, remembering whatever you had to remember, savoring life.

We sat in silence after the girls had gone to sleep. Once I asked, "How long does it take?"

"I never heard," she answered. "Don't think about it."

I slept after a while, with my chin on my chest.

Mary's moving around brought me wide-awake. The black of night was fading.

"I guess it's all right," Mary said. "I'd be able to tell by now, wouldn't I?"

I answered gruffly, "I don't know."

Mary stood in the doorway for a while, looking out at the dripping world as if she found it beautiful. Then she fried slices of the mushroom while the little girls danced with anxiety.

We feasted, we three, my sisters and I, until Mary ruled, "That'll hold you," and would not cook any more. She didn't touch any of the mushroom herself.

That was a strange day in the moldy cabin. Mary laughed and was gay; she told stories, and we played "Who's Got the Thimble?" with a pine cone.

In the afternoon we heard a shout, and my sisters screamed and I ran ahead of them across the clearing.

The rain had stopped. My father came plunging out of the woods leading a pack horse—and well I remember the treasures of food in that pack.

He glanced at us anxiously as he tore at the ropes that bound the pack.

"Where's the other one?" he demanded.

Mary came out of the cabin then, walking sedately. As she came toward us, the sun began to shine.

My stepmother was a wonderful woman.

- savoring (SAY vur ing) **taking delight in**
- sedately (suh DAYT lee) **calmly; in a quiet and serious way**

ALL THINGS CONSIDERED

1. The family in "Too Soon a Woman" is traveling (a) by stagecoach. (b) with several other families in a Conestoga wagon train. (c) in an old farm wagon drawn by a horse.

2. Pa doesn't want Mary to join them as they move West because he (a) knows the supply of food is low. (b) believes she isn't strong enough to help with the heavy work. (c) is afraid he'd be accused of kidnapping her.

3. Pa leaves the children and Mary at a deserted cabin so that he can (a) get medical attention. (b) have some fun in town. (c) find food.

4. Mary cooks up part of a huge mushroom she found but won't give any to the hungry children because (a) she's afraid it might be poisonous. (b) she wants it all for herself. (c) she knows children don't like mushrooms.

5. Mary stays awake most of the night before Pa gets back because (a) she's worried about Pa. (b) she wants to think about her life. (c) she has a stomach ache.

THINKING IT THROUGH

1. Why do you think the family left where they had been living? Point to facts in the story that lead you to your conclusion.

2. The narrator states, "It was a cruel thing, what she did then. She sliced that big, solid mushroom and heated grease in the pan. . . ." The narrator's feelings toward Mary change dramatically a short while later. Explain how his feelings are different, and tell what caused the change.

3. The general mental picture that a certain word creates is called a **stereotype** (STER ee uh typ). A stereotype usually is an unfair representation. The mental picture results in a distorted judgment of a certain group of people. For instance, right now you probably have some kind of stereotype for the words "model," "professor," and "suburb." (a) When Pa first meets Mary, he reacts to her as a *stereotype*, not as a different, unique person. What kind of stereotype? (b) Pa's feelings toward Mary gradually change. What is the first indication that he's seeing her differently?

4. The last line of the story states, "My stepmother was a wonderful woman." (a) Why does the narrator end with that statement? (b) What inference do you make from reading it?

Reading and Analyzing

Noting Comparison and Contrast

A **comparison** shows usually how two (or more) things, ideas, or feelings are alike. A **contrast**, on the other hand, shows how they are different. Dorothy Johnson uses contrast to heighten interest in "Too Soon a Woman." She develops Mary, as the main character, by contrasting the way she is seen by the narrator and Pa at the beginning of the story and later on in the story.

1. The narrator mentions that when Pa first sees Mary, he doesn't want her traveling with them. Contrast his feelings toward Mary at the beginning of the story with the way he feels when he leaves her and the children at the deserted cabin. What speech of his indicates that his feelings have changed somewhat? Quote the speech.

2. How does Pa feel toward Mary at the very end of the story? Which two sentences give you clues as to how his feelings have changed?

3. The narrator also has different ideas and feelings about Mary. Contrast the way he feels when Mary brings back the mushroom and doesn't share it with the way he feels about her later that evening and the next day.

4. Mary is an example of a dynamic character. She "grows" as a person in a short period of time. Contrast Mary, the runaway teenager, with Mary, the responsible young woman.

Composition

1. Think of someone you know well. (a) Write two sentences comparing yourself to this person. (b) Write two more sentences contrasting yourself with this same person.

2. Think over the past year of your life. Have you discovered some differences in yourself within the last year? (a) Fold a piece of paper in half lengthwise; on the top line of the left-hand side write your name and the date a year ago; head the right-hand side with your name and today's date. Make two parallel lists to show what you were like then contrasted with what you are like today. (b) Using this information, write a well-developed paragraph.

VOCABULARY AND SKILL REVIEW

Before completing the exercise that follows, you may wish to review the **bold-faced** words on pages 71 to 95.

I. On a separate sheet of paper, write the *italicized* word that best fills the blank in each sentence. Use each word only once.

amiable	*contempt*
gaunt	*tyranny*
cowering	*spouse*
gaudy	*valor*
infirmary	*colleague*

1. "I love _____ clothes," she cried as she buckled the wide fluorescent pink belt over her purple and red striped dress.

2. I'm not going to hit you. Why are you _____?

3. What an _____ hostess your mother is!

4. Joe's _____ suggested a surprise birthday party for him at the office.

5. "I feel nothing but _____ for your proposal," she sneered.

6. She's not my _____—she's married to my uncle.

7. Because she had a horrible case of the flu, Mary had to stay in the _____ for over a week.

8. After three months of dieting, Robert looks _____.

9. For his great _____ in World War II, Audie Murphy was awarded the Medal of Honor.

10. The schoolyard bully's _____ made the children afraid to go out at recess.

II. Read the following poem on page 97 carefully before answering the questions that follow it.

THE SUDDEN SIGHT

by Mari Evans

My eye
walked lightly over their faces
until it stopped
short
at him
and my breathing was not the same
ever again
even after we became
lovers the sudden
sight—
and my breathing
was not the same

1. Young people are often warned to beware of "love at first sight."
   What does this poem say on the subject?

2. What do you visualize as the setting? Where do you see the
   speaker when her eye "walked lightly over their faces"? For example, do you see her coming into a classroom? A party? A job
   interview? Explain your choice.

3. To whom does the pronoun "their" (line 2) refer?

4. Look at the fourth line. Why do you think the poet chose not to
   make this line longer?

5. To whom does the pronoun "him" refer? How does the narrator
   feel about this person?

6. Is "The Sudden Sight" of the title only the first sight, or something more? Explain.

7. Notice how the poet manages to convey an overwhelming emotion through characterization. (a) What does the term "walked
   lightly" indicate about the narrator's mood and expectations at
   the beginning? (b) Note that after she sees "him," her "breathing
   was not the same." What does this physical clue tell the reader
   about the speaker's emotional state?

Bonus questions: Read the definitions on the next page from *The
Devil's Dictionary* by Ambrose Bierce (1842–1914?). From reading
the definitions, see if you can infer what kind of person Bierce was.
Then read the statements about Bierce that follow the definitions.
On a separate sheet of paper, copy each statement. Mark each item
true or *false*. If it is *false*, explain what is wrong.

admiration: our polite way of saying that someone resembles us.

bore: a person who talks when you want him to listen.

clarinet: an instrument of torture operated by someone with cotton in his ears. There are two instruments that are worse than a clarinet—two clarinets.

coward: one who, in an emergency, thinks with his legs.

peace: in international affairs, a period of cheating between two periods of fighting.

positive: mistaken at the top of your voice.

selfish: to have no consideration for the selfishness of others.

1. Bierce's favorite musical instrument was the clarinet.
2. Bierce had a good sense of humor.
3. Bierce enjoyed listening to people more than he enjoyed talking himself.
4. At times Bierce probably felt quite depressed.

The date of Bierce's death is given as "1914?" Research Bierce's life in a good reference work and find why the question mark is there. It's an interesting story.

Dick Gregory (Born 1932)

Dick Gregory, whose boyhood was spent in poverty, grew up to be a writer, comedian, and worker for civil rights. In his autobiography, he tells how, as a child, he was a target for neighborhood bullies because he was undernourished and small for his age. One day, instead of crying over the taunts about his uniform-like relief clothes or his absent father, he made a joke—and the bullies laughed!

From that time on, Dick Gregory saw humor as a way of easing the pain in his own life. Later he used his humor to help others understand the agony many people endure because of racial discrimination.

SHAME

by Dick Gregory

▶ Do you remember the first time you ever felt ashamed? Dick Gregory remembers the first time—vividly.

I never learned hate at home, or shame. I had to go to school for that. I was about seven years old when I got my first big lesson. I was in love with a little girl named Helene Tucker, a light-complected little girl with pigtails and nice manners. She was always clean and she was smart in school. I think I went to school then mostly to look at her. I brushed my hair and even got me a little old handkerchief. It was a lady's handkerchief, but I didn't want Helene to see me wipe my nose on my hand. The pipes were frozen again, there was no water in the house, but I washed my socks and shirt every night. I'd get a pot, and go over to Mister Ben's grocery store, and stick my pot down into his soda machine. Scoop out some chopped ice. By evening the ice melted to water for washing. I got sick a lot that winter because the fire would go out at night before the clothes were dry. In the morning I'd put them on, wet or dry, because they were the only clothes I had.

Everybody's got a Helene Tucker, a symbol of everything you want. I loved her for her goodness, her cleanness, her popularity. She'd walk down my street and my brothers and sisters would yell, "Here comes Helene," and I'd rub my tennis sneakers on the back of my pants and wish my hair wasn't so nappy and the white folks' shirt fit me better. I'd run out on the street. If I knew my place and didn't come too close, she'd wink at me and say hello. That was a good feeling. Sometimes I'd follow her all the way home, and shovel the snow off her walk and try to make friends with her Momma and her aunts. I'd drop money on her stoop late at night on my way back from shining shoes in the taverns. And she had a Daddy, and he had a good job. He was a paper hanger.

I guess I would have gotten over Helene by summertime but something happened in that classroom that made her face hang in front of me for the next twenty-two years. When I played the drums in high school it was for Helene and when I broke track records in college it was for Helene and when I started standing behind microphones and heard applause I wished Helene could hear it, too. It wasn't until I was twenty-nine years old and married and making money that I finally got her out of my system. Helene was sitting in that classroom when I learned to be ashamed of myself.

It was on a Thursday. I was sitting in the back of the room, in a seat with a chalk circle drawn around it. The idiot's seat, the trouble-maker's seat.

The teacher thought I was stupid. Couldn't spell, couldn't read, couldn't do arithmetic. Just stupid. Teachers were never interested in finding out that you couldn't concentrate because you were so hungry, because you hadn't had any breakfast. All you could think about was noontime, would it ever come? Maybe you could sneak into the cloakroom and steal a bite of some kid's lunch out of a coat pocket. A bite of something. Paste. You can't really make a meal of paste, or put it on bread for a sandwich, but sometimes I'd scoop a few spoonfuls out of the paste jar in the back of the room. Pregnant people get strange tastes. I was pregnant with poverty. Pregnant with dirt and pregnant with smells that made people turn away, pregnant with cold and pregnant with shoes that were never bought for me, pregnant with five other people in my bed and no Daddy in the next room, and pregnant with hunger. Paste doesn't taste too bad when you're hungry.

The teacher thought I was a troublemaker. All she saw from the front of the room was a little black boy who squirmed in his idiot's seat and made noises and poked the kids around him. I guess she couldn't see a kid who made noises because he wanted someone to know he was there.

• pregnant (PREG nunt) **full of meaning**

It was on a Thursday, the day before the Negro payday. The eagle always flew on Friday. The teacher was asking each student how much his father would give to the Community Chest. On Friday night, each kid would get the money from his father, and on Monday he would bring it to the school. I decided I was going to buy me a Daddy right then. I had money in my pocket from shining shoes and selling papers, and whatever Helene Tucker pledged for her Daddy I was going to top it. And I'd hand the money right in. I wasn't going to wait until Monday to buy me a Daddy.

I was shaking, scared to death. The teacher opened her book and started calling out names alphabetically.

"Helene Tucker?"

"My Daddy said he'd give two dollars and fifty cents."

"That's very nice, Helene. Very, very nice indeed."

That made me feel pretty good. It wouldn't take too much to top that. I had almost three dollars in dimes and quarters in my pocket. I stuck my hand in my pocket and held onto the money, waiting for her to call my name. But the teacher closed her book after she called everybody else in the class.

I stood up and raised my hand.

"What is it now?"

"You forgot me."

She turned toward the blackboard. "I don't have time to be playing with you, Richard."

"My Daddy said he'd . . . "

"Sit down, Richard, you're disturbing the class."

"My Daddy said he'd give . . . fifteen dollars."

She turned around and looked mad. "We are collecting this money for you and your kind, Richard Gregory. If your Daddy can give fifteen dollars you have no business being on relief."

"I got it right now, I got it right now, my Daddy gave it to me to turn in today, my Daddy said . . ."

"And furthermore," she said, looking right at me, her nostrils getting big and her lips getting thin and her eyes opening wide, "we know you don't have a Daddy."

Helene Tucker turned around, her eyes full of tears. She felt sorry for me. Then I couldn't see her too well because I was crying, too.

"Sit down, Richard."

And I always thought the teacher kind of liked me. She always picked me to wash the blackboard on Friday, after school. That was a big thrill, it made me feel important. If I didn't wash it, come Monday the school might not function right.

"Where are you going, Richard?"

I walked out of school that day, and for a long time I didn't go back very often. There was shame there.

Now there was shame everywhere. It seemed like the whole world had been inside that classroom, everyone had heard what the teacher had said, everyone had turned around and felt sorry for me. There was shame in going to the Worthy Boys Annual Christmas Dinner for you and your kind, because everybody knew what a worthy boy was. Why couldn't they just call it the Boys Annual Dinner, why'd they have to give it a name? There was shame in wearing the brown and orange and white plaid mackinaw the welfare gave to 3,000 boys. Why'd it have to be the same for everybody so when you walked down the street people could see you were on relief? It was a nice warm mackinaw and it had a hood, and my Momma beat me and called me a little rat when she found out I stuffed it in the bottom of a pail full of garbage way over on Cottage Street. There was shame in running over to Mister Ben's at the end of the day and asking for his rotten peaches, there was shame in asking Mrs. Simmons for a spoonful of sugar, there was shame in running out to meet the relief truck. I hated that truck, full of food for you and your kind. I ran into the house and hid when it came. And then I started to sneak through alleys, to take the long way home so the people going into White's Eat Shop wouldn't see me. Yeah, the whole world heard the teacher that day, we all know you don't have a Daddy.

● **mackinaw** (MAK uh naw) man's short heavy coat

ALL THINGS CONSIDERED

1. Dick Gregory couldn't get Helene Tucker out of his system until he was 29 years old because (a) he saw her often. (b) she was in the classroom when he learned to feel shame. (c) he remembers his embarrassment when she beat him up on the playground.

2. Dick Gregory had trouble in school because (a) the teachers were all men. (b) he was stupid. (c) he was so hungry he couldn't concentrate.

3. Gregory said he made noises and poked the kids around him because he (a) wanted someone to know he was there. (b) enjoyed making the teacher angry. (c) was practicing to become a comedian.

4. When Gregory announced that his father would give 15 dollars to the Community Chest, Helene Tucker (a) laughed at him. (b) ignored him. (c) felt sorry for him.

5. Dick Gregory threw his warm mackinaw in a garbage can because (a) it wasn't in style. (b) he thought everyone who saw him wearing it would know he got it from the welfare. (c) Helene Tucker told him it was ugly.

THINKING IT THROUGH

1. What facts does Gregory give in his **autobiography,** a personal account of his life, to show that his family was very poor when he was growing up?

2. What specific differences does Gregory see between himself and Helene Tucker? Name at least three.

3. After the Community Chest incident, Gregory says, "Now there was shame everywhere." He meant that now shame was a part of his mental map. What incidents particularly caused him to feel shame?

4. When she collected money for the Community Chest, the teacher asked the children individually—in front of the whole class—how much their fathers would give. (a) What do you see wrong with the teacher's method? (b) How might you do it differently if you were the teacher?

5. In your opinion, did the teacher react to the young Dick Gregory as a different, unique person or as a *stereotype* (see page 94)? Support your answer with a fact from the selection.

Reading and Analyzing

Interpreting Symbols and Symbolic Action

A **symbol** is something that stands for something else. In everyday life, common objects used as symbols are easily recognized: a dove (peace), a heart (love), a cross or Star of David (religion).

In literature, however, most symbols are not easily recognized. A person, a place, an object, an action, or even an idea can take on special *symbolic meaning* in a piece of literature. For instance, a hubcap (an object) is usually just a hubcap. But a young man in a story might keep an old hubcap from a small sporty 1973 car nailed over the garage door. He might even clean and wax it regularly. In such a case, the hubcap might symbolize happy memories of his first car.

Symbolic action is important in literature, too. Suppose that one day the hubcap owner takes the hubcap down and throws it in the trash can. He mounts a magazine photograph of a long, sleek expensive automobile on the refrigerator. His actions may symbolize the end of a significant memory and the beginning of a new dream. The action has symbolic meaning.

Think about "Shame" in terms of symbols and symbolic action.

1. Reread the first paragraph of "Shame." What does the handkerchief symbolize for Gregory?

2. Gregory writes, "I stood up and raised my hand." What does this action symbolize in American classrooms?

3. Gregory's teacher always picked him to wash the blackboards after school on Friday. What two things does this action symbolize to him?

4. "I walked out of school that day, and for a long time I didn't go back." Why does Gregory do this? What does his action symbolize?

5. What does the brown and orange and white plaid mackinaw symbolize to Gregory?

Composition

1. Dick Gregory writes, "Everybody's got a Helene Tucker, a symbol of everything you want." Think of someone you regard as a symbol of everything you want or want to be. Write a description of that person, explaining why you think that person is special.

Give at least two examples to support your reasons.

2. To which three items in your own life do you attach the most symbolic importance? Explain the meaning and history of these items in a way that will interest other people.

Kate Chopin (1851-1904)

A street scene in St. Louis, Missouri, 1903

What was wrong with Kate Chopin's career as an author can hardly be called her own fault. She was simply born 50 years ahead of her time.

The daughter of a wealthy Irish immigrant, Katherine O'Flaherty Chopin grew up in St. Louis, Missouri. Even as a girl, she loved to read and write. At 20 she married a banker and moved to Louisiana. In the next ten years, there was little time for writing as her family grew larger and larger. Then, quite suddenly, her husband died of swamp fever. Chopin decided that if she was ever going to become a successful writer, she had to do it then.

Success came slowly at first, but by the 1890s, she was selling bold, daring stories to *Vogue* and other magazines. In a tight, modern style, she told the truth about life as she saw it. However, it was too much truth for many people of that era. "Too strong drink," one critic wrote. "Poison!" added another. By 1900, her very name had become a danger sign, and no editor would touch her stories. She published nothing the last four years of her life.

THE STORY OF AN HOUR

by Kate Chopin

Because Louise Mallard had heart trouble, great care was taken to break the news of her husband's death as gently as possible.

It was her sister Josephine who told her, in broken sentences, in hints that revealed in half concealing. Her husband's friend Richards was there, too, near her. It was he who had been in the newspaper office when news of the railroad disaster was received, with Brently Mallard's name leading the list of "killed." He had only taken the time to make sure of the name by telegram. Then he had rushed to beat any less careful, less tender friend in bearing the sad message.

She did not hear the story as many women have heard the same sad news, with a paralyzed failure to accept its truth. She wept at once, with sudden, wild abandon in her sister's arms. When the storm of grief had spent itself, she went away to her room alone. She would have no one follow her.

There stood, facing the open window, a comfortable, roomy armchair. Into this she sank, pressed down by a physical exhaustion that haunted her body and seemed to reach into her soul.

She could see in the open square before her house the tops of trees that were all quivering with the new spring life. The delicious breath of rain was in the air. The notes of a distant song that someone was singing reached her faintly, and countless sparrows were twittering in the eaves.

There were patches of blue sky showing here and there through the clouds that had piled up in the west facing her window.

She sat with her head thrown back upon the cushion of the chair. She remained quite motionless, except when a sob came up into her throat and shook her, as a child who has cried itself to sleep continues to sob in its dreams.

She was young, with a fair, calm face, whose lines revealed repression and even a certain strength. But now there was a dull stare in her eyes. Her gaze was fixed away off on one of those patches of blue sky. It was not a glance of reflection, but rather indicated a suspension of intelligent thought.

- repression (ri PRESH un) **keeping down; habit of keeping feelings and desires under control**
- **reflection** (ri FLEK shun) **serious thought**

There was something coming to her and she was waiting for it, fearfully. What was it? She did not know; it was too subtle and new to name. But she felt it, creeping out of the sky, reaching toward her through the sounds, the scents, the color that filled the air.

Now her chest rose and fell tumultuously. She was beginning to recognize this thing that was approaching to possess her, and she was striving to beat it back with her will—as powerless as her two white slender hands would have been.

When she managed to relax, a little whispered word escaped her slightly parted lips. She said it over and over under her breath: "Free, free, free!" The vacant stare and the look of terror that had followed it went from her eyes. They stayed keen and bright. Her pulse beat fast, and the racing blood warmed and relaxed every inch of her body.

She did not stop to ask if it were not a monstrous joy that held her. A clear and thrilling perception enabled her to dismiss the suggestion as trivial.

- subtle (SUT ul) **having fine shades of meaning; mysterious**
- **tumultuously** (too MUL choo us lee) **violently; in a very disturbed fashion; stormily**
- **perception** (pur SEP shun) **awareness; understanding**
- trivial (TRIV ee ul) **not important; insignificant**

She knew that she would weep again when she saw the kind, tender hands folded in death—the face that had never looked except with love upon her, fixed and gray and dead. But she saw beyond that bitter moment a long procession of years to come that would belong to her absolutely. And she opened and spread her arms out to them in welcome.

There would be no one to live for during those coming years; she would live for herself. There would be no powerful will bending her in the way that men and women believe they have a right to impose a private will upon a fellow creature. A kind intention or a cruel intention made the act seem no less a crime as she looked upon it in that brief moment of illumination.

And yet she had loved him—sometimes. Often she had not. What did it matter! What could love, the unsolved mystery, count for in the face of this new self-assertion, which she suddenly recognized as the strongest force of her being!

"Free! Body and soul free!" she kept whispering.

Josephine was kneeling before the closed door with her lips to the keyhole, pleading for admission. "Louise, open the door! I beg, open the door—you will make yourself ill. What are you doing, Louise? For heaven's sake open the door."

"Go away. I am not making myself ill." No; she was drinking in a very elixir of life through that open window.

Her fancy was running riot along those days ahead of her. Spring days, and summer days, and all sorts of days that would be her own. She breathed a quick prayer that life might be long. It was only yesterday she had thought with a shudder that life might be long.

She arose at length and opened the door to her sister. There was a feverish triumph in her eyes, and she carried herself like a goddess of Victory. She clasped her sister's waist, and together they descended the stairs. Richards stood waiting for them at the bottom.

Someone was opening the front door with a latchkey. It was Brently Mallard who entered, a little travel-stained and tired, carrying his little suitcase and umbrella. He had been far from the scene of accident, and did not even know there had been one. He stood amazed at Josephine's piercing cry, at Richards's quick motion to screen him from the view of his wife.

But Richards was too late.

When the doctors came they said she had died of a heart attack—of joy that kills.

- self-assertion (self uh SUR shun) **willingness to express one's wishes and desires; personal and strong declaration**
- elixir (i LIK sur) **cure-all; health-giving tonic**

ALL THINGS CONSIDERED

1. Louise Mallard's first reaction to the report of her husband's death is to (a) weep wildly. (b) disbelieve the news. (c) ask for companionship.

2. Her second reaction is to fall into a dull, unthinking state, shown by her (a) sinking into an armchair. (b) remaining motionless except for an occasional sob. (c) having a dull stare in her eyes. (d) all of the above.

3. Her third and last reaction is signaled by the words, "Free, free, free." She feels she is free to (a) look for another husband. (b) begin a career in the theater. (c) live for herself.

4. Guilt does not bother her too much because she (a) is so sure her new feelings are good and right. (b) is not a moral person. (c) puts all the blame on others.

5. The doctors' opinion at the end—death by "joy that kills"—is (a) correct. (b) incorrect. (c) based entirely on medical evidence.

THINKING IT THROUGH

1. It is often said that you can see the end of a good story in its beginning (and vice versa). What fact in the first paragraph relates directly to the last paragraph?

2. If the mistaken news of Brently Mallard's death had never arrived, what would the rest of Louise's life have probably been like? Prove your answer with at least two clues from the story.

3. Although the author states that Louise did *not* view her new state as one of "monstrous joy," she might have. Why? What in the story might make you think her joy was "monstrous"?

4. (a) At the beginning of the story, how does Louise see herself? (b) How does her awareness of herself change near the end of the story?

5. Why might "The Story of an Hour" have been considered "dangerous" by some readers in the 1890s? What message might the author be giving to women readers?

Literary Skills

Subject and Theme

Pairs of literary terms are sometimes used inexactly or confused with each other. One such pair is *mood* and *tone* (see page 49). Another pair is *subject* and *theme*. When you use these terms, have the meaning of each one clearly in mind.

The **subject** of a piece of literature is simply what it is about. For instance, the subject of a certain poem might be *a mouse*. The subject of a short story might be *heroism* or *self-sacrifice*. It often happens that two (or more) subjects are combined. For example, a poem about *a mouse* could also be about *plans for the future*. If you were asked to name the subject of a piece of literature, it would only take a word, or just a few words.

The word *theme* refers to a larger idea than the word *subject*. A **theme** is an underlying meaning within a piece of literature. The theme of a poem might be this one: *Even the most sensible plans for the future can come to a sudden, sad end.* A story theme might be the following: *Taking a risk to benefit others may make you an appreciated hero in their eyes.* If you were asked to explain the theme of a piece of literature, it would probably require a full sentence. A story can have more than a single theme, but usually only one is the major theme.

1. Each of the following terms might be used as the subject of a story. Change three of them into sentences that could be used as the theme of the story.

Example subject: *heart attack*
Example theme: *A heart attack can force a person to slow down, relax, and find new meaning in life.*

Subjects: (a) *basketball,* (b) *anger,* (c) *cheating,* (d) *taking risks,* (e) *stolen jewelry.*

2. Now think about "The Story of an Hour." In your opinion, what is the subject? In other words, what is the story about? (You may suggest two or more subjects if you wish; members of your class may have additional suggestions.)

3. In your opinion, what is the theme of "The Story of an Hour"? First think about what Louise Mallard learns about herself and her marriage. Then consider the end of the story. What does this mean to you as a reader? In a complete sentence, try to express what you see as the underlying meaning of the story.

4. It is sometimes said that, in a way, most human beings are simply themes walking around on two legs. School yearbooks, for instance, often use a quotation to give some general insight or meaning about the life of each graduate. For example, one caption for a student may say: "Still waters run deep." Another may say: "Let a smile be your umbrella" and still another, "My mind is made up; don't bother me with facts." So . . . when it comes time for *your* theme, what might it be?

Literary Skills

Conflict

One of the reasons a reader becomes involved in a good short story is that the story plot itself involves **conflict.** A conflict develops when two opposing forces meet. It is possible to have more than one kind of conflict in a story, but usually one is the *main* conflict.

There are four main kinds of conflict.

A. Conflict between people. (An example would be one person opposing another person because of something that happened.)

B. Conflict within a single person. (For instance, an athlete might ponder whether or not to accept a bribe.)

C. Conflict between people and things. (An example would be a person trying to deal with a robot that has gone berserk.)

D. Conflict between people and nature. (For example, a person becomes stranded in freezing temperatures far from civilization with no means to build a fire.)

1. Which of the four kinds of conflict described above is the main conflict in "The Story of an Hour"?

2. Which other kind of conflict is involved in the story?

Composition

1. Look back at the descriptions of the four kinds of conflict. Unit II contains good examples of three of the kinds of conflict. The main conflict in "A Kind of Murder" is between the students and Mr. Warren, an example of conflict A—between people. In "The False Gems," M. Lantin is undergoing conflict B—within himself—as he discovers new information about his wife. And in "Too Soon a Woman," the main character is in conflict D—with nature: the only food is a possibly poisonous mushroom, and she and the children are starving. Come up with your own example of conflict C— between people and things. Make up a title and then, in a few sentences, explain the conflict.

2. Part of the conflict in "Story of an Hour" is within Louise Mallard: on one hand, she is experiencing the joy of knowing she can live the rest of her life for herself, but on the other hand, she knows that society would find much fault with her thoughts. You have probably been in this position more than once. For example, have you ever been in conflict because deep inside you felt you were right— but "society" (peers, parents, the church, the school system, or other) would brand you as wrong? Choose one experience you are willing to share. Write a paragraph describing your conflict.

SWEET POTATO PIE

by Eugenia Collier

▶ In this story, Buddy tells about his very loving, very giving older brother. See if you don't find Charley as remarkable a person as Buddy does.

From up here on the fourteenth floor, my brother Charley looks like an insect scurrying among other insects. A deep feeling of love surges through me. Despite the distance, he seems to feel it, for he turns and scans the upper windows, but failing to find me, continues on his way. I watch him moving quickly—gingerly, it seems to me—down Fifth Avenue and around the corner to his shabby taxicab. In a moment he will be heading back uptown.

I turn from the window and flop down on the bed, shoes and all. Perhaps because of what happened this afternoon or maybe just because I see Charley so seldom, my thoughts hover over him like hummingbirds. The cheerful, impersonal tidiness of this room is a world away from Charley's walk-up flat in Harlem and a hundred worlds from the bare, noisy shanty where he and the rest of us spent what there was of childhood. I close my eyes, and side by side I see the Charley of my boyhood and the Charley of this afternoon, as clearly as if I were looking at a split TV screen. Another surge of love, seasoned with gratitude, wells up in me.

As far as I know, Charley never had any childhood at all. The oldest children of sharecroppers never do. Mama and Pa were shadowy figures whose voices I heard vaguely in the morning when sleep was shallow and whom I glimpsed as they left for the field before I was fully awake or as they trudged wearily into the house at night when my lids were irresistibly heavy.

They came into sharp focus only on special occasions. One such occasion was the day when the crops were in and the sharecroppers were paid. In our cabin there was so much excitement in the air that even I, the "baby," responded to it. For weeks we had been running out of things that we could neither grow nor get on credit. On the evening of that day we waited anxiously for our parents' return. Then

---

- gingerly (JIN jur lee) **with great caution or care**
- sharecropper (SHAYR crahp ur) **someone who farms land for the landowner**

we would cluster around the rough wooden table—I on Lil's lap or clinging to Charley's neck, little Alberta nervously tugging her plait, Jamie crouched at Mama's elbow, like a panther about to spring, and all seven of us silent for once, waiting. Pa would place the money on the table—gently, for it was made from the sweat of their bodies and from their children's tears. Mama would count it out in little piles, her dark face stern and, I think now, beautiful. Not with the hollow beauty of well-modeled features but with the strong radiance of one who has suffered and never yielded.

"This for store bill," she would mutter, making a little pile. "This for c'llection. This for piece o' gingham . . ." and so on, stretching the money as tight over our collective needs as Jamie's outgrown pants were stretched over my bottom. "Well, that's the crop." She would look up at Pa at last. "It'll do." Pa's face would relax, and a general grin flitted from child to child. We would survive, at least for the present.

The other time when my parents were solid entities was at church. On Sundays we would don our threadbare Sunday-go-to-meeting clothes and tramp, along with neighbors similarly attired, to the Tabernacle Baptist Church, the frail edifice of bare boards that was all that my parents ever knew of security and future promise.

- plait (PLAYT) **braid**
- entity (EN ti tee) **actual being; something that has real and distinct existence**
- edifice (ED i fis) **building**

Being the youngest and therefore the most likely to err, I was plopped between my father and my mother on the long wooden bench. They sat huge and eternal like twin mountains at my sides. I remember my father's still, black profile silhouetted against the sunny window, looking back into dark recesses of time, into some dim antiquity, like an ancient ceremonial mask. My mother's face, usually sternly set, changed with the varying nuances of her emotion, its planes shifting, shaped by the soft highlights of the sanctuary, as she progressed from a subdued "amen" to a loud "Help me, Jesus," wrung from the depths of her gaunt frame.

My early memories of my parents are associated with special occasions. The contours of my every day were shaped by Lil and Charley, the oldest children, who rode herd on the rest of us while Pa and Mama toiled in fields not their own. Not until years later did I realize that Lil and Charley were little more than children themselves.

Lil had the loudest, screechiest voice in the county. When she yelled, "Boy, you better git yourself in here!" you *got* yourself in there. It was Lil who caught and bathed us, Lil who fed us and sent us to school. Lil who punished us when we needed punishing and comforted us when we needed comforting. If her voice was loud, so was her laughter. When she laughed, everybody laughed. And when Lil sang, everybody listened.

Charley was taller than anybody in the world. From his shoulders, where I spent considerable time in the earliest years, the world had a different perspective: I looked down at tops of heads rather than at the undersides of chins. As I grew older, Charley became more father than brother. Those days return in fragments of splintered memory: Charley's slender dark hands whittling a toy from a chunk of wood, his face thin and intense, brown as the loaves Lil baked when there was flour; Charley's quick fingers guiding a stick of charred kindling over a bit of scrap paper, making a wondrous picture take shape—Jamie's face or Alberta's rag doll or the spare figure of our bony brown dog. Charley's voice low and terrible in the dark, telling ghost stories so delightfully dreadful that later in the night the moan of the wind through the chinks in the wall sent us scurrying to the security of Charley's pallet. Charley's sleeping form.

Some memories are more than fragmentary. I can still feel the *whap* of the wet dishrag across my mouth. Somehow I developed a stutter, which Charley was determined to cure. Someone had told him that an effective cure was to slap the stutterer across the mouth

---

- err (UR) **make a mistake; go wrong**
- antiquity (an TIK wuh tee) **olden times**
- nuance (NOO ahns) **a shade of difference**
- pallet (PAL ut) **small, hard bed or a straw-filled mattress**

with a sopping wet dishrag. Thereafter whenever I began, "Let's
g-g-g——," *whap!* from nowhere would come the ubiquitous rag.
Charley would always insist, "I don't want hurt you none, Buddy——"
and *whap* again. I don't know when or why I stopped stuttering. But I
stopped.

Already laid waste by poverty, we were easy prey for ignorance
and superstition, which hunted us like hawks. We sought education
feverishly—and, for most of us, futilely, for the sum total of our
combined energies was required for mere brute survival. Inevitably
each child had to leave school and bear his share of the eternal
burden.

Eventually the family's hopes for learning fastened on me, the
youngest. I remember—I *think* I remember, for I could not have
been more than five—one frigid day Pa, huddled on a rickety stool
before the coal stove, took me on his knee and studied me gravely. I
was a skinny little thing, they tell me, with large, solemn eyes.

"Well, boy," Pa said at last, "if you got to depend on your looks
for what you get out'n this world, you just as well lay down right
now." His hand was rough from the plow, but gentle as it touched
my cheek. "Lucky for you, you got a *mind.* And that's something
ain't everybody got. You go to school, boy, get yourself some learning. Make something out'n yourself. Ain't nothing you can't do if you
got learning."

Charley was determined that I would break the chain of poverty,

---

- ubiquitous (yoo BIK wuh tus) **present everywhere**
- feverishly (FEEV uh rish lee) **hurriedly**
- **futilely** (FYOO tuh lee) **uselessly**
- brute (BROOT) **of unrelieved harshness**

that I would "be somebody." As we worked our small vegetable garden in the sun or pulled a bucket of brackish water from the well, Charley would tell me, "You ain gon be no poor farmer, Buddy. You gon be a teacher or maybe a doctor or a lawyer. One thing, bad as you is, you ain gon be no preacher."

I loved school with a desperate passion, which became more intense when I began to realize what a monumental struggle it was for my parents and brothers and sisters to keep me there. The cramped, dingy classroom became a battleground where I was victorious. I stayed on top of my class. With glee I out-read, out-figured, and out-spelled the country boys who mocked my poverty, calling me "the boy with eyes in back of his head"—the "eyes" being the perpetual holes in my hand-me-down pants.

As the years passed, the economic strain was eased enough to make it possible for me to go on to high school. There were fewer mouths to feed, for one thing: Alberta went North to find work at sixteen; Jamie died at twelve.

I finished high school at the head of my class. For Mama and Pa and each of my brothers and sisters, my success was a personal triumph. One by one they came to me the week before commencement bringing crumpled dollar bills and coins long hoarded, muttering, "Here, Buddy, put this on your graduation clothes." My graduation suit was the first suit that was all my own.

On graduation night our cabin (less crowded now) was a frantic collage of frayed nerves. I thought Charley would drive me mad.

"Buddy, you ain pressed out them pants right. . . . Can't you git a better shine on them shoes? . . . Look how you done messed up that tie!"

Overwhelmed by the combination of Charley's nerves and my own, I finally exploded. "Man, cut it out!" Abruptly he stopped tugging at my tie, and I was afraid I had hurt his feelings. "It's okay, Charley. Look, you're strangling me. The tie's okay."

Charley relaxed a little and gave a rather sheepish chuckle. "Sure, Buddy." He gave my shoulder a rough joggle. "But you gotta look good. You *somebody.*"

My valedictory address was the usual idealistic, sentimental nonsense. I have forgotten what I said that night, but the sight of Mama

---

- brackish (BRAK ish) **somewhat salty; distasteful**
- monumental (MAHN yu ment ul) **great and lasting**
- collage (kuh LAHZH) **assembly of a variety of fragments; design of pasted pieces**
- **frayed** (FRAYD) **ragged and torn; worn into shreds**
- valedictory address (val uh DIK tor ee) **farewell speech given by the student having the highest rank in a graduating class**

and Pa and the rest is like a lithograph burned on my memory; Lil, her rough face made beautiful by her proud smile; Pa, his head held high, eyes loving and fierce; Mama radiant. Years later when her shriveled hands were finally still, my mind kept coming back to her as she was now. I believe this moment was the apex of her entire life. All of them, even Alberta down from Baltimore—different now, but united with them in her pride. And Charley, on the end of the row, still somehow the protector of them all. Charley, looking as if he were in the presence of something sacred.

As I made my way through the carefully rehearsed speech it was as if part of me were standing outside watching the whole thing— their proud, work-weary faces, myself wearing the suit that was their combined strength and love and hope: Lil with her lovely, low-pitched voice, Charley with the hands of an artist, Pa and Mama with heaven knows what potential lost with their sweat in the fields. I realized in that moment that I wasn't necessarily the smartest—only the youngest.

And the luckiest. The war came along, and I exchanged three years of my life (including a fair amount of my blood and a great deal of pain) for the GI Bill and a college education. Strange how time can slip by like water flowing through your fingers. One by one the changes came—the old house empty at last, the rest of us scattered; for me, marriage, graduate school, kids, a professorship, and by now a thickening waistline and thinning hair. My mind spins off

● lithograph (LITH uh graf) **kind of picture**

the years, and I am back to this afternoon and today's Charley—still long and lean, still gentle-eyed, still my greatest fan.

I didn't tell Charley I would be at a professional meeting in New York and would surely visit; he and Bea would have spent days in fixing up, and I would have had to be company. No, I would drop in on them, take them by surprise before they had a chance to stiffen up. I was anxious to see them—it had been so long. Yesterday and this morning were taken up with meetings in the posh Fifth Avenue hotel—a place we could not have dreamed in our boyhood. Late this afternoon I shook loose and headed for Harlem, hoping that Charley still came home for a few hours before his evening run. Leaving the glare and glitter of downtown, I entered the subway. When I emerged, I was in Harlem.

Whenever I come to Harlem I feel somehow as if I were coming home—to some mythic ancestral home. The problems are real, the people are real—yet there is some mysterious epic quality about Harlem, as if all black people began and ended there, as if each had left something of himself. As if in Harlem the very heart of blackness pulsed its beautiful tortured rhythms. Joining the throngs of people that saunter Lenox Avenue late afternoons, I headed for Charley's apartment. Along the way I savored the panorama of Harlem— women with shopping bags trudging wearily home; little kids flitting saucily through the crowd; groups of adolescent boys striding boldly along—some boisterous, some ominously silent; tables of merchandise spread on the sidewalks with hawkers singing their siren songs of irresistible bargains; a blaring microphone sending forth waves of words to draw passersby into a restless bunch around a slender young man whose eyes have seen Truth; defeated men standing around on street corners or sitting on steps, heads down, hands idle; posters announcing Garvey Day,* "Buy Black" stamped on pavements; store windows bright with things African; stores still boarded up, a livid scar from last year's rioting. There was a terrible tension in the air; I thought of how quickly dry timber becomes a roaring fire from a single spark.

I mounted the steps of Charley's building—old and in need of paint, like all the rest—and pushed the button to his apartment.

- posh (PAHSH) **smart and expensive**
- epic (EH pik) **about heroic events**
- **saunter** (SAWN tur) **stroll**
- **savor** (SAYV ur) **taste with pleasure**
- ominously (AHM uh nus lee) **threateningly**

*Garvey Day—Marcus Garvey (1880–1940) was a black leader who organized the first important American black nationalist movement (1919–1926); the movement was based in New York City's Harlem section.

Charley's buzzer rang. I pushed open the door and mounted the stairs.

"Well, it's Buddy!" roared Charley as I arrived on the third floor. "Bea! Bea! Come here, girl, it's Buddy!" And somehow I was simultaneously shaking Charley's hand, getting clapped on the back, and being buried in the fervor of Bea's gigantic hug. They swept me from the hall into their dim apartment.

"Buddy, what you doing here? Whyn't you tell me you was coming to New York?" His face was so lit up with pleasure that in spite of the inroads of time, he still looked like the Charley of years gone by, excited over a new litter of kittens.

"The place look a mess! Whyn't you let us know?" put in Bea, suddenly distressed.

"Looks fine to me, girl. And so do you!"

And she did. Bea is a fine-looking woman, plump and firm, with rich brown skin and thick black hair.

"Mary, Lucy, look, Uncle Buddy's here!" Two neat little girls came shyly from the TV. Uncle Buddy was something of a celebrity in this house.

I hugged them heartily, much to their discomfort. "Charley, where you getting all these pretty women?"

We all sat in the warm kitchen, where Bea was preparing dinner. It felt good there. Beautiful odors mingled in the air. Charley sprawled in a chair near mine, his long arms and legs akimbo. No longer shy, the tinier girl sat on my lap, while her sister darted here and there like a merry little water bug. Bea bustled about, managing to keep up with both the conversation and the cooking.

I told them about the conference I was attending and, knowing it would give them pleasure, I mentioned that I had addressed the group that morning. Charley's eyes glistened.

"You hear that, Bea?" he whispered. "Buddy done spoke in front of all them professors!"

"Sure I hear," Bea answered briskly, stirring something that was making an aromatic steam. "I bet he weren't even scared. I bet them professors learnt something, too."

For a fleet second I wondered—could my reality ever really filter through to those who could never, in their most distorted dreams, conceive of my world? And without sensing my Self, *could they hear me at all?*

"Well, anyway," I said. "I hope they did."

- fervor (FUR vur) **zeal; intensity of feeling or expression**
- inroads (IN rohdz) **advances at the expense of someone or something**
- akimbo (uh KIM boh) **set in a bent position (for example, hands on hips)**
- **aromatic** (AR uh MAT ik) **fragrant**

We talked about a hundred different things after that—Bea's job in the school cafeteria, my Jess and the kids, our scattered family.

"Seems like we don't git together no more, not since Mama and Pa passed on," said Charley sadly. "I ain't even got a Christmas card from Alberta for three-four year now."

"Well, ain't no two a y'all in the same city. An' everybody scratchin to make ends meet," Bea replied. "Ain't nobody got time to git together."

"Yeah, that's the way it goes, I guess," I said.

"But it sure is good to see you, Buddy. Say, look, Lil told me about the cash you sent the children last winter when Jake was out of work all that time. She sure preciated it."

"Why, man, as close as you and Lil stuck to me when I was a kid, I owed her that and more. Say, Bea, did I ever tell you about the time——" and we swung into the usual reminiscences.

They insisted that I stay for dinner. Persuading me was no hard job: fish fried golden, ham hocks and collard greens, corn bread—if I'd *tried* to leave, my feet wouldn't have taken me. It was good to sit there in Charley's kitchen, my coat and tie flung over a chair surrounded by soul food and love.

"Say, Buddy, a couple months back I picked up a kid from your school."

"No stuff."

"I axed him did he know you. He say he was in your class last year."

"Did you get his name?"

"No, I didn't ax him that. Man, he told me you were the best teacher he had. He said you were one smart cat!"

"He told you that cause you're my brother."

"Your *brother*—I didn't tell him I was your brother. I said you was a old friend of mine."

I put my fork down and leaned over. "What you tell him *that* for?"

Charley explained patiently as he had explained things when I was a child and had missed an obvious truth. "I didn't want your students to know your brother wasn't nothing but a cabdriver. You *somebody.*"

"You're a nut," I said gently. "You should've told that kid the truth." I wanted to say, I'm proud of you, I wouldn't have been anything at all except for you. But he would have been embarrassed.

Bea brought in the dessert—homemade sweet potato pie! "Buddy, I must of knew you were coming! I just had a mind I wanted to make some sweet potato pie."

There's nothing in this world I like better than Bea's sweet potato pie! "Bea, how you expect me to eat all that?"

The slice she put before me was outrageously big—and moist and covered with a light, golden crust—I ate it all.

As we were finishing up, Charley said wistfully, "Buddy, you recollect when we was all home—even 'fore Jamie died, poor little fellow—you recollect, at Christmas time Mama always used to make us a sweet potato pie?"

"Sure I do. I don't guess we had much, come to think of it, but when that good old pie came on, smelling like heaven, I thought we had us a feast."

Charley's grin was seasoned with sadness. "I can just see y'all little fellows now. And Mama and Pa and Lil——"

Bea cut in, "And all that good pie!"

And we all laughed, softer this time.

"Bea, I'm gonna have to eat and run," I said at last.

Charley guffawed. "Much as you et, I don't see how you gonna *walk*, let alone *run*." He went out to get his cab from the garage several blocks away.

Bea was washing the tiny girl's face. "Wait a minute, Buddy. I'm gon give you the rest of that pie to take with you."

"Great!" I'd eaten all I could hold, but my *spirit* was still hungry for sweet potato pie.

Bea got out some waxed paper and wrapped up the rest of the pie. "That'll do you for a snack tonight." She slipped it into a brown paper bag.

I gave her a long goodbye hug. "Bea, I love you for a lot of things. Your cooking is one of them!" We had a last comfortable laugh together. I kissed the little girls and went outside to wait for Charley, holding the bag of pie reverently.

In a minute Charley's ancient cab limped to the curb. I plopped into the seat next to him, and we headed downtown. Soon we were assailed by the garish lights of New York on a sultry spring night. We chatted as Charley skillfully managed the heavy traffic. I looked at his long hands on the wheel and wondered what they could have done with artists' brushes.

We stopped a bit down the street from my hotel. I invited him in, but he said he had to get on with his evening run. But as I opened the door to get out, he commanded in the old familiar voice, "Buddy, you wait!"

"What's wrong?"

"What's that you got there?"

I was bewildered. "That? You mean this bag? That's a piece of sweet potato pie Bea fixed for me."

"You ain't going through the lobby of no big hotel carrying no brown paper bag."

"Man, you *crazy!* Of course I'm going——Look, Bea fixed it for me—*That's my pie*——"

● guffaw (gu FAW) **laugh loudly**

● garish (GAR ish) **tastelessly showy**

Charley's eyes were miserable. "Folks in that hotel don't go through the lobby carrying no brown paper bags. That *country*. And you can't neither. You *somebody*, Buddy. You got to be *right*. Now, gimme that bag."

"I want that pie, Charley. I've got nothing to prove to anybody——"

I couldn't believe it. But there was no point in arguing. Foolish as it seemed to me, it was important to him.

"You got to look *right*, Buddy. Can't nobody look dignified carrying a brown paper bag."

So finally, thinking how tasty it would have been and how seldom I got a chance to eat anything that good, I handed over my bag of sweet potato pie. If it was that important to him——

I tried not to show my irritation. "Okay, man—take care now." I slammed the door harder than I had intended, walked rapidly to the hotel, and entered the brilliant, crowded lobby.

"That Charley!" I thought. Walking slower now, I crossed the carpeted lobby toward the elevator, still thinking of my lost snack. I had to admit that of all the herd of people who jostled each other in the lobby, not one was carrying a brown paper bag. Or anything but expensive attaché cases or slick packages from exclusive shops. I suppose we all operate according to the symbols that are meaningful to us, and to Charley a brown paper bag symbolizes the humble life he thought I had left. I was *somebody*.

I don't know what made me glance back, but I did. And suddenly the tears and laughter, toil and love of a lifetime burst around me like fireworks in a night sky.

For there, following a few steps behind, came Charley, proudly carrying a brown paper bag full of sweet potato pie.

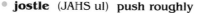

• jostle (JAHS ul) push roughly

ALL THINGS CONSIDERED

1. While Buddy (the narrator) was growing up, his parents worked as (a) grocers. (b) teachers. (c) sharecroppers.

2. In order to help Buddy stop stuttering, his brother Charley would (a) slap him across the mouth with a wet dishrag. (b) keep telling him to slow down. (c) listen patiently to him and never interrupt him.

3. Charley fusses over Buddy's graduation clothes because he (a) thinks Buddy is so ugly he has to do *something* to make him look good. (b) thinks Buddy should look good because he's *somebody*. (c) doesn't want Buddy to disgrace the family.

4. When he gives the valedictory address at graduation, Buddy looks down at his family, his parents and his six brothers and sisters, and realizes he is the (a) smartest in the family. (b) bravest in the family. (c) luckiest in the family.

5. After graduating from college and attending graduate school, Buddy becomes a (a) cabdriver. (b) professor. (c) lawyer.

THINKING IT THROUGH

1. It is obvious that Buddy has deep feelings for Charley. Referring to what Buddy tells the reader in the part of the story about his youth, explain why Charley is so important to him.

2. Why doesn't Buddy tell Charley and Bea that he plans to be in New York City and wants to visit them?

3. Charley tells Buddy that he gave a cab ride to a student of his and that the student had told him that Buddy was the best teacher he had. Buddy modestly says, "He told you that cause you're my brother." But Charley replies, "I didn't tell him I was your brother. . . ." Why didn't he?

4. Charley refuses to let Buddy carry the brown bag containing the sweet potato pie into the hotel, and yet Charley himself carries it into the hotel. (a) In Buddy's opinion, Charley sees the bag as a symbol (see page 104). A symbol of what? (b) Explain Charley's reasons for carrying the brown bag himself.

Literary Skills

Flashback

Most stories that you read take place in **chronological order,** the order that events take place in real life. When stories are written in chronological order, the reader expects the plot to be a continual sequence of beginning, middle, and end: the beginning starts the action, the middle continues the action and requires something to follow, and the end follows from what has gone before but requires nothing further.

Some authors, however, make use of a device called **flashback.** In a flashback, the author interrupts the natural time sequence of a story to relate an episode or scene that occurred prior to the opening situation. In this way the author can make the reader aware of some background information important to the story's action, characterization, and/or theme.

1. "Sweet Potato Pie" begins in the present as Buddy is thinking about his afternoon with his brother Charley. But you are hardly into the story before the narration is interrupted by a long flashback. Find where the flashback begins and write the first five words of that paragraph.

2. Write the last five words in the paragraph to show where the flashback ends.

3. What reason might the author have had for using a flashback rather than straight chronological order?

Composition

1. The story begins in the present, contains a flashback, then ends in the present—but earlier in the day than the opening scene in the story. In one paragraph of no more than six sentences, describe what happens in the flashback in "Sweet Potato Pie."

2. Use Collier's story as a model for a brief story of your own. The story should contain a flashback. Follow this procedure: (a) Think of someone who is as special to you as Charley is to Buddy. Write an opening paragraph in which you tell of seeing this person recently. (b) In a second paragraph, use flashback. Tell an anecdote about something the two of you did together as children. Choose an event that will show why you consider the person special. (c) In your final paragraph, continue with the action in the present. (For example, you could tell why both you and your friend remember and value the event(s) you experienced when you were younger.)

Before completing the exercises that follow, you may wish to review the **bold-faced** words on pages 102 to 124.

I. On a separate sheet of paper, write the term in each line that means the same, or nearly the same thing, as the word in *italics*.

1. *mackinaw:* umbrella, short coat, rain hat, scarf
2. *reflection:* serious thought, joking speech, brass mirror, loving response
3. *tumultuously:* happily, joyfully, beautifully, violently
4. *savor:* throw away, taste pleasurably, move quickly, dislike
5. *frayed:* worn through, scattered, amazed, brand new
6. *jostle:* make happy, entertain, push roughly, annoy
7. *perception:* awareness, poise, intelligence, honor
8. *futilely:* angrily, hopefully, sweetly, uselessly
9. *aromatic:* lovely, fragrant, ironic, fortunate
10. *saunter:* walk quickly, wink, wave, stroll

II. Read the following poem carefully before answering the questions on page 126.

BATTLE WON IS LOST

by Phil George

They said, "You are no longer a lad."
    I nodded.
They said, "Enter the council lodge."
    I sat.
They said, "Our lands are at stake."
    I scowled.
They said, "We are at war."
    I hated.
They said, "Prepare red war symbols."
    I painted.
They said, "Count coups."
    I cringed.
They said, "Desperate warriors fight best."
    I charged.
They said, "Some will be wounded."
    I bled.
They said, "To die is glorious."
    They lied.

1. What do you infer about the speaker from terms like "council lodge" and "red war symbols"? To which group of people does he belong?

2. Each line in the poem starts with "I" or "They." (a) What can you infer about the "I"? (b) What can you infer about the "They"?

3. The speaker is being told to accept certain group beliefs. Note the order of the statements he is told to believe. (a) In your opinion, do the statements become successively easier or more difficult to believe? (b) Which statement does the speaker disbelieve?

4. Review the four kinds of conflict on page 111. Which kinds of conflict are expressed in this poem?

UNIT REVIEW

I. Match the terms in Column A with their definitions in Column B.

<table>
<tr><td align="center">A</td><td align="center">B</td></tr>
</table>

A

1. character clues
2. conflict
3. flashback
4. characterization
5. chronological order
6. compare
7. contrast
8. stanza

B

a) the clash between opposing forces that gets the reader involved in a story

b) a division of a poem

c) showing how two things are alike

d) the hints the author gives the reader about a character through actions and speeches

e) showing the differences between two or more things

f) the ways in which authors bring the people in their stories to life

g) in the order of time; that is, the order that events take place in real life

h) interrupts chronological order in a story to show something that happened earlier

II. Look over Unit II and find the story you liked the best. Then pick the story you thought was least interesting. Fold a piece of paper in half lengthwise to make two columns. On the top left, write the title of the story you liked best. On the top right, put the title of the story you liked least. Analyze what it was about the two stories that created such a different reaction in you. Compare and contrast the two stories. Try to use at least three of the following terms: *plot* (including rising action, resolution, climax), *narrator, characterization, conflict, character clues, mood.* (You may first wish to review these terms by referring to the glossary that begins on page 393.)

Bonus questions: Comment on the cartoon below in terms of stereotyped thinking.

1. How may the girl have stereotyped B.D.?

2. B.D. suggests three ways that he might not fit the stereotype. What are they?

3. The girl then suggests ways that she sees B.D. as not fitting into the stereotype. (a) What are these? (b) Do you think she is correct in her evaluation? Explain why you think so.

Doonesbury, Copyright, 1971, G. B. Trudeau. Reprinted with permission of Universal Press Syndicate. All rights reserved.

SPEAKING UP

Roleplaying for an Interview

Roleplaying is an excellent way to practice speaking before a group because it's often easier to play a part than to be yourself. In this exercise, you'll play either an *interviewer* or the person being interviewed. Work with a partner. Choose one of the situations.

First Situation—based on "A Kind of Murder": Mr. Warren is about to be interviewed for a job at another prep school. The headmaster, who is the interviewer, knows the events that led to the last dismissal. What might happen in the interview?

Second Situation—based on "Sweet Potato Pie": A reporter for a magazine plans to interview an important member of the Black community. Through the interview, the reporter hopes to learn how Buddy reached such an important position. What was it in his background that helped him to become successful?

Third Situation—(of your own invention) based on a different type of interview from one of the selections mentioned or from another selection in the unit.

Use the following steps to develop the interview:

1. Reread the story to refresh your memory so that you can roleplay the situation effectively. As you read, jot down notes that might be useful as you develop the interview.

2. Discuss possible questions and answers with your fellow roleplayer. Be sure that each question will encourage the person being interviewed to give interesting answers. Avoid questions that can be answered by only a *yes* or a *no*.

3. Organize your questions and answers in some logical order. Rehearse an introduction. The interviewer may begin with a few pleasant remarks to help put the person being interviewed at ease.

4. Once you and your partner have the questions and answers organized, look over your plan once again. When you can, have the answer to one question lead to the next question. Make any necessary revisions at this time.

5. Decide who will be the interviewer and who will be the person interviewed. If you are the person being interviewed, study that character thoroughly. When you roleplay, try to *become* that character.

6. Practice your interview. The questions should be written out. For the answers, notes are sufficient. Each person should be prepared so that the interview can move along at a smooth pace.

WRITING A FICTIONAL DIARY

Prewriting

As a warm-up activity, jot down answers to the following questions. Express your feelings and thoughts freely. Imagine that you are writing in your own personal—and private—diary.

- What event stands out in your mind for today?
- What did you accomplish? (Accomplishments could include completing an assignment for school, helping a friend with a problem, doing a necessary chore around the house—anything you felt good about.)
- What minor events do you want to record?
- Did you think through any problems? Hope any hopes? Have any interesting ideas? Dream any dreams?
- Now look through the stories in Unit II to find a character who interested you. Reread the story to remind yourself what the character was like. As you read, jot down notes about (a) personality traits; (b) special interests; (c) accomplishments; (d) problems; (e) hopes and dreams. (You may not find information on all of the above. Just take notes on what you *do* find.)

Writing

1. First, write your title: The Diary of _____
2. Date your first entry. (This may take some thought. Only "A Kind of Murder" and possibly "Sweet Potato Pie" could be considered as taking place in the present. The rest of the stories take place in the 1800s; you'll have to come up with an appropriate exact date.)
3. Using the questions requested in the prewriting activities begin writing the first diary entry. You may wish to begin by writing only a sentence or two for each of the questions listed. (You'll be improving these during the revision process.)
4. You may be wondering, "But what do I do if the story gives no clue as to a hope or dream of the character?" Or "The story only mentioned one problem! What do I do?" The answer is "Use your imagination." Imagine what the character is feeling and is thinking.
5. When the first entry is completed, draw a line of asterisks (***) under it.

6. Date and write your second entry. This entry does not have to be for the very next day. You might even wish to have the entries several months apart to show how the character's problem has been solved, how dreams have changed, and so on.

The Diary of Mary

Sept. 14, 1842

Yesterday I got a ride with some folks going West. They seem like good people. The man was grumpy at first, and he didn't want to take me with them. I told him I could help by watching the children. That convinced him!

✳   ✳   ✳

October 9, 1842

Revising

1. Probably the most difficult aspect of this assignment is *voice:* Does the diary entry sound as though *you* are talking? It shouldn't! You have to sound like a fragile nineteenth-century woman ("The Story of an Hour"), or a warm, loving, but not-very-well-educated cabdriver (Charley in "Sweet Potato Pie")—or whatever character you've chosen.

2. You have been writing only the main ideas for the diary entries. Now see if you can make the entries more colorful. By improving word choices, you can create pictures for your readers and bring your characters to life.

   a. First look at the nouns in your diary entries. Have you included exact, detailed adjectives? For example, you may have written for Madame Lantin, *I wore a beautiful dress to the opera tonight.* "Beautiful" is an adjective, but it doesn't show much. Try to be specific: *I wore my blue-green silk gown cut low on the bosom to the opera; I do love that dress so because it rustles and gives off shimmers of light as I move.*

   b. Verbs (action words) can also help to create pictures. Instead of writing, *After the opera, I walked home,* show Madame Lantin's mood by the *way* she walked. You could write, *I flew home from the opera on winged feet.*

UNIT · 3

CHANGE

Nothing is permanent except change.

—Heraclitus

The words of Heraclitus (her uh KLY tus), a Greek philosopher who lived nearly 2,500 years ago, are truer than ever. Even change has changed for it now occurs faster. In the time of Heraclitus, it took thousands of years for the earth's population to double. Now it takes less than 40 years. More people . . . more cars . . . more cities . . . more discoveries . . . more challenges . . . more, more, more . . . faster, faster, faster. It's not surprising that people often feel confused!

This unit demonstrates an important rule of clear thinking: *territories change constantly, but our mental maps can be frozen in time.* You'll start by reading about a scientific genius who tries to improve his body's health—and slow its rate of change. During the reading of other selections, you'll have an opportunity to think about *time* and *change* from different points of view.

Once again: *Nothing is permanent except change.*

▶ Suppose you could find a way to slow down the effects of time in your own life. Why, you might decide to live forever! What else might happen to you? The amazing details are revealed in . . .

THE MANUSCRIPT OF DR. ARNESS

by Gahan Wilson

Before I do what I must do, I suppose it would be a good idea to leave behind an explanation.

Please understand that I do love life. I am not happy at the idea of giving it up. If I could discover any other choice, I would take it. But there is no other choice.

My main reason for writing this is to leave behind a warning. Even now, some brilliant minds like my own might be engaged in a similar experiment, unaware of where it will lead. I address myself to these minds.

It is ironic that I have been pushed into suicide because of an attempt to prolong my life. From childhood I have been consumed with this single goal. It is infuriating to consider what Mozart* or Emily Dickinson† or Isaac Newton‡ could have accomplished if their creative years had been prolonged. Imagine how much richer our heritage would now be.

I am, as I said, brilliant. I am not boasting, for it isn't something I've accomplished but merely something I was born with. I did, however, make full use of my mind to crowd a large amount of learning into a short period of time. I wanted, you see, to cheat the time trap as much as possible.

Despite a quick start, I was into my mid 30's before I completed my theories and well into my 40's before I could start the actual test.

My aim was to improve my body's health and to slow its rate of

---

● consumed (kun SOOMD) **absorbed; taken up**

*Wolfgang Amadeus Mozart (WOOLF gang am uh DAY us MOHT sart) (1756–1791) Austrian composer

†Emily Dickinson (1830–1886) American poet

‡Isaac Newton (1642–1727) English mathematician and scientist, discoverer of laws of gravity

change. In this way I could prolong my active mental and physical life well beyond the normal span. And I succeeded—by a process described in the notebook I shall leave behind with this note.

I proceeded in the usual way, testing my theories on animals and keeping careful records. I began with mice, went on to guinea pigs, and worked the final experiments on a group of chimpanzees.

Everything worked, and I was filled with joy. The dream of my life was proving itself before my eyes—I had achieved the power to work the miracle for which I had been born. I could become immortal.

It was at this point that I erred, and the error was haste. But can you blame me? The years were passing—each one, it seemed, faster than the year before. Freedom from time was in my grasp. I could not resist the temptation to reach out and take it. Even now, I cannot blame myself too much.

I began to apply the treatment to myself. As with my animals, there was no noticeable change at first. But then I became aware of a growing peace and contentment, and my body improved dramatically. I had worn thick glasses. In four weeks I had no further need of them. My digestion had been faulty. Now it was perfect. I could hardly believe the image in my mirror. It was like some before-and-after ad in the back pages of a magazine. I positively radiated health.

By now the lack of aging in my animals had become evident. The mice, which would have died long ago under normal conditions, were all alive and thriving. They could be killed by any normal means, but if they were only wounded, their rate of recovery was staggering. A scalpel cut that would ordinarily take weeks to mend would heal in a matter of days. My triumph was past all belief.

Now I proceed to the less happy events that followed.

It was my habit to run my mice through mazes to check their reaction time. At the start of the experiment, their increased ability gave me much satisfaction. Now, to my growing concern, I saw that the time they needed to run the mazes was growing longer.

I examined the mice carefully. I dissected a few to see if anything had gone wrong with their internal organs. They were all in flawless shape. But still each day they took a little longer to find their way through the maze.

At the end of one month, to my great discomfort, they needed twice as much time as they had at the beginning.

By this time my guinea pigs and even the chimps were showing the same loss of ability. There was not the slightest thing wrong with

---

- **err** (UR) make a mistake; go wrong; violate an accepted standard of conduct
- **radiate** (RAY dee ayt) send forth in rays
- **maze** (MAYZ) puzzle made of network of paths

any of them except that they needed more and more time to accomplish any task.

In another month the condition of my mice had become positively scary. At their peak, they had needed a minute and a half to make their trek through the mazes. Now they needed two hours. It was the same with all their activities. They ate and played and fought, but my patience wore thin trying to watch them because they took so much time. I can only compare the effect to that of a slow-motion movie.

I attached an ink marker to the tail of one mouse so the creature would leave a thin black line behind itself as it moved. After a full week the trail was only one inch long.

DR. A. ARNESS

All of my mice remained in the best of health. The only trouble was that, to a casual observer in my laboratory, the mice would have appeared to be stuck in one spot.

As the reader might have guessed, I was not exempt from this slowing process. To me everything seemed normal. But by timing my actions with my watch, I could see only too well that my movements had become increasingly slower.

Then I no longer needed a clock to remind myself of my condition. I could not strike a match fast enough to ignite it. By counting the sunsets through my window I saw that it took me nine days to arrange my typewriter so that I could type this note.

I decided to end my life after what might seem a trivial incident. I gave one of my chimps a banana and observed that it took him an entire afternoon to peel it. He looked so happy, so blissfully unaware of his snail-paced condition, that I began to laugh at him. My laughter became hysterical, and I ended by crying.

I have no idea how long ago this happened, as I have lost all track of ordinary time. It has become a foreign thing to me.

I can see no point in becoming a comical object. The chimps now look like stuffed monkeys, and I have no intention of joining their ranks. I shall now take the gun, which I have placed beside my typewriter, and end this endless existence. I wonder how long it will take me to do it. As I said earlier, the situation is not without iron

Thus ends the manuscript of Dr. Arness. The last page remains, as you can see for yourself, on exhibit in his typewriter. The placement of the typewriter in relation to the gun and to Dr. Arness himself is exactly the same as when he and the other objects were discovered in his laboratory.

Although Dr. Arness appears to be—as he put it—"stuffed," he is not. He is alive, in good health, and he is moving. His index finger is actually approaching the *y* key so that he can finish the *y* in *irony*. His speed, however, can be measured only with the most delicate of instruments. Dr. Arness is now 250 years old.

The animals referred to in his manuscript are also all alive and well. They have been moved to the Hall of Mammals in the city museum. Attractive models of the chimps are available, in various sizes, at the museum store.

You are welcome to view Dr. Arness in his laboratory. Public visiting hours are 9 A.M. to 4 P.M. on every day of the week except Monday. You needn't worry about not finding the doctor on hand.

● **trivial** (TRIV ee ul) unimportant; of little worth

ALL THINGS CONSIDERED ───────────────────

1. As he starts writing the manuscript, Dr. Arness intends to (a) live forever. (b) commit suicide. (c) become a hero of modern science.

2. Arness makes the mistake of (a) using chimps instead of rabbits. (b) beginning his manuscript too soon. (c) treating himself before fully testing the animals.

3. The first result of the scientist's self-treatment is (a) an increase in health and happiness. (b) some loss of memory. (c) an immediate slowdown in activity.

4. The scientist begins to worry when he (a) finds he can no longer type. (b) observes the chimps fighting. (c) notices that the mice are slowing down.

5. The story ends with Dr. Arness (a) in complete control of himself. (b) unable to function at all. (c) alive and healthy but not moving normally.

THINKING IT THROUGH ───────────────────

1. Dr. Arness writes about the "time trap" and his wish to gain "freedom from time." What does he mean?

2. If the story were continued, what would you expect the rest of Dr. Arness's life to be like? For instance, how long would you expect him to live?

3. (a) Why does the narrator change in the last four paragraphs of the story? (b) How do these paragraphs add interest to the story?

4. At the end of the story, Dr. Arness indicates that although the chimps seem happy and blissful, he himself is unhappy and miserable. Why do these differences exist?

5. Explain this sentence: "It is ironic that I have been pushed into suicide because of an attempt to prolong my life" (page 134). You may first wish to reread the definition of *irony of situation* on page 58.

Literary Skills

Point of View

The **point of view** is the position from which a story is told. The two most common points of view are the *first person* and the *third person.*

First-Person Point of View

In the **first-person** point of view, the narrator is a character in the story. This character uses the words *I, me,* and *my* frequently. Everything that happens in the story must be presented as observed and interpreted by this one character. *I don't know what has become of Mr. Silas Warner, but I have lived for many years with the burden on my conscience . . .* (page 68).

Third-Person Point of View

In the **third-person** point of view, the narrator, or storyteller, is *not* a character in the story. *She sat with her head thrown back upon the cushion of the chair.* (page 106).

Both points of view—first person and third person—allow for a variety of storytelling techniques. In some stories told in the first person, the narrator is the main character. In others, the narrator is not the main character but another character who always happens to be around when the important action takes place.

In stories told from the third-person point of view, sometimes the narrator presents the feelings and thoughts of a single character. This is called **third-person limited point of view.** At other times, the narrator skips around and enters the mind of one character and then another character at will. The reader learns what each character thinks and feels. This is called **third-person omniscient point of view.**

1. "The Manuscript of Dr. Arness" is unusual in that one part is told in the first person and another part is told in the third person. (a) Briefly describe the events in each part. (b) How does the plot demand that the story be told in this odd way?

2. In your opinion, is it easier to write by using the first person or by using the third person? Explain why you think so.

3. Think about the story again. Are the *author,* Gahan Wilson, and the *narrator,* Dr. Arness, the same person? Explain why or why not.

4. In a piece of literature, can the *author* and the *narrator* be the same person? If so, give an example.

Composition

1. Write a paragraph of no more than ten sentences in the third-person point of view summarizing "The Manuscript of Dr. Arness." Since you are writing from the third-person point of view, use the words *Dr. Arness, he, the animals,* and *they* throughout your paragraph.

2. Think of reasons why writers often use the first-person point of view. Write a paragraph explaining your reasons. Refer to one specific story written from the first-person point of view that seems realistic to you. (Choose a story from another unit that you have read.)

139

APRIL

by Lois Duncan

▶ *The author introduces her own story:* Back in my grammar-school days, I had ridden the school bus with a girl named Martha Dunning. Dunning wasn't her last name; it went with the Martha. People called her Martha Dunning when they spoke to her. I was horrified by the idea of being known by such a mouthful, and once I timidly asked her how she felt about it. She told me it was a family name and she was used to it, and then added, after a short pause, "You should hear what our folks named my sister."

I didn't have the nerve to ask her, and I'd wondered about it ever since. Was the sister's name longer or shorter? Prettier or uglier? The question had hung dormant in the back of my mind for over twelve years. Now it came popping forth to give me a jump-off point for a story.

My sister's name is April. She was born in the spring. Mother says it was the first real day of spring when the air was suddenly warm and soft and fresh and dandelions popped out on the lawn and the first group of birds invaded the birdbath in the backyard. Mother isn't usually the romantic type, but when she heard the birds and felt springtime pouring in the open window she completely forgot the baby was to be named Martha Dunning after an aunt.

She said, "Her name is April."

So when I came along a year later, the Martha Dunning name was still lying around waiting to be used. I was born in the hottest part of August, so there was no inspiration for anything else.

I've often wondered whether, if things had been different—if I had been the springtime baby and April had come in dead summer and been Martha Dunning—maybe we would have been different people too. I've wondered how much being named April had to do with making April look like springtime. Because she does. Even when we were very little, people would look at April with her soft, light hair shining silver over her shoulders and her eyes a dark, dark blue, almost a purple blueness, and smile. As she grew older the loveliness did not fade the way it does with so many pretty children. If anything, she grew more beautiful each day.

Sometimes I would catch Mother and Daddy looking at her and then glancing at each other and shaking their heads as though to say, "How in the world did we—two quite average people—ever produce anything like this!" And aside from being exquisite to look at, April is sweet. It is a

---

● **dormant** (DOR munt) inactive; at rest

gentle, childlike sweetness that makes her like and trust everybody, and when she was little, Mother and Daddy were fiercely protective. Although she was the older, I always felt as though she were my younger sister, and in all our games I was the one who led and made the rules. She was a year ahead of me in school, but it was I who taught her to read, carefully pointing out the letters and pronouncing the words.

"Oh, Martha," April would sigh, staring at the page in bewilderment, "I'll never be able to do it. All those letters making words and the words making sense . . . How do you ever remember what they all are! I'm so dumb!"

"No," I would say quickly, "of course, you're not dumb, April. You'll learn. It just takes time."

"But look at you!" April would exclaim. "You've been able to read practically since you were a baby!"

Which was true. I loved books with a passionate devotion, and the problems of reading never held any terrors for me.

"Oh, some people are good at some things," I would say, "and some at others. Come on and try again."

At last she did learn to read, at least well enough to get by, but she never liked it. I don't believe I have ever seen April pick up a book for pleasure. And then came a worse step—multiplication tables—and then long division and fractions and algebra, and finally Latin and biology and chemistry. Through them all, April struggled earnestly, and I spent hours with her at home, and finally, when our report cards came, she would produce D's and C's, and Mother and Daddy would always say, "Well, that's fine, dear."

And to my straight A's they would say, "That's fine, dear," in exactly the same tone of voice. And April would smile with such radiant relief that they would kiss her impulsively. Because, after all, she did try so hard and was so beautiful.

Our house was a good-sized one and April and I each had our own room.

● **impulsively** (im PUL siv lee) **with a sudden tendency**

April's room was the smaller, but it had a window overlooking the backyard garden and in summer it always smelled of flowers and freshly cut grass. It was done in pink and white with fluffy curtains at the windows and a dressing table with a ruffle around it covered and pink rosebuds. My room was yellow and brown, with a chocolate rug and sunny curtains and several rows of bookshelves and a large desk. The rooms were as different as we were, but they were both nice in their own ways.

"Your room looks so comfortable in winter," April would say, wandering in to toss herself across the foot of the bed where I lay reading. "I think it's the yellow—it seems so warm and friendly."

"Well, you can spend the winter with me," I would answer, "and I'll come visit your room in the spring."

Then we would both laugh, for we knew how hopeless our sharing a room would be—like trying to mix orange sherbet with mashed potatoes.

I liked my room. It suited me, and there was plenty of room for the books I loved so much and for my desk, which would never have fitted into April's room. Even so, sometimes I would pass her door and glance in and see the fluff of curtains and the rosebud dressing table, and I would wonder what it would be like to have such a dainty room and to fit in it as perfectly as April did.

We both had our boys. April, of course, had admirers in droves from the time she started kindergarten, and by the time she reached high school she never had a choice of less than three or four invitations to the school dances. I went to the dances too, although my admirers seemed to consist of only one boy at a time. I was never actually jealous, because April whisked back and forth from one boy to another so gaily that it made it all seem like a game.

Until the arrival of Jeff Reigle.

Jeff was much older than the boys we were used to dating. We would never have known him at all if Daddy had not been introduced to him at Rotary. He was a fine young man, Daddy told us, in business for himself, and Daddy had invited him over to visit.

"April's a senior now—eighteen years old," he told us. "It's time she met somebody besides the high school crowd."

"How old is he?" we asked in amazement. Daddy had always been so strict about our dating boys our own age.

"Oh, twenty-five or twenty-six," Daddy said slowly.

April and I were stunned. "Ancient!" we whispered to each other.

But when Jeff arrived he was not ancient at all. Nor was he handsome. He was tall and sturdy with a square, stubborn chin, and he was wearing a slightly surly expression, as though he were not in the least happy about being dragged to meet a couple of high school girls. But there was something about him—a strength and maturity—that was very attractive.

"—my daughters . . ." Daddy was saying, "April and Martha Dunning."

Jeff nodded politely to April and then to me, and then his eyes shifted back to April, and the sullen expression left his face. Instead there came into his eyes the look that boys always got when they

- **drove** (DROHV) crowd; large numbers of people
- Rotary (ROH tuh ree) **club of business and professional people**
- surly (SUR lee) **bad-tempered**

looked at April. I had never minded before, but now suddenly I felt a sudden heaviness in the pit of my stomach.

He said, "How do you do, Martha Dunning . . . April . . ." and his voice lingered on the "April" as though surprised at how well the name fitted the girl. I thought what a perfectly ghastly name Martha Dunning was in comparison.

April smiled. Her smile is wonderful, like a flood of sunlight. She always smiles at everybody, but anyone on the receiving end is always absolutely sure that she has been waiting her whole lifetime just to smile at him.

I don't remember exactly what we talked about that evening. I know that Jeff was wonderfully polite; he divided his attention equally between us. He asked me if I liked sports and where I wanted to go to college and what books I read. He even seemed to be interested in my answers, but then his eyes would wander back to April.

After Jeff left and April and I were upstairs getting ready for bed, I tried to think of some way to bring the conversation around to Jeff, but I did not have to, for April mentioned him herself.

"He's nice, isn't he?" she said dreamily. "Jeff Reigle, I mean."

"Yes." I glanced sideways at her standing in front of my mirror, brushing her hair.

"He asked me for a date," she said. "When he was saying good night. For this Friday. I think it should be fun, don't you?"

I nodded, feeling my throat tighten.

"You have a date Friday night too, don't you, Martha?"

"Yes," I said. "I do." It was with Timmy Kendal, one of the boys in my class. Timmy was pleasant and I had been looking forward to the evening, but now suddenly I didn't think I could bear to have Friday come.

As it happened, Timmy arrived early, so I never got to see Jeff. We got home around eleven-thirty and I said a hurried good night and went upstairs. April was not home yet. I went to my room and set my hair and got ready for bed and tried to settle down to read, but I could not concentrate. It was almost one o'clock before I heard the tap of April's feet in the hall.

She hesitated by my door, saw the light, and came in.

She was wearing a green dress that swished about her like spring breezes and her hair was rippling silver across her shoulders. She smiled at me, and I knew how she must have looked to Jeff.

I said, "Hi. Did you have a nice time?"

"Oh, yes," breathed April. "It was marvelous! We had dinner on the terrace of the San Carlos Hotel. There was dancing, and there's nothing but sky over you up there and when you look down off the edge, you can see lights all the way down to the river."

"What's Jeff like?" I asked, trying to keep my voice casual.

"Jeff? Oh, Martha," and her voice was singing in a way I had never heard before, "Martha, he's wonderful! He's not like anybody I've ever known! He treated me like . . . as if I was going to break any minute . . . and he thinks I'm beautiful!"

She said it with such wonder and joy that I was able to keep my resentment out of my voice.

"Of course he does," I said. "Because you are. You're innocent and sweet and springtime. You're"—I managed to smile—"you're April."

April smiled too, not really understanding.

"Well, of course, I'm April," she said. "And you're Martha. And you must have had quite an evening yourself to be talking like such a nut! Good night."

After she was gone I lay there for a long time, thinking. April was beautiful and unspoiled, but was that really enough? Oh, for the high school boys, yes. But Jeff Reigle was a grown man with his school days far behind him, es-tablished in his own business, used to adult companionship. What really did he and April have to talk about? April was never tongue-tied—she could chatter gaily along about school and parties and movie stars, but surely after a while this could become boring to a man like Jeff. I, on the other hand, had read so much; I had opinions on so many things that school boys shrugged off as silly, but things a man would respond to and find interesting.

It wouldn't hurt to try anyway, I thought defensively. After all, April had so many boys in love with her, and Jeff Reigle was the first man I'd ever felt this way about. If I could get him interested in me intellectually, surely it wouldn't hurt April . . .

I don't know, thinking back on it, if my plan would have worked. Sometimes I think it would have; other times I don't. There were occasions, I know, there in the beginning before their love was established and final when Jeff did seem a little bored with April's chatter. I tried to make the most of these opportunities. I would ask Jeff something about a book we'd both read—about art or politics or philosophy—something that would leave April out of the conversation or would cause her to make some remark to show her ignorance. And Jeff would be interested. He liked stimulating conversation, and he would turn to me eagerly.

April didn't know what was going on. She is never suspicious of anyone, least of all me.

Mother, however, is not gullible. She drew me aside one day and said quietly, "Martha Dunning, I know what you are

---

- **philosophy** (fi LOS uh fee) the study of ideas, such as the nature of truth
- gullible (GUL uh bul) **easily fooled or deceived**

doing, or trying to do, and I don't want to see any more of it."

"What do you mean?" I asked, a little frightened by Mother's tone of voice.

"Jeff," she said decidedly, "is April's beau. He is right for April; he is old enough and strong enough to take care of her the way your father and I have always done. I don't want you spoiling things for them, Martha Dunning."

"But, Mother," I gasped in amazement. "You sound as though you want them to get married."

"Well," Mother said thoughtfully, "Jeff would make April a good husband."

At first I was too stunned to reply. Finally I said, "What about me? Don't you care about my having a good husband too?"

"Oh, for goodness sake," said Mother impatiently, "you just think you care for Jeff because he's the first mature man you've known. You'll find somebody at college or afterward; you have all the time in the world, Martha Dunning."

And that, of course, was the end of my plan.

Jeff and April were married that spring right after April's graduation. The wedding was in the little church two blocks over, and we had the reception in the garden afterward, and people said it was the loveliest they had ever seen. April looked like an angel drifting down the aisle in her wedding gown with her hair shimmering in the sunlight that flowed through the open windows, and afterward when she threw back her veil and lifted her radiant face to Jeff's, there wasn't a person in the church who did not catch his breath.

I glanced across at Mother and Daddy, and they were standing very close together, hand in hand, watching her with a glow on their faces that nearly matched her own. And standing there in

my new pink gown, I thought resentfully, Why did April have to insist on her maid of honor's wearing pink when she knew yellow was my best color? I felt a surge of bitterness toward April for being so beautiful and toward Jeff for marrying her, and toward Mother and Daddy for loving her so much. It was an ugly feeling. I knew it, and I was ashamed of it, but I could not drive it away.

There was one moment during the reception when I almost lost it. It was when April flew up to me, her face glowing, and impulsively seized my hands and said in that soft sweet way of hers, "Oh, Martha, I only hope you're as happy on your wedding day as I am now!"

I squeezed her hands and said, "You deserve to be happy, honey." But then, as she turned away, the envy returned in a vicious surge, because I saw Mother standing by the buffet table, beaming at her.

145

During the next year it was hard to believe that April was now Mrs. Jeff Reigle. She and Jeff had an apartment of their own, but it was only a block away and April was always popping in and out of our house almost as though she still lived there. She would arrive in the morning after Jeff left for work and sit around the kitchen chatting with Mother, or she would dash in for lunch, or she would stop by on her way to market to see if one of us wanted to go along. I was surprised at the delight she took in the apartment. At home she had never shown much liking for domestic things, but now with her own four rooms to decorate and care for she was like a child with a new toy. Mother spent a good deal of each day over at the apartment, teaching her how to do things—how to cook Jeff's favorite dishes and how to wax a wooden floor and what to do when the toilet was stopped up or the refrigerator wouldn't defrost. She and April worked together for a full week making curtains, and they would phone each other to swap recipes and talk "woman talk." It was as though, suddenly, April and Mother were on one step of a ladder and I was alone on another, and I hated it.

"You know," I said one day at dinner, "I think I'll move into April's old room. I've always liked it, and it would be nice having a window out over the garden."

Mother said, "Martha, that's ridiculous! Where on earth would you put all your books and your desk and things if you moved into April's little room?"

"I'll leave them in my old room," I said. "I can always go in and get anything I need or work at my desk in there. I'll have April's room as a bedroom and my old room as a kind of study."

"Oh, no, you don't!" exclaimed Mother. "Two rooms indeed! One of those rooms is going to be a guest room, Martha Dunning. I've never had a guest room, and I've always wanted one. You just stay in your own nice room, just as you always have."

"You'll be going away to college next year anyway," added Daddy.

"Going to college?" I repeated. I felt a wave of laughter welling up within me. For once I was going to be the center of as much astonishment, confusion and incredulous delight as April. I hesitated, wondering if this was the time to tell them. Perhaps it wasn't, but I knew I could not hold my secret any longer.

"I'm not going to college next fall," I announced triumphantly. "I'm going to be married!"

"What!"

Never in my wildest dreams had I imagined the amazement that covered their faces. I was so happy I could hardly continue.

"Yes," I said, "to Timmy. He asked me several weeks ago, but I was waiting to surprise you. His dad has promised him a job in his men's store after graduation. We're going to get an apartment, maybe in the same building with April and Jeff, and fix it all up and"—I hesitated, realizing the surprise on their faces had given way to a look that was far from the delight I had anticipated—"and everything," I finished lamely.

"Well," said Daddy as soon as I stopped talking, "you certainly are not! Throw over college and marry a shirt salesman the minute you get out of high school! That's the craziest thing I ever heard."

I felt my face growing hot with anger.

- domestic (doh MES tik) **of the home; housekeeping**
- incredulous (in KREJ uh lus) **unbelieving; doubtful**

"You didn't say that when *April* wanted to get married! In fact, you did everything you possibly could to get her married to Jeff. And she wasn't a bit older than I am."

"That was different," said Mother. "Now, you just forget this getting married business, Martha Dunning, and buckle down to your studies and get yourself ready for the college entrance exams."

And that was all they would say. They refused to discuss it anymore. Timmy and I toyed with the idea of eloping, but we were both well under age and we knew our parents could have the marriage annulled as soon as they located us. Besides, when I thought about getting married I visualized a lovely wedding reception in the garden, just like April's, with Mother and Daddy beaming proudly and people surging all over the place, gasping and exclaiming about what a beautiful (well, at least "attractive") bride I was. And then the apartment with Mother making a grand fuss over me and helping me fix it up. Somehow when my parents drained all the excitement from the idea, my enthusiasm for Timmy began to wane also. By springtime we weren't even going steady any longer.

With spring came June and my graduation. I was valedictorian of our class and had a speech to make at Commencement. Mother and Daddy seemed very pleased, but at the last moment, as it turned out, even this day of glory was not fully my own. April chose that time to announce that she was going to have a baby.

"I know I should have told you sooner," she said happily, "but I thought it would be just perfect to wait and tell you tonight so the news would be a kind of special graduation present for Martha Dunning. It's due in October. Isn't it marvelous!"

"Yes," I agreed, "marvelous."

I knew in my heart that what April said was true. She had saved the news to tell tonight only because she thought I would be pleased to have it for part of my graduation excitement. Her joy was pure and complete and I knew she expected mine to be too, but it was not. Somehow the evening was no longer mine—it was April's. When I rose that night to give my speech, I looked over the audience and saw my family sitting there, watching me, but even as I spoke I saw Mother turn and look sideways at April as though wondering how she felt. And afterward, when I was preparing for bed and passed Mother's and Daddy's room on the way to the bathroom, I heard them talking. It was not about my speech or how nice I had looked in my cap and gown or how proud they were of my honors.

"A baby!" Mother was saying. "Why, she doesn't know the first thing about babies! How will she manage—the responsibility—"

"There now," Daddy said reassuringly, "it'll work out. We'll be here to help her, just as we always have. It'll be sort of nice having a baby in the family again, won't it? April's baby?"

"Yes," Mother said softly.

I went on into the bathroom and brushed my teeth so hard they bled. When I passed their door again, I did not stop to say good night; I went straight to my room and shut the door and lay there on the bed, hating April with all my might. Later there were footsteps in the

---

- annulled (uh NULD) **canceled; declared illegal or not valid**
- valedictorian (val i dik TOR ee un) **high-ranking student who gives farewell speech at graduation**

hall and a light tap at my door, but I did not answer. I knew it was Mother, and I did not want to talk to her. After a few moments the footsteps went away.

That was the longest, slowest summer I can remember. Mother spent most of her time at April's apartment, cleaning and cooking and doing the things she thought it best that April not try to do. And April herself, to my disgust, had never looked lovelier.

"Martha," she said to me once, "I may never have been good in school, but I do think I'll do a good job having a baby."

"Yes," I said shortly, "you undoubtedly will."

There was no gentleness in my voice, and April looked at me in surprise. Then she smiled.

"Honestly," she said, "I think you've suffered through this pregnancy much more than I have. Martha Dunning, I've never seen you so snappish as you've been lately. Are you worried about me, honey? Please don't be. I'm just fine, really."

"No," I said truthfully, "I'm not worried about you at all."

In September college started. Mother did not go with me to buy my college wardrobe; she just had Daddy give me a check and told me to buy anything I thought I would need. Any other time the idea of such independence would have filled me with delight, but now as I drove into town I kept thinking about Mother and April, rushing about from shop to shop together, buying things for the baby. At least, I thought, Mother might have shown enough interest to want to go with me.

I shopped all day and came home with a nice assortment of clothes. Mother nodded when she saw them and said I had good taste and had found excellent values for the money, and April exclaimed over my new satin evening dress and laughed about how wonderful it would be to be able to fit into something like that again. But when they got out a bunch of little nighties they were embroidering with daisies and began to discuss whether to use pink or blue for the centers of the flowers, I went alone to carry the clothes up to my room and put them away.

The first weeks of college were pleasant ones and I would have really enjoyed them if I had been able to relax and forget about April and all the excitement that was going on at home without me. April's baby was due the twelfth of October, and I wrote Mother that I had reservations home the afternoon of the eleventh.

"I know you'll need me," I wrote, "to help around the house and take care of April's apartment while she is in the hospital and give you both a hand with the baby when she gets it home. I can use all my semester cuts, plus the weekend, and spend a full week there."

I waited a week for what I thought would be Mother's grateful and joyful reply, but when it came it was highly unenthusiastic.

"We appreciate your wanting to help," she wrote, "but, truly, dear, the fewer people here the less confusion there will be. Besides, Jeff is going to be staying with us while April is in the hospital. Then she and the baby will stay on here until she is back on her feet again, so we will need your room. Study hard and have a good time at college, and we will telegraph you as soon as the baby arrives."

As I read the letter I felt more left out and unwanted than I ever had before, and then more angry. There was nothing to be done but wait for the telegram.

LOIS DUNCAN

The twelfth came, and the thirteenth, and the fourteenth. A week passed, and then another. And no telegram.

I burst forth with my bitterness to my roommate.

"They promised!" I raged. "They gave their word that they'd telegraph me immediately!"

"Oh, don't get so upset about it," my roommate soothed. "After all, there's probably so much confusion. . . . Why don't you phone them?"

I phoned that night. I meant it to be a short call. I meant to ask in a quiet, injured voice whether I had a niece or nephew. Instead, when I heard Mother's voice on the other end of the line, the anger that had been pent up in me for so long burst over and I found myself saying things I could never have imagined myself saying.

"You didn't telegraph!" I stormed. "You didn't even bother to think I might be wondering what was going on. You were so wrapped up in your precious April! All my life it's been 'April, April, April.' April gets the garden room! April gets to get married when she wants to! April gets any little thing she wants, always! Well, I'm sick and tired of it. I may not be as pretty as April but I'm your daughter too. I'm sick of April—sick to death of her—and I hope her baby turned out to be a two-headed monster!"

I clamped the receiver down on the hook and stood there in the booth, shaking with fury, and then suddenly the full horror of what I had done—of what I had said—swept over me. I leaned back against the wall of the booth and heard the words again, rasping in my ears. "I'm sick to death of April—I hope her baby—"

"No," I whispered. "Oh, no, I didn't mean that. Mother, I didn't mean that at all!"

But the receiver was back on the hook and Mother was hundreds of miles away.

149

I turned and went up to my dorm room, knowing that any love my parents had ever had for me would be gone after this, and I couldn't blame them. This I could not blame on April. Only on myself.

I went to class the next morning just as I always did. I can't pretend I listened carefully to the lectures. And afterward I walked over to the cafeteria and forced myself to eat a decent lunch before going back to the dorm to study. I walked to the dormitory, still alone, for my roommate had an afternoon lab, and opened the door to the room.

There, sitting in the chair by the window, was Mother.

"Mother!" I gasped. "What are you doing here! Is anything the matter! Is—" and suddenly my knees were so weak I could not stand. I stumbled forward and sat down on the end of the bed. "It's April," I whispered. "April—the baby—something happened."

Terror shot through me, sharp and icy, with a pain so great I could hardly breathe. My stomach lurched and I thought, I'm going to be sick—all that lunch I ate—and I reached out my hand crazily for the bedside table, for something to hold onto, but the table was farther away than I thought and I could not reach it. The whole room was a million miles away—the chair—the desk—even Mother, and all I could see was April's face dancing before my eyes. I could hear her laughter, bright and careless, filling the room with the sound of springtime and see her turn to me with that puzzled expression in her eyes, the way she did when she could not understand something and wanted me to help her.

"April," I whispered. "The baby is . . ."

Mother was beside me on the bed with her arms tight around me.

"No, Martha," she was saying over and over again. "Honey, no. Nothing's the matter with April. I'm sorry I frightened you—I didn't realize—" She was shaking me, trying to get me to listen to her. "Martha, listen, dear—April's all right. The baby's overdue, that's all. It very often happens with first babies.

Why, when I left last night April was at a shower over at Nancy's house."

Slowly her words penetrated and the world began to fall back into place.

"She's all right," I repeated. "And the baby—it hasn't even been born yet."

"No," said Mother. "At least, it hadn't when I left."

I stared at her. "Then what are you doing here! You left April when her baby's due any minute?"

Mother's arms were still around me. "April's all right," she said quietly. "She's got Jeff. I think my other daughter is the one who needs me right now."

I don't know exactly when I started to cry, but now I was conscious of the tears streaming down my face. I buried my face against Mother's shoulder and let them come, and it was as though all the tension and resentment and jealousy that had built up for so long were pouring out with the tears. I cried for a long time, and after I grew quiet, Mother began to talk.

"I didn't know," she said. "Until you called last night, I didn't have any idea how you felt about April. I took it for granted you understood. You're so smart, Martha Dunning—why, sometimes when you came to us with a poem you'd written or a book you wanted to discuss, Daddy and I would look at each other in amazement—we just couldn't believe that a child of ours could have a mind like yours. So maybe I assumed that you understood things when you really didn't.

"Do you remember," she asked, "the Christmas we gave you the Mickey Mouse watch?"

"No . . ." I said hesitantly, and then, "Yes." For suddenly I did remember. I had not thought of it in years, but out of the past came the memory of that wondrous moment when I pulled aside the tissue paper and saw the watch—a real one with hands that moved. "I was six years old."

"Yes." Mother nodded. "April didn't get a watch. Do you remember why?"

"She couldn't tell time," I said immediately, "and I could."

"Yes," Mother said again. "Poor April, in the second grade, and she still couldn't tell time. I think we gave her a baby doll that Christmas. But it wasn't because we loved you better that we gave you the better gift—it was because the watch was right for you and it wasn't right for April.

"No two children," she continued slowly, "are the same. The things that are good for one may not do for another, and parents have to decide what is best for each. Sometimes they are wrong, but at least they have to try.

"When April wanted to marry Jeff it seemed like a good thing. We've always known April would marry early (can you imagine her trying to go to college or have a career?) and we were glad for it to be a mature, responsible man who would take care of her instead of one of the boys her own age. Jeff had a business right in town so we knew April would be close enough for us to help her with any problems, just as we've always done, and she could have her pretty apartment and her babies, which are all April needs to make her happy. But you, honey—why, you need more than that! You need a chance to use your mind, to see and do things by yourself, to meet boys with education and ambition! You'd go crazy with a husband who sold shirts in a men's store! You'd be bored to death with nothing to do but hem curtains and change babies. Not," she added quickly, "that you won't want babies, but you must have a chance at something else first."

She stopped and drew back a little so she could see my face.

"It had nothing to do with loving April more. Or you more. Can you see that, Martha Dunning?"

I felt so ashamed of myself I could hardly speak.

"Yes," I said. "I can see."

Mother was starting to say something more when there was a quick rap at the door and one of the girls stuck her head in.

"Martha?" she said. "Is your mother in the dorm? There's a long distance call for her at the desk."

Mother practically flew into the telephone booth. It was a full five minutes later that she emerged, triumphant.

"April's baby!" she exclaimed. "It's come! A seven pound, six ounce girl! April's fine, and the delivery was an easy one. Everything's perfect!"

Her face was radiant with happiness, the same happiness she would feel, someday, at the birth of my baby. And looking at her I felt joy flowing through me—a mixture of wonder and pride and relief—and my own love for April which I had pushed from me for so long rose up within me.

"Oh," I whispered. "I'm so glad. A girl! I wonder what they will name her!"

"Well," Mother said, "that was Jeff on the phone. He says that if it's all right with you, April wants to name her baby Martha Dunning. She says she's always thought it was the most beautiful name she ever heard."

ALL THINGS CONSIDERED

1. The older of the two girls is (a) April. (b) Martha Dunning. (c) not made clear in the story.

2. When Jeff becomes interested in April, Martha Dunning (a) thinks only of her sister's happiness. (b) tries to warn April that Jeff is too old for her. (c) tries to get Jeff interested in her intellectually.

3. Martha Dunning feels that her graduation is ruined by (a) April's failure to graduate. (b) her speech as valedictorian. (c) April's announcement that she is expecting a baby.

4. Throughout the story, April—but not Martha Dunning—can be described as (a) well meaning but envious. (b) honest, sweet, and straightforward. (c) a quick learner and topnotch student.

5. A surprise at the end of the story is that the (a) mother loves both girls equally. (b) baby will be named Martha Dunning. (c) narrator agrees to continue college.

THINKING IT THROUGH

1. The story is about the growth of two sisters as time takes them in different directions. From the facts given in the story, what do you think the future will hold for Martha Dunning? For April?

2. Early in the story, the parents look at very different report cards but say the same thing to each girl: "That's fine, dear." (a) In your opinion, why do the parents do this? (b) Do you agree with their attitude? Why or why not?

3. Near the end, the mother confesses that she has always made a mistaken assumption about Martha Dunning. She says, "I didn't have any idea how you felt about April. I took it for granted you understood." Exactly what is it that Martha Dunning has not understood?

4. Nearer to the end, the narrator realizes her own love for April, which she has pushed aside for so long. What causes this change?

5. It is important to the story that the mother actually travels hundreds of miles to see Martha Dunning. What does this action prove?

Reading and Analyzing

Understanding Imagery

In everyday language, the word *image* refers to something that can be seen or imagined as being seen. For example, the photographs on the covers of this book are images you can actually see. On the other hand, at this exact moment you can only imagine the Statue of Liberty, but you can probably visualize how it looks. The whole subject of images is called *imagery* (IM uj ree).

In literary use, however, *image* and *imagery* have wider meanings. Authors and poets often use words or phrases to create **images,** or vivid sensory impressions, for the reader. **Imagery** refers not only to what the reader can see but also to what the reader can hear, smell, taste, and feel.

Skillful writers know that it's not enough to tell the reader that a certain day was hot. It's better to make the reader *smell* the melting tar on a steaming street, *feel* moist around the collar, and *taste* the sweat as it drips onto the lips. Imagery allows the reader to experience what is being described by the writer.

Part of Lois Duncan's popularity as a modern writer comes from her skill with imagery. What kinds of images (sight, hearing, smell, taste, or feeling) are involved in these sentences from "April"?

1. Mother says it was the first real day of spring when the air was suddenly warm and soft and fresh and dandelions popped out on the lawn and the first group of birds invaded the birdbath in the backyard (page 140).

2. "I think it's the yellow—it seems so warm and friendly" (page 142).

3. Then we would both laugh, for we knew how hopeless our sharing a room would be—like trying to mix orange sherbet with mashed potatoes (page 142).

4. Her smile is wonderful, like a flood of sunlight (page 143).

5. Terror shot through me, sharp and icy, with a pain so great I could hardly breathe (page 150).

Composition

1. Put yourself in Martha Dunning's place. You are preparing to visit April, Jeff, and your namesake, Martha Dunning. What thoughts are racing through your head? Tell about them in a short paragraph.

2. Describe a recent experience by creating a strong image that appeals to one or more of the five senses. Make your images so sharp that the reader can actually relive your experience. The choice of subject is up to you—a tense moment at a local ballgame, a bad ten minutes on a babysitting job, or another subject.

OZYMANDIAS

by Percy Bysshe Shelley (1792–1822)

▶ This poem takes you back to two different periods in time. Percy Bysshe Shelley, one of the great English romantic poets, wrote the poem in 1817. Its subject is Ozymandias (oz uh MAN dee us), a powerful Egyptian king who died about 1258 B.C. Ozymandias was a great builder of palaces, temples, and statues of himself.

"Ozymandias" deals with the way time often treats the reputations of tyrants. Lines 6–8 may cause some trouble. Read them this way: *The sculptor well understood the passions of the king, passions that now stamped on stone, survive or outlive the sculptor's hand that mocked or made fun of them, and the king's heart that fed or proudly doted on them.*

I met a traveler from an antique land
Who said: "Two vast and trunkless legs of stone
Stand in the desert. . . . Near them, on the sand,
Half sunk, a shattered visage lies, whose frown,
5 And wrinkled lip, and sneer of cold command
Tell that its sculptor well those passions read
Which yet survive, stamped on these lifeless things,
The hand that mocked them, and the heart that fed;
And on the pedestal these words appear:
10 'My name is Ozymandias, king of kings;
Look on my works, ye Mighty, and despair!'
Nothing beside remains. Round the decay
Of that colossal wreck, boundless and bare
The lone and level sands stretch far away."

- **romantic** (roh MAN tik) **creative; imaginative; free from traditional rules**
- **trunkless** (TRUNK les) **without the torso, or main part of the body**
- **visage** (VIZ ij) **face**
- **pedestal** (PED uh stul) **base of a statue**

155

WAYS OF KNOWING

1. (a) What is the "antique land" (line 1)? (b) Whose is the "shattered visage" (line 4)?

2. In your own words explain lines 5 through 8. How did the sculptor feel about the king? How did he show his feelings?

3. How did the king feel about himself?

4. Reread the last three lines, which give the setting. Do you suppose the setting was the same in the time of Ozymandias? Explain.

5. The introduction mentions "the way time often treats the reputations of tyrants." How has time treated the reputation of Ozymandias?

6. In what way is the poem an excellent example of irony of situation (page 58)? Think about the difference between what Ozymandias expected and what really happened.

7. **Alliteration** (uh lit uh RAY shun) is the repetition of consonant sounds, usually at the beginning of words, for poetic effect. Examples are the hard *c* sound in "cold command" (line 5) and the *l* sound in "*l*one and *l*evel" (line 14). (a) What examples of alliteration can you find in lines 7, 10, and 13? (b) Why might the poet have used alliteration? In other words, what effect does alliteration have on this poem?

VOCABULARY AND SKILL REVIEW

Before completing the exercises that follow, you may wish to review the **bold-faced** words on pages 134 to 156.

I. Mark each item *true* or *false*. If it is false, explain in your own words exactly what is wrong.

1. Many reptiles and some mammals become *dormant* during the cold winter season.
2. You *err* when you make a mistake.
3. *Romantic* poets write mainly love poems.
4. *Pedestal* is to *statue* as *foundation* is to *house*.
5. The Super Bowl attracts *droves* of people to the city where it's played.
6. People who *radiate* friendship are not generally liked by others.
7. The older sections of some cities contain a *maze* of little streets.
8. People who act *impulsively* ought to remember the saying, "Look before you leap."
9. The study of *philosophy* requires excellent reading and thinking skills.
10. A presidential election is a *trivial* event.

II. Match the terms in Column A with their definitions in Column B.

A	**B**
1. point of view	a) a vivid sensory impression
2. first person	b) told by an author/narrator who keeps out of the story
3. third person	c) repetition of consonant sounds for poetic effect
4. alliteration	d) position or viewpoint from which a story is told
5. image	e) involving the storyteller as a character

III. Although both of the poems on the next page concern love, they treat the subject in very different ways. Read each poem carefully before answering the questions that follow.

WHEN I WAS ONE-AND-TWENTY

by A. E. Housman

When I was one-and-twenty
    I heard a wise man say,
"Give crowns and pounds and guineas
    But not your heart away;
Give pearls away and rubies
    But keep your fancy free."
But I was one-and-twenty,
    No use to talk to me.

When I was one-and-twenty
    I heard him say again,
"The heart out of the bosom
    Was never given in vain;
'Tis paid with signs a plenty
    And sold for endless rue."
And I am two-and-twenty,
    And oh, 'tis true, 'tis true.

1. Is the poem written in the first person or the third person?
2. A(fred) E(dward) Housman (1859–1936) was a well-known English poet. In your opinion, is the speaker the same person as the poet?
3. At the end of the poem, how old is the speaker?
4. (a) In your own words, what advice did the speaker receive from the "wise man"? (b) How did the speaker regard that advice?
5. (a) What has the speaker learned during the past year? (b) What kind of experience might have caused the change in the speaker's feelings?

- crowns, pounds, guineas (GIN eez) **units of English money**
- rue (ROO) **sorrow; regret**

NEW FACE

by Alice Walker

I have learned not to worry about
love, but to honor its coming
with all my heart.
To examine the dark mysteries
of the blood
with headless heed and
swirl,
to know the rush of feelings
swift and flowing
as water.

The source appears to be
some inexhaustible
spring
within our twin and triple
selves;
the new face I turn up
to you
no one else on earth
has ever
seen.

1. Judging by the first few lines, the speaker used to "worry about love." What might these worries have been?
2. In just a few words, explain how the speaker now feels about being in love?
3. The speaker talks about examining "the dark mysteries of the blood." What does the speaker put first, *feelings* or *thoughts?*
4. The lines "within our twin and triple/selves" seem to indicate that the speaker feels like more than one person. This is a common experience. Note that the speaker does not say "within *my* twin and triple self." How does the word "our" add to the meaning?
5. In what way is the speaker's face a "new" one that has never before been seen?
6. What is one example of *alliteration* (see page 156) in the poem?
7. What are two examples of *imagery* (see page 154) in the poem?
8. Contrast the poem with Housman's "When I Was One-and-Twenty." Which speaker would you rather be? Explain why.

TIME REMEMBERED

by Four Poets

▶ Think about this statement: *the past exists only in the present*. That sounds odd, but it's logically true. What you know, or think you know, about the past is knowledge you have at the present moment. Memories are mental maps not of the past as it really existed but of times remembered.

Here are four poems—each one written in the first person point of view—that deal with the relationship between past and present. The first three poets are modern Americans. The last, William Wordsworth (1770—1850), was a leading British romantic poet. Read each poem thoughtfully at least three times before you answer the questions.

THE 1ST

by Lucille Clifton

What I remember about that day
is boxes stacked across the walk
and couch springs curling through the air
and drawers and tables balanced on the curb
and us, hollering,
leaping up and around
happy to have a playground;

nothing about the emptied rooms
nothing about the emptied family

WAYS OF KNOWING

1. The speaker in the poem is an adult remembering an incident from childhood days. In your opinion, what had just happened to the child's family?

2. According to the speaker, now aware of what actually happened on "that day" long ago, young children are often unaware of the real meaning of events. Do you agree with this? Explain.

3. A **précis** (PRAY see) is a very short summary of a literary selection. Write a one-sentence précis of Clifton's "The 1st."

BLACK HAIR

by Gary Soto

At eight I was brilliant with my body.
In July, that ring of heat
We all jumped through, I sat in the bleachers
Of Romain Playground, in the lengthening
Shade that rose from our dirty feet.
The game before us was more than baseball.
It was a figure—Hector Montejano,
Quick and hard with turned muscles,
His crouch the one I assumed before an altar
Of worn baseball cards, in my room.

I came here because I was Mexican, a stick
Of brown light in love with those
Who could do it—the triple and hard slide,
The gloves eating balls into double plays.
What could I do with 50 pounds, my shyness,
My black torch of hair, about to go out?
Father was dead, his face no longer
Hanging over the table or sleep,
And mother was the terror of mouths
Twisting hurt by butter knives.

In the bleachers I was brilliant with my body,
Waving players in and stomping my feet,
Growing sweaty in the presence of white shirts.
I chewed sunflower seeds. I drank water,
And bit my arm through the late innings.
When Hector lined balls into deep
Center, in my mind I rounded
The bases with him, my face flared,
My hair lifting beautifully, because we were
Coming home to the arms of brown people.

- figure (FIG yur) **well-known person**
- turned (TURND) **as if turned on a lath**
- assume (uh SOOM) **take on for oneself; imitate**

WAYS OF KNOWING

1. The speaker remembers himself as an eight-year-old who worshiped a certain ballplayer. Why did the child admire Hector Montejano so much? Name at least two reasons.
2. The speaker twice says, "I was brilliant with my body." However, the boy himself was not playing baseball. What do you think he means?
3. Describe the scene remembered in the last two lines in your own words.
4. A **metaphor** (MET uh for) is a figure of speech in which one person or thing is compared to something else usually by suggesting that the one *is* the other. Sometimes a metaphor creates a picture by saying, in a figurative way, that a person or thing *is doing* something. Look, for instance, at the first three lines of the poem. The month of July is called a "ring of heat" that could be "jumped through." Since July is not *really* a "ring" of anything, the words starting with "ring" form a metaphor. (a) Identify the metaphor in the last two lines of stanza 1. What is being compared to what? (b) Identify the metaphor in the first two lines of stanza 2. What is being compared to what?
5. Write a short précis of "Black Hair." You might wish to write your précis in the first person and begin, "When I was eight, I. . . ."

GRANDMOTHER, ROCKING

by Eve Merriam

Last night I dreamed of an old lover,
I had not seen him in forty years.
When I awoke,
I saw him on the street:
his hair was white,
his back stooped.
How could I say hello?
He would have been puzzled all day
about who the young girl was
who smiled at him.

So I let him go on his way.

WAYS OF KNOWING

1. Is the man dreamed of in the first line old or young? How do you know?

2. (a) About how old is the speaker? (b) Why does she call herself a "young girl" near the end of the poem?

3. In your own words, explain the last line. Why does the speaker "let him go on his way"?

DAFFODILS

by William Wordsworth

I wandered lonely as a cloud
That floats on high o'er vales and hills,
When all at once I saw a crowd,
A host, of golden daffodils;
Beside the lake, beneath the trees,
Fluttering and dancing in the breeze.

Continuous as the stars that shine
And twinkle on the milky way,
They stretched in never-ending line
Along the margin of a bay:
Ten thousand saw I at a glance,
Tossing their heads in sprightly dance.

The waves beside them danced; but they
Out-did the sparkling waves in glee:
A poet could not but be gay,
In such a jocund company:
I gazed—and gazed—but little thought
What wealth the show to me had brought:

For oft, when on my couch I lie
In vacant or in pensive mood,
They flash upon that inward eye
Which is the bliss of solitude;
And then my heart with pleasure fills,
And dances with the daffodils.

- vale (VAYL) **small valley**
- host (HOHST) **great number**
- sprightly (SPRYT lee) **lively; joyful**
- jocund (JAHK und *or* JOH kund) **joyous; jolly**
- pensive (PEN siv) **deeply thoughtful**

WAYS OF KNOWING

1. The first three stanzas describe a happy experience remembered by the speaker. (a) What was the speaker's mood when the remembered experience first began? (b) What happened to change this mood?

2. At the end of the third stanza, the speaker refers to something not realized at the time of the incident. What is the unrealized "wealth"?

3. "They flash upon that inward eye. . . ." When you read those words, did your "inward eye" actually see the image pictured in the first three stanzas? If not, read the poem again and try to have this experience.

4. The poem was written long before the first three poems in this section. How does it differ in form and technique from the others?

5. A **personification** (pur son uh fuh KAY shun) is a figure of speech in which something nonhuman is given human qualities and abilities. Look, for example, at the last line of stanza 2. Do daffodils really have "heads"? Of course not. The poet is *personifying* the daffodils. (a) Identify another personification in the last line of stanza 2. (b) Identify at least one other personification in the poem.

Bonus question: Poets tell us that the memory of an event can be as enjoyable as the event itself. Moreover, the passage of time brings new meanings and values to memories. (a) What single event in your life do you think you will remember most happily in 50 years? (b) In what way, if any, will the memory differ from the experience?

Oliver Goldsmith (1730?-1774)

An engraving of the Mansion House in London, 1750

Seldom has success and failure fought for control of a person's life as in the case of the Irish-born author Oliver Goldsmith. Early in life, Goldsmith studied religion, but he was never permitted to become a clergyman, partly because of his fun-loving and careless habits. He moved to England and studied medicine, only to fail as a doctor. He turned to teaching, with no success. When he was nearly 30, he began writing. At first he lived in poverty in London, peddling an assortment of writings to magazines.

Then, quite suddenly, a literary genius emerged. A long poem, "The Deserted Village," was an instant success. *The Vicar of Wakefield* became the most popular novel of the eighteenth century. Plays he wrote, such as *She Stoops to Conquer,* moved audiences to tears and laughter. Goldsmith even wrote a two-volume *History of the World.*

Success with money did not come as easily, however. It seemed to flow through Goldsmith's fingers as quickly as it came. Some of the money he gambled away. Some he spent on pleasures. Much he simply gave away to people in need. His habits kept him a poor man, and he died at an early age.

Today, Goldsmith lives on through his words. Like William Shakespeare (page 233), he is sometimes quoted unknowingly. In the play that follows, for instance, you'll read "the very pink of perfection" and "Ask me no questions, and I'll tell you no fibs."

Two lines of Goldsmith's poetry seem to fit his own life well:

His best companions, innocence and
   health;
And his best riches, ignorance of
   wealth.

Oral Interpretation

Oral interpretation means reading aloud with expression. As you know, the first literature was oral literature—intended for the ear, not for the eye. Today, of course, people tend to think of literature, first of all, as words on paper. Even today, however, good oral interpretation is often required for complete understanding. This is true of most poems, and is especially true of plays.

If you can, read the following play aloud with some classmates. If this is not possible, try to imagine each speech in your "mind's ear." The following procedures will help.

1. Study the cast of characters carefully. Draw a diagram on a separate sheet of paper to make the relationships between the characters clear. Try to visualize the characters (the play was written in 1773, so think of George Washington's time). Look at the illustrations that accompany the play. Don't go on until each name on the list brings a picture of a definite character to mind.

2. Read through the first scene silently. Try to "hear" the dialogue as if spoken by living persons. Form images of the action. "See" the faces and the body movements of each character.

3. Prepare to read the first scene aloud, if possible. Since there are five main characters, get together in groups of five and decide who will play each character. (Whether you are male, or female, you can play *any* character—just act in a way that the character might act.)

4. Practice your part. Don't rush through all the lines. Pauses often add meaning. If you expect a laugh, stop for it.

5. As you act out the scene, try not to stop and reread when you make a little mistake. Your words don't have to be *exactly* those in the script.

If you follow the above suggestions, you'll probably find at some point that you've stopped the "interpretation" and that the characters themselves have taken over. When that happens, just let them speak. Enjoy the play. It's a good one.

SHE STOOPS TO CONQUER

or

The Mistakes of a Night

by Oliver Goldsmith

▶ History books can tell you *about* the past. However, only literature can really bring a bygone age to life. As you read this eighteenth-century play, note the differences in language, customs, and manners between Goldsmith's age and the present. You may find words used in unfamiliar ways, but the meanings are not hard to understand.

CHARACTERS

Mr. Hardcastle—*Squire of an English manor house*
Miss Kate Hardcastle—*Mr. Hardcastle's daughter by a previous marriage*
Mrs. Hardcastle—*Wife of the squire*
Tony Lumpkin—*Mrs. Hardcastle's son by a previous marriage*
Miss Constance Neville—*Mrs. Hardcastle's niece*
Charles Marlow—*Suitor of Miss Hardcastle*
Sir Charles Marlow—*Young Marlow's father and a friend of Mr. Hardcastle*
George Hastings—*Suitor of Miss Neville and a friend of Charles Marlow*
Servants, Maid, Landlord, and Others

ACT ONE

Scene 1: a room in HARDCASTLE'S manor

(*Enter* Mrs. Hardcastle *and* Mr. Hardcastle)

Mrs. Hardcastle: I say again, Mr. Hardcastle, you're very particular. Is there a creature in the whole county but ourselves that doesn't take a trip to London now and then, to rub off the rust a little? There's our neighbor, Mrs. Grigsby—she goes for a month's polishing every winter.

Hardcastle: Aye, and brings back enough fine clothes and foolishness to last the whole year. I wonder why London cannot keep its own fools at home. In my time, the follies of the town crept slowly among us, but now they travel faster than a stagecoach.

Mrs. Hardcastle: Aye, *your* times were

- **squire** (SKWYR) country gentleman
- **suitor** (SOO tur) man who courts a woman

167

very fine times, indeed. You have been telling us of *them* for many a long year. Here we live in an old rambling mansion, that looks for all the world like an inn, but we never see company. All our entertainment is your old stories of Prince Eugene and the Duke of Marlborough. I hate such old-fashioned nonsense.

Hardcastle: And I love it! I love everything that's old: old friends, old times, old manners, old books, old wine. And, I believe, Dorothy (*taking her hand*), you'll agree I've been pretty fond of an old wife.

Mrs. Hardcastle: Lord, Mr. Hardcastle! I'm not so old as you'd make me by more than one good year. Add twenty to twenty, and make money of that.

Hardcastle: Let me see: twenty added to twenty—makes just fifty and seven!

Mrs. Hardcastle: It's false, Mr. Hardcastle! I was but twenty when I gave birth to Tony, that I had by Mr. Lumpkin, my first husband. And he's not come to years of discretion yet.

Hardcastle: Nor ever will, I say.

Mrs. Hardcastle: No matter. Tony Lumpkin has a good fortune. I don't think a boy needs too much discretion to spend fifteen hundred a year. Come, Mr. Hardcastle, you must allow the boy a little fun.

Hardcastle: If burning the footman's shoes, frightening the maids, and worrying the kittens is fun, he has it! It was only yesterday he fastened my wig to the back of my chair, and when I went to make a bow, I popped my bald head in Mrs. Frizzle's face!

Mrs. Hardcastle: Am I to blame? The poor boy was always too sickly to do any good, even to go to school.

Hardcastle: School for him! A cat and a fiddle! No, no, the alehouse and the stable are the only schools he'll ever go to.

Mrs. Hardcastle: Well, we must not snub the poor boy now, for I believe we shan't have him long among us. Anybody that looks in his face can see he's consumptive.

Hardcastle: Aye, if growing too fat is one of the symptoms.

Mrs. Hardcastle: He coughs sometimes.

Hardcastle: Yes, when his liquor goes the wrong way. Sometimes he whoops like a trumpet, too. (Tony *whoops behind the scene.*) Oh, here he comes.

(*Enter* Tony, *crossing the stage*)

Mrs. Hardcastle: Tony, where are you going, my charmer? Won't you give

- **discretion** (dis KRESH un) good judgment; freedom of choice
- **consumptive** (kun SUMP tiv) afflicted with tuberculosis, a serious lung disease

Papa and me a little of your company?

Tony: I'm in haste, Mother. I cannot stay.

Mrs. Hardcastle: You shan't venture out on this raw evening, my dear.

Tony: I can't stay, I tell you. *The Three Pigeons* expects me down any moment. There's some fun going on.

Hardcastle: Aye, the alehouse. I thought so.

Mrs. Hardcastle: Please, my dear, disappoint your friends for one night, at least.

Tony: As for disappointing *them*, I shouldn't much mind. But I can't stand to disappoint *myself.*

Mrs. Hardcastle (*grabbing his arm*): You shan't go!

Tony: I will, I tell you!

Mrs. Hardcastle: I say you shan't!

Tony: We'll see who is stronger, you or I! (*Exit, hauling her out*)

Hardcastle (*to himself*): Aye, there goes a pair that only spoil each other. But isn't the whole age we live in enough to drive sense and discretion out of anyone? Ah, (*looking off*) there's my pretty darling, Kate. The fashions of the times have infected her, too. By living a year or two in London, she's as fond of silk and French foolishness as the best of them.

(*Enter* Miss Hardcastle, *very dressed up*)

Hardcastle: Dressed up as usual, my Kate! Goodness!

Miss Hardcastle: You know our agreement, sir. You allow me in the morning to receive and pay visits, and to dress in my own manner. And in the evening, I put on my plain old housedress, to please you.

Hardcastle: Well, remember I insist on the terms of our agreement. And by the way, I believe I'll have a chance to test your obedience this very evening.

Miss Hardcastle: What, sir? I don't understand your meaning.

Hardcastle: Then, to be plain with you, Kate, I expect the young gentleman I have chosen to be your husband to arrive this very day. I have his father's letter, in which he informs me that his son has set out from London, and that he intends to follow shortly after.

Miss Hardcastle: Indeed! I wish I had known something of this before. How shall I behave? It's a thousand to one I shan't like him. Our meeting will be so formal, so like a thing of business. I fear I shall find no room for friendship, not to speak of love.

Hardcastle: Depend upon it, child, I'll never control your choice. But Mr. Marlow, whom I have picked for you, is the son of my old friend, Sir Charles Marlow. The young man has been a good student and is headed for excellent employment. I'm told he's a man of generous character.

Miss Hardcastle: Is he?

Hardcastle: Very generous.

Miss Hardcastle: I believe I shall like him.

Hardcastle: Young and brave.

Miss Hardcastle: I'm sure I shall like him!

Hardcastle: And very handsome.

Miss Hardcastle: My dear Papa, say no more (*kissing his hand*). He's mine! I'll have him!

Hardcastle: And to top it all, Kate, he's one of the most bashful and reserved young fellows in all the world.

Miss Hardcastle: You have frozen me to death again. That word *reserved* has undone all the rest. A reserved

---

• reserved (ri ZURVD) **quiet and formal in manner**

lover, it is said, always makes a suspicious husband.

Hardcastle: No, just the opposite. Modesty seldom occurs in a dishonest or suspecting person. It was this very feature of his character that first struck me.

Miss Hardcastle: He must have more striking features to catch me, I promise you. However, if he's so young, so handsome, and so everything, I think I'll have him. At least, I'll have a look.

Hardcastle: That's the spirit! I'll go prepare the servants for his arrival. As we seldom have company, they'll need some training. (*Exit*)

Miss Hardcastle (*to herself*): *Young, handsome*—these he put last. But I put them first. *Sensible, good natured*—I like all that. But then *reserved* and *sheepish*—that's much against him.

(*Enter* Miss Neville)

Miss Hardcastle: I'm glad you've come, Neville, my dear. Tell me, Constance, how do I look today? Is this one of my better days? Am I in face?

Miss Neville: You look fine, my dear. Yet, now I look again—bless me!— you *do* look excited. Has the cat or your brother been meddling? Or has the last novel been too moving?

Miss Hardcastle: No, nothing like that. I have been threatened—I can scarcely get it out—I have been threatened with a lover!

Miss Neville: And his name—

Miss Hardcastle: Is Marlow.

Miss Neville: Indeed!

Miss Hardcastle: The son of Sir Charles Marlow.

Miss Neville: As I live, he's the best friend of Mr. Hastings, *my* admirer! I believe you must have seen him when we lived in London.

Miss Hardcastle: Never.

Miss Neville: He's a very strange character, I assure you. Among women of reputation and virtue, he's the most modest man alive. But I hear he has a very different character among women of another kind. You understand me?

Miss Hardcastle: An odd character, indeed! What shall I do? Oh, I'll think no more of him, but trust to luck for success. But how goes your own

NEVILLE

affair, my dear? Has my mother been courting you for my brother Tony, as usual?

Miss Neville: Yes, I've just come from her. She's been saying a hundred tender things, and setting off her monster of a son as the very pink of perfection.

Miss Hardcastle: And she actually thinks him so! A fortune like yours is no small temptation. Besides, as she still has control over it, she'll do all she can to keep it in the family. That's one reason she wants you to marry your cousin.

Miss Neville: A fortune like mine, which is mostly jewels, is no such huge temptation. And at any rate, my dear Hastings is the one I hope to marry. But to keep the peace, I let Mrs. Hardcastle think that I'm in love with her son Tony, and she never once dreams that I dream of another.

Miss Hardcastle: My good brother holds out against her plans, though. I could almost love him for hating you so.

Miss Neville: There—my aunt's bell rings for our afternoon walk. Good-bye. Courage is necessary, as our lives are nearing an important point. (*Exit*)

Miss Hardcastle: I wish it all were over, and all were well.

Scene 2: an alehouse room, with Tony *and his friends*

Tony *is at the head of a table.*

All: Hurrah, hurrah, bravo!

First Fellow: Now, gentlemen, silence for a song. Our friend Tony Lumpkin is going to knock himself out with a song.

Second Fellow: Aye, a song, a song.

Tony: Then I'll sing you a song I just made up about this alehouse, *The Three Pigeons* (*sings*): Let schoolmasters puzzle their brains, with grammar, and nonsense, and learning (*looks off and stops*). Well, Stingo, what's the matter?

(*Enter* Landlord)

Landlord: There are two gentlemen in a large carriage at the door. They have lost their way, and they are saying something about Mr. Hardcastle.

Tony: As sure as can be, one of them must be the gentleman that's coming down to court my sister. Do they seem like Londoners?

Landlord: I believe so.

Tony: Then ask them to step this way, and I'll set them right in a flash. (*Exit* Landlord) Gentlemen, they might not be good enough company for you. If you step out a moment, I'll be with you in the squeezing of a lemon. (*Exeunt all but* Tony)

Tony (*to himself*): My stepfather has been calling me a lazy dog this half year. Now, if I pleased, I could get my revenge. But then I'm afraid—afraid of what? I shall soon be worth fifteen hundred a year, and let him frighten me out of *that* if he can!

(*Enter* Landlord, *with* Marlow *and* Hastings)

● exeuent (EK see unt) **they go offstage (a kind of plural of** *exit*)

Marlow: What a day we've had of it! We were told it was forty miles across the county, and we've come more than sixty.

Hastings: And all, Marlow, because of that shyness of yours. It wouldn't let us inquire more often along the way.

Tony: No offense, gentlemen. But I'm told you've been inquiring for one Mr. Hardcastle in these parts. Do you know what part of the county you are in?

Hastings: Not in the least, sir. But we would thank you for information.

Tony: Nor the way you came?

Hastings: No, sir. But if you can inform us—

Tony: Why, gentlemen, if you know neither the road you are on, nor where you are, the first thing I have to inform you is that—you have lost your way.

Marlow: We needed no genius to tell us that.

Tony: Gentlemen, may I be so bold as to ask the place you came from?

Marlow: That is not necessary for directing us where we want to go.

Tony: No offense. But question for question is fair, you know. Now, gentlemen, is not this same Hardcastle an old-fashioned, stubborn fellow with an ugly face, a daughter, and a handsome son?

Hastings: We have not seen the gentleman, but he has the family you mention.

Tony: The daughter, a tall, talkative beanpole. The son, a well-bred, agreeable youth that everybody is fond of.

Marlow: Our information differs. The daughter is said to be well-bred and beautiful; the son, an awkward fool, reared up and spoiled at his mother's apron string.

Tony: He-he-hem—then, gentlemen, all I have to tell you is this: You won't reach Mr. Hardcastle's house this night, I believe.

Hastings: Unfortunate!

Tony: It's a long, dark, dirty, and dangerous way.

Hastings: What's to be done, Marlow?

Marlow: Perhaps this landlord can put us up.

Landlord: No, master. We have but one spare bed in the whole house.

Tony: And to my knowledge, that's taken up by three guests already. (*After a pause*) I have it! Don't you think, Stingo, that you could let these gentlemen have the fireside, with three chairs and a pillow?

Hastings: I hate sleeping by the fireside.

Marlow: And I detest your three chairs and a pillow.

Tony: You do, do you? Then let me see—if you go on a mile farther, to the Buck's Head. . . . Yes, the old Buck's Head Inn, one of the best in the whole county!

Landlord (*apart to* Tony): Surely, you aren't sending them to your step-father's house as an inn, are you?

Tony: Mum's the word, you. Let *them* find that out. (*To them*) You have only to keep on straight forward till you come to a large old house by the roadside. You'll see a pair of large horns over the door. That's the sign. Drive up in the yard, and call loudly.

Hastings: Sir, we're obliged to you. Our servants can't miss the way?

Tony: No, no. But let me warn you about the landlord at the Buck's Head. He's grown rich, and he's going to get out of the business soon. So he wants to be thought of as a gentleman, he! he! he! He'll be for giving you his company, as well as his rooms.

Landlord: A troublesome old fool, to be sure. But he keeps as good meat and beds as any in the county.

Marlow: Well, if he supplies us with those, we shall want no more. We are to turn to the right, did you say?

Tony: No, no, straight forward. I'll just step outside myself and show you a piece of the way. (*To* Landlord) Mum, now.

Landlord: Ah, bless your heart. (*Exeunt*)

CHECKPOINT

Answer the following questions before going on with the play. If you have trouble with any of the answers, go back and review the first act before you continue reading.

1. Hardcastle tells his daughter Kate that (a) Charles Marlow, a suitor chosen by him, is coming from London. (b) she must wear a plain housedress at all times. (c) he will force Constance Neville to marry Tony Lumpkin.
2. Constance Neville (a) hopes to marry Tony Lumpkin. (b) hopes to marry Hastings but pretends to love Tony Lumpkin. (c) detests both Hastings and Lumpkin.
3. Tony Lumpkin is (a) Mr. Hardcastle's son by a previous marriage. (b) Constance Neville's cousin and Mrs. Hardcastle's brother. (c) Mrs. Hardcastle's son, Kate Hardcastle's (step)brother, and Constance Neville's cousin.
4. Tony Lumpkin plays a joke on Marlow and Hastings (a) to get revenge on Hardcastle. (b) because he dislikes both of them. (c) after Kate Hardcastle asks him to.
5. What might happen in Act Two when Marlow and Hastings arrive at Hardcastle's manor thinking it's an inn?

ACT TWO

Back at Hardcastle's *manor house*

(*Enter* Hardcastle, *followed by three or four awkward* Servants)

Hardcastle: Well, I hope you're perfect in the table exercises I have been teaching you. You all know your places, and can act as if you've been used to good company.

All: Aye, aye.

Hardcastle: When company comes, you're not to pop out and stare, and then run in again, like frighted rabbits.

All: No, no.

Hardcastle: You, Diggory, whom I have taken from the barn, are to make a show at the side table. And you, Roger, whom I have advanced from the plow, are to place yourself behind *my* chair. But you're not to stand so, with your hands in your pockets. Take your hands from your pockets, Roger. And from your head, you blockhead, you. But don't I hear a coach drive into the yard? To your posts, you blockheads! I'll go in the meantime and give my old friend's son a warm reception at the gate. (*Exit*)

First Servant: What now? My place is gone quite out of my head!

Second Servant: I know that my place is to be everywhere!

Third Servant: Where the devil is mine?

Fourth Servant: My place is to be nowhere at all, and so I'll go about my business! (*Exeunt* Servants, *running about as if frighted, different ways*)

(*Enter* Servant *with candles, showing in* Marlow *and* Hastings)

Servant: Welcome, gentlemen, very welcome. This way.

Hastings: After the disappointments of the day, welcome once more, Charles, to the comforts of a clean room and a good fire. Upon my word, a very good-looking house. Antique but comfortable.

Marlow: The usual fate of a large mansion. Having first ruined the master with expenses, it at last comes to collect contributions as an inn.

Hastings: You have lived at inns a good deal. In truth, I have been surprised that a person like you, who has seen so much of the world, never became more self-confident.

Marlow: The Englishman's malady. But tell me, George, where could I have learned that self-confidence you talk of? Most of my life has been spent at schools, or staying at an inn. I've always lived far from that lovely part of the creation that chiefly teaches men confidence. I don't know that I was ever really acquainted with a single modest woman—except my mother. But among females of another class, you know—

Hastings: Aye, among them you are confident enough!

Marlow: They are like *us*, you know.

Hastings: But in the company of women of reputation I never saw such an idiot. You look for all the world as if you wanted a chance to sneak out of the room.

Marlow: Why, man, that's because I *do* want to sneak out of the room. I have often made a resolution to break the ice, and rattle away at a great rate.

* malady (MAL uh dee) **disease or other complaint**

But I don't know how. A single glance from a pair of fine eyes has totally ruined my resolutions. A confident fellow can fake modesty, but I'll be hanged if a modest man can ever fake confidence.

Hastings: If you could only say half the things to them that I have heard you say to the barmaid of an inn, or even to a college cleaning—

Marlow: But, George, I *can't* say *anything* to them! I freeze. They petrify me. To me, a modest woman, dressed out in all her finery, is the most frightening object of the whole creation.

Hastings: Ha! ha! ha! At this rate, man, how can you ever expect to marry!

Marlow: Never, unless, as among kings and princes, my bride were just to be given to me. If one were to be introduced to a wife he never saw before, it might be endured. But to go through all the terrors of a formal courtship, together with the aunts, grandmothers and cousins, and at last to blurt out the question, *Madam, will you marry me?* No, no, that's a strain much above me, I assure you!

Hastings: I pity you. But how do you intend behaving to the lady you have come down to visit at the request of your father?

Marlow: As I behave to all other ladies. Bow very low. Answer yes, or no, to all her demands. But for the rest, I don't think I'll dare to look at her face till I see my father's again.

Hastings: I'm surprised that one who is so warm a friend can be so cool a lover.

Marlow: To be clear, my dear Hastings,

my chief reason for coming was your happiness, not my own. Miss Neville loves you, the family doesn't know you, as my friend you are sure of a welcome. Aw, this fellow again to interrupt us!

(*Enter* Hardcastle)

Hardcastle: Gentlemen, once more you are welcome. Which is Mr. Marlow? Sir, you're most welcome. It's not my way, you see, to receive my friends with my back to the fire. I like to give them a good reception, in the old style, at my gate. I like to see their horses and trunks taken care of.

Marlow (*aside*): He has got our names from the servants already. (*To him*) We approve your hospitality, sir. (*To Hastings*) I have been thinking, George, of changing our traveling clothes in the morning. I'm growing ashamed of mine.

Hardcastle: Mr. Marlow, you'll not have to dress up in this house.

Hastings: George, you're right. With the women, your first appearance is important. The first shot is half the battle. I intend opening the campaign with the white and gold.

Hardcastle: Mr. Marlow—Mr. Hastings—gentlemen—please be informal in this house. This is Liberty Hall, gentlemen. You may do just as you please here.

Marlow: Yet, George, if we start the campaign with too much strength, we may need ammunition before it is over. I think I'll reserve the gold for after a retreat.

Hardcastle: Your talking of a retreat, Mr. Marlow, puts me in mind of the

---

• aside (uh SYD) **actor's words heard by the audience but supposedly not heard by certain other actors**

Duke of Marlborough, when we went to conquer Denain. He first summoned the garrison—

Marlow: Don't you think my yellow jacket will do with the brown pants?

Hardcastle: He first summoned the garrison, which consisted of about five thousand men—

Hastings: I think not. Brown and yellow mix very poorly.

Hardcastle: I say, gentlemen, as I was telling you, he summoned the garrison, about five thousand men—

Marlow: The girls like yellow.

Hardcastle: About five thousand men, well provided with ammunition. "Now," says the Duke of Marlborough to George Brooks, who stood next to him—you must have heard of George Brooks. "I'll pawn my dukedom," says he, "but I'll take that garrison without spilling a drop of blood!" So—

Marlow (*to* Hardcastle): What, my good friend? If you gave us a glass of punch in the meantime, it would help us to carry on the battle with vigor.

Hardcastle (*aside*): Punch, sir!—This is the strangest kind of modesty I ever met with!

Marlow: Yes, sir, punch! A glass of punch, after our journey, will be comfortable. This is Liberty Hall, you know.

Hardcastle (*filling three glasses*): I hope you'll find this to your liking. I have prepared it with my own hands, and I believe you'll agree the ingredients are good. Here, Mr. Marlow, here is to our better acquaintance! (*Drinks*)

Hastings (*aside*): I see this fellow wants to give us his company, and forgets that he's only an innkeeper, not a gentleman. Here's your health, my philosopher. (*Drinks*)

Hardcastle: Good, very good, thank you; ha! ha! Your talk puts me in mind of Prince Eugene, when he fought the Turks at the battle of Belgrade. You shall hear—

Marlow: Instead of the battle of Belgrade, I believe it's almost time to talk about supper. What has your philosophy got in the house for supper?

Hardcastle (*aside*): For supper, sir!—Was there ever such a request to a man in his own house!

Marlow: Yes, sir, supper, sir; I begin to feel an appetite.

Hardcastle (*aside*): Such a demanding dog, surely, never my eyes beheld. (*To him*) Why, really, sir, as for supper I can't well tell. My wife Dorothy and the cook settle these things between them. I leave these kinds of things entirely to them.

Marlow: You do, do you?

Hardcastle: Entirely. By the way, I believe they are talking about what's for supper this moment in the kitchen.

Marlow: Then I beg they'll admit *me* to their meeting. It's a way I have. When I travel, I always choose to regulate my own supper.

Hardcastle: I beg you'll leave all that to me. You shall not stir a step.

Marlow: Leave that to you! I protest, sir. You must excuse me, I always look to these things myself.

Hardcastle (*aside*): Well, sir, I'm determined at least to go with you. This may be modern modesty, but I never saw anything look so like old-fashioned rudeness. (*Exeunt* Marlow *and* Hardcastle)

---

garrison (GAR i sun) group of soldiers stationed in a certain place

Hastings (*to himself*): I find this fellow's friendship begins to grow troublesome. Ha! What do I see? Miss Neville, by all that's happy!

(*Enter* Miss Neville)

Miss Neville: My dear Hastings! What unexpected good fortune! What accident have I to thank for this happy meeting?

Hastings: Rather let *me* ask the same question. I could never have hoped to meet my dearest Constance at this inn.

Miss Neville: An inn! Surely you make a mistake! My aunt and guardian, Mrs. Hardcastle, lives here. What could make you think this house an inn?

Hastings: My friend, Mr. Marlow, and I have been sent here as to an inn, I assure you. A young fellow we accidentally met at an alehouse directed us here.

Miss Neville: Oh, no! This must be one of my nasty cousin's tricks, ha! ha! ha! ha!

Hastings: The cousin your aunt intends for you to marry? The one I'm worried about?

Miss Neville: You have nothing to fear from him, I assure you. You'd adore him if you knew how much he despises me.

Hastings: You must know, Constance, of my plans. I have used the excuse of my friend's visit to get admittance into the family. The horses that brought us down will soon be refreshed. And then my dearest girl must trust in her faithful Hastings. We shall soon be landed in France, where the laws of marriage are respected as well as here.

Miss Neville: Mr. Hastings, I have often told you that I'm ready to obey you. But I don't want to leave my little fortune behind. The greatest part of it was left me by my uncle, and chiefly consists of jewels. I have been for some time persuading my aunt to let me wear them. I think I'm very near succeeding. The instant they are put into my hands, you shall find me ready to make them and myself yours.

Hastings: Forget the jewels! Your person is all I desire. In the meantime, my friend Marlow must not know about this mistake. I know the strange shyness of his nature. If suddenly informed of it, he would instantly leave the house before our plan was ripe.

Miss Neville: But Miss Hardcastle has just returned from walking. This, this way—(*They confer*)

(*Enter* Marlow)

Marlow: The fine friendship of these people is more than I can take. My host seems to think it ill manners to leave me alone. He and his old-fashioned wife talk of coming to eat with us, too. What have we got here!

Hastings: My dear Charles! Let me congratulate you!—The most fortunate accident! Who do you think has just arrived?

Marlow: Cannot guess.

Hastings: Our mistresses, boy, Miss Hardcastle and Miss Neville. Give me leave to introduce Miss Constance Neville to your acquaintance. They happened to dine in the neighborhood. Then they stopped, on their return, to take fresh horses here. Miss Hardcastle has just stepped into the next room, and will be back in an instant. Wasn't it lucky?

Marlow (*aside*): Here comes something to complete my embarrassment.

Hastings: Well! But wasn't it the most fortunate thing in the world?

Marlow: Oh, yes! Very fortunate—most joyful. But our clothes, George, you know, are in disorder. What if we should postpone the happiness till tomorrow? Tomorrow at her own house—It will be every bit as convenient—Tomorrow let it be. (*Starts to go*)

Miss Neville: By no means, sir. Your leaving will displease her. The disorder of your clothes will show the force of your impatience. Besides, she knows you are in the house, and will permit you to see her.

Marlow: Oh, the devil! Hem! hem! Hastings, you must not leave me. You are to assist me, you know. I shall look ridiculous. Yet, hang it, I'll take courage! Hem!

Hastings: Man, it's but the first plunge, and all's over! She's but a woman, you know.

Marlow: And of all women she that I dread most to meet!

(*Enter* Miss Hardcastle, *as returned from walking, wearing a large bonnet that nearly hides her face*)

Hastings (*introducing them*): Miss Hardcastle, Mr. Marlow. I'm proud of bringing two persons of such merit together.

Miss Hardcastle (*aside*): Now for meeting my modest gentleman. And I must meet him in quite his own manner. (*After a pause, in which he appears very uneasy*) I'm glad of your safe arrival, sir. I'm told you had some accidents on the way.

Marlow (*hardly looking at her directly, as throughout the meeting*): Only a few, madam. Yes, we had some. Yes, madam, a good many accidents, but should be sorry—madam—or rather glad of any accidents—that are so wonderfully ended. Hem!

Hastings (*to him*): You never spoke better in your whole life! Keep it up, and I'll guarantee you the victory.

Miss Hardcastle: I'm afraid you flatter, sir. You who have seen so much of the finest company can find little entertainment in this forgotten corner of the country.

Marlow (*gathering courage*): I have lived, indeed, in the world, madam. But I have kept very little company. I have been but an observer upon life, madam, while others were enjoying it.

Miss Neville: But that, I am told, is the way to enjoy it at last.

Hastings (*to him*): No one ever spoke better. Once more, and you are a confident man for life.

Marlow (*to him*): Hem! Stand by me, then, and when I'm down, throw in a word or two to set me up again.

Hastings: Well, Miss Hardcastle, I see that you and Mr. Marlow are going to be very good company. I believe our being here will only embarrass the two of you.

Marlow: Not in the least, Mr. Hastings. We like your company! (*To him*) Zounds, George! How can you leave us?

Hastings: Our presence will only spoil conversation, so we'll retire to the next room. (*To him*) Don't you realize, man, that we want a little meeting of our own? (*Exeunt* Hastings *with* Miss Neville)

Miss Hardcastle (*after a pause*): But you have not always been just an observer upon life, sir. The ladies, I should hope, have received some part of your attention.

Marlow (*again very timid*): Pardon me, madam, I—I—I—as yet have tried—only—to—deserve them.

Miss Hardcastle: And that, some say, is the very worst way to please them.

Marlow: Perhaps so, madam. But I love to converse only with the more serious and sensible members of the sex. Ah, I'm afraid I grow tiresome.

Miss Hardcastle: Not at all, sir. There is nothing I like so much as serious conversation myself. I could hear it forever. Indeed, I have often been surprised how a man of *quality* could ever admire those light, airy pleasures, where nothing reaches the heart.

Marlow: It's—a disease—of the mind, madam. In the variety of tastes there must be some who, wanting—um-a-um.

Miss Hardcastle: I understand you, sir. There must be some, who, wanting certain pleasures, pretend to despise what they are not capable of getting.

Marlow: My meaning, madam, but much better expressed. And I can't help observing—a—

Miss Hardcastle (*aside*): Who could ever suppose this fellow rude upon some occasions? (*To him*) You were going to observe, sir—

Marlow: I was observing, madam—I protest, madam. I forget what I was going to observe.

Miss Hardcastle: You were observing, sir, that in this age of hypocrisy—something about hypocrisy, sir.

Marlow: Yes, madam. In this age of hypocrisy, there are few who do not—a—a—

Miss Hardcastle: I understand you perfectly, sir.

Marlow (*aside*): Egad, and that's more than I do myself!

Miss Hardcastle: You mean that in this age of hypocrisy, there are few who do not condemn in public what they practice in private.

Marlow: True, madam. Those who have most—a—a—virtue in their—um, a—But I'm sure I tire you, madam.

Miss Hardcastle: Not in the least, sir. There's something so agreeable and lively in your manner, such life and force! Please, sir, go on.

Marlow: Yes, madam, I was saying—that there are some occasions—when a total lack of courage, madam, destroys all the—and puts us—upon a—a—a—

Miss Hardcastle: I agree with you entirely. A lack of courage sometimes looks like ignorance, and makes us fail when we most want to succeed. I beg you to proceed.

Marlow: Yes, madam. But I see Miss Neville wants us in the next room. I would not wish to keep her waiting.

Miss Hardcastle: I protest, sir. I never was more agreeably entertained in all my life. Please go on.

Marlow: Yes, madam. I was—but she waves for us to join her.

Miss Hardcastle: Well, then, I'll follow.

Marlow (*aside*): This conversation has ruined my chances. (*Exit*)

Miss Hardcastle (*to herself*): Ha! ha! ha! Was there ever such a sober, serious interview? I'm certain he scarcely looked at my face the whole time. Yet the fellow, but for his bashfulness, has good sense. If I could teach him a little confidence, it would be doing somebody that I know of a favor. But who is that somebody? Well, that's a question I can scarcely answer. (*Exit*)

(*Enter* Tony *and* Miss Neville, *followed by* Mrs. Hardcastle *and* Hastings)

Tony: What do you follow me for, Cousin Con?

Miss Neville: I hope, cousin, that I can speak to one of my own relations, and not be to blame.

Tony: Aye, I know what sort of a relation you want to make me! But it won't do. I tell you, Cousin Con, it won't do; so I beg you to keep your distance. I want no nearer relationship. (*She follows him to the back scene.*)

Mrs. Hardcastle: Well! Mr. Hastings, you are very entertaining. There's nothing in the world I love to talk of so much as London, and the fashions, though I was never there myself.

Hastings: Never there! You amaze me! From your air and manner, I concluded you went to London often.

Mrs. Hardcastle: Please, Mr. Hastings, what do you take to be the most fashionable age in London now?

Hastings: Some time ago forty was all the style. But I'm told the ladies intend to bring up fifty for the coming winter.

Mrs. Hardcastle: Seriously? Then I shall be too young for the fashion!

Hastings: No real lady now wears jewels till she's past forty. For instance, that young women there, in London society, would be considered a child.

Mrs. Hardcastle: And yet my niece thinks herself as a woman. Why, she's as fond of jewels as the oldest of us all.

Hastings: Your niece, is she? And that young gentleman—a brother of yours, I should think?

Mrs. Hardcastle: My son, sir. They are engaged to each other. Observe their little games. They fall in and out ten times a day, as if they were man and wife already. (*To them*) Well, Tony my child, what soft things are you saying to your Cousin Constance this evening?

Tony: I have been saying no soft things!

Mrs. Hardcastle: Never mind him, Con, my dear. He's another person behind your back.

Tony: That's a—crack.

Mrs. Hardcastle: Ah, he's a sly one! Don't you think they resemble each other about the mouth, Mr. Hastings? They're of a size too. Back to back, my pretties, so Mr. Hastings may see you. Come, Tony.

Tony: You had better not make me, I tell you.

Mrs. Hardcastle: Was ever the like? But I see he wants to break my heart, I see he does.

Hastings: Dear madam, permit me to lecture the young gentleman a little. I'm certain I can persuade him to do his duty.

Mrs. Hardcastle: Well! I must go. Come Constance, my love. You see, Mr.

Hastings, the misery of my situation. Was ever a poor woman so bothered by a dear, sweet, undutiful boy? (*Exeunt* Mrs. Hardcastle *and* Miss Neville)

Tony: Don't mind her. Let her cry. It's the comfort of her heart. I have seen her and sister cry over a book for an hour together, and they said they liked the book the better the more it made them cry.

Hastings: Then you're no friend to the ladies, my young gentleman?

Tony: Well, I'm a friend to *some*.

Hastings: Not to her of your mother's choosing, then. And yet she appears to me a pretty, well-tempered girl.

Tony: That's because you don't know her as well as I do.

Hastings: Well, but you must allow her a little beauty.—Yes, you must allow her some beauty.

Tony: Make-up! She's all a made-up thing, man. Ah! If you could see Bet Bouncer of these parts, you might then talk of beauty. She has two eyes as black as sloes, and cheeks as broad and red as a pulpit cushion. She'd make two of Cousin Con.

Hastings: Well, what would you think of a friend who would take this bitter bargain off your hands?

Tony: Speak on.

Hastings: Would you thank someone who would take Miss Neville, and leave you to happiness and your dear Betsy?

Tony: Aye, but where is there such a friend? Who would take *her*?

Hastings: I am he. If you'll only help me, I'll try to whip her off to France, and you'll never hear more of her.

Tony: Assist you! I will, to the last drop of my blood. I'll get you a pair of horses that shall carry you off in a twinkling. And maybe, I'll get you a part of her fortune besides, in jewels that you little dream of.

Hastings: My dear friend, you look like a lad of spirit.

Tony: Come along then, and you shall see more of my spirit before you have done with me.

● sloe (SLOH) **kind of small black fruit**

182

ACT THREE

The house

(*Enter* Hardcastle, *alone*)

Hardcastle: What could my old friend Sir Charles mean by recommending his son as the most modest young man in town? That fellow, modest? He has taken over my easy chair by the fireside already. He took off his boots, and told me to take care of them. I'm curious to know how his rudeness affects my daughter. She will certainly be shocked at it.

(*Enter* Miss Hardcastle, *quite simply dressed*)

Hardcastle: Well, my Kate, I see you have changed your dress as I told you. And yet, I believe there was no great reason—particularly when I recommended my *modest* gentleman to you as a lover today.

Miss Hardcastle: You taught me to expect something unusual, and I found that the original was even more than the description!

Hardcastle: I was never so surprised in my life!

Miss Hardcastle: I never saw anything like it! And a man of the world, too!

Hardcastle: Aye, he learned it all abroad. What a fool was I, to think a young man could learn modesty by traveling. I fear he's been a good deal assisted by bad company and a French dancing master!

Miss Hardcastle: You're mistaken, Papa! A French dancing master could never have taught him that timid look—that awkward speech—that bashful manner—

Hardcastle: Whose look? Whose manner, child?

Miss Hardcastle: Mr. Marlow's. His timidity struck me at the first sight.

Hardcastle: Then your first sight deceived you.

Miss Hardcastle: He met me with a respectful bow, a stammering voice, and a look fixed on the ground.

Hardcastle: He met me with a loud voice, a lordly air, and a friendliness that made my blood freeze.

Miss Hardcastle: One of us must certainly be mistaken.

Hardcastle: If he really is what he has shown himself to be, he shall never have my consent.

Miss Hardcastle: And if he really is the sheepish thing I saw, he shall never have mine.

Hardcastle: In one thing then we are agreed—to reject him.

Miss Hardcastle: Yes. But upon conditions. For you might find him less rude, and I more confident—I don't know—the fellow *is* good looking.

Hardcastle: If we should find him so— but that's impossible!

Miss Hardcastle: And as one of us must be mistaken, what if we go on to make further discoveries?

Hardcastle: Agreed. But depend on it— I'm in the right.

Miss Hardcastle: And depend on it— I'm not much in the wrong. (*Exeunt*)

(*Enter* Tony, *running in with a box*)

Tony: I have got them! Here they are. My Cousin Con's jewels, necklaces and all. My mother shan't cheat the poor souls out of their fortune now. Oh! Is that you?

(*Enter* Hastings)

Hastings: My dear friend, how have you managed with your mother? I hope you have amused her with pretending love for your cousin Constance. Our horses will be ready in a short time, and we shall soon set off.

Tony: And here's something to take with you (*giving the box*), your sweetheart's jewels.

Hastings: But how have you got them from your mother?

Tony: Ask me no questions, and I'll tell you no fibs. If I didn't have a key to every drawer in Mother's bureau, how could I go to the alehouse so often as I do? Zounds! Here they are! Go! Hurry! (*Exit* Hastings)

(*Enter* Mrs. Hardcastle *and* Miss Neville)

Mrs. Hardcastle: Indeed, Constance, you amaze me. Such a girl as you want jewels? There will be time enough for jewels, my dear, twenty years from now, when your beauty begins to want repairs.

Miss Neville: But what will repair beauty at forty will certainly improve it at twenty, madam.

Mrs. Hardcastle: Besides, I believe I can't easily get at them. They may be missing, for all I know.

Tony (*apart to* Mrs. Hardcastle): Then why don't you tell her so at once? Say they're lost, and call me to bear witness.

Mrs. Hardcastle (*apart to* Tony): You know, my dear, I'm only keeping them for you, when you two marry. So if I say they're gone, you'll bear me witness, will you? He! he! he!

Tony (*apart to* Mrs. Hardcastle): Never fear! I'll say I saw them taken with my own eyes.

Miss Neville: I desire them but for a day, madam. Just to look at.

Mrs. Hardcastle: My dear Constance, if I could find them, you should have them. They're missing, I assure you. Lost, for all I know. But we must have patience, wherever they are.

Tony: That I can bear witness to. They are missing, and not to be found.

Mrs. Hardcastle: You must learn patience, my dear. For though we lose our fortune, we should not lose our patience. See me, how calm I am.

Miss Neville: Aye, people are generally calm at the misfortune of others.

Mrs. Hardcastle: We shall soon find them. In the meantime, you shall make use of my garnets till your jewels are found.

Miss Neville: I detest garnets!

Mrs. Hardcastle: I will get them. (*Exit*)

Miss Neville: I dislike them of all things.

Tony: Don't be a fool. If she gives you the garnets, take what you can get. The jewels are your own already. I have stolen them out of her bureau, and she doesn't know it. Fly to your Hastings. He'll tell you more of the matter. Leave me to manage here.

Miss Neville: My dear cousin!

Tony: Vanish! She's here, and has missed them already. (*Exit* Miss Neville)

(*Enter* Mrs. Hardcastle)

Mrs. Hardcastle: Confusion! Thieves! Robbers! We are cheated, broke open, undone!

Tony: What's the matter, Mamma?

Mrs. Hardcastle: My bureau has been broke open, the jewels taken out, and I'm undone!

Tony: Stick to that! Ha, ha, ha! Stick to

• **garnet** (GAHR nit) kind of red gem

that! I'll bear witness, you know. Call me to bear witness.

Mrs. Hardcastle: I tell you, Tony, by all that's precious, the jewels are gone!

Tony: Sure, I know they're gone, and I am here to say so.

Mrs. Hardcastle: My dearest Tony, hear me! They're *gone,* I say.

Tony: That's right!—that's right! Keep being that disturbed about it, and nobody will suspect either of us. I'll bear witness that they are gone.

Mrs. Hardcastle: Oh! Was ever poor woman so beset with fools on one hand, and thieves on the other?

Tony: I can bear witness to that. (*He runs off; she follows him*)

(*Enter* Miss Hardcastle *and* Maid)

Miss Hardcastle: What a character that brother of mine is, to send them to this house as an inn! Ha! ha! I don't wonder at Mr. Marlow's behavior.

Maid: But what's more, as you passed by in that dress you have on now, Mr. Marlow asked me if you were the barmaid. He mistook you for the barmaid, madam!

Miss Hardcastle: Did he? Then as I live, I'm going to keep the fun alive. Are you sure he doesn't remember my face or size?

Maid: Certain of it!

Miss Hardcastle: I think so too. For though we spoke for some time together, his fears were such that he never once looked at me. Indeed, if he had, my bonnet would have kept him from seeing my face.

Maid: But are you sure you can act your part? Can you disguise your voice? He has to mistake that now too, you know.

Miss Hardcastle: Never fear. I think I know how to speak bar language. (*Acting the part*)—Did your honor call?—Attend the gentleman there.—Pipe and tobacco for the squire.

Maid: It will do, madam. But he's here. (*Exit* Maid)

(*Enter* Marlow)

Marlow: What an inn this is! I have scarcely a moment's peace. If I go to

---

 • beset (be SET) **bothered; troubled**

185

the best room, there I find my host and his stories. If I fly to the gallery, there we have my hostess with all her courtesy. Finally I have a moment to myself, and now for some thought. (*Walks and muses*)

Miss Hardcastle: Did you call, sir? Did your honor call?

Marlow (*musing*): As for Miss Hardcastle, she's much too serious for me.

Miss Hardcastle: Did your honor call? (*She places herself before him, he turning away.*)

Marlow: No, child! (*Musing*) Besides, from the glimpse I had of her, I think she squints.

Miss Hardcastle: I'm sure, sir, that I heard the bell ring.

Marlow: No, no! (*Musing*) I have pleased my father, however, by coming down here. And tomorrow I'll please myself by returning.

Miss Hardcastle: Perhaps the other gentleman called, sir?

Marlow: I tell you no.

Miss Hardcastle: I should be glad to know, sir.

Marlow: No, no, I tell you. (*Looks full in her face*) Yes, child, I think I did call. I wanted—I wanted—I see, child, you are a real beauty.

Miss Hardcastle: Oh la, sir, you'll make me ashamed.

Marlow: I never saw a more lively, devilish eye. Yes, yes, my dear. I did call. Suppose I should call for a taste, just by way of trial, of the nectar of your lips. Might I be disappointed in that?

Miss Hardcastle: Nectar? Nectar? That's a drink there's no call for in these parts. French, I suppose. We keep no French wines here, sir.

Marlow: Of true English growth, I assure you.

Miss Hardcastle: Then it's odd I should not know it. We brew all sorts of wines in this house, and I have lived here these eighteen years.

Marlow: Eighteen years! Why one would think, child, you kept the bar before you were born. How old are you?

Miss Hardcastle: Oh, sir! I must not tell my age. They say women and music should never be dated.

Marlow: To guess at this distance, you can't be much above forty. (*Approaching*) Yet nearer, I think not so old. (*Approaching*) By coming close to some women, they look younger still. But when we come very close indeed—(*Attempting to kiss her*)

Miss Hardcastle: Pray, sir, keep your distance. One would think you wanted to know a person's age as they do horses, by checking their teeth.

Marlow: I protest, child. If you keep me at this distance, how is it possible you and I can be ever acquainted?

Miss Hardcastle: And who wants to be acquainted with you? I want no such acquaintance, not I. I'm sure you didn't treat Miss Hardcastle a while ago in this flirtatious manner. Before her you looked embarrassed, and kept bowing to the ground.

Marlow: Before Miss Hardcastle, child? Ha! ha! ha! She's only an awkward, squinting thing! No, no! I find you don't know me. I laughed and cheered her up a little. But I was unwilling to be as serious as she was.

Miss Hardcastle: Then, sir, you're a real favorite among the ladies?

Marlow: Yes, my dear, a great favorite.

- muse (MYOOZ) **think; ponder**
- nectar (NEK tur) **in mythology, the life-giving drink of the gods**

And yet, I don't really see what they find in me. At the Ladies Club in town I'm called their agreeable Rattle. Rattle, child, is not my real name, but one I'm known by. My name is Solomons. Mr. Solomons, my dear, at your service. (*Making a sweep with his arm before reaching for her shoulders*)

Miss Hardcastle (*stepping back*): Wait, sir! You were introducing me to your club, not to yourself. And you're a great favorite there, you say?

Marlow: Yes, my dear. There's Mrs. Mantrap, Lady Betty Blackleg, the Countess of Sligo, Mrs. Longhorns, Miss Biddy Buckskin, and your humble servant, to keep up the spirit of the place.

Miss Hardcastle: Then it's a very merry place, I suppose.

Marlow: Yes, as merry as cards, suppers, and women can make me.

Miss Hardcastle: And their agreeable Rattle. Ha! ha! ha!

Marlow (*aside*): Egad! I don't quite like this talk. She looks knowing, I think. (*To her*) You laugh, child!

Miss Hardcastle: I can't help laughing when I think what little time all those ladies have for their work or their family.

Marlow: (*aside*): All's well. She doesn't laugh at me. (*To her*) Do *you* ever work, child?

Miss Hardcastle: Aye, sure. There's not a pillow or a quilt in the whole house but what can bear witness to that.

Marlow: Oh, so! Then you must show me your embroidery. I embroider and draw patterns myself a little. If you want a judge of your work you must apply to me. (*Seizing her hand*)

(*Enter Hardcastle, who stands in surprise*)

Miss Hardcastle: Aye, but the colors don't look well by candlelight. You shall see all in the morning. (*Struggling*)

Marlow: And why not now, my angel? Such beauty fires up beyond my power to resist. Oh, no! The innkeeper here! My old luck. (*Exit*)

Hardcastle: So, madam! So I find *this* is your *modest* lover! This is your humble admirer who kept his eyes on the ground and only adored at distance. Kate, Kate, aren't you ashamed to deceive your father so?

Miss Hardcastle: Trust me, dear Papa, that he's still the modest man I first took him for. You'll be convinced of it soon, I promise.

Hardcastle: But didn't I see him seize your hand? Didn't I see him haul you about like a milkmaid? And now you talk of his respect and his modesty!

Miss Hardcastle: But soon I'll convince you of his modesty. If you see that his faults will pass off with time, and that his virtues will improve with age, I hope you'll forgive him.

Hardcastle: This girl would actually make me run mad! I tell you, I'll not be convinced. Or rather, I *am* convinced. My son-in-law, madam, must have very different qualifications.

Miss Hardcastle: Sir, I ask only this evening to convince you.

Hardcastle: You shall not have half the time. I have thoughts of turning him out of my house this very hour.

Miss Hardcastle: Give me that hour then, and I hope to satisfy you.

Hardcastle: Well, an hour let it be then. But I'll have no trifling with your father. All fair and open, do you hear me?

Miss Hardcastle: Of course, sir. I have always considered your commands to be your kindness.

CHECKPOINT

ACT FOUR

The house

(*Enter* Hastings *and* Miss Neville)

Hastings: You surprise me! Sir Charles Marlow expected here this night? Where have you got your information?

Miss Neville: You may depend upon it. I just saw his letter to Mr. Hardcastle. Sir Charles writes that he intends setting out a few hours after his son.

Hastings: Then, my Constance, all must be completed before he arrives. He knows me. If he should find me here, he might tell my plans to the rest of the family.

Miss Neville: The jewels, I hope, are safe.

Hastings: Yes, yes. I have sent them to Marlow, who keeps the keys of our baggage. In the meantime, I'll go to prepare for our elopment. I have had the promise of a fresh pair of horses. (*Exit*)

Miss Neville: Well, success be with you! In the meantime, I'll go amuse my aunt with the old story of a violent passion for my cousin. (*Exit*)

(*Enter* Marlow, *followed by a* Servant)

Marlow: I wonder what Hastings could mean by sending a valuable box of jewels to keep for him. Have you deposited the box with the landlady, as

I ordered you? Have you put it into her own hands?

Servant: Yes, your honor.

Marlow: She said she'd keep it safe, did she?

Servant: Yes. Those were her very words: "*I'll* keep it safe enough." (*Exit*)

Marlow: Ha! Ha! Ha! They're safe, however. What a set of people at this inn. That little barmaid, though, runs in my head most strangely. She's mine, she must be mine, or I'm greatly mistaken!

(*Enter* Hastings)

Hastings: Bless me! Marlow here, and looking happy too.

Marlow: Give me joy, George! Crown me! After all, we modest fellows don't always lack success among the women.

Hastings: But what success?

Marlow: Didn't you see the tempting, brisk, lovely little thing that runs about the house with a bunch of keys?

Hastings: Well! And what then?

Marlow: She's mine, you rascal, you. Such fire, such motion, such eyes, such lips! But egad! She would not let me kiss them though.

Hastings: But are you sure, so very sure of her?

Marlow: Why, man, she talked of showing me her embroidery upstairs.

Hastings: Well—we'll see what happens. You have taken care, I hope, of the box I sent you to lock up? It's in safety?

Marlow: Yes, yes. It's safe enough. I have taken care of it. But how could you think our baggage a place of safety? Ah! I have taken even better care of it—I have—

Hastings: What?

Marlow: I have sent it to the landlady to keep for you.

Hastings: To the landlady!

Marlow: The landlady.

Hastings: You did!

Marlow: Wasn't I right?

Hastings (*aside*): He must not see my uneasiness.

Marlow: You seem a little disturbed, I think. Surely nothing has happened?

Hastings: No, nothing. I was never in better spirits in all my life. After all, the jewels are safe.

Marlow: As in a miser's purse.

Hastings (*aside*): So now all hopes of fortune are at an end, and we must elope without it. (*To him*) Well, Charles, I'll leave you to your pretty barmaid. He! he! he! May you be as successful for yourself as you have been for me. (*Exit*)

Marlow: Thanks, George! I ask no more. Ha! ha! ha! (*Enter* Hardcastle)

Hardcastle (*to himself*): I no longer know my own house. It's turned all topsy-turvy. His servants have got drunk already. I'll stand it no longer— and yet, from my respect for his father, I'll be calm. (*To him*) Mr. Marlow, I have submitted to your rudeness for more than four hours. I see no likelihood of its coming to an end. I'm the master here, sir. And I desire that you and your drunken pack leave my house directly.

Marlow: Leave your house! Surely, you cannot be serious! At this time of night, and such a night!

Hardcastle: I tell you, sir, I'm serious. I say this house is mine, sir. This house is mine, and I command you to leave it directly.

Marlow: Ha! ha! ha!

Hardcastle: Young man, young man, listen. From your father's letter to me, I was led to expect a well-bred, modest man as a visitor here. But now I find him no better than a bully. I tell you, Sir Charles will be here soon, and he shall hear all of it! (*Exit*)

Marlow: How's this! Surely, I have not mistaken the house. Everything looks like an inn. The servants cry, "Coming." The barmaid, too, to attend us. But she's here, and will tell me more.

(*Enter* Miss Hardcastle)

Marlow: Why so fast, child? A word with you.

Miss Hardcastle: Let it be short then. I'm in a hurry. (*Aside*) I believe he begins to find out his mistake.

Marlow: Child, answer me one question. Who are you, and what may your business in this house be?

Miss Hardcastle: A relation of the family, sir.

Marlow: What! A poor relation?

Miss Hardcastle: Yes, sir. A poor relation appointed to keep the keys, and to see that the guests lack nothing in my power to give them.

Marlow: That is, you act as the barmaid of this inn.

Miss Hardcastle: Inn! What brought that in your head? Does one of the best families in the county keep an inn? Ha, ha, ha. Old Mr. Hardcastle's house an inn!

Marlow: Mr. Hardcastle's house! Is this house Mr. Hardcastle's house, child?

Miss Hardcastle: Aye, sure. Whose else would it be?

Marlow: So then all's out in the open. I have been fooled for some reason. I shall be laughed at forever. To mistake this house, of all others, for an inn! And my father's old friend for an innkeeper! What a rude bully must he take me for! What a silly puppy do I find myself! There again, may I be hanged, my dear, but I mistook you for a common barmaid! And you're really a relation of Mr. Hardcastle's!

Miss Hardcastle: Dear me! I'm sure there was nothing in my *behavior* to make you think—

Marlow: Nothing, my dear, nothing. I was in for a list of mistakes. My stupidity saw everything the wrong way. But it's over—this house I'll no more show *my* face in!

Miss Hardcastle: I hope, sir, I have done nothing to displease you. I'm sure I should be sorry to anger any gentleman who has said so many nice things to me. I'm sure I should be sorry (*pretending to cry*) if he left the family upon my account.

Marlow (*aside*): By heaven, she weeps! This is the first sign of tenderness I ever had from a modest woman, and it touches me. (*To her*) Excuse me, my lovely girl. You are the only part of the family I leave with pain. But the difference of our birth, fortune, and education makes an honorable connection impossible. And I could never think of bringing ruin upon one whose only fault was being too lovely.

Miss Hardcastle (*aside*): Generous man! I now begin to admire him. (*To him*) But I'm sure my family is as good as Miss Hardcastle's. And though I'm poor, that's no great misfortune. Why, until this moment, I never thought that it was bad to lack a fortune.

Marlow: And why now, my pretty one?

Miss Hardcastle: Because it puts me at a distance from a person whom, if I had a thousand pounds, I would give it all to.

Marlow (*aside*): This girl bewitches me!

If I stay, I'm undone! I must make one bold effort and leave her. (*To her*) Your words, my dear, touch me most tenderly. If I could live for myself alone, I could easily fix my choice. But I owe too much to the opinion of the world, too much to the authority of a father.—I can scarcely speak of how—all this—affects me! Farewell! (*Exit*)

Miss Hardcastle: I never knew half his merit till now. He shan't go. Not if I can help it. I'll still keep the character in which I stooped to conquer. But I'll tell all to my father, who perhaps can laugh him out of his plans. (*Exit*)

(*Enter* Tony, Miss Neville)

Tony: Aye, you may steal for yourselves the next time. I have done my duty. My mother has got the jewels again, that's a sure thing. But she believes it was all a mistake of the servants.

Miss Neville: My dear cousin, surely you won't forsake us in this distress. If she suspects that I am going off, I shall certainly be locked up—or sent to my Aunt Pedigree's, which is ten times worse.

Tony: But what can I do? I have got you a pair of horses that will fly. Here she comes. We must act our parts a bit more, or she'll suspect us. (*They retire, and seem to fondle.*)

(*Enter* Mrs. Hardcastle)

Mrs. Hardcastle: Well, I was greatly annoyed, to be sure. But my son tells me it was all a mistake of the servants. Ah, what do I see! Fondling together, as I'm alive! Ah, have I caught you, my pretty doves?

Miss Neville: Cousin Tony promises to give us more of his company at home. Indeed, he shan't leave us any more.

Tony: I'm sure I always loved Cousin Con's hazel eyes, and her pretty long fingers. Oh, pretty creature.

Mrs. Hardcastle: Ah, he would charm the bird from the tree. I was never so happy before. The jewels, my dear Con, shall be yours. You shall have them. Isn't he a sweet boy, my dear? You shall be married tomorrow.

(*Enter* Servant)

Servant (*to* Tony): I have a letter for your worship.

Tony: Give it to my mamma. She reads all my letters first.

Servant: I had orders to deliver it into your own hands. (*Exit*)

Miss Neville (*aside*): Undone, undone! A letter to him from Hastings. I know the hand. If my aunt sees it, we are ruined forever!

Tony: Here, mother. (*Giving* Mrs. Hardcastle *the letter*)

Mrs. Hardcastle: How's this! (*Reads*) "Dear Tony, I'm now waiting for Miss Neville at the bottom of the garden. But I find my horses yet unable to perform the journey. I expect you'll assist us with a pair of fresh horses, as you promised. Speed is necessary, as the *hag*, (*aye, the hag*) your mother, will otherwise suspect me. Yours, Hastings." Give me patience! My rage chokes me!

Miss Neville: I hope, madam—

Mrs. Hardcastle (*to* Tony): And you, you great oaf! Were you, too, joined against me? But I'll defeat all your plots in a moment. As for you, madam, since you have a pair of fresh horses ready, it would be cruel to disappoint them. So, if you please, forget your plan of running away with your Hastings. Instead, prepare, this very moment, to run off with *me*. Your old Aunt Pedigree will keep you secure, I'm sure. You too, my son, may mount your horse, and guard us upon the way. (*Exit*)

Miss Neville: So now I'm completely ruined.

Tony: Aye, that's a sure thing.

Miss Neville: What better could be expected from such a stupid fool as you!

Tony: No miss, it was your own cleverness, not my stupidity. You were so nice and smiling with me—I thought you could never be making believe. And her words: "Married tomorrow!"

(*Enter* Hastings)

Hastings: So, sir, I find from my servant that you have shown my letter and betrayed us!

Tony: Ask miss there who betrayed you. It was her doing, not mine.

(*Enter* Marlow)

Marlow: So I have been laughed at here among you! Made to look the fool! Insulted!

Miss Neville: And there, sir, is the gentleman who caused every part of this madness.

Tony: Baw!

Marlow: What can I say to him, a mere boy, an idiot!

Hastings: A poor fool, not worth my breath.

Miss Neville: Yet with enough evil tricks to make himself merry with all our embarrassments.

(*Enter* Servant)

Servant: My mistress desires you'll get ready immediately, madam. The horses are ready. Your hat and things are in the next room. We are to go thirty miles before morning.

Miss Neville: Well, I'll come presently.

Marlow (*to* Hastings): Was it all done, sir, to make me look ridiculous? Depend upon it, sir, I shall expect an explanation.

Miss Neville: Mr. Hastings. Mr. Marlow. Why will you increase my distress by this silly dispute? I beg you—

Servant: Your cloak, madam. My mistress is impatient.

Miss Neville: Oh, Mr. Marlow! If you knew all my poor Mr. Hastings has been through, I'm sure it would change your anger into pity.

Marlow: I don't know what I know. Forgive me, madam. George, forgive me. You know my hasty temper.

Hastings: The torture of my situation is my only excuse.

Mrs. Hardcastle (*within*): Miss Neville! Constance, why, Constance, I say.

Miss Neville: I'm coming. (*Exit, followed by* Servant)

Hastings: My heart! How can I stand this! To be so near happiness, and such happiness!

Marlow (*to* Tony): You see now, young gentleman, the results of your tricks. What might be amusement to you is here disappointment, and even distress.

Tony (*from a trance*): Egad, I have hit it! It's here! Your hands. Yours, and yours (*shaking hands with both*). Meet me two hours from now at the bottom of the garden. And if you don't find Tony Lumpkin a better fellow than you thought, I'll give you my best horse, and Bet Bouncer in the bargain! Come along. (*Exeunt*)

ACT FIVE

Scene 1: the house

(*Enter* Hastings *and* Servant)

Hastings: You saw the old lady and Miss Neville drive off, you say?

Servant: Yes, your honor. They went off in a coach, and master Tony Lumpkin went on horseback. They're thirty miles off by this time.

Hastings: Then all my hopes are over.

Servant: Yes, sir. Old Sir Charles Marlow has arrived. He and the old gentleman of the house have been laughing at young Marlow's mistakes. Oh, they're coming this way.

Hastings: Then I must not be seen. So now to my fruitless appointment at the bottom of the garden. This is about the time. (*Exit*)

(*Enter* Sir Charles *and* Hardcastle)

Hardcastle: Ha! ha! ha! The tone in which he gave me his commands! And yet he might have seen something in me above the common innkeeper, too.

Sir Charles: Yes, Dick, but he mistook you for an uncommon innkeeper, ha! ha! ha!

Hardcastle: Well, I'm too happy now to

think of anything but joy. Yes, my dear friend, this union of our families will make our personal friendship hereditary. And though my daughter's fortune is but small—

Sir Charles: Why, Dick, will you talk of fortune to *me*? My son has more than a little money already. He can want nothing but a good and virtuous girl to share his happiness and increase it. If they like each other, as you say they do—

Hardcastle: *If,* man. I tell you they *do* like each other. My daughter as good as told me so.

Sir Charles: But girls are apt to flatter themselves, you know.

Hardcastle: I saw him grasp her hand in the warmest manner myself. And here he comes to put you out of your *ifs.* (*Enter* Marlow)

Marlow: I come, sir, once more, to ask pardon for my very strange conduct.

Hardcastle: It was nothing, boy. You take it too seriously. An hour or two of laughing with my daughter will set all to rights again. She'll never like you the worse for it.

Marlow: Sir, I shall always be proud of her approval.

Hardcastle: *Approval* is too cold a word, Mr. Marlow. If I'm not deceived, you have something more than just approval from her right now. You understand me?

Marlow: Really, sir, I have not that happiness.

Hardcastle: Come, boy. I'm an old fellow, but I know what's what as well as a younger man. I know what has passed between you two.

Marlow: Sir, nothing has passed between us but the most profound respect and serious discussion. You can't think, sir, that my impudence to you has been passed on to the rest of the family.

Hardcastle: Impudence? No, I don't say that—it's not quite impudence. Girls like to be flirted with, and rumpled a little, too, sometimes. But she has told no tales, I assure you.

Marlow: I never gave her the slightest cause.

Hardcastle: Well, well, I like modesty in its place. But this is over-acting, my young gentleman. You may be honest with us. Your father and I will like you the better for it.

Marlow: Dear sir—I protest, sir—

Hardcastle: I see no reason why you two should not be joined as fast as the parson can tie you.

Marlow: But hear me, sir—

Hardcastle: Your father approves the match, and I admire it.

Marlow: But why won't you hear me? By all that's just and true, I never gave Miss Hardcastle the most distant hint of affection. We had but one interview, and that was formal and uninteresting.

Hardcastle (*aside*): This fellow's formal, modest impudence is beyond bearing.

Sir Charles: And you never grasped her hand or made any talk of love?

Marlow: As Heaven is my witness, *no!* (*Exit*)

Sir Charles: I'm astonished at the air of sincerity with which he parted.

Hardcastle: And I'm astonished that his odd behavior goes on and on.

Sir Charles: I dare pledge my life and honor upon his truth.

Hardcastle: Here comes my daughter, and I would stake my happiness upon *her* truth.

• impudence (IM pyoo duns) rudeness; disregard of others

(*Enter* Miss Hardcastle)

Hardcastle: Kate, come here, child. Answer us sincerely. Has Mr. Marlow made to you any show of love and affection?

Miss Hardcastle: The question is very abrupt, sir! But since you require sincerity, I think he has.

Hardcastle (*to* Sir Charles): You see!

Sir Charles: And tell us, madam, have you and my son had more than one interview?

Miss Hardcastle: Yes, sir, several.

Hardcastle (*to* Sir Charles): You see!

Sir Charles: But did he talk of love?

Miss Hardcastle: Much sir.

Sir Charles: Amazing. And all this in earnest?

Miss Hardcastle: In earnest.

Hardcastle: Now, my friend, I hope you are satisfied.

Sir Charles: And how did he behave, madam?

Miss Hardcastle: As most admirers do. Said some nice things about my face; talked much of his lack of merit, and the greatness of mine; mentioned his heart; gave a short speech of pretended—

Sir Charles: *Indeed, no!* I know his conversation with women to be most modest. This bold, talkative manner by no means describes him. I am confident he never sat for the picture.

Miss Hardcastle: Then what, sir, if I should convince you of my sincerity? If you and my papa, in about half an hour, will place yourselves behind that screen, you shall hear him declare his passion to me in person.

Sir Charles: Agreed. And if I find him what you describe, all my happiness in him must have an end. (*Exit*)

Miss Hardcastle: And if you don't find him what I described—I fear my happiness will never have a beginning. (*Exeunt*)

Scene 2: the back of the garden

(*Enter* Hastings)

Hastings: What an idiot I am, to wait here for a fellow who probably takes great delight in tricking me.

(*Enter* Tony, *booted and spattered*)

Hastings: My honest friend! I now find you a man of your word!

Tony: Aye, I'm your friend.

Hastings: But where did you leave your fellow travelers? Are they in safety?

Tony: Leave them? Why, where should I leave them but where I found them?

Hastings: This is a riddle.

Tony: Riddle me this, then. What goes round and round the house, and never touches the house?

Hastings: I'm still astray.

Tony: You shall hear. First I took them round and round the house on this dark night. They've been within five miles these two hours. At the end, I nearly dumped them in the horse pond over there.

Hastings: By no accident, I hope.

Tony: No, no. Only Mother is frightened. She thinks herself forty miles off. So, if your own horses are ready, you can whip off with Cousin Con toward France. I'll be sure that no one here will follow you.

Hastings: My dear friend, how can I show my gratitude? (*Exit*)

(*Enter* Mrs. Hardcastle)

Mrs. Hardcastle: Oh Tony, I'm killed! Shook! Battered to death! I shall never survive it.

Tony: Alas, Mama, it was all your own fault. You would be for running away by night, without knowing one inch of the way.

Mrs. Hardcastle: I wish we were at home again. I never met so many accidents on such a short journey. Overturned in a ditch, stuck fast in the mud, jolted to a jelly, and at last to lose our way! Where do you think we are, Tony?

Tony: By my guess we should be upon Crackskull Common, about forty miles from home.

(*Enter* Hardcastle, *holding lamp, to one side*)

Hardcastle: I thought I heard a voice down here. I'd be glad to know where it came from.

Mrs. Hardcastle: Mr. Hardcastle, as I'm alive! My fears blinded me. But who, my dear, could have expected to meet you here, in this frightful place, so far from home? What has brought you to follow us?

Hardcastle: Surely, Dorothy, you have not lost your wits! So far from home, when you are within forty yards of your own door! (*To* Tony) This is one of your old tricks, you rascal, you. (*To* her) Don't you know the gate, and the mulberry tree? And don't you remember the horse pond, my dear?

Mrs. Hardcastle: That's—that's *our* horse pond? Then I shall remember the horse pond as long as I live! I have caught my death in it! (*To* Tony) And it is to you, you graceless son of mine, that I owe all this? I'll teach you to abuse your mother, I will!

Tony: Now, Mother, all the county says you spoiled me, and so you must take the results of it.

Mrs. Hardcastle: I'll spoil you, I will! (*Chases him off the stage*)

Hardcastle: There's some sense, however, in his reply. (*Exit*)

(*Enter* Hastings *and* Miss Neville)

Hastings: My dear Constance, if we delay a moment, all is lost forever. Pluck up a little courage, and we shall soon be out of her reach.

Miss Neville: No, I find it impossible. My spirits are so sunk with all I have suffered. I am unable to face any new danger.

Hastings: Let us fly, my charmer. Let us date our happiness from this very moment. Forget your fortune. Love and joy will increase what we possess beyond the fortune of a king.

Miss Neville: No, Mr. Hastings, no. Good sense once more comes to my relief, and I will obey it. In a moment of passion, fortune may be despised, but it can never be regained. I'm determined to apply to Mr. Hardcastle's justice and sense of fair play.

Hastings: I have no hopes. But since you insist, I must obey you. (*Exeunt*)

Scene 3: a room at Mr. Hardcastle's

(*Enter* Hardcastle, Sir Charles *and* Miss Hardcastle)

Sir Charles (*to* Miss Hardcastle): What a situation I am in! If what you say is true, I shall then find a guilty son. But if what he says is true, I shall then lose the girl I most wanted for a daughter.

Miss Hardcastle: I am proud of your approval. And to show I merit it, if you place yourself as I directed, you shall hear his very declaration of love to me. But he comes!

Hardcastle: Quick, my friend, behind the screen. (*They go there.*) (*Enter* Marlow)

Marlow: Though prepared for setting out, I come once more to say goodbye. Till this moment, I never knew the pain I'd feel in separation.

Miss Hardcastle (*in her own natural manner*): I believe your suffering cannot be very great, sir. Why, you can so easily remove the pain. Staying a day or two longer, perhaps, might bring some relief.

Marlow (*aside*): This girl every moment improves upon me. (*To her*) That must not be, madam. I have already played too long with my heart. My very pride begins to submit to my passion. The difference between us in education and fortune, and the anger of a parent, begin to lose their weight. Nothing can ease the situation now—but that I leave.

Miss Hardcastle: Then go, sir. I'll not detain you. Remember, though, that my family is as good as hers you came down to visit. And my education, I hope, is not inferior. But what are these things worth without an equal fortune? I must be content with only the sight of your back as you leave, while all your serious aims are fixed on fortune.

Sir Charles (*from behind*): Ah, what is this?

Hardcastle: Shhh, make no noise. I'll bet my Kate covers him with confusion at last.

Marlow: By the heavens, madam! Fortune was ever my smallest thought. Your beauty first caught my eye. Who could see that without emotion? Even now, every moment that I converse with you brings some new attraction.

Sir Charles: What can it mean? He amazes me!

Hardcastle: I told you how it would be. Hush.

Marlow (*with great self-confidence*): I am now determined to stay, madam. The fortune means nothing. And I think I know my father's taste in women. When he sees you, his approval is certain.

Miss Hardcastle: No, Mr. Marlow. I will not, I cannot detain you. How could I agree to a connection with the slightest room for doubt? How could I take advantage of a passing passion to load you with confusion? Do you think I could ever enjoy my own happiness by lessening yours?

Marlow: By all that's good, I can have no happiness but what's in your power to give me! I will stay, even against your wishes. And even if you shun me, my behavior will make up for the levity of my past conduct.

Miss Hardcastle: Sir, I must beg you to change your mind. As our acquaintance began, so let it end—with no strong attachment. Once, I might have given an hour or two to levity. But seriously, Mr. Marlow, do you think I could ever agree to a connection? What would people think? I might appear greedy for money, and you lacking in judgment.

Marlow (*kneeling*): Does this look like poor judgment? No, madam, your merit only increases my confidence that my judgment is—

Sir Charles (*coming from behind screen*): I can hold it no longer. Charles! How you have deceived me! Is this what you call uninteresting conversation?

Hardcastle: Your cold behavior! Your formal interview! What have you to say now?

Marlow: That I'm all amazement. What can this mean?

Hardcastle: It means that you can say and unsay things as you wish. That you can court a lady in private, and deny it in public. That you have one story for us, and another for my daughter!

Marlow: Daughter!—this lady, your daughter!

Hardcastle: Yes, sir, my only daughter, my Kate. Whose else should she be?

Marlow: Oh, the devil!

Miss Hardcastle: Yes, sir, the very same tall, squinting lady you were pleased to take me for. (*Curtsying*) She that you approached as the mild, shy, and serious man, and also as the bold, confident, Rattle of the Ladies Club, ha! ha! ha!

Marlow: I can't stand this. It's worse than death!

Miss Hardcastle: In which of your characters, sir, shall we now address you? As the gentleman who looks on the ground, speaks just to be heard, and hates hypocrisy? Or as the loud, confident creature that rattles away with Mrs. Mantrap and Miss Biddy Buckskin till three in the morning, ha! ha! ha!

Marlow: Oh, curse my noisy head. I must be gone.

Hardcastle: By the hand of my body, you shall not go! I see it was all a mistake, and I am happy to find it so. You shall not go, sir, I tell you. I know she'll forgive you. Won't you forgive him, Kate? We all forgive you. Take courage, man. (Marlow *and* Miss Hardcastle *retire, talking together, to the back of the scene.*)

(*Enter* Mrs. Hardcastle *and* Tony)

● levity (LEV i tee) lightness of mind; lack of seriousness

Mrs. Hardcastle: So, so, they've gone off. Let them go. I care not.

Hardcastle: Who gone?

Mrs. Hardcastle: My niece Constance and her gentleman, Mr. Hastings.

Sir Charles: Who? My honest George Hastings? As worthy a fellow as lives, and the girl could not have made a better choice.

Hardcastle: Then, by the hand of my body, I'm proud of the connection.

Mrs. Hardcastle: Well, if he has taken away the lady, he has not taken her fortune. That remains in this family to make up for her loss.

Hardcastle: Surely, Dorothy, you would not be so money-minded.

Mrs. Hardcastle: Aye, and that's my affair, not yours.

Hardcastle: But you know, if your son, when he comes of age, refuses to marry his cousin, her whole fortune is then her own.

Mrs. Hardcastle: Aye, but he's not of age, and Constance has not thought proper to wait for his refusal.

(*Enter* Hastings *and* Miss Neville)

Mrs. Hardcastle: What! Returned so soon? I begin not to like it.

Hastings (*to* Hardcastle): Sir, I regret my recent attempt to fly off with your niece. Let my present confusion be my punishment. We have now come back, to appeal to your justice and your humanity.

Miss Neville: In an hour of folly, I was even ready to give up my fortune to marry Mr. Hastings. But I'm now recovered, and appeal to your tenderness.

Mrs. Hardcastle: Oh, all this sounds like the whining end of a modern novel.

Hardcastle: Be it what it will, I'm glad they've come back to make things right. Come here, Tony, boy. Do you refuse to marry this lady I now offer you?

Tony: What means my refusing? You know I can't refuse her till I'm of legal age, Father.

Hardcastle: Boy, when I thought that hiding your age was likely to lead to your improvement, I agreed with your mother's desire to keep it a secret. But since I find she turns it to a wrong use, I must now declare that you have been of age for three months.

Tony: Of age? Am I of legal age, Father?

Hardcastle: More than three months.

Tony: Then you'll see the first use I make of my liberty. (*Taking* Miss Neville's *hand*) Witness all men, that I, Anthony Lumpkin, of BLANK place, now refuse you Constance Neville, of no place at all, for my true and lawful wife. So Constance Neville may marry whom she pleases, and Tony Lumpkin is his own man again!

Sir Charles: O brave young man!

Hastings: My worthy friend!

Mrs. Hardcastle: My undutiful child!

Marlow: Joy, my dear George, I give you joy sincerely. And if I could persuade my little tyrant here to now accept *me,* I would be the happiest man alive.

Hastings: (*to* Miss Hardcastle): Come, madam, you are now driven to the very last scene of all your play acting.

I know you love him. I'm sure he loves you. Now, you must and shall have him.

Hardcastle (*joining their hands as Miss Hardcastle smiles*): And I say so too. Mr. Marlow, if she makes as good a wife as she has a daughter, I don't believe you'll ever regret your bargain. So now to supper. Tomorrow we shall gather all the neighborhood together, and the Mistakes of the Night shall be crowned with a merry morning. So, boy, take her. And as you have been mistaken in the mistress, my wish is that you'll never be mistaken in the wife.

ALL THINGS CONSIDERED

1. "She Stoops to Conquer": in other words, _____ stoops to conquer _____ . (a) Constance Neville . . . George Hastings. (b) Kate Hardcastle . . . Charles Marlow. (c) Mrs. Hardcastle . . . Tony Lumpkin.

2. Constance Neville's journey to her Aunt Pedigree's (a) ends her plans for marriage. (b) turns out to end at home. (c) takes longer than planned.

3. When Charles Marlow drops to his knees and declares his love for Kate Hardcastle, he (a) knows who she really is. (b) thinks she's a poor relative of the Hardcastle's. (c) probably doesn't like her at all.

4. Tony Lumpkin's refusal to marry Constance Neville (a) disappoints her greatly. (b) pleases Mrs. Hardcastle. (c) clears the way for her to marry Hastings.

5. At the very end, when Charles Marlow and Kate Hardcastle join hands, (a) each has to forgive the other. (b) only she has to forgive him. (c) only he has to forgive her.

6. Most of "The Mistakes of the Night" are started by (a) Tony Lumpkin. (b) George Hastings. (c) Constance Neville.

7. The character who probably learns most from the changing situation is (a) Mr. Hardcastle. (b) Charles Marlow. (c) Constance Neville.

8. A character who is thoroughly honest throughout the play is (a) Tony Lumpkin. (b) Mrs. Hardcastle. (c) Mr. Hardcastle.

9. The play makes good use of (a) the flashback. (b) real historical characters. (c) mistaken identity.

10. Goldsmith's main purpose in writing the play seems to have been to (a) teach people the value of honesty. (b) have fun. (c) let future generations know what eighteenth-century life was like.

THINKING IT THROUGH

1. "She Stoops to Conquer" offers an actress one of the top roles in famous dramatic literature. (a) What is this part? (b) Why do you suppose it has long been a favorite for leading actresses to play?

2. Like many longer literary selections, this play contains a **subplot,** or a minor plot related in some way to the main plot. (a) If Kate Hardcastle and Marlow are the chief characters in the main plot, who are the two chief characters in the subplot? (b) In what ways are the subplot and the main plot the same? How are they different?

3. The introduction asked you to be alert for differences between Goldsmith's day and the present. Consider the language used. Give examples of (a) expressions that are no longer used today, and (b) words whose meanings seem to have changed somewhat.

4. What are some differences between eighteenth-century courtship and marriage as portrayed in the play and courtship and marriage today?

5. The most important difference involves social classes. Clearly, in eighteenth-century England there was a huge difference between ladies and gentlemen as one class of people and servants and other workers as another class. (a) How did people from these two classes talk to each other? (Think of Hardcastle and his servants at the beginning of Act II.) (b) How does Marlow's feeling about the "barmaid" begin to change when he learns she's educated and from a "good family"?

Reading and Analyzing

Making Predictions

Making **predictions,** or judgments about future events, is a reading skill that adds enjoyment to any reading experience. It makes reading a kind of game between writer and reader. The writer puts forth certain statements, happenings, and clues that the reader uses to predict what is going to happen. A good reader is constantly rewarded as many predictions come to pass.

To help the reader make reasonable predictions, authors often use a technique called **foreshadowing** so that certain *shadows* of possibility are cast before an event happens. For example, in just the third speech of the play, Mrs. Hardcastle happens to say that their mansion "looks for all the world like an inn." Later Tony directs Marlow and Hastings to the mansion as an inn. In this way Goldsmith foreshadows the likelihood that the two suitors will, in fact, mistake the house for an inn.

1. To accept the play as a series of events that might have really happened, the reader (or viewer) has to believe that Marlow sees no similarity between Kate Hardcastle and the "barmaid." How does Goldsmith foreshadow such an improbable happening so that it becomes a likely possibility? (Think about her clothing, her demonstrated acting ability, and Marlow's behavior with certain kinds of women.)

2. Although Kate Hardcastle mocks and embarrasses Marlow after he learns the whole truth, you can probably predict that she will accept him at the end. How is this final acceptance foreshadowed throughout the play?

3. In Act V, you learn of Mrs. Hardcastle's dishonesty about Tony's age. Explain how this is foreshadowed by the discussion of *her* age in Act I.

Composition

1. Summarize the main plot of the play in one or two sentences. Then summarize the subplot in one or two sentences.

2. Our country is a wonderful "melting pot" of many races and nationalities. "She Stoops to Conquer," of course, gives the background of only one of these groups—people with wealthy pre-Revolutionary British ancestors. What do you know of your own background? In a short paragraph, describe several differences, real or as you imagine them, between your life and that of an ancestor who lived a long time ago.

VOCABULARY AND SKILL REVIEW

Before completing the exercises that follow, you may wish to review the **bold-faced** words on pages 160 to 203.

I. On a separate sheet of paper, write the *italicized* term that best fills the blank in each sentence.

trivial	*squire*	*garrison*	*suitor*	*interpretation*
prediction	*garnet*	*foreshadowing*	*précis*	*discretion*

1. Good oral _____ makes reading plays more interesting.

2. A weather report is a _____ about the weather.

3. A _____ is a short summary of a literary selection.

4. In old England, a _____ usually owned a large house and had several servants.

5. A _____ often becomes a husband.

6. _____ is a technique authors use to hint about the future or to make future events more believable.

7. The lost ring contained a large red _____ .

8. At Fort Ticonderoga, Ethan Allen captured the British _____ .

9. People with _____ seldom get in needless trouble.

10. The newspaper article contained _____ items along with important facts.

II. A metaphor, you will remember, is a figure of speech in which one person or thing is compared to something else by saying that the one *is* the other. Here's a riddle that asks you to make a *prediction* about the speaker. Feel very proud of yourself if you can infer the answer before reading the questions that follow the poem.

METAPHORS

by Sylvia Plath (1932–1963)

I'm a riddle in nine syllables,
An elephant, a ponderous house,
A melon strolling on two tendrils.
O red fruit, ivory, fine timbers!
This loaf's big with its yeasty rising.
Money's new-minted in this fat purse.
I'm a means, a stage, a cow in calf.
I've eaten a bag of green apples,
Boarded the train there's no getting off.

A. Here are the clues. Think about each one before going on to the next.

1. Count the "nine syllables" in the first line. (a) Does every line have nine syllables? (b) What "special" event in some people's lives involves nine _____ ?

2. (a) How many lines are in the poem? (b) Again, does this clue confirm your prediction?

3. Think about the words "ponderous," "big," and "fat." During what special time might these words fit a particular person's body?

4. (a) How does eating "a bag of green apples" make a person feel? (b) What other cause might make certain people feel the same way?

5. Here's the last clue. A "cow in calf" means a cow (not a bull) carrying a calf. What is your prediction?

B. Reread the poem. Choose five lines that you think create strong visual images. Explain how each line is a good metaphor for the speaker's condition.

- ponderous (PAHN dur us) **heavy; cumbersome and awkward**
- tendril (TEN dril) **part of climbing plant that attaches itself to something and supports the plant**

UNIT REVIEW

I. Match the terms in Column A with their definitions in Column B.

A	**B**
1. précis	a) reading aloud with expression
2. image	b) short summary of a literary selection
3. alliteration	c) told by author/narrator who keeps out of story
4. metaphor	d) involving the storyteller as the ``I/me'' character
5. prediction	e) repetition of consonant sounds
6. point of view	f) viewpoint or position from which story is told
7. first person	g) a vivid sensory impression
8. third person	h) providing hints or clues about the future
9. foreshadowing	i) judgment about what is going to happen
10. oral interpretation	j) a figure of speech

II. This unit has stressed two key words: *time* and *change.* You have read about characters who learn—or fail to learn—that change is an unavoidable fact of life. Think about the selections listed below. Pick five of them that you remember well. Then state what the character experienced about time and change. Example: "When I Was One-and-Twenty": A proud, self-assured young man learns that falling in love can lead to a painful experience.

"The Manuscript of Dr. Arness" (story)
"April" (story)
"Ozymandias" (poem)
"New Face" (poem)
"The 1st" (poem)
"Black Hair" (poem)
"Grandmother, Rocking" (poem)
"Daffodils" (poem)
"She Stoops to Conquer" (play)
"Metaphors" (poem)

206

SPEAKING UP

Oral Interpretation of a Poem

Look back at the poems in this unit and choose one of them. (If you prefer, you may select a poem from a book of poetry.) Then follow the guidelines below to prepare for reading the poem aloud to the class.

1. First of all, copy the poem onto a piece of paper.
2. Read through the poem to make sure you can pronounce all the words correctly.
3. Read the poem again, looking for natural phrasing or groups of words that seem to go together. Separate the phrases into groups by inserting a slash mark, as shown below. (Use two slash marks to indicate where you want to pause longer to catch your breath.)

> In the bleachers/ I was brilliant with my body,//
> Waving players in/ and stomping my feet, . . .

4. Which words should be emphasized? Look for the words that help to convey meaning. Underline those words and remember to emphasize them.

> In the <u>bleachers</u> I was <u>brilliant</u> with my <u>body</u>,
> <u>Waving</u> <u>players</u> in and <u>stomping</u> my feet, . . .

5. Although you don't need to memorize your poem, you will need to be thoroughly familiar with it. After you have prepared your poem for reading, practice it many times.
6. Stand with your weight balanced on both feet. Hold your paper so that you can read the poem easily. Be sure that you can see your audience. Also decide on the appropriate tone. Do you want to show excitement, dignity, horror, sympathy, or some other tone? Do a few final practice readings in front of a mirror. Pay special attention to your body language.
7. The day before you read your poem to the class, find a sympathetic critic listener. Read your selected poem to that person. Ask your listener for suggestions to help you improve your presentation.

As an extension of this activity, write an original poem. Then proceed through the steps in the guidelines in preparation for reading your own poetic creation to the class.

WRITING ABOUT CHARACTERS

Prewriting

1. Fold a sheet of notebook paper lengthwise. In the middle of the left side of the sheet, write *April.* In the middle of the right side, write *Martha Dunning.*

2. Reread the short story "April." As you read, jot down any facts that you are given about April and Martha Dunning.

   a. As you begin to list items, you may place them *anywhere* on the proper side of the sheet.

   b. As you find additional items that belong to a certain category, list them close by. This is called **clustering.** For example, you might list all items pertaining to the physical description of April in one bunch, or cluster.

After reading the first few pages, one half of your clustering sheet might look something like this:

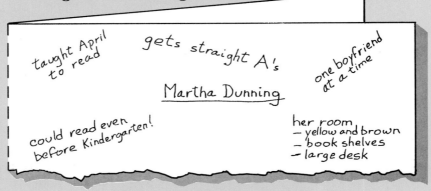

3. *Sorting your information:* Take a separate sheet of lined paper and fold it in half lengthwise. Head the left side *April* and the right side *Martha Dunning.* Look at your "cluster sheet." Find parallel items (those on the same topic) for both April and Martha Dunning. List the first parallel facts as #1 in both columns. Your list should consist of items of similarities as well as of differences. Your list might begin like the one below.

April	*Martha Dunning*
1. Gets C's and D's in school	1. Gets straight A's
2. Has droves of boyfriends	2. Has one boyfriend at a time

4. Reread your list. In front of each number write either "S" for similarity or "D" for difference.

Writing

1. First, write a topic sentence about the two sisters. State the topic clearly and tell exactly what you are going to explain in your paragraph. A sample topic sentence is: *The story "April" is about two sisters who are similar in some ways but quite different in other ways.*

2. To make the work of writing your paragraph easier, try to start with any similarities you found in the two characters. You might start sentences containing similarities with *Both, Another similarity between,* or other words and phrases that let the reader know you are about to make a comparison.

3. After showing comparisons, move on to the contrasts. What are the most important differences you found? Try to cover each difference in one complete sentence.

4. In order to make your paragraph read as clearly as possible, begin each comparison and each contrast with the same story character.

5. Write a concluding sentence summarizing the main point of your paragraph and giving a finished feeling. This sentence should let the reader know the paragraph has been completed without coming out and saying "The End."

Revising

1. Look at your topic sentence. Does it really indicate what the rest of the paragraph is to be about? If not, revise it.

2. Read through your paragraph. Where the subject matter is not completely clear, a transition word or phrase may help. The following transition words and phrases are useful to introduce sentences showing contrasts.

however	even though	in contrast
although	in spite of	unlike

A word of caution: Only use transitional words when you need to make your writing clearer.

3. Read over your concluding sentence. Does it summarize the main point of your paragraph? That is, does it include the information from your topic sentence? Does it give a finished feeling to your paragraph?

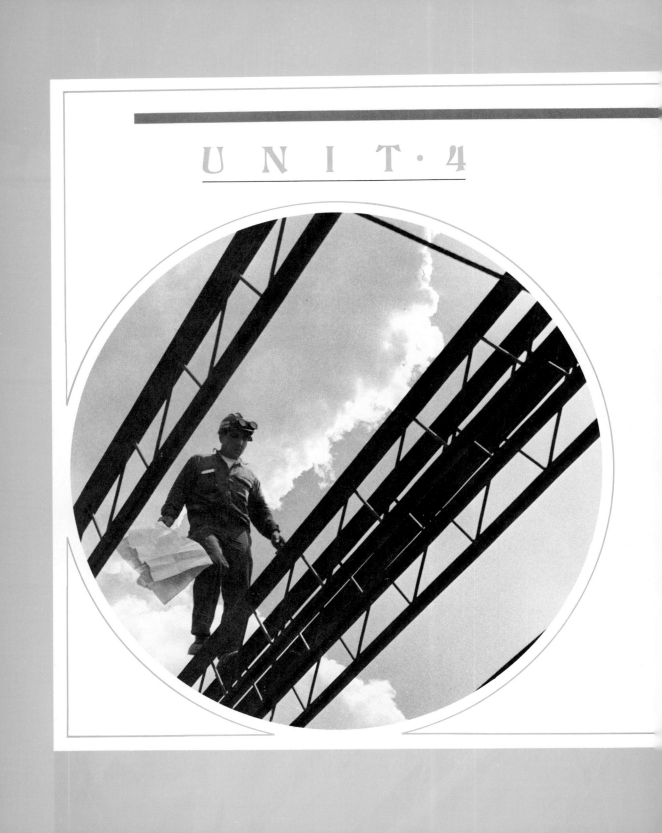

U N I T · 4

SOME MATTERS

OF

JUDGMENT

There's a big difference between intelligence and the ability to make good judgments. Thousands of bright people, after all, are now behind bars. They failed to make their most critical decisions in the right way. It's clear that if critical thinking is to help a person, it must involve not only reasoning but sound judgment.

When faced with a decision, one must put each possible solution to two tests: (1) How well will it work? (2) Is it the right thing to do? The second question is often harder to answer than the first, for it involves a whole series of related questions. Is it fair to others? Would it be fair to myself? Will it solve one problem but create another one? Is it a temporary solution or will it last?

As you read the selections that follow, think about the ways the characters make judgments that affect themselves and others. You'll have an opportunity to judge Shakespeares's Macbeth as a decision-maker. Selections from Africa, China, Russia, and other places show the hard decisions that people sometimes face. You be the judge of the winners.

HEAVEN AND HELL

by Isabelle C. Chang

▶ Folktales often reveal the basic common sense of the ordinary people who first told them. Here's a folk tale from China with a **moral**, or lesson, to be drawn from it.

A Chinese angel visited hell. He saw many people seated around a table covered with delicious food of every description. Beside each person was a pair of yard-long chopsticks. But everyone there was wasting away with starvation, because no one was able to manipulate the clumsy chopsticks adequately to feed himself.

Then the angel went to visit heaven. There he saw another table piled with all kinds of wholesome, delicious food. Each person seated around the table was also provided with yard-long chopsticks. These people were happy and contented. They were feeding each other across the table with their yard-long chopsticks.

The difference between heaven and hell is the people.

1. The difference is the people, of course. In exactly what way are the two groups of people who are mentioned different?
2. In your judgment, what single word or short phrase best sums up the meaning of this folktale?

THE POT OF GOLD

by Salvador Salazar Arrué

▶ Here's a folktale from Central America. The author is a native of El Salvador who lived for years in the United States. The story itself is far from a happy one, but its meaning can help bring happiness to the thoughtful reader.

José Pashaca was a body that had been tossed into a skin; the skin was a skin that had been tossed into a shanty; the shanty was a *rancho* tossed on to the side of a hill.

Petrona Pulunto was the mother of that mouth.

"Son, open your eyes; I've even forgot what color they are."

José Pashaca wriggled and sometimes even stretched a leg.

"What you want, Mamma?"

"Son, you've got to find some work to do. You're just bone-lazy."

But the good-for-nothing showed a slight improvement; from sleeping he took to sitting around, frowning, yawning.

One day Ulogio Isho came by with a thing he had found. It was of stone, shaped like a toad, which he had turned up while plowing. It had a chain of round pebbles about its neck and three holes in its head, one for the mouth and two for the eyes.

"Did you ever see anything so ugly? It looks just like one-eyed Cande," he said with a guffaw.

And he left it for María Elena's children to play with.

But two days later old Bashuto happened by, and when he saw the toad, he said:

"These things were made a long time ago in the days of our grandparents. You bring up a lot of them plowing. And pots of gold too."

José Pashaca deigned to wrinkle the skin between his eyes, where other people have their forehead.

"What's that you say, *Ño* Bashuto?"

Bashuto took his homemade cigar out of his mouth and spat noisily and far.

"Just luck, my boy. You're going along plowing, and all of a sudden—*ploc osh*—you turn up a buried pot. And there you are, rich as cream."

- ● rancho (RAHN choh) **Spanish for farm or ranch**
- ● guffaw (guh FAW) **loud laugh**
- ● deign (DAYN) **agree to as a favor**
- ● Ño (NYO) **probably short for señor (Mr.)**

213

"No! You mean it, *Ño* Bashuto?"

"Just as sure as I'm sitting here."

Bashuto dragged at his cigar again with all the strength of his wrinkles, and became a cloud of smoke. Why, he'd seen people find pots of gold a thousand times, with his very own eyes. When he left, he left without realizing that he had scattered the seeds of what he had said behind him.

It so happened that about this time Petrona Pulunto died. José lifted up his mouth and carried it all around the neighborhood without any nutritive results. He lived on bananas he managed to steal, and decided he would look for buried pots of gold. To accomplish this, he got behind the tail of a plow and pushed. Both his eyes and the plowshare furrowed the earth. It was thus that José Pashaca became at one and the same time the laziest and the hardest-working person in the whole neighborhood. He worked without working, at least without realizing that he was working, and he worked so much that the colored hours always found him with his eyes on the furrow and his hands on the plow handle.

Like a louse of the hillside, he crawled up and down the black loam, always gazing so intently at the ground that it seemed he was planting his very soul in the soil. To be sure, nothing but laziness would have come up, because Pashaca knew he was the most worthless person in the valley. He was not working. He was looking for pots full of golden coins which went *plocosh* when the plow hit against them and vomited forth silver and gold.

As he grew, so did his obsession. Ambition more than hunger had straightened him up in his skin, and drove him to the slopes of the hills, where he plowed and plowed.

Pashaca shaved the hillsides clean. The *patrón,* awed by the miracle that had turned José into the best renter he had, gladly gave him all the land he wanted. And the renter, musing on the buried treasure, furrowed the earth with eye ever alert to inform the eager heart waiting for the pot of gold like an enchanted carpet on which it should find its rest.

And Pashaca had to plant the fields, because the owner demanded his share. And for the same reason Pashaca had to harvest and sell the grain of his bountiful crops, carelessly tucking the money into a hole in the floor of the house, "just in case."

- **nutritive** (NOO tri tiv) healthful (of food); nourishing
- plowshare (PLOU shair) blade of a plow
- **obsession** (ub SESH un) overpowering desire or idea
- patrón (pah TRON) Spanish for landowner
- awed (AWD) amazed; overcome
- musing (MYOOZ ing) thinking; dreaming
- **bountiful** (BOUN tuh ful) plentiful; abundant

There was not another renter the equal of José. "He's made of iron," people said. "Look how he settled down once he set his heart on earning money. He must have a nice little pile laid by."

But José Pashaca never realized that he had a nice little pile. What he was looking for was that pot of gold, and as they were said to be buried in the fields, sooner or later he'd find it.

He had not only become a hard worker; in his neighbors' opinion he had even become generous. On days when he had no land of his own to plow, he helped out the others, telling them to go off and rest and he'd do their plowing. And he did a good job; his furrows were always so straight and deep it was a pleasure to look at them.

"Now, where the devil are you hiding?" he muttered to himself, refusing to give up. "I'm going to find you, whether you like it or not, even if I kill myself in these furrows."

And that was just what happened. Not that he found the buried treasure, but that he killed himself.

One day, at the hour when the sky turns a tender green and the rivers are white stripes upon the plains, José Pashaca realized that for him there would be no pots of gold. His first warning was a fainting spell; he fell forward over the plow handle, and the oxen came to a halt as though the plowshare had caught in the roots of darkness.

José Pashaca was a sick man. But he did not want anyone to look after him. Ever since Petrona died, he had lived all by his lone.

One night, gathering up his little strength, he slipped out of the house, carrying all his money in an old jug. With his grubbing machete he began to dig a hole, slinking behind the bushes when-

---

- grubbing (GRUB ing) **digging; clearing land of roots, stumps, and so on**
- **machete** (muh SHET ee) **kind of large knife**

ever he heard a noise. Every now and then he had to stop because of the pain, but then he would go back to work with renewed zeal. He set the pot in the hole, covered it carefully, patted down the dirt over it, and effaced all traces of his digging. Then raising his arms, aged before their time, to the stars, he uttered these words swathed in a deep sigh:

"Now nobody can say there are no more pots of gold to be found in the fields."

ALL THINGS CONSIDERED

1. In the first half of the story, José Pashaca changes from (a) stupid to intelligent. (b) lazy to hard working. (c) generous to selfish.
2. Pashaca differs from other workers in that he (a) gives his money to the poor. (b) refuses to work on religious days. (c) does not work mainly for the money received.
3. At the end, Pashaca (a) finds his pot of gold. (b) decides that wealth is not a good aim in life. (c) buries his money.
4. It is *most* accurate to say that Pashaca (a) works himself to death. (b) commits suicide. (c) dies as a result of his disappointment.
5. The "pot of gold" symbolizes (a) a carefully considered goal. (b) the rewards of hard work. (c) unexpected good fortune.

THINKING IT THROUGH

1. The ending of the story can be interpreted in several ways: (1) Pashaca hides his money so that he can prove to the world that at least one "pot of gold" exists. (2) Pashaca places the money so that another person, more fortunate than he, will find it. Which interpretation of the story do you accept? Tell why. (If you have another interpretation, explain why you think it is so.)
2. What defects in Pashaca's character lead to the tragic ending? Try to name at least two.
3. The introduction stated that the story's message "can help bring happiness to the thoughtful reader." What advice concerning good judgment can you draw from the story?

- **zeal** (ZEEL) eager desire
- efface (i FAYS) wipe out; do away with
- **swathed** (SWAHTHD) wrapped

Literary Skills

Figurative Language in Prose

Figurative language is language that does not really mean what it seems to say. Poetry is often rich in figurative language. *Simile* (page 39) and *metaphor* (page 162) are often found in poetry. If you do not remember what these terms mean, go back and review them now.

Because similes and metaphors are often studied along with poetry, students often forget that prose, too, can *sparkle* with figurative language or figurative expressions. Think, for instance, about the very first sentence of "Pot of Gold." Of course, a "body" cannot really be "tossed into a skin." Neither is a human skin "tossed" into a shanty, or a farm on a hillside. The author is using figurative language to suggest that there is some accidental quality about life that has resulted in Pashaca's circumstances.

Here are five figurative expressions from the story. In each case, (a) tell whether the item is a simile or metaphor, and (b) explain how the figurative lan-

guage adds excitement or interest to the underlying real meaning.

1. Bashuto left without knowing that he had "scattered the seeds of what he had said behind him."

2. (Of Pashaca) "Both his eyes and the plowshare furrowed the earth."

3. Pashaca worked "like a louse of the hillside."

4. People said that Pashaca was "made of iron."

5. The oxen stopped "as though the plowshare had caught in the roots of darkness."

Some figurative expressions are new and fresh; others have been used many, many times. An overworked figurative expression is called a **cliché** (klee SHAY). In your opinion, can any of the five figurative expressions above be called a cliché? If so, explain.

Composition

1. The following are clichés. Change at least three of them into fresh figurative expressions by substituting your own words for the italicized parts. Example: happy *as a lark* could become *happy as an escaped balloon in a spring breeze.*
   a) dead as *a doornail*
   b) slow as *molasses in January*
   c) fresh as *a cucumber*
   d) dry as *a bone*
   e) thin as *a rail*

2. Find two more examples of figurative language in the story. Copy them on your paper. Then explain why the author might have used the figurative expression rather than plain language.

217

RED

by Yevgeny Yevtushenko

▶ In this short autobiographical selection, a well-known Russian poet tells how he felt forced to fight his own private battle while still a teenager during World War II. The young Yevtushenko's decision now becomes a matter for your own judgment.

In 1944 I was living alone in an empty apartment in a small quiet Moscow street, Chetvertaya Meshchanskaya.

My parents were divorced. My father was somewhere in Kazakhstan* with his new wife and their two children. I seldom received letters from him.

My mother was at the front. She had given up her work as a geologist to become a singer and was giving concerts for the troops.

My education was left to the street. The street taught me to swear, smoke, spit elegantly through my teeth, and to keep my fists up, always ready for a fight—a habit that I have kept to this day.

The street taught me not to be afraid of anything or anyone—this is another habit I have kept.

I realized that what mattered in the struggle for existence was to overcome my fear of those who were stronger.

The ruler of our street, Chetvertaya Meshchanskaya, was a boy of about sixteen who was nicknamed Red.

Red's shoulders were incredibly broad for a boy of his age.

Red walked masterfully up and down our street, his legs wide apart and with a slightly rolling gait, like a seaman on the deck of his ship.

From under his peaked cap, always worn back to front, his forelock tumbled down in a fiery cascade, and out of his round pockmarked face, green eyes, like a cat's, sparkled with scorn for everything and everyone crossing his path. Two or three lieutenants, in peaked caps back to front like Red's, trotted at his heels.

- **gait** (GAYT) manner of walking
- **forelock** (FOHR lok) lock of hair just above the forehead
- **cascade** (kas KAYD) something falling like a waterfall
- pockmarked (PAHK markt) scarred with small pits

*Kazakhstan (kah zahk STAHN) a southeastern republic of the Soviet Union bordering on China

Red could stop any boy and say impressively the one word "money." His lieutenants would turn out the boy's pockets, and if he resisted they gave him a real beating.

Everyone was afraid of Red. I too was afraid. I knew he carried heavy brass knuckles in his pocket.

I wanted to conquer my fear of Red.

So I wrote a poem about him.

This was my first piece of journalism in verse.

By the next day the whole street knew the piece by heart and relished it with triumphant hatred.

One morning on my way to school I suddenly came upon Red and his lieutenants. His eyes seemed to bore through me. "Ah, the poet," he drawled, smiling crookedly. "So you write verses. Do they rhyme?"

Red's hand darted into his pocket and came out armed with its brass knuckles; it flashed like lightning and struck my head. I fell down streaming with blood and lost consciousness.

This was my first payment as a poet.

I spent several days in bed.

When I went out, with my head still bandaged, I again saw Red. I struggled with instinctive fear but lost and took to my heels.

I ran all the way home. There I rolled on my bed, biting my pillow and pounding it with my fists in shame and impotent fury at my cowardice.

But then I made up my mind to vanquish it at whatever cost.

I went into training with parallel bars and weights, and after every session I would feel my muscles. They were getting harder, but slowly. Then I remembered something I had read in a book about a miraculous Japanese method of wrestling that gave an advantage to the weak over the strong. I sacrificed a week's ration card for a textbook on jujitsu.

For three weeks I hardly left home—I trained with two other boys. Finally I felt I was ready and went out.

Red was sitting on the lawn in our yard, playing Twenty-one with his lieutenants. He was absorbed in the game.

Fear was still in me and it ordered me to turn back. But I went up to the players and kicked the cards aside with my foot.

Red looked up, surprised at my impudence after my recent flight.

He got up slowly. "You looking for more?" he asked menacingly.

- **instinctive** (in STINGK tiv) **natural; not learned**
- impotent (IM poh tunt) **powerless; weak**
- **vanquish** (VANG kwish) **overcome; defeat**
- Twenty-one—**card game like blackjack**
- impudence (IM pyoo duns) **rudeness**

As before, his hand dived into his pocket for the brass knuckles. But I made a quick jabbing movement, and Red, howling with pain, rolled on the ground. Bewildered, he got up and came at me, swinging his head furiously from side to side like a bull.

I caught his wrist and squeezed slowly, as I had read in the book, until the brass knuckles dropped from his limp fingers. Nursing his hand, Red fell down again. He was sobbing and smearing the tears over his pockmarked face with his grimy fist. His lieutenants discreetly withdrew.

That day Red ceased to rule our street.

And from that day on I knew for certain that there is no need to fear the strong. All one needs is to know the method of overcoming them. There is a special jujitsu for every strong man.

What I also learned that day was that, if I wished to be a poet, I must not only write poems but also know how to stand up for what I have written.

● discreetly (dis KREET lee) **with wise caution**

ALL THINGS CONSIDERED

1. Early in the selection, Yevtushenko states that during the time described he got his education (a) from his parents. (b) in a high school for the gifted. (c) in the streets.

2. The poet's "first piece of journalism in verse" was (a) on World War II. (b) an angry letter to Red. (c) a poem about Red.

3. The first fight ended in (a) a quick victory for Red. (b) no real victor. (c) a well-planned victory for the author/narrator.

4. The second fight ended in (a) a quick victory for Red. (b) no real victor. (c) a well-planned victory for the author/narrator.

5. At the end, the author/narrator says that the experience taught him (a) to dislike most people. (b) to stand up for what he has written. (c) the wisdom of running away.

THINKING IT THROUGH

1. Which was actually harder for the author/narrator, overcoming his fear of Red or the fight itself?

2. What did Yevtushenko do to help overcome his fear?

3. Poets are sometimes *stereotyped* (see page 94) as rather shy, timid people. Does the selection support the stereotype or does it show the stereotype to be false? Explain.

4. Near the end, the author writes, "There is a special jujitsu for every strong man." In your opinion, what is the *figurative meaning* (see page 217) of this sentence?

5. What is *your* judgment of Yevtushenko's decision as revealed in the selection? That is, did Yevtushenko do the right thing as a teenager in 1944? Whether your answer is *yes* or *no*, explain it fully, justifying the poet's actions or showing how they were wrong.

Critical Thinking

Cause and Effect

"A **cause** is an event or idea that leads to a certain result, which is called an **effect.**"

Definitions like this one are common. The only trouble is that in the real world, things aren't quite so simple. Just consider this "simple" question: *What causes you to be sitting in this particular room right now reading this particular book?*

You might say, "The government, because it requires young people to go to school"—but that is hardly the only cause. Why *this* room and not another or why *this* book and not another? The questions could go on and on. Why *this* copy of the book and not your friend's? Why *right now* instead of yesterday? Why, even, in a school in *this* city and not another?

Your mental maps should not always link single causes to single effects because that's not always the way cause and effect are related in the real world.

It's better to consider that nearly every result (effect) may have had several causes. Also, every cause leads to more than one effect.

What causes the second fight between the author/narrator and Red? Try to think of at least five causes. In forming your answers, ask yourself some questions, including these: *Would the fight have happened—*

(a) *if a horrible war had not left civilians largely on their own, with little police protection?*

(b) *if the narrator and Red had lived normal family lives?*

(c) *if education had come from the school, not the street?*

(d) *if the narrator had not wanted to master his fear?*

(e) *if the narrator had not trained himself?*

(f) *if Red had been smart enough to foresee his own defeat?*

Composition

1. Items (a) through (f) above suggest causes for a certain effect. But note that each of these causes could have had other effects as well. Choose (a), (c), or (e), and explain two other possible effects. If you choose (a), for example, you might begin your answer this way: *If a horrible war had*

not left civilians on their own with little police protection, . . .

2. Turn back to page 21 and reread the fallacy of logic called "After the fact, therefore because of the fact." Then explain this fallacy in terms of *cause and effect.* If you can, include an original example.

William Shakespeare (1564-1616)

The Globe Theater—home of Shakespeare's theatrical company

William Shakespeare was probably the greatest writer ever to use the English language. He left 37 plays and a book of poems. Unfortunately, he wrote almost nothing about his own life, and what little we know comes from sketchy 400-year-old official records and the writings of a few friends.

Shakespeare was born in Stratford, England, in April, 1564. His father, a glove maker, was an active town leader. The boy probably went to the free local school, but nothing is known for sure about his education. Records show that at 18 he married Anne Hathaway, a woman of 26. The births of three children are recorded. The next facts about Shakespeare's life come from London. He is referred to as an actor in 1592, and soon after as a playwright. He was also part owner of the theater company with which he worked. His plays were popular, and about 1612 he retired to Stratford a wealthy man. In the words of his friends, he was "handsome," "open and free," "very good company," and "gentle"—but "a poor speller."

Shakespeare usually wrote in **blank verse,** or unrhymed poetry with five strong vocal stresses per line. Although he wrote for the common playgoer, his language is sometimes hard for the reader of today to understand. This is because English is in a constant process of change.

In the play that follows, you'll read words like *ere, withal,* and *on's,* all common in Shakespeare's time. (On the other hand, many of our most-used words, including *its,* were not used by Shakespeare.) In spite of the change in language, however, many words and expressions invented by Shakespeare live on in our everyday speech: "flaming youth," "method in his madness," "an itching palm," "a fool's paradise," "cold comfort," "out of the question," "a spotless reputation," and even "it was Greek to me."

THE MACBETH EXPERIENCE

from the tragedy by William Shakespeare

> ▶ By employing your imagination, try to go back in time—way, way back to the year 1606. Imagine yourself on your way to the bustling city of London, England. You've decided that you're old enough to travel a hundred miles from the country area to visit the wicked yet wonderful city of London.

Upon arrival at the inn, you learn that one of the things to do is to visit the famous Globe Theater. "The Globe's on the opposite bank of the Thames River," the innkeeper tells you. He adds, with a laugh, "You see, playhouses and actors are considered rather sinful, so they're not allowed in the city of London itself."

You set out right after lunch. You stroll across London Bridge, crowded on both sides with shops and merchants hawking their wares. Then you turn right, and it's only a short walk to the Globe. You can't mistake the building—a tall, wooden, eight-sided structure. Above its thatched roof, a flag signals that this is a play day. As you draw near, a sign announces _The Tragedie of Macbeth,_ a new play by William Shakespeare. The play must be popular, you believe, for you have to wait in line to pay and enter.

Once inside, you look around in wonder. The center of the theater is open to the sky. ("Of course!" you think. "How else could such a large area be lit up with safety?") Three of the eight sides form a kind of stage. The two outside portions of this stage are similar, walls with doors and balconies above. ("Behind the doors, the dressing rooms? Where else?") The center of the stage is backed by a curtain, which, you realize, can be pulled aside for a setting such as a small room or a cave. There is no painted scenery, and a large platform stage juts out into the area where you are standing.

You are standing since there are no seats for most of the audience. By this time, the area around the platform stage is crowded with "groundlings," milling about, talking, and laughing as they wait for the play to start. The people who do have seats sit in tiers of narrow platforms against the walls. Those people look well dressed and rich. You go on standing there, jostled by the impatient crowd. What will the play be about? You remember only that Macbeth was a Scottish lord sometime in the dim, dark past. You _think_ you remember that he became

- hawking (HAWK ing) **trying to sell**
- **jut** (JUT) **stick out; extend**
- **milling** (MIL ing) **moving aimlessly**
- jostle (JOS ul) **push roughly**

King of Scotland by murdering the previous king. "Was his name Duncan? And how will the play get started? There are no house lights to lower, no curtain to rise."

Suddenly, you know. From offstage come roll after roll of thunder. ("Drums," you realize, "but very well done.") Then a jet of steam or smoke clouds one side of the stage. In it appear three creatures that look like women, except that they have beards. They have withered faces and are dressed like witches. Yes—they *are* witches!

First Witch: When shall we three meet again
        In thunder, lightning, or in rain?
Second Witch: When the hurlyburly's done
        When the battle's lost and won.
Third Witch: That will be ere set of sun.
First Witch: Where the place?
Second Witch: Upon the heath.
Third Witch: There to meet with Macbeth.
All: Fair is foul, and foul is fair;
        Hover through the fog and filthy air.

The witches leave, and as the smoke drifts up and away, the next scene starts almost at once. King Duncan, his son Malcolm, and a group of soldiers enter. Now you learn about the battle mentioned by the witches. A rebellion has just been put down. The rebellious Thane of Cawdor has just been defeated in battle by two of King Duncan's loyal lords, Macbeth (Thane of Glamis) and a general named Banquo. Macbeth, it seems, has fought most valiantly. In gratitude, King Duncan orders that the title Thane of Cawdor now be given to Macbeth.

More thunder, more smoke, and the scene shifts back to the witches on the heath:

First Witch: Where hast thou been, sister?
Second Witch: Killing swine.
Third Witch: Sister, where thou?
First Witch: Here I have a pilot's thumb,
        Wrecked as homeward he did come.
Third Witch: A drum, a drum!
        Macbeth doth come.

(*Enter* Macbeth *and* Banquo)

- **hurlyburly** (HUR lee BUR lee) **uproar; confusion; (as used here) the battle**
- ere (AIR) **before**
- heath (HEETH) **area of open wasteland**
- thane (THAYN) **rank of high noble in old Scotland**
- pilot—**(as used here) any guide or leader**

Macbeth (*entering into smoke*): So foul and fair a day I have
    not seen.
Banquo (*seeing witches*): What are these,
    So withered, and so wild in their attire,
    That look not like th' inhabitants o' th' earth,
    And yet are on't? You should be women,
    And yet your beards forbid me to interpret
    That you are so.
Macbeth: Speak if you can. What are you?
First Witch: All hail Macbeth, hail to thee, Thane of Glamis!
Second Witch: All hail Macbeth, hail to thee, Thane of Cawdor!
Third Witch: All hail Macbeth, that shalt be King hereafter.

Both Macbeth and Banquo are amazed at these prophecies. Macbeth, long the Thane of Glamis, has yet had no way to learn that he's just been named Thane of Cawdor, too. And as for being "King hereafter," Macbeth can only marvel at the news.

Banquo then asks the witches what is in store for him. He learns that although he himself will not be the king, he shall be the father of a king. The witches vanish. Macbeth and Banquo start to discuss the prophecies when a messenger from King Duncan arrives. Now Macbeth learns that he has, in fact, been named Thane of Cawdor.

Thane of Cawdor! So the witches told the truth! At first, Macbeth finds himself speechless. Might the prediction of the third witch also come true? Might Macbeth soon find himself king? He becomes obsessed with the thought. He hardly listens to Banquo's warning that "the instruments of darkness tell us truths, win us with honest trifles, only to betray us when it comes to more important matters." He resolves to stop at nothing on his path to the crown. Sending the news ahead to his wife by speedy messenger, he proceeds to his castle at Dunsinane.

Lady Macbeth is overjoyed at the news. Her husband a king! And herself a queen! Yet she has one worry:

Glamis thou art, and Cawdor, and shalt be
What thou art promised; yet I do fear thy nature,
It is too full o' th' milk of human kindness
To catch the nearest way.

To Lady Macbeth, "the nearest way" means only one thing: the murder of King Duncan. Even before Macbeth arrives, she works herself into a state of frenzy on the subject:

- **attire** (uh TYR) **clothing**
- **obsessed** (ahb SEST) **dominated; completely ruled in thought and feeling**
- **frenzy** (FREN zee) **wild excitement**

> Come thick night,
> That my keen knife see not the wound it makes,
> Nor heaven peep through the blanket of the dark,
> To cry, hold, hold!

Macbeth then arrives—with more startling news. The king himself is following on his heels, to honor him with an overnight visit. Lady Macbeth's eyes gleam with evil. She declares that King Duncan "never shall sun tomorrow see." Further, she advises her husband to carry "welcome in your eye, your hand, your tongue; look like th' innocent flower, but be the serpent under 't." Seeing that Macbeth is undecided, she tells him that all he has to do is act like an untroubled host: "Leave all the rest to me."

When the good and gentle Duncan arrives, however, Macbeth realizes that he cannot go through with his wife's plan:

> He's here in double trust;
> First, I am his kinsman, and his subject,
> Strong both against the deed; then, as his host,
> Who should against his murderer shut the door,
> Not bear the knife myself.

But Lady Macbeth has no patience for such talk. She calls her husband a coward. She pours into his ears reason after reason for proceeding with the murder. Why, the action of just one short night will give all their nights and days the sway and power of royalty! And the deed can be done so easily! For protection, two of Duncan's grooms always sleep in his room. All she has to do is to give these two servants enough drugged wine to ensure a "swinish sleep."

Macbeth, better than his wife, knows the risks involved. He knows that King Duncan is so fine a man that his subjects will spare no effort to revenge his murder. He knows, too, that he himself has attained his present place only through Duncan's trust. Yet he cannot resist the pull of his own powerful ambition and the pleas of his wife. Suddenly he finds himself part of the plot. Won't people think, he asks, "when we have marked with blood those sleepy two of his own chamber, and used their very daggers, that they have done't?"

Suspense heightens as the hours drive on toward the murder. Much care is needed: Macbeth knows that the King's son, Malcolm, is also sleeping within his walls. The plan must wait till all is quiet. Then Banquo and his son Fleance arrive unexpectedly. They must be greeted and shown to bed. Macbeth and his wife agree that when everyone seems asleep, she will ring a little bell. That will be the signal.

When silence finally falls upon the castle, Macbeth slowly steals through the dark toward Duncan's room. But suddenly he stops, alarmed. Seemingly suspended in the air ahead of him is a shining, ghostly object.

Is this a dagger which I see before me,
The handle toward my hand? Come let me clutch thee.
I have thee not, and yet I see thee still.
Art thou not, fatal vision, sensible
To feeling as to sight? Or art thou but
A dagger of the mind, a false creation,
Proceeding from a heat-oppressed brain?
  (A bell rings in the distance.)
I go, and it is done. The bell invites me.
Hear it not Duncan, for it is a knell
That summons thee to heaven, or to hell.

As Macbeth leaves the stage, you, along with the rest of the audience, await the next scene: the murder. But this is not to be. Instead, the setting shifts to Lady Macbeth's room. She is nervously awaiting Macbeth's return.

Macbeth (*off stage*): Who's there? What ho!
Lady Macbeth: Alack, I am afraid they have awakened,
  And 'tis not done. Th' attempt, and not the deed,
  Confounds us. Hark! I laid their daggers ready,
  He could not miss 'em.—Had he not resembled
  My father as he slept, I had done't.
    (*Macbeth enters, carrying bloody daggers.*)
                                        My husband!
Macbeth: I have done the deed. (*Looks at his hands.*)
  This is a sorry sight.
Lady Macbeth: These deeds must not be thought
  After these ways; so, it will make us mad.
Macbeth: Methought I heard a voice cry, sleep no more.
  Macbeth does murder sleep, the innocent sleep,
  Sleep that knits up the ravelled sleave of care,
  The death of each day's life, sore labor's bath,
  Balm of hurt minds, great nature's second course,
  Chief nourisher of life's feast.
Lady Macbeth: What do you mean?

- sensible—(as used here) able to be sensed; perceptible
- knell (NEL) warning bell
- alack (uh LAK) alas; oh my
- confound (kun FOUND) confuse; bewilder
- ravelled (RAV uld) frayed
- sleave (SLEEV) tangle of threads
- **balm** (BAHM) soothing ointment

Macbeth: Still it cried, sleep no more, to all the house.
Glamis hath murdered sleep, and therefore Cawdor
Shall sleep no more. Macbeth shall sleep no more.

Lady Macbeth: Go get some water,
And wash this filthy witness from your hands.
Why did you bring these daggers from the place?
They must lie there. Go carry them, and smear
The sleepy grooms with blood.

Macbeth: I'll go no more.
I am afraid, to think what I have done.
Look on't again I dare not.

Lady Macbeth: Infirm of purpose!
Give me the daggers. If he do bleed,
I'll gild the faces of the grooms withal,
For it must seem their guilt.

(As she leaves, a loud knocking begins far off.)

Macbeth: To know my deed, 'twere best not know myself.
Wake Duncan with thy knocking. I would thou coulds't.

The next scene is an odd one. In another part of the castle, a drunken porter, lantern in hand, staggers to answer the knocking. He talks to himself—on and on and on. Most of the audience howls with laughter, but you find yourself wondering: "What's this Shakespeare up to? Comedy in the midst of tragedy?" Then you realize that this is the first time since the play started that your attention has left the stage. You haven't even marveled at the way some young actor convinced you that he really *was* Lady Macbeth. (You know, of course, that acting is so degrading an occupation that all parts are played by men.)

At last the knocking is answered, the door opened. The early morning visitor turns out to be Macduff, a respected thane. Soon the murder is discovered. At once the castle bustles with activity. Macbeth and his wife make a great show of grief. Macduff, the dead king's son Malcolm, Banquo and his son Fleance, and others enter and exit in tumultuous order. Although the evidence seems to be against the two grooms, suspicion begins to fall on Macbeth. Malcolm, fearing for his own life, flees to the south, to England.

Since Malcolm, King Duncan's natural heir, has fled the country, Macbeth, next in line for the throne, is crowned King—but entirely without honor. His troubles continue. He and Lady Macbeth realize they have bloodied their hands

---

- witness—(**as used here**) evidence; proof of guilt
- infirm (in FURM) **weak; sickly**
- gild (GILD) (**as used here**) cover with blood
- withal (with AWL) **with it all**
- **tumultuous** (too MUL choo us) **disorderly; noisy**

for what may be an empty victory. Moreover, they remember the witch's prophecy that Banquo's son—Fleance—will someday become king. What to do? Get rid of Banquo and Fleance, of course!

A great feast is planned, to which Banquo and Fleance are invited. Macbeth hires murderers to kill his two enemies on their way to the castle. In a thrilling night scene, Banquo is killed, but young Fleance escapes.

Right afterward Macbeth greets his guests with warm praise. As they are about to sit down at the banquet, Macbeth expresses his regrets that his good friend Banquo is not yet present. But almost as he says these words, the ghost of Banquo, pale and bloody, enters and sits at the table. (You, as a member of the audience, see this ghost. So does Macbeth—but others on the stage do not.) The guests sit down. Macbeth remains standing, staring at the ghost, his face blanching.

Macbeth (*to* Banquo's *ghost*): Thou canst not say I did it;
Never shake thy gory locks at me.
Ross (*a guest*): Gentlemen rise, his Highness is not well.
Lady Macbeth: Sit worthy friends; my lord is often thus,
And hath been from his youth. Pray you keep seat,
The fit is momentary, upon a thought
He will be well again. (*She pulls* Macbeth *aside.*)
This is the very painting of your fear.
This is the air-drawn dagger which you said
Led you to Duncan.

Macbeth speaks to the ghost again before it silently rises and leaves. Then, trying to pull himself together, he excuses his behavior as a "strange infirmity, which is nothing to those that know me." But Lady Macbeth wants to take no more chances. She cancels the banquet at once, and the guests leave in a rush.

Now Macbeth and his lady are troubled by bloody dreams and fears of the future. Macbeth's odd behavior has increased the suspicions of the great lords of Scotland. Moreover, Malcolm and Fleance are still alive and dangerous. Still worse, Macduff has gone to England to raise an army that will put Malcolm on the throne. In desperation, Macbeth decides to return to the witches, and learn from them the worst.

With thunder and a cloud of smoke, the three witches appear once again. They are in a cave, preparing a witches' brew in a large caldron.

First Witch: Round about the caldron go;
In the poisoned entrails throw.
All: Double, double toil and trouble;
Fire burn, and caldron bubble.

- blanching (BLANCH ing) **turning white**
- **infirmity** (in FUR mi tee) **weakness; disease**
- caldron (KAWL drun) **large open kettle or boiler**
- entrails (EN traylz) **internal parts of body; intestines**

Second Witch: Eye of newt, and toe of frog,
Wool of bat, and tongue of dog,
Third Witch: Slivered in the moon's eclipse,
Nose of Turk, and Tartar's lips.
All: Double, double toil and trouble;
Fire burn, and caldron bubble.
Second Witch: Cool it with a baboon's blood,
Then the charm is firm and good. . . .
By the pricking of my thumbs,
Something wicked this way comes.
Open locks,
Whoever knocks.

(Macbeth *enters.*)

Macbeth: How now, you secret, black, and midnight hags?
What is't you do?
All: A deed without a name.

Macbeth loses no time in asking the witches about his future. In reply, they produce three apparitions. The first is the likeness of an armed head. It calls Macbeth by name, and tells him to beware of the Thane of Fife (Macduff). The second, which resembles a bloody child, also addresses Macbeth by name. It tells him to be bloody and fearless, "for none of woman born shall harm Macbeth." The third, a crowned child holding a tree, tells him to "take no care" and that he will be safe "until great Birnam Wood to high Dunsinane Hill shall come."

All in all, the messages please Macbeth. If he can be harmed "by none of woman born," why then he can be harmed by no one, for all people have been born of a woman. He knows, too, that Birnam Wood, a forest, can never "unfix his earth-bound root" and move to his castle at nearby Dunsinane. It is only the first message that worries Macbeth: to beware of Macduff, the Thane of Fife. He decides to act at once.

Thereupon Macbeth, seething with rage, marches his men to Macduff's castle at Fife. Macduff is not there, but Lady Macduff, her children, and all relations lose their lives.

Back at Dunsinane, Lady Macbeth, left alone with her guilt, seems more and more oppressed by all the blood she has helped to spill. She sleeps poorly. A woman of her retinue has observed her talking and even writing while sleepwalking. She has asked Lady Macbeth's doctor to witness this behavior.

- newt (NOOT) **salamander; small lizard-like creature**
- tartar (TAR tur) **member of old eastern-European tribe**
- apparition (ap uh RISH un) **phantom; spirit**
- **seething** (SEETH ing) **very angry**
- retinue (RET uh noo) **group of servants of important person**

Doctor: I have two nights watched with you, but can perceive no truth in your report. When was it she last walked?

Woman: Since his Majesty went into the field. I have seen her rise from her bed, throw her nightgown upon her, unlock her closet, take forth paper, write upon it, read it, afterward seal it, and again return to bed; yet all this while in a most fast sleep.

Doctor: What at any time have you heard her say?

Woman: That, sir, I will not report after her.

(Lady Macbeth *enters with a candle.*)

Lo you, here she comes. Observe her, stand close.

Doctor: You see her eyes are open.

Woman: Ay, but their sense are shut.

Doctor: What is it she does now? Look how she rubs her hands.

Woman: It is an accustomed action with her. I have known her to continue in this a quarter of an hour.

Lady Macbeth: Yet here's a spot.

Doctor: Hark, she speaks.

Lady Macbeth: Out damned spot, out I say! What need we fear who knows it, when none can call our power into account? Yet who would have thought the old man to have so much blood in him?

Doctor: Do you mark that?

Lady Macbeth: The Thane of Fife had a wife; where is she now? What, will these hands ne'er be clean?

Doctor (*thoughtfully, to himself*): You have known what you should not.

Woman: She has spoke what she should not, I am sure of that. Heaven knows what she has known.

Lady Macbeth: Here's the smell of the blood still: all the perfumes of Arabia will not sweeten this little hand. Oh, oh, oh!

Doctor: This disease is beyond my practice.

Lady Macbeth: Wash your hands, put on your nightgown, look not so pale. I tell you again Banquo's buried; he cannot come out on's grave.

Doctor: Even so?

Lady Macbeth: To bed, to bed; there's knocking at the gate. Come, come, come, come, give me your hand. What's done cannot be undone. To bed, to bed, to bed.

Doctor: Will she go now to bed?

Woman: Directly.

● on's (AHNZ) **of his**

Doctor: Foul whisperings are abroad. Unnatural deeds
Do breed unnatural troubles; infected minds
To their deaf pillows will discharge their secrets.
More needs she the divine than the physician.
God, God forgive us all. Look after her.
I think, but dare not speak.

Woman: Good night good doctor.

Little time is left. Macbeth, back at Dunsinane, learns that an army led by Malcolm and Macduff is approaching. Even worse, that army is getting ever larger as lords from all over Scotland join it to oppose Macbeth. Now the army has reached Birnam Wood. Now it is marching on the castle. Macbeth tries to take comfort in the memory of the words about "none of woman born" and "Birnam Wood." He assures his forces that the attackers will be defeated.

Just at this tense moment, word reaches Macbeth that Lady Macbeth has killed herself. He is stunned:

She should have died hereafter;
There would have been a time for such a word.
To-morrow, and to-morrow, and to-morrow,
Creeps in this petty pace from day to day,
5   To the last syllable of recorded time;
And all our yesterdays have lighted fools
The way to dusty death. Out, out, brief candle!
Life's but a walking shadow, a poor player,
That struts and frets his hour upon the stage,
10   And then is heard no more. It is a tale
Told by an idiot, full of sound and fury
Signifying nothing.

Life has now lost all meaning for Macbeth, and the audience senses that the play is nearly over. Macbeth learns that Malcolm's troops have cut limbs off trees in Birnam Wood to camouflage themselves as they march on the castle. Thus, Birnam Wood *has* come to Dunsinane.

When the attack comes, Macduff seeks out Macbeth to personally avenge the killing of his wife and children. The two draw swords, and Macbeth taunts Macduff by boasting that no man "of woman born" can kill him. Macduff shouts back that he was "from his

---

- abroad (uh BRAWD) (as used here) about; spread around
- divine (di VYN) priest or other clergyman
- petty (PET ee) small or slow
- taunt (TAWNT) tease

mother's womb untimely ripped" by Caesarean section, not born in the natural way. Macduff slays Macbeth, the rest of his force is defeated, and Malcolm is hailed as the new king.

As you leave the theater, you find yourself saddened—and yet strangely thrilled at the same time. This Shakespeare will go places! It's great to be living in the modern world!

ALL THINGS CONSIDERED

1. Macbeth is encouraged to believe the witches when he suddenly learns that (a) their prophecy that he would become Thane of Cawdor has come true. (b) they are really human beings. (c) King Duncan has asked him to take over the kingdom.

2. At first, the leader in the plot to murder Duncan is (a) Macbeth. (b) Lady Macbeth. (c) Banquo.

3. Macbeth might have gotten away with his evil deed had it not been for (a) Banquo and Fleance. (b) a drunken porter. (c) Macduff and Malcolm.

4. The messages given Macbeth by the three apparitions turn out to be (a) false. (b) true, but not as Macbeth understands them. (c) intended for someone else.

5. The correct order in which three of the characters die is (a) Banquo, Duncan, Macbeth. (b) Duncan, Macbeth, Lady Macbeth. (c) Banquo, Lady Macbeth, Macbeth.

THINKING IT THROUGH

1. (a) Before the murder of Duncan, what reasons does Macbeth give himself for *not* proceeding with the plan? (b) In your judgment, are these reasons good ones?

2. Right after the murder, why does Macbeth refuse to reenter Duncan's room?

3. How does Macbeth's behavior at the banquet help convince the other lords of his guilt?

4. In Lady Macbeth's famous sleepwalking scene (page 234), what is the "spot" that concerns her so much?

5. Lady Macbeth's last speech in the sleepwalking scene begins, "To bed, to bed." Go back and find that speech now (page 234). What is its significance?

6. The so-called heroes in tragedies often have a **tragic flaw,** or a personality defect that forces them to act in ways that lead to their downfall. Most tragic flaws involve an excess of some quality—for example, too much ambition, pride, or suspicion. Clearly, Macbeth has at least one tragic flaw. Name one—or more.

7. Macbeth is a classic example of a person with very poor judgment. (a) In your opinion, what are his two most important mistakes in judgment? (b) In each case, what causes him to make these mistakes?

8. Both Shakespeare's "Macbeth" and Yevtushenko's "Red" (page 218) contain much violence. In your opinion, can any of this violence be justified? Explain.

9. Macbeth's speech that starts "She should have died hereafter" (page 235) is one of the best-known passages in world literature. Demonstrate your understanding of the speech by answering the following questions:

(a) As it is used, what is the meaning of the word "hereafter" (line 1)?

(b) What is the meaning of "such a word" in line 2? (Hint: it is one of the five words in line 1.)

(c) In your opinion, why is the word "to-morrow" repeated three times in line 3?

(d) What do the terms "creeps" and "petty pace" (line 4) suggest about the passage of time?

(e) Does "the last syllable of recorded time" (line 5) mean the end of the earth or the end of intelligent human life on earth?

(f) Does the word "fools" (line 6) mean people, in general, or only the kind of people who are thought foolish?

(g) Much has been written on Shakespeare's use of "brief candle" (line 7) for the course of a human life. What are some ways a person's life is like a candle?

(h) Most of lines 8 to 10 give another comparison for human life. What is this comparison, and why is it a good one?

(i) The last sentence in the speech (lines 10 to 12) says, in effect, that life is pointless and meaningless. Consider the most recent event in the play, and the effect it probably had on Macbeth's mood at that time. How does Macbeth feel?

Critical Thinking

Application of Knowledge

Knowledge should never be sealed up in neat metal boxes labeled "History," "Biology," "English," and so on. No such tidy divisions exist in your brain or in the real world. To make full use of your thinking abilities, you constantly have to apply knowledge. In other words, you must put to use the knowledge learned in one field by applying it to other fields.

Here are five items that might be labeled "Social Studies." Apply each of them to literature by explaining what they have to do with Shakespeare's *Macbeth*.

1. Throughout history, even among primitive tribes, kindness to guests has generally been considered a virtue, and unkindness a vice, or even a sin.

2. Carrying branches or shrubs as camouflage has been a common military practice from ancient times to Vietnam.

3. Today we tend to think of witches as costumed figures at Halloween. Years ago, people took them much more seriously. Many people really believed that witches could predict the future and cause animals to die (see pages 225–226).

4. Tourists visiting Scotland today often try to see Birnam Wood, Dunsinane, and Cawdor Castle.

5. Raphael Holinshed's *Chronicles of England and Ireland*, a history book written in 1587, states that Banquo was in on the plot to kill King Duncan. (Relate this to the fact that in 1606 Shakespeare wanted to write a Scottish play to honor the new British king, James I. This king was proud of his Scottish ancestors—including the very same Banquo!)

Composition

1. Look back at the famous speech beginning, "She should have died hereafter" (page 235). Review the questions on it (page 237) carefully. Then **paraphrase** the speech. (To paraphrase means to rewrite by using mostly your own words.) Use simple language that is easy to understand.

2. Some readers (and viewers) think that the really fascinating character is not Macbeth but Lady Macbeth. Decide which of the two characters you find more interesting and write a paragraph explaining why you find yourself more interested in one than in the other.

VOCABULARY AND SKILL REVIEW

Before completing the exercises that follow, you may wish to review the **bold-faced** words on pages 212 to 238.

I. On a separate sheet of paper, write the term on each line that means the same, or nearly the same, as the word in *italics*.

1. *hurlyburly:* garden tool, confusion, accent, children's game
2. *cascade:* winter sport, something falling like a waterfall, type of cloud, disease
3. *vanquish:* defeat, overeat, make neat, make disappear
4. *attire:* appear, grow tired, clothing, anticipate
5. *swathed:* soothed, washed, annoyed, wrapped
6. *seething:* scorching, very angry, frightened, daydreaming
7. *frenzy:* fringe, foolish mistake, peasant, wild excitement
8. *infirmity:* importance, friendship, loneliness, weakness
9. *nutritive:* nourishing, dangerous, exciting, difficult
10. *tumultuous:* ugly, disorderly, lazy, exhausted

II. Write the *italicized* word that best fills the blank in each sentence.

jut	*balm*
instinctive	*forelock*
obsession	*machete*
cliché	*milling*
gait	*bountiful*

1. A powerful _____ can force everything else from your mind.
2. Farmers always hope for a(n) _____ harvest.
3. *Sparrow* is to *ostrich* as *penknife* is to _____ .
4. Anita walked down the street with a fast _____ .
5. Blinking your eyes is a(n) _____ action.
6. I put some _____ on Dad's burned hand.
7. The horse's _____ fell nearly to its eyes.
8. A(n) _____ is an overused expression such as "(I) saw red."
9. The new dock will _____ 150 feet into the harbor.
10. We were told to stop _____ around near the school after dismissal.

III. Read this famous poem carefully and notice the advice it contains. Then answer the questions.

A PSALM OF LIFE

by Henry Wadsworth Longfellow (1807—1882)

Tell me not, in mournful numbers,
    Life is but an empty dream!—
For the soul is dead that slumbers,
    And things are not what they seem.

5   Life is real! Life is earnest!
    And the grave is not its goal;
Dust thou art, to dust returnest,
    Was not spoken of the soul.

Not enjoyment, and not sorrow,
10   Is our destined end or way;
But to act, that each to-morrow
    Find us farther than to-day.

Art is long, and Time is fleeting,
    And our hearts, though stout and brave,
15   Still, like muffled drums, are beating
    Funeral marches to the grave.

In the world's broad field of battle,
    In the bivouac of Life,
Be not like dumb, driven cattle!
20   Be a hero in the strife!

Trust no Future, howe'er pleasant!
    Let the dead Past bury its dead!
Act—act in the living Present!
    Heart within, and God o'erhead!

- destined (DES tind) **fated; bound to happen**
- fleeting (FLEET ing) **soon gone; fast disappearing**
- stout (STOUT) **bold; firm; strong**
- bivouac (BIV oo ak) **temporary shelter or encampment**

25   Lives of great men all remind us
            We can make our lives sublime,
     And, departing, leave behind us
            Footprints on the sands of time;

     Footprints, that perhaps another,
30   Sailing o'er life's solemn main,
     A forlorn and shipwrecked brother,
            Seeing, shall take heart again.

     Let us, then, be up and doing,
            With a heart for any fate;
35   Still achieving, still pursuing,
            Learn to labor and to wait.

1. Look at the first few lines. To what kind of person does the poem seem to be addressed?

2. Think about lines 7 and 8. What *was* originally "spoken of" in "Dust thou art, to dust returneth"?

• sublime (suh BLYM) **grand; lofty; on high level**
• main (MAYN) **open sea**

3. When asked about the goal of life, most people answer "happiness." (a) What does the third stanza say on this subject? (b) Might "happiness" be involved here in any way?

4. Explain the figurative language in lines 17 to 19.

5. (a) Would the speaker in the poem have the reader place attention on the past, the present, or the future? (b) Which lines in the poem give the answer?

6. Lines 25 to 28 contain a famous example of figurative language. In fact, it is so well known that it has nearly become a cliché. Did you spot it? If not, take a guess.

7. Reread the last line of the poem. How do you interpret its meaning?

8. A hundred years ago, Longfellow was *by far* the most popular poet in the United States. People respected his judgment on many subjects. What do you think of the advice in his poem? Be honest, but give at least one reason for your opinion.

IV. In the following paragraph there are a number of clichés. Find at least five of them. (a) Change each cliché into a fresh figurative expression by substituting your own words in the comparison. (b) Rewrite the paragraph using your new figurative expressions.

The classroom was as silent as a tomb. Students were working diligently on their history assignment while the teacher, busy as a bee, sat at her desk correcting papers. Jerry heard his stomach growl. He was as hungry as a horse. Finally the lunch bell rang, and Jerry, clumsy as an ox, lurched out of his seat, tripping over the girl who sat in front of him. Why did I have to trip over Ellen, he thought in dismay. She's so beautiful and as graceful as a gazelle. Quick as a wink a thought came to him. Offer to buy her lunch! Great idea! Then a second thought stopped him: he remembered that his wallet was as flat as a pancake.

▶ Lottie and Bess were sisters who went separate ways—until the bond that relatives feel for one another brought them together again. Sound like the plot of a 600-page novel? It could be. It could also be the plot of a meaningful five-page story called

THE RICHER, THE POORER

by Dorothy West

Over the years Lottie had urged Bess to prepare for her old age. Over the years Bess had lived each day as if there were no other. Now they were both past sixty, the time for summing up. Lottie had a bank account that had never grown lean. Bess had the clothes on her back, and the rest of her worldly possessions in a battered suitcase.

Lottie had hated being a child, hearing her parents' skimping and scraping. Bess had never seemed to notice. All she ever wanted was to go outside and play. She learned to skate on borrowed skates. She rode a borrowed bicycle. Lottie couldn't wait to grow up and buy herself the best of everything.

As soon as anyone would hire her, Lottie put herself to work. She minded babies, she ran errands for the old.

She never touched a penny of her money, though her child's mouth watered for ice cream and candy. But she could not bear to share with Bess, who never had anything to share with her. When the dimes began to add up to dollars, she lost her taste for sweets.

By the time she was twelve, she was clerking after school in a small variety store. Saturdays she worked as long as she was wanted. She decided to keep her money for clothes. When she entered high school, she would wear a wardrobe that neither she nor anyone else would be able to match.

But her freshman year found her unable to indulge so frivolous a whim, particularly when her admiring instructors advised her to think seriously of college. No one in her family had ever gone to college, and certainly Bess would never get there. She would show them all what she could do, if she put her mind to it.

- indulge (in DULJ) **yield to a desire**
- **frivolous** (FRIV uh lus) **silly; unimportant**
- **whim** (HWIM) **odd notion or desire**

She began to bank her money, and her bank account became her most private and precious possession.

In her third year high she found a job in a small but expanding restaurant, where she cashiered from the busy hour until closing. In her last year high the business increased so rapidly that Lottie was faced with the choice of staying in school or working full-time.

She made her choice easily. A job in hand was worth two in the future.

Bess had a beau in the school band, who had no other ambition except to play a horn. Lottie expected to be settled with a home and family while Bess was still waiting for Harry to earn enough to buy a marriage license.

That Bess married Harry straight out of high school was not surprising. That Lottie never married at all was not really surprising either. Two or three times she was halfway persuaded, but to give up a job that paid well for a homemaking job that paid nothing was a risk she was incapable of taking.

Bess's married life was nothing for Lottie to envy. She and Harry lived like gypsies, Harry playing in second-rate bands all over the country, even getting himself and Bess stranded in Europe. They were often in rags and never in riches.

Bess grieved because she had no child, not having sense enough to know she was better off without one. Lottie was certainly better off without nieces and nephews to feel sorry for. Very likely Bess would have dumped them on her doorstep.

That Lottie had a doorstep they might have been left on was only because her boss, having bought a second house, offered Lottie his first house at a price so low and terms so reasonable that it would have been like losing money to refuse.

She shut off the rooms she didn't use, letting them go to rack and ruin. Since she ate her meals out, she had no food at home, and did not encourage callers, who always expected a cup of tea.

Her way of life was mean and miserly, but she did not know it. She thought she lived frugally in her middle years so that she could live in comfort and ease when she most needed peace of mind.

The years, after forty, began to race. Suddenly Lottie was sixty, and retired from her job by her boss's son, who had no sentimental feeling about keeping her on until she was ready to quit.

She made several attempts to find other employment, but her dowdy appearance made her look old and inefficient. For the first

---

- in hand—**really existing at the moment**
- mean (MEEN) **stingy; shabby**
- **miserly** (MY zur lee) **like a miser; stingy**
- **frugally** (FROO gul ee) **in an economical, thrifty manner**
- **dowdy** (DOU dee) **shabby; not stylish**

time in her life Lottie would gladly have worked for nothing, to have some place to go, something to do with her day.

Harry died abroad, in a third-rate hotel, with Bess weeping as hard as if he had left her a fortune. He had left her nothing but his horn. There wasn't even money for her passage home.

Lottie, trapped by the blood tie, knew she would not only have to send for her sister, but take her in when she returned. It didn't seem fair that Bess should reap the harvest of Lottie's lifetime of self-denial.

It took Lottie a week to get a bedroom ready, a week of hard work and hard cash. There was everything to do, everything to replace or paint. When she was through the room looked so fresh and new that Lottie felt she deserved it more than Bess.

She would let Bess have her room, but the mattress was so lumpy, the carpet so worn, the curtains so threadbare that Lottie's conscience pricked her. She supposed she would have to redo that room, too, and went about doing it with an eagerness that she mistook for haste.

- **self-denial** (SELF di NY ul) **sacrifice; refusing personal desires**
- threadbare (THRED bair) **worn out**

When she was through upstairs, she was shocked to see how dismal downstairs looked by comparison. She tried to ignore it, but with nowhere to go to escape it, the contrast grew more intolerable.

She worked her way from kitchen to parlor, persuading herself she was only putting the rooms to right to give herself something to do. At night she slept like a child after a long and happy day of playing house. She was having more fun than she had ever had in her life. She was living each hour for itself.

There was only a day now before Bess would arrive. Passing her gleaming mirrors, at first with vague awareness, then with painful clarity, Lottie saw herself as others saw her, and could not stand the sight.

She went on a spending spree from specialty shops to beauty salon, emerging transformed into a woman who believed in miracles.

She was in the kitchen basting a turkey when Bess rang the bell. Her heart raced, and she wondered if the heat from the oven was responsible.

She went to the door, and Bess stood before her. Stiffly she suffered Bess's embrace, her heart racing harder, her eyes suddenly smarting from the onrush of cold air.

"Oh, Lottie, it's good to see you," Bess said, but saying nothing about Lottie's splendid appearance. Upstairs Bess, putting down her shabby suitcase, said, "I'll sleep like a rock tonight," without a word of praise for her lovely room. At the lavish table, top-heavy with turkey, Bess said, "I'll take light and dark both," with no marveling at the size of the bird, or that there was turkey for two elderly women, one of them too poor to buy her own bread.

With the glow of good food in her stomach, Bess began to spin stories. They were rich with places and people, most of them lowly, all of them magnificent. Her face reflected her telling, the joys and sorrows of her remembering, and above all, the love she lived by that enhanced the poorest place, the humblest person.

Then it was that Lottie knew why Bess had made no mention of her finery, or the shining room, or the twelve-pound turkey. She had not even seen them. Tomorrow she would see the room as it really looked, and Lottie as she really looked, and the warmed-over turkey in its second-day glory. Tonight she saw only what she had come seeking, a place in her sister's home and heart.

She said, "That's enough about me. How have the years used you?"

- suffer (SUF ur) **allow; permit; endure**
- **lavish** (LAV ish) **having great amounts; generous**
- enhance (en HANS) **make better; magnify**

"It was me who didn't use them," said Lottie wistfully. "I saved for them. I forgot the best of them would go without my ever spending a day or a dollar enjoying them. That's my life story in those few words, a life never lived. Now it's too near the end to try."

Bess said, "To know how much there is to know is the beginning of learning to live. Don't count the years that are left us. At our time of life it's the days that count. You've too much catching up to do to waste a minute of a waking hour feeling sorry for yourself."

Lottie grinned, a real wide open grin, "Well, to tell the truth I felt sorry for you. Maybe if I had any sense I'd feel sorry for myself, after all. I know I'm too old to kick up my heels, but I'm going to let you show me how. If I land on my head, I guess it won't matter. I feel giddy already, and I like it."

• **wistfully** (WIST ful ee) longingly; with envy

ALL THINGS CONSIDERED

1. At different times in her life, Lottie's long-range plans include (a) college and marriage. (b) buying the house of her dreams. (c) moving to Europe to be near Bess.

2. Throughout her life, Lottie's judgments always favor (a) her sister's welfare. (b) taking reasonable risks. (c) safety and her bank account.

3. The words "the love she lived by that enhanced the poorest place, the humblest person" apply to (a) Lottie. (b) Bess. (c) both Lottie and Bess.

4. Bess comes to live with Lottie (a) because it's her best choice at the time. (b) only after Lottie's repeated pleading. (c) as the result of a long-range plan.

5. At the end, (a) Bess changes more than Lottie. (b) both women change a great deal. (c) Lottie changes more than Bess.

THINKING IT THROUGH

1. The very different lives of the two sisters both have advantages and disadvantages. (a) What is one advantage, as well as one disadvantage, in Lottie's life? (b) What is one advantage, as well as one disadvantage, in Bess's life?

2. Tell how the following sentence applies to the story: "Some people spend their lives making 'important' decisions, while others let life make the decisions for them."

3. In your opinion, why doesn't Bess immediately notice and comment on all the preparations Lottie has made for her arrival?

4. (a) What decision does Lottie make at the end of the story? (b) In your opinion, will she be successful, or is she too old and set in her ways to change? Explain.

5. After reading the story, you may find yourself wondering about the title. It may have more than one meaning. What does the title mean to you?

Critical Thinking

Denotation and Connotation

Words may have two kinds of meanings. The first is a word's **denotation** (de noh TAY shun), or dictionary meaning. The second is the word's **connotation** (kon uh TAY shun), or everything that the word suggests or brings to the mind of the reader (or listener). When writers use words mainly for their connotations, they expect the reader to infer various feelings and ideas that wouldn't be found in a dictionary.

For example, consider the words *house* and *home*. Their denotations are about the same: "enclosed structure," "self-contained group of rooms," and so forth. But the connotations of *home* go far beyond those of *house*. *Home* suggests a family unit, people who care, and security.

Explain the connotations of the following *italicized* expressions from "The Richer, the Poorer." In each case, ask yourself what the *italicized* term suggests that the inserted term [in brackets] does not.

Example: Lottie would wear a *wardrobe* [clothing] that no one else would be able to match. (*A wardrobe* suggests a total, well-coordinated selection of clothing and accessories.)

1. Lottie began to *bank* [save] her money.
2. Very likely Bess would have *dumped* [left] her children with Lottie.
3. Lottie's way of life was *mean and miserly* [modest and thrifty].
4. At night Lottie slept like a *child* [tired person].
5. Bess's stories were *rich with* [full of] places and people.

Composition

1. Here are five slang expressions followed by their current meanings in brackets. For each expression, write a sentence explaining what connotations the words in italics suggest to you.
   (a) to *pig out* [overeat]
   (b) *bubble-gummers* [junior high students—as referred to by senior high students]
   (c) to *ace* a test [get a high mark]
   (d) to be *grounded* [forced to stay at home]
   (e) you *turkey!* [stupid person]

2. Think of five slang expressions that are very new. Write each one on your paper. Then translate it into common English and explain why its connotation makes it effective and popular.

249

MARRIAGE IS A PRIVATE AFFAIR

by Chinua Achebe

▶ Should a person's actions be based on a judgment of what is right, if what is "right" conflicts with traditions? This question has troubled millions of people the world over. It's the basic question in this story by one of present-day Africa's leading writers.

"**H**ave you written to your dad yet?" asked Nene one afternoon as she sat with Nnaemeka in her room at 16 Kasanga Street, Lagos.*

"No. I've been thinking about it. I think it's better to tell him when I get home on leave!"

"But why? Your leave is such a long way off yet—six whole weeks. He should be let into our happiness now."

Nnaemeka was silent for a while, and then began very slowly as if he groped for his words: "I wish I were sure it would be happiness to him."

"Of course it must," replied Nene, a little surprised. "Why shouldn't it?"

"You have lived in Lagos all your life, and you know very little about people in remote parts of the country."

"That's what you always say. But I don't believe anybody will be so unlike other people that they will be unhappy when their sons are engaged to marry."

"Yes. They are most unhappy if the engagement is not arranged by them. In our case it's worse—you are not even an Ibo."

This was said so seriously and so bluntly that Nene could not find speech immediately. In the cosmopolitan atmosphere of the city it had always seemed to her something of a joke that a person's tribe could determine whom he married.

At last she said, "You don't really mean that he will object to your marrying me simply on that account? I had always thought you Ibos

---

- **cosmopolitan** (kahz muh PAHL i tun) **composed of people from many parts of the world**
- **disposed** (dis POHZD) **inclined to act in a certain manner**

*Lagos (LAH gohs) the capital of Nigeria, the narrator's homeland

were kindly-disposed to other people."

"So we are. But when it comes to marriage, well, it's not quite so simple. And this," he added, "is not peculiar to the Ibos. If your father were alive and lived in the heart of Ibibio-land he would be exactly like my father."

"I don't know. But anyway, as your father is so fond of you, I'm sure he will forgive you soon enough. Come on then, be a good boy and send him a nice lovely letter . . ."

"It would not be wise to break the news to him by writing. A letter will bring it upon him with a shock. I'm quite sure about that."

"All right, honey, suit yourself. You know your father."

As Nnaemeka walked home that evening he turned over in his mind different ways of overcoming his father's opposition, especially now that he had gone and found a girl for him. He had thought of showing his letter to Nene but decided on second thoughts not to, at least for the moment. He read it again when he got home and couldn't help smiling to himself. He remembered Ugoye quite well, an Amazon of a girl who used to beat up all the boys, himself included, on the way to the stream, a complete dunce at school.

> I have found a girl who will suit you admirably—Ugoye Nweke, the eldest daughter of our neighbor, Jacob Nweke. She has a proper Christian upbringing. When she stopped schooling some years ago her father (a man of sound judgment) sent her to live in the house of a pastor where she has received all the training a wife could need. Her Sunday School teacher has told me that she reads her Bible very fluently. I hope we shall begin negotiations when you come home in December.

- Amazon (AM uh zahn) **mythological race of female warriors; a tall, strong female**

251

On the second evening of his return from Lagos, Nnaemeka sat
with his father under a cassia tree. This was the old man's retreat
where he went to read his Bible when the parching December sun
had set and a fresh, reviving wind blew on the leaves.

"Father," began Nnaemeka suddenly, "I have come to ask for
forgiveness."

"Forgiveness? For what, my son?" he asked in amazement.

"It's about this marriage question."

"Which marriage question?"

"I can't—we must—I mean it is impossible for me to marry
Nweke's daughter."

"Impossible? Why?" asked his father.

"I don't love her."

"Nobody said you did. Why should you?" he asked.

"Marriage today is different . . ."

- cassia (KASH uh) **kind of tropical tree**
- retreat (ri TREET) **safe, peaceful place**
- **reviving** (ri VYV ing) **bringing new life and health**

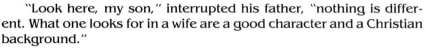

"Look here, my son," interrupted his father, "nothing is different. What one looks for in a wife are a good character and a Christian background."

Nnaemeka saw there was no hope along the present line of argument.

"Moreover," he said, "I am engaged to marry another girl who has all of Ugoye's good qualities, and who . . ."

His father did not believe his ears. "What did you say?" he asked slowly and disconcertingly.

"She is a good Christian," his son went on, "and a teacher in a Girls' School in Lagos."

"Teacher, did you say? If you consider that a qualification for a good wife I should like to point out to you, Emeka, that no Christian woman should teach. St. Paul in his letter to the Corinthians says that women should keep silence." He rose slowly from his seat and paced forwards and backwards. This was his pet subject, and he condemned vehemently those church leaders who encouraged women to teach in their schools. After he had spent his emotion on a long homily he at last came back to his son's engagement, in a seemingly milder tone.

"Whose daughter is she, anyway?"

"She is Nene Atang."

"What!" All the mildness was gone again. "Did you say Neneataga, what does that mean?"

"Nene Atang from Calabar. She is the only girl I can marry." This

---

- disconcertingly (dis kun SURT ing lee) **in a manner that confuses and disturbs**
- vehemently (VEE uh munt lee) **forcefully; earnestly**
- homily (HAHM uh lee) **sermon; sermon-like speech**

was a very rash reply and Nnaemeka expected the storm to burst. But it did not. His father merely walked away into his room. This was most unexpected and perplexed Nnaemeka. His father's silence was infinitely more menacing than a flood of threatening speech. That night the old man did not eat.

When he sent for Nnaemeka a day later he applied all possible ways of dissuasion. But the young man's heart was hardened, and his father eventually gave him up as lost.

"I owe it to you, my son, as a duty to show you what is right and what is wrong. Whoever put this idea into your head might as well have cut your throat. It is Satan's work." He waved his son away.

"You will change your mind, Father, when you know Nene."

"I shall never see her," was the reply. From that night the father scarcely spoke to his son. He did not, however, cease hoping that he would realize how serious was the danger he was heading for. Day and night he put him in his prayers.

Nnaemeka, for his own part, was very deeply affected by his father's grief. But he kept hoping that it would pass away. If it had occurred to him that never in the history of his people had a man married a woman who spoke a different tongue, he might have been less optimistic. "It has never been heard," was the verdict of an old man speaking a few weeks later. In that short sentence he spoke for all of his people. This man had come with others to commiserate with Okeke when news went round about his son's behavior. By that time the son had gone back to Lagos.

"It has never been heard," said the old man again with a sad shake of his head.

"What did Our Lord say?" asked another gentleman. "Sons shall rise against their Fathers; it is there in the Holy Book."

"It is the beginning of the end," said another.

Six months later, Nnaemeka was showing his young wife a short letter from his father:

It amazes me that you could be so unfeeling as to send me your wedding picture. I would have sent it back. But on further thought I decided just to cut off your wife and send it back to you because I have nothing to do with her. How I wish that I had nothing to do with you either.

When Nene read through this letter and looked at the mutilated picture her eyes filled with tears, and she began to sob.

- **perplex** (pur PLEKS) puzzle; confuse
- dissuasion (di SWAY zhun) **advising against**
- commiserate (kuh MIZ uh rayt) **sympathize**

"Don't cry, my darling," said her husband. "He is essentially good-natured and will one day look more kindly on our marriage." But years passed and that one day did not come.

For eight years, Okeke would have nothing to do with his son, Nnaemeka. Only three times (when Nnaemeka asked to come home and spend his leave) did he write to him.

"I can't have you in my house," he replied on one occasion. "It can be of no interest to me where or how you spend your leave—or your life, for that matter."

The prejudice against Nnaemeka's marriage was not confined to his little village. In Lagos, especially among his people who worked there, it showed itself in a different way. Their women, when they met at their village meeting, were not hostile to Nene. Rather, they paid her such excessive deference as to make her feel she was not one of them. But as time went on, Nene gradually broke through some of this prejudice and even began to make friends among them. Slowly and grudgingly they began to admit that she kept her home much better than most of them.

The story eventually got to the little village in the heart of the Ibo country that Nnaemeka and his young wife were a most happy couple. But his father was one of the few people in the village who knew nothing about this. He always displayed so much temper whenever his son's name was mentioned that everyone avoided it in his presence. By a tremendous effort of will he had succeeded in pushing his son to the back of his mind. The strain had nearly killed him but he had persevered, and won.

Then one day he received a letter from Nene, and in spite of himself he began to glance through it perfunctorily until all of a sudden the expression on his face changed and he began to read more carefully.

. . . Our two sons, from the day they learnt that they have a grandfather, have insisted on being taken to him. I find it impossible to tell them that you will not see them. I implore you to allow Nnaemeka to bring them home for a short time during his leave next month. I shall remain here in Lagos . . .

The old man at once felt the resolution he had built up over so many years falling in. He was telling himself that he must not give in. He tried to steel his heart against all emotional appeals. It was a

---

- deference (DEF ur uns) **courteous respect**
- persevere (pur suh VEER) **continue; keep trying**
- perfunctorily (pur FUNGK tuh ri lee) in an uninterested manner
- **implore** (im PLOHR) **ask urgently; beg**
- **steel** (STEEL) **harden**

reenactment of that other struggle. He leaned against a window and looked out. The sky was overcast with heavy black clouds and a high wind began to blow filling the air with dust and dry leaves. It was one of those rare occasions when even Nature takes a hand in a human fight. Very soon it began to rain, the first rain in the year. It came down in large sharp drops and was accompanied by the lightning and thunder which mark a change of season. Okeke was trying hard not to think of his two grandsons. But he knew he was now fighting a losing battle. He tried to hum a favorite hymn but the pattering of large rain drops on the roof broke up the tune. His mind immediately returned to the children. How could he shut his door against them? By a curious mental process he imagined them standing, sad and forsaken, under the harsh angry weather—shut out from his house.

That night he hardly slept, from remorse—and a vague fear that he might die without making it up to them.

ALL THINGS CONSIDERED ————————————

1. It was a custom in Nigeria for (a) marriage ceremonies to be private. (b) parents to arrange marriages. (c) women to propose to men.

2. Nigeria is divided by (a) rivers and mountain ranges. (b) military leaders with political differences. (c) tribal and language differences.

3. When Nene and Nnaemeka learn of Okeke's opposition to their engagement, they (a) never consider changing their plans. (b) discuss calling the wedding off. (c) decide to wait a year or more.

4. When Okeke receives the wedding picture, he sends back the (a) part showing Nene. (b) part showing his son. (c) whole picture.

5. At the end, Okeke's resolution to have nothing to do with his son's marriage is overcome by (a) a tearful speech by Nene. (b) his desire to see his grandsons. (c) the arguments of a few friends.

THINKING IT THROUGH ————————————

1. The story shows that two well-meaning people can make judgments that put them on a collision course with each other. (a) Why does Okeke think *his* judgment is right? (b) Why does Nnaemeka think *his* judgment is right?

2. (a) What does Nnaemeka do to overcome Okeke's refusal to see them? (b) What does Nene do in an effort to change Okeke's mind?

3. What do you think might have happened if the story had continued? For instance, might Okeke and Nene meet? What might they have said to one another?

4. In your judgment, is Nnaemeka right and his father wrong? Is the father right and Nnaemeka wrong? Or do you see the situation in some other way?

Critical Thinking

Supporting Hypotheses With Facts

A **hypothesis** (hy POTH uh sis) is a possible answer to some question, or a possible explanation for something. Most people frequently use **hypotheses** (hy POTH uh seez—the plural form). Suppose, for instance, a plant on a schoolroom windowsill begins to droop and lose some of its leaves. An interested person might immediately form several of the following hypotheses: (1) It hasn't been watered enough. (2) It's been over-watered. (3) It needs fertilizer. (4) It's become rootbound and needs a larger pot. (5) The same thing happens to this kind of plant every year at this time. (6) A fungus or insect is to blame. Once the hypotheses have been formed, the next step is to find the facts that might support one or more of the hypotheses.

The reader who tries to analyze or evaluate a piece of literature must do much the same thing. It is one thing to simply say that a story is "interesting," "terrific," or "boring." But it's quite another to explain *why*. To do this, you have to make several hypotheses about what might be true of a good story and then test the story against them.

Here are nine hypotheses that may or may not help explain your reaction to "Marriage Is a Private Affair." For each, ask yourself two questions: (1) Can the hypothesis be properly applied to the story? (2) If so, exactly *what* in the story supports the hypothesis?

1. The characters are developed so well that the reader soon gets to "know" them.

2. The characters are a lot like me.

3. The characters are very different from me.

4. The writing is crisp, fast, and easy to read.

5. The plot keeps the reader curious to know what will happen.

6. The setting is familiar.

7. The setting is unfamiliar and there-fore interesting.

8. Humor adds a pleasant mood to the story.

9. The story makes the reader think about something important.

Composition

1. From the list of hypotheses above, select the one that you think best applies to "Marriage Is a Private Affair." Then support it with as many details as you can.
2. Explain your overall reaction to the story by discussing some of the hy-potheses listed above. Your reaction may be positive, negative, or a mixture of both. Use facts for support. In some cases, you may want to object to the story in some respect because it *lacks* details that would support a hypothesis you think is important.

VOCABULARY AND SKILL REVIEW

Before completing the exercises that follow, you may wish to review the **bold-faced** words on pages 243 to 258.

I. On a separate sheet of paper, write the letter of the word or phrase that best completes each sentence.

1. One result of a *miserly* life would probably be (a) lung and heart trouble. (b) a fat bank account. (c) many grateful friends.
2. A *frivolous whim* is (a) a dangerous mental condition. (b) an evil plan. (c) a silly notion.
3. Problems that *perplex* you (a) are easy to solve. (b) puzzle and confuse you. (c) make you furious with anger.
4. A *lavish* party would probably (a) cost quite a lot of money. (b) include swimming. (c) leave some guests hungry.
5. If you *steel* your heart, you (a) give it to a loved one. (b) avoid physical exercise. (c) harden your determination.
6. To look at something *wistfully* is to look (a) longingly. (b) scornfully. (c) proudly.
7. *Seize* is to *grasp* as *implore* is to (a) *forbid.* (b) *offend.* (c) *beg.*
8. A fresh, *reviving* breeze is most commonly associated with (a) fall. (b) winter. (c) spring.
9. To spend money *frugally* is to (a) throw it away on pleasures. (b) watch every penny. (c) risk being arrested by the police.
10. The italicized words above most commonly associated with *self-denial* are (a) *frivolous* and *lavish.* (b) *reviving* and *whim.* (c) *miserly* and *frugally.*

II. The poem on page 260 recalls a very repulsive event in American history. During the spring and summer of 1963, the city of Birmingham, Alabama, swarmed with civil rights activity. Marching for freedom, Dr. Martin Luther King, Jr. and other black leaders were arrested and hauled off to jail. Other marchers—adults and children alike—were met with clubs, dogs, and fire hoses. Then, one Sunday in September, a bomb exploded in the Sixteenth Avenue Baptist Church. When the smoke cleared, four young black girls were found dead.

BALLAD OF BIRMINGHAM

by Dudley Randall

"Mother dear, may I go downtown
Instead of out to play,
And march the streets of Birmingham
In a Freedom March today?"

"No, baby, no, you may not go,
For the dogs are fierce and wild,
And clubs and hoses, guns and jails
Aren't good for a little child."

"But, mother, I won't be alone,
Other children will go with me,
And march the streets of Birmingham
To make our country free."

"No, baby, no, you may not go,
For I fear those guns will fire.
But you may go to church instead
And sing in the children's choir."

She has combed and brushed her night-dark hair.
And bathed rose petal sweet,
And drawn white gloves on her small brown hands,
And white shoes on her feet.

The mother smiled to know her child
Was in the sacred place,
But that smile was the last smile
To come upon her face.

For when she heard the explosion,
Her eyes grew wet and wild.
She raced through the streets of Birmingham
Calling for her child.

She clawed through bits of glass and brick,
Then lifted out a shoe.
"O, here's the shoe my baby wore,
But, baby, where are you?"

1. (a) What did the mother expect to happen to her daughter that day? (b) What actually did happen?

2. Reread the historical background that precedes the poem. Which *hypothesis* best explains the bombing? (a) The bomb was dropped from a police helicopter. (b) Racial prejudice resulted in the senseless slaughter of innocent people. (c) Churches that mix violence with religion get what they deserve.

3. The words *dogs, clubs, hoses, guns,* and *jails* have *denotations* that can be found in any dictionary. Yet taken together in the context of this particular poem, they take on special *connotations.* Explain why.

4. Look at the first line of the last stanza. What connotation does *clawed* have that a word like *dug* or *poked* would lack?

5. President John Kennedy, who was assassinated about a month later, said at the time of the bombing that events like the bombing actually *advanced* the cause of civil rights. What could he have possibly meant?

Bonus question: Think about the cartoon below in terms of denotation and connotation. First, consider the scene represented. Then, consider the caption. The speaker's words are funny only because the connotations of the word *tobacco* have changed in the last 350 years. Explain.

"Don't worry. If it turns out tobacco is harmful, we can always quit."

FLOWERS FOR ALGERNON

by Daniel Keyes

▶ What determines the way a person evaluates and judges something? As this story indicates, intelligence, personality, and experience all play a part. Get ready to meet Charlie Gordon, a retarded person who is in for a big surprise.

Part I

progris riport 1—martch 5 19——

Dr. Strauss says I shud rite down what I think and evrey thing that happins to me from now on. I dont know why but he says its importint so they will see if they will use me. I hope they use me. Miss Kinnian says maybe they can make me smart. I want to be smart. My name is Charlie Gordon. I am 37 years old and 2 weeks ago was my brithday. I have nuthing more to rite now so I will close for today.

progris riport 2—martch 6

I had a test today. I think I faled it. and I think that maybe now they wont use me. What happind is a nice young man was in the room and he had some white cards with ink spillled all over them. He sed Charlie what do you see on this card. I was very skared even tho I had my rabits foot in my pockit because when I was a kid I always faled tests in school and I spillled ink to.

I told him I saw a inkblot. He said yes and it made me feel good. I thot that was all but when I got up to go he stopped me. He said now sit down Charlie we are not thru yet. Then I dont remember so good but he wantid me to say what was in the ink. I dint see nuthing in the ink but he said there was picturs there other pepul saw some picturs. I coudnt see any picturs. I reely tryed to see. I held the card close up and then far away. Then I said if I had my glases I coud see better I usally only ware my glases in the movies or TV but I said they are in the closit in the hall. I got them. Then I said let me see that card agen I bet Ill find it now.

I tryed hard but I still coudnt find the picturs I only saw the ink. I told him maybe I need new glases. He rote something down on a paper and I got skared of faling the test. I told him it was a very nice inkblot with littel points all around the eges. He looked very sad so that wasnt it. I said please let me try agen. Ill get it in a few minits becaus Im not so fast sometimes. Im a slow reeder too in Miss Kinnians class for slow adults but I'm trying very hard.

He gave me a chance with another card that had 2 kinds of ink spilled on it red and blue.

He was very nice and talked slow like Miss Kinnian does and he explaned it to me that it was a *raw shok*. He said pepul see things in the ink. I said show me where. He said think. I told him I think a inkblot but that wasnt rite eather. He said what does it remind you—pretend something. I closd my eyes for a long time to pretend. I told him I pretned a fowntan pen with ink leeking all over a table cloth. Then he got up and went out.

I dont think I passd the *raw shok* test.

progris report 3—martch 7

Dr Strauss and Dr Nemur say it dont matter about the inkblots. I told them I dint spill the ink on the cards and I couldn't see anything in the ink. They said that maybe they will still use me. I said Miss Kinnian never gave me tests like that one only spellin and reading. They said Miss Kinnian told that I was her bestist pupil in the adult nite scool becaus I tryed the hardist and I reely wantid to lern. They said how come you went to the adult nite scool all by yourself Charlie. How did you find it. I said I askd pepul and sumbody told me where I shud go to lern to read and spell good. They said why did you want to. I told them becaus all my life I wantid to be smart and not dumb. But its very hard to be smart. They said you know it will probly be tempirery. I said yes. Miss Kinnian told me. I dont care if it herts.

Later I had more crazy tests today. The nice lady who gave it me told me the name and I asked her how do you spellit so I can rite it in my progris riport. THEMATIC APPERCEPTION TEST. I dont know the frist 2 words but I know what *test* means. You got to pass it or you get bad marks. This test lookd easy becaus I coud see the picturs. Only this time she dint want me to tell her the picturs. That mixd me up. I said

---

- raw shok, *really* Rorschach (ROHR shahk) test —a test of a person's underlying personality in which the subject is asked to explain what is seen in a series of ten ink blots
- Thematic (thee MAT ik) Apperception (a pur SEP shun) test —a test in which a subject's feelings and personality are revealed by stories made up about a series of pictures of people interacting

the man yesterday said I shoud tell him what I saw in the ink she said that dont make no difrence. She said make up storys about the pepul in the picturs.

I told her how can you tell storys about pepul you never met. I said why shud I make up lies. I never tell lies any more becaus I always get caut.

She told me this test and the other one the raw-shok was for getting personalty. I laffed so hard. I said how can you get that thing from inkblots and fotos. She got sore and put her picturs away. I dont care. It was sily. I gess I faled that test too.

Later some men in white coats took me to a difernt part of the hospitil and gave me a game to play. It was like a race with a white mouse. They called the mouse Algernon. Algernon was in a box with a lot of twists and turns like all kinds of walls and they gave me a pencil and a paper with lines and lots of boxes. On one side it said START and on the other end it said FINISH. They said it was *amazed* and that Algernon and me had the same *amazed* to do. I dint see how we could have the same *amazed* if Algernon had a box and I had a paper but I dint say nothing. Anyway there wasnt time because the race started.

One of the men had a watch he was trying to hide so I wouldnt see it so I tryed not to look and that made me nervus.

Anyway that test made me feel worser than all the others because they did it over 10 times with difernt *amazeds* and Algernon won every time. I dint know that mice were so smart. Maybe thats because Algernon is a white mouse. Maybe white mice are smarter then other mice.

progis riport 4—Mar 8

Their going to use me! Im so exited I can hardly write. Dr Nemur and Dr Strauss had a argament about it first. Dr Nemur was in the office when Dr Strauss brot me in. Dr Nemur was worryed about using me but Dr Strauss told him Miss Kinnian rekemmended me the best from all the people who she was teaching. I like Miss Kinnian becaus shes a very smart teacher. And she said Charlie your going to have a second chance. If you volenteer for this experament you mite get smart. They dont know if it will be perminint but theirs a chance. Thats why I said ok even when I was scared because she said it was an operashun. She said dont be scared Charlie you done so much with so little I think you deserv it most of all.

So I got scaird when Dr Nemur and Dr Strauss argud about it. Dr Strauss said I had something that was very good. He said I had a good *motor-vation.* I never even knew I had that. I felt proud when he said that not every body with an eye-q of 68 had that thing. I dont know what it is or where I got it but he said Algernon had it too. Algernons *motor-vation* is the cheese they put in his box. But it cant be that because I didnt eat any cheese this week.

Then he told Dr Nemur something I dint understand so while they were talking I wrote down some of the words.

He said Dr Nemur I know Charlie is not what you had in mind as the first of your new brede of intelek** (coudnt get the word) superman. But most people of his low ment** are host** and uncoop** they are usualy dull apath** and hard to reach. He has a good natcher hes intristed and eager to please.

Dr Nemur said remember he will be the first human beeng ever to have his intelijence trippled by surgicle meens.

Dr Strauss said exakly. Look at how well hes lerned to read and write for his low mentel age its as grate an acheve** as you and I lerning einstines therey of **vity without help. That shows the intenss motor-vation. Its comparat** a tremen** achev** I say we use Charlie.

I dint get all the words and they were talking to fast but it sounded like Dr Strauss was on my side and like the other one wasnt.

• motivation (moh ti VAY shun) **desire to do something**

Then Dr Nemur nodded he said all right maybe your right. We will use Charlie. When he said that I got so exited I jumped up and shook his hand for being so good to me. I told him thank you doc you wont be sorry for giving me a second chance. And I mean it like I told him. After the operashun Im gonna try to be smart. Im gonna try awful hard.

progris ript 5—Mar 10

Im skared. Lots of people who work here and the nurses and the people who gave me the tests came to bring me candy and wish me luck. I hope I have luck. I got my rabits foot and my lucky penny and my horse shoe. Only a black cat crossed me when I was comming to the hospitil. Dr Strauss says dont be supersitis Charlie this is sience. Anyway Im keeping my rabits foot with me.

I asked Dr Strauss if Ill beat Algernon in the race after the operashun and he said maybe. If the operashun works Ill show that mouse I can be as smart as he is. Maybe smarter. Then Ill be abel to read better and spell the words good and know lots of things and be like other people. I want to be smart like other people. If it works perminint they will make everybody smart all over the wurld.

They dint give me anything to eat this morning. I dont know what that eating has to do with getting smart. Im very hungry and Dr Nemur took away my box of candy. That Dr Nemur is a grouch. Dr Strauss says I can have it back after the operashun. You cant eat befor a operashun . . .

Progress Report 6—Mar 15

The operashun dint hurt. He did it while I was sleeping. They took off the bandijis from my eyes and my head today so I can make a PROGRESS REPORT. Dr Nemur who looked at some of my other ones says I spell PROGRESS wrong and he told me how to spell it and REPORT too. I got to try and remember that.

I have a very bad memary for spelling. Dr Strauss says its ok to tell about all the things that happin to me but he says I shoud tell more about what I feel and what I think. When I told him I dont know how to think he said try. All the time when the bandijis were on my eyes I tryed to think. Nothing happened. I dont know what to think about. Maybe if I ask him he will tell me how I can think now that Im suppose to get smart. What do smart people think about. Fancy things I suppose. I wish I knew some fancy things alredy.

Progress Report 7—mar 19

Nothing is happining. I had lots of tests and different kinds of races with Algernon. I hate that mouse. He always beats me. Dr

Strauss said I got to play those games. And he said some time I got to take those tests over again. Thse inkblots are stupid. And those pictures are stupid too. I like to draw a picture of a man and a woman but I wont make up lies about people.

I got a headache from trying to think so much. I thot Dr Strauss was my friend but he dont help me. He dont tell me what to think or when Ill get smart. Miss Kinnian dint come to see me. I think writing these progress reports are stupid too.

Progress Report 8—Mar 23

Im going back to work at the factery. They said it was better I shud go back to work but I cant tell anyone what the operashun was for and I have to come to the hospitil for an hour evry night after work. They are gonna pay me mony every month for lerning to be smart.

Im glad Im going back to work because I miss my job and all my frends and all the fun we have there.

Dr Strauss says I shud keep writing things down but I dont have to do it every day just when I think of something or something speshul happins. He says dont get discoridged because it takes time and it happins slow. He says it took a long time with Algernon before he got 3 times smarter then he was before. Thats why Algernon beats me all the time because he had that operashun too. That makes me feel better. I coud probly do that *amazed* faster than a reglar mouse. Maybe some day Ill beat Algernon. Boy that would be something. So far Algernon looks like he mite be smart perminent.

Mar 25   (I dont have to write PROGRESS REPORT on top any more just when I hand it in once a week for Dr Nemur to read. I just have to put the date on. That saves time)

We had a lot of fun at the factery today. Joe Carp said hey look where Charlie had his operashun what did they do Charlie put some brains in. I was going to tell him but I remembered Dr Strauss said no. Then Frank Reilly said what did you do Charlie forget your key and open your door the hard way. That made me laff. Their really my friends and they like me.

Sometimes somebody will say hey look at Joe or Frank or George he really pulled a Charlie Gordon. I don't know why they say that but they always laff. This morning Amos Borg who is the 4 man at Donnegans used my name when he shouted at Ernie the office boy. Ernie lost a packige. He said Ernie for godsake what are you trying to be a Charlie Gordon. I dont understand why he said that. I never lost any packiges.

Mar 28   Dr Strauss came to my room tonight to see why I dint come in like I was suppose to. I told him I dont like to race with Algernon any more. He said I dont have to for a while but I shud come in. He had a present for me only it wasnt a present but just for lend. I thot it was a little television but it wasnt. He said I got to turn it on when I go to sleep. I said your kidding why shud I turn it on when Im going to sleep. Who ever herd of a thing like that. But he said if I want to get smart I got to do what he says. I told him I dint think I was going to get smart and he put his hand on my sholder and said Charlie you dont know it yet but your getting smarter all the time. You wont notice for a while. I think he was just being nice to make me feel good because I dont look any smarter.

Oh yes I almost forgot. I asked him when I can go back to the class at Miss Kinnians school. He said I wont go their. He said that soon Miss Kinnian will come to the hospitil to start and teach me speshul. I was mad at her for not comming to see me when I got the operashun but I like her so maybe we will be frends again.

Mar 29 That crazy TV kept me up all night. How can I sleep with something yelling crazy things all night in my ears. And the nutty pictures. Wow. I dont know what it says when Im up so how am I going to know when Im sleeping.

Dr Strauss says its ok. He says my brains are lerning when I sleep and that will help me when Miss Kinnian starts my lessons in the hospitl (only I found out it isnt a hospitil its a labatory). I think its all crazy. If you can get smart when your sleeping why do people go to school. That thing I dont think will work. I use to watch the late show and the late late show on TV all the time and it never made me smart. Maybe you have to sleep while you watch it.

PROGRESS REPORT 9—April 3

Dr Strauss showed me how to keep the TV turned low so now I can sleep. I dont hear a thing. And I still dont understand what it says. A few times I play it over in the morning to find out what I lerned when I was sleeping and I dont think so. Miss Kinnian says Maybe its another langwidge or something. But most times it sounds american. It talks so fast faster then even Miss Gold who was my teacher in 6 grade and I remember she talked so fast I coudnt understand her.

I told Dr Strauss what good is it to get smart in my sleep. I want to be smart when Im awake. He says its the same thing and I have two minds. Theres the *subconscious* and the *conscious* (thats how you spell it). And one dont tell the other one what its doing. They don't even talk to each other. Thats why I dream. And boy have I been having crazy dreams. Wow. Ever since that night TV. The late late late late late show.

I forgot to ask him if it was only me or if everybody had those two minds.

(I just looked up the word in the dictionary Dr Strauss gave me. The word is *subconscious. adj. Of the nature of mental operations yet not present in consciousness; as, subconscious conflict of desires.*) Theres more but I still dont know what it means. This isnt a very good dictionary for dumb people like me.

Anyway the headache is from the party. My frends from the factery Joe Carp and Frank Reilly invited me to go with them to Muggsys Saloon for some drinks. I dont like to drink but they said we will have lots of fun. I had a good time.

Joe Carp said I shoud show the girls how I mop out the toilet in the factory and he got me a mop. I showed them and everyone laffed when I told that Mr Donnegan said I was the best janiter he ever had because I like my job and do it good and never come late or miss a day except for my operashun.

I said Miss Kinnian always said Charlie be proud of your job because you do it good.

Everybody laffed and we had a good time and they gave me lots of drinks and Joe said Charlie is a card when hes potted. I dont know what that means but everybody likes me and we have fun. I cant wait to be smart like my best frends Joe Carp and Frank Reilly.

I dont remember how the party was over but I think I went out to buy a newspaper and coffe for Joe and Frank and when I came back there was no one their. I looked for them all over till late. Then I dont remember so good but I think I got sleepy or sick. A nice cop brot me back home. Thats what my landlady Mrs Flynn says.

But I got a headache and a big lump on my head and black and blue all over. I think maybe I fell but Joe Carp says it was the cop they beat up drunks some times. I don't think so. Miss Kinnian says cops are to help people. Anyway I got a bad headache and Im sick and hurt all over. I dont think Ill drink anymore.

April 6   I beat Algernon! I dint even know I beat him until Burt the tester told me. Then the second time I lost because I got so exited I fell off the chair before I finished. But after that I beat him 8 more times. I must be getting smart to beat a smart mouse like Algernon. But I dont *feel* smarter.

I wanted to race Algernon some more but Burt said thats enough for one day. They let me hold him for a minit. Hes not so bad. Hes soft like a ball of cotton. He blinks and when he opens his eyes their black and pink on the eges.

I said can I feed him because I felt bad to beat him and I wanted to be nice and make frends. Burt said no Algernon is a very specshul mouse with an operashun like mine, and he was the first of all the animals to stay smart so long. He told me Algernon is so smart that every day he has to solve a test to get his food. Its a thing like a lock on a door that changes every time Algernon goes in to eat so he has

to lern something new to get his food. That made me sad because if he couldnt lern he would be hungry.

I dont think its right to make you pass a test to eat. How woud Dr Nemur like it to have to pass a test every time he wants to eat. I think Ill be frends with Algernon.

April 9   Tonight after work Miss Kinnian was at the laboratory. She looked like she was glad to see me but scared. I told her dont worry Miss Kinnian Im not smart yet and she laffed. She said I have confidence in you Charlie the way you struggled so hard to read and right better than all the others. At werst you will have it for a littel wile and your doing something for sience.

We are reading a very hard book. I never read such a hard book before. Its called *Robinson Crusoe* about a man who gets merooned on a dessert Iland. Hes smart and figers out all kinds of things so he can have a house and food and hes a good swimmer. Only I feel sorry because hes all alone and has no frends. But I think their must be somebody else on the iland because theres a picture with his funny umbrella looking at footprints. I hope he gets a frend and not be lonely.

CHECKPOINT

Answer the following questions before going on with the story.

1. Charlie Gordon is keeping a diary because (a) it's an assignment in Miss Kinnian's adult education class. (b) Dr. Strauss asked him to keep it. (c) he wants to record the events of his life to save for his grandchildren.
2. The Thematic Apperception Test and the Rorschach (*raw shok*) Test that Charlie takes are designed to test a person's (a) personality. (b) motor skill development. (c) reading skills.
3. Charlie goes to the adult night school because (a) he has to as part of his parole conditions. (b) he's the janitor. (c) he wants to be smart.
4. A person who tests 100 on an I.Q. test is said to have average intelligence. Charlie has an I.Q. of 68. But after the operation, Charlie's intelligence will be tripled. (a) What will that make his I.Q.? (b) How much more intelligent than the average person will he be?
5. In "progris riport 4—Mar 8" there are a number of difficult words that Charlie can't figure out. (a) The first is *motor-vation*. What is this word, really? (b) A number of words are only partly spelled out and are finished with two asterisks (**). Why? Name the words as they should appear if correctly spelled. Ask your teacher about those you can't figure out.
6. Why do you think Dr. Strauss brought Charlie a special kind of TV that he is supposed to play only when he's asleep?
7. In the diary entries for April 6 and April 9 one can see that Charlie is beginning to make good inferences—a sign of intelligence. Name one inference he makes in his report of April 6 and one in his report of April 9.
8. A clue about what might happen in the story, or foreshadowing, is given in the following diary entry by Charlie: "They said you know it will probly be tempirery. I said yes. Miss Kinnian told me. I dont care if it herts." What do you think will happen?

Part II

April 10 Miss Kinnian teaches me to spell better. She says look at a word and close your eyes and say it over and over until you remember. I have lots of truble with *through* that you say *threw* and *enough* and *tough* that you dont say *enew* and *tew.* You got to say *enuff* and *tuff.* Thats how I use to write it before I started to get smart. Im confused but Miss Kinnian says theres no reason in spelling.

Apr 14 Finished *Robinson Crusoe.* I want to find out more about what happens to him but Miss Kinnian says thats all there is. *Why.*

Apr 15 Miss Kinnian says Im lerning fast. She read some of the Progress Reports and she looked at me kind of funny. She says Im a fine person and Ill show them all. I asked her why. She said never mind but I shoudnt feel bad if I find out that everybody isnt nice like I think. She said for a person who god gave so little to you done more then a lot of people with brains they never even used. I said all my frends are smart people but there good. They like me and they never did anything that wasnt nice. Then she got something in her eye and she had to run out to the ladys room.

Apr 16 Today, I lerned, the *comma,* this is a comma (,) a period, with a tail, Miss Kinnian, says its important, because, it makes writing better, she said, somebody, coud lose, a lot of money, if a comma, isnt, in the, right place, I dont have, any money, and I dont see, how a comma, keeps you from losing it,

But she says, everybody, uses commas, so Ill use, them too,

Apr 17 I used the comma wrong. Its punctuation. Miss Kinnian told me to look up long words in the dictionary to lern to spell them. I said whats the difference if you can read it anyway. She said its part of your education so now on I'll look up all the words Im not sure how to spell. It takes a long time to write that way but I think Im remembering. I only have to look up once and after that I get it right. Anyway thats how come I got the word *punctuation* right. (Its that way in the dictionary). Miss Kinnian says a period is punctuation too, and there are lots of other marks to lern. I told her I thot all the periods had to have tails but she said no.

You got to mix them up, she showed? me" how. to mix! them(up,. and now; I can! mix up all kinds" of punctuation, in! my writing? There, are lots! of rules? to lern; but Im gettin'g them in my head.

One thing I? like about, Dear Miss Kinnian: (thats the way it goes in a business letter if I ever go into business) is she, always gives me' a reason" when—I ask. She's a gen'ius! I wish! I cou'd be smart' like, her;

(Punctuation, is; fun!)

April 18 What a dope I am! I didn't even understand what she was talking about. I read the grammar book last night and it explanes the whole thing. Then I saw it was the same way as Miss Kinnian was trying to tell me, but I didn't get it. I got up in the middle of the night, and the whole thing straightened out in my mind.

Miss Kinnian said that the TV working in my sleep helped out. She said I reached a plateau. Thats like the flat top of a hill.

After I figgered out how punctuation worked, I read over all my old Progress Reports from the beginning. Boy, did I have crazy spelling and punctuation! I told Miss Kinnian I ought to go over the pages and fix all the mistakes but she said, "No, Charlie, Dr. Nemur wants them just as they are. That's why he let you keep them after they were photostated, to see your own progress. You're coming along fast, Charlie."

That made me feel good. After the lesson I went down and played with Algernon. We don't race any more.

April 20 I feel sick inside. Not sick like for a doctor, but inside my chest it feels empty like getting punched and a heartburn at the same time.

I wasn't going to write about it, but I guess I got to, because it's important. Today was the first time I ever stayed home from work.

Last night Joe Carp and Frank Reilly invited me to a party. There were lots of girls and some men from the factory. I remembered how sick I got last time I drank too much, so I told Joe I didn't want anything to drink. He gave me a plain Coke instead. It tasted funny, but I thought it was just a bad taste in my mouth.

We had a lot of fun for a while. Joe said I should dance with Ellen and she would teach me the steps. I fell a few times and I couldn't understand why because no one else was dancing besides Ellen and me. And all the time I was tripping because somebody's foot was always sticking out.

Then when I got up I saw the look on Joe's face and it gave me a funny feeling in my stomack. "He's a scream," one of the girls said. Everybody was laughing.

Frank said, "I ain't laughed so much since we sent him off for the newspaper that night at Muggsy's and ditched him."

"Look at him. His face is red."

"He's blushing. Charlie is blushing."

"Hey, Ellen, what'd you do to Charlie? I never saw him act like that before."

I didn't know what to do or where to turn. Everyone was looking at me and laughing and I felt naked. I wanted to hide myself. I ran out into the street and I threw up. Then I walked home. It's a funny

---

• photostat (FOH toh stat) **make a photographic copy**

thing I never knew that Joe and Frank and the others liked to have me around all the time to make fun of me.

Now I know what it means when they say "to pull a Charlie Gordon."

I'm ashamed.

PROGRESS REPORT 11

April 21 Still didn't go into the factory. I told Mrs. Flynn my landlady to call and tell Mr. Donnegan I was sick. Mrs. Flynn looks at me very funny lately like she's scared of me.

I think it's a good thing about finding out how everybody laughs at me. I thought about it a lot. It's because I'm so dumb and I don't even know when I'm doing something dumb. People think it's funny when a dumb person can't do things the same way they can.

Anyway, now I know I'm getting smarter every day. I know punctuation and I can spell good. I like to look up all the hard words in the dictionary and I remember them. I'm reading a lot now, and Miss Kinnian says I read very fast. Sometimes I even understand what I'm reading about, and it stays in my mind. There are times when I can close my eyes and think of a page and it all comes back like a picture.

Besides history, geography, and arithmetic, Miss Kinnian said I should start to learn a few foreign languages. Dr. Strauss gave me some more tapes to play while I sleep. I still don't understand how that conscious and unconscious mind works, but Dr. Strauss says not to worry yet. He asked me to promise that when I start learning college subjects next week I wouldn't read any books on psychology—that is, until he gives me permission.

I feel a lot better today, but I guess I'm still a little angry that all the time people were laughing and making fun of me because I wasn't so smart. When I become intelligent like Dr. Strauss says, with three times my I.Q. of 68, then maybe I'll be like everyone else and people will like me and be friendly.

I'm not sure what an I.Q. is. Dr. Nemur said it was something that measured how intelligent you were—like a scale in the drugstore weighs pounds. But Dr. Strauss had a big argument with him and said an I.Q. didn't weigh intelligence at all. He said an I.Q. showed how much intelligence you could get, like the numbers on the outside of a measuring cup. You still had to fill the cup up with stuff.

Then when I asked Burt, who gives me my intelligence tests and works with Algernon, he said that both of them were wrong (only I had to promise not to tell them he said so). Burt says that the I.Q. measures a lot of different things including some of the things you learned already, and it really isn't any good at all.

So I still don't know what I.Q. is except that mine is going to be over 200 soon. I didn't want to say anything, but I don't see how if they don't know *what* it is, or *where* it is—I don't see how they know *how much* of it you've got.

Dr. Nemur says I have to take a *Rorshach Test* tomorrow. I wonder what *that* is.

April 22 I found out what a *Rorshach* is. It's the test I took before the operation—the one with the inkblots on the pieces of cardboard. The man who gave me the test was the same one.

I was scared to death of those inkblots. I knew he was going to ask me to find the pictures and I knew I wouldn't be able to. I was thinking to myself, if only there was some way of knowing what kind of pictures were hidden there. Maybe there weren't any pictures at all. Maybe it was just a trick to see if I was dumb enough to look for something that wasn't there. Just thinking about that made me sore at him.

"All right, Charlie," he said, "you've seen these cards before, remember?"

"Of course I remember."

The way I said it, he knew I was angry, and he looked surprised. "Yes, of course. Now I want you to look at this one. What might this be? What do you see on this card? People see all sorts of things in these inkblots. Tell me what it might be for you—what it makes you think of."

I was shocked. That wasn't what I had expected him to say at all. "You mean there are no pictures hidden in those inkblots?"

He frowned and took off his glasses. "What?"

"Pictures. Hidden in the inkblots. Last time you told me that everyone could see them and you wanted me to find them too."

He explained to me that the last time he had used almost the exact same words he was using now. I didn't believe it, and I still have the suspicion that he misled me at the time just for the fun of it. Unless—I don't know any more—could I have been *that* feeble-minded?

We went through the cards slowly. One of them looked like a pair of bats tugging at something. Another one looked like two men fencing with swords. I imagined all sorts of things. I guess I got carried away. But I didn't trust him any more, and I kept turning them around and even looking on the back to see if there was anything there I was supposed to catch. While he was making his notes, I peeked out of the corner of my eye to read it. But it was all in code that looked like this:

WF + A DdF-Ad orig. WF-A SF + obj

The test still doesn't make sense to me. It seems to me that anyone could make up lies about things that they didn't really see.

How could he know I wasn't making a fool of him by mentioning things that I didn't really imagine? Maybe I'll understand it when Dr. Strauss lets me read up on psychology.

April 25   I figured out a new way to line up the machines in the factory, and Mr. Donnegan says it will save him ten thousand dollars a year in labor and increased production. He gave me a twenty-five-dollar bonus.

I wanted to take Joe Carp and Frank Reilly out to lunch to celebrate, but Joe said he had to buy some things for his wife, and Frank said he was meeting his cousin for lunch. I guess it'll take a little time for them to get used to the changes in me. Everybody seems to be frightened of me. When I went over to Amos Borg and tapped him on the shoulder, he jumped up in the air.

People don't talk to me much any more or kid around the way they used to. It makes the job kind of lonely.

April 27   I got up the nerve today to ask Miss Kinnian to have dinner with me tomorrow night to celebrate my bonus.

At first she wasn't sure it was right, but I asked Dr. Strauss and he said it was okay. Dr. Strauss and Dr. Nemur don't seem to be getting along so well. They're arguing all the time. This evening when I came in to ask Dr. Strauss about having dinner with Miss Kinnian, I heard them shouting. Dr. Nemur was saying that it was *his* experiment and *his* research, and Dr. Strauss was shouting back that he contributed just as much, because he found me through Miss Kinnian and he performed the operation. Dr. Strauss said that someday thousands of neurosurgeons might be using his technique all over the world.

Dr. Nemur wanted to publish the results of the experiment at the end of this month. Dr. Strauss wanted to wait a while longer to be sure. Dr. Strauss said that Dr. Nemur was more interested in the Chair of Psychology at Princeton than he was in the experiment. Dr. Nemur said that Dr. Strauss was nothing but an opportunist who was trying to ride to glory on *his* coattails.

When I left afterwards, I found myself trembling. I don't know why for sure, but it was as if I'd seen both men clearly for the first time. I remember hearing Burt say that Dr. Nemur had a shrew of a wife who was pushing him all the time to get things published so that he could become famous. Burt said that the dream of her life was to have a big-shot husband.

- neurosurgeon (NOOR oh SUR jun) **surgeon specializing in nervous structures (as nerves, the brain, or the spinal cord)**
- opportunist (op ur TOON ist) **one who strives for success with little regard for right and wrong**
- shrew (SHROO) **bad-tempered woman**

Was Dr. Strauss really trying to ride on his coattails?

April 28 I don't understand why I never noticed how beautiful Miss Kinnian really is. She has brown eyes and feathery brown hair that comes to the top of her neck. She's only thirty-four! I think from the beginning I had the feeling that she was an unreachable genius—and very, very old. Now, every time I see her she grows younger and more lovely.

We had dinner and a long talk. When she said that I was coming along so fast that soon I'd be leaving her behind, I laughed.

"It's true, Charlie. You're already a better reader than I am. You can read a whole page at a glance while I can take in only a few lines at a time. And you remember every single thing you read. I'm lucky if I can recall the main thoughts and the general meaning."

"I don't feel intelligent. There are so many things I don't understand."

She took out a cigarette and I lit it for her. "You've got to be a *little* patient. You're accomplishing in days and weeks what it takes normal people to do in half a lifetime. That's what makes it so amazing. You're like a giant sponge now, soaking things in. Facts, figures, general knowledge. And soon you'll begin to connect them, too. You'll see how the different branches of learning are related. There are many levels, Charlie, like steps on a giant ladder that take you up higher and higher to see more and more of the world around you.

"I can see only a little bit of that, Charlie, and I won't go much higher than I am now, but you'll keep climbing up and up, and see

more and more, and each step will open new worlds that you never even knew existed." She frowned. "I hope . . . I just hope to God—"

"What?"

"Never mind, Charles. I just hope I wasn't wrong to advise you to go into this in the first place."

I laughed. "How could that be? It worked, didn't it? Even Algernon is still smart."

We sat there silently for a while and I knew what she was thinking about as she watched me toying with the chain of my rabbit's foot and my keys. I didn't want to think of that possibility any more than elderly people want to think of death. I *knew* that this was only the beginning. I knew what she meant about levels because I'd seen some of them already. The thought of leaving her behind made me sad.

I'm in love with Miss Kinnian.

PROGRESS REPORT 12

April 30 I've quit my job with Donnegan's Plastic Box Company. Mr. Donnegan insisted that it would be better for all concerned if I left. What did I do to make them hate me so?

The first I knew of it was when Mr. Donnegan showed me the petition. Eight hundred and forty names, everyone connected with the factory, except Fanny Girden. Scanning the list quickly, I saw at once that hers was the only missing name. All the rest demanded that I be fired.

Joe Carp and Frank Reilly wouldn't talk to me about it. No one else would either, except Fanny. She was one of the few people I'd known who set her mind to something and believed it no matter what the rest of the world proved, said, or did—and Fanny did not believe that I should have been fired. She had been against the petition on principle and despite the pressure and threats she'd held out.

"Which don't mean to say," she remarked, "that I don't think there's something mighty strange about you, Charlie. Them changes. I don't know. You used to be a good, dependable, ordinary man—not too bright maybe, but honest. Who knows what you done to yourself to get so smart all of a sudden. Like everybody around here's been saying, Charlie, it's not right."

"But how can you say that, Fanny? What's wrong with a man becoming intelligent and wanting to acquire knowledge and understanding of the world around him?"

She stared down at her work and I turned to leave. Without looking at me, she said: "It was evil when Eve listened to the snake and ate from the tree of knowledge. It was evil when she saw that she was naked. If not for that none of us would ever have to grow old and sick, and die."

Once again now I have the feeling of shame burning inside me. This intelligence has driven a wedge between me and all the people I once knew and loved. Before, they laughed at me and despised me for my ignorance and dullness; now, they hate me for my knowledge and understanding. What in God's name do they want of me?

They've driven me out of the factory. Now I'm more alone than ever before . . .

May 15 Dr. Strauss is very angry at me for not having written any progress reports in two weeks. He's justified because the lab is now paying me a regular salary. I told him I was too busy thinking and reading. When I pointed out that writing was such a slow process that it made me impatient with my poor handwriting, he suggested that I learn to type. It's much easier to write now because I can type nearly seventy-five words a minute. Dr. Strauss continually reminds me of the need to speak and write simply so that people will be able to understand me.

I'll try to review all the things that happened to me during the last two weeks. Algernon and I were presented to the American Psychological Association sitting in convention with the World Psychological Association last Tuesday. We created quite a sensation. Dr. Nemur and Dr. Strauss were proud of us.

I suspect that Dr. Nemur, who is sixty—ten years older than Dr. Strauss—finds it necessary to see tangible results of his work. Undoubtedly the result of pressure by Mrs. Nemur.

Contrary to my earlier impressions of him, I realize that Dr. Nemur is not at all a genius. He has a very good mind, but it struggles under the specter of self-doubt. He wants people to take him for a genius. Therefore, it is important for him to feel that his work is accepted by the world. I believe that Dr. Nemur was afraid of further delay because he worried that someone else might make a discovery along these lines and take the credit from him.

Dr. Strauss on the other hand might be called a genius, although I feel that his areas of knowledge are too limited. He was educated in the tradition of narrow specialization; the broader aspects of background were neglected far more than necessary—even for a neurosurgeon.

I was shocked to learn that the only ancient languages he could read were Latin, Greek, and Hebrew, and that he knows almost nothing of mathematics beyond the elementary levels of the calculus of variations. When he admitted this to me, I found myself al-

- tangible (TAN juh bul) **solid and substantial; real; actual**
- specter (SPEK tur) **something that haunts the mind**
- calculus (KAL kyoo lus)   of   variations (ver ee AY shuns) **highly complex branch of mathematics**

most annoyed. It was as if he'd hidden this part of himself in order to deceive me, pretending—as do many people I've discovered—to be what he is not. No one I've ever known is what he appears to be on the surface.

[Note: From this point on, some rare technical words that only a specialist would know will not be defined. To demonstrate Charlie's increasing intelligence, the author deliberately uses words that are unfamiliar to most readers. Just make a good guess and read on.]

Dr. Nemur appears to be uncomfortable around me. Sometimes when I try to talk to him, he just looks at me strangely and turns away. I was angry at first when Dr. Strauss told me I was giving Dr. Nemur an inferiority complex. I thought he was mocking me and I'm oversensitive at being made fun of.

How was I to know that a highly respected psychoexperimentalist like Nemur was unacquainted with Hindustani and Chinese? It's absurd when you consider the work that is being done in India and China today in the very field of his study.

I asked Dr. Strauss how Nemur could refute Rahajamati's attack on his method and results if Nemur couldn't even read them in the first place. That strange look on Dr. Strauss' face can mean only one of two things. Either he doesn't want to tell Nemur what they're saying in India, or else—and this worries me—Dr Strauss doesn't know either. I must be careful to speak and write clearly and simply so that people won't laugh.

May 18 I am very disturbed. I saw Miss Kinnian last night for the first time in over a week. I tried to avoid all discussions of intellectual concepts and to keep the conversation on a simple, everyday level, but she just stared at me blankly and asked me what I meant about the mathematical variance equivalent in Dorbermann's *Fifth Concerto.*

When I tried to explain she stopped me and laughed. I guess I got angry, but I suspect I'm approaching her on the wrong level. No matter what I try to discuss with her, I am unable to communicate. I must review Vrostadt's equations on *Levels of Semantic Progression.* I find that I don't communicate with people much any more. Thank God for books and music and things I can think about. I am alone in my apartment at Mrs. Flynn's boardinghouse most of the time and seldom speak to anyone.

- refute (ri FYOOT) **prove wrong by evidence**
- concept (KON sept) **idea**

CHECKPOINT

Answer the following questions before going on with the story.

1. Look at Charlie's entry for April 15. (a) Why is Miss Kinnian upset by some of Charlie's Progress Reports? (b) Why do you think she has to "run out to the ladys room"?

2. In his entry for April 21, Charlie writes, "When I become intelligent like Dr. Strauss says, with three times my I.Q. of 68, then maybe I'll be like everyone else and people will like me and be friendly." Do you think this inference will prove to be correct? Explain.

3. (a) What new information does Charlie discover about Miss Kinnian and his feelings for her (April 28)? (b) What does he mean by "The thought of leaving her behind made me sad"?

4. In the entry for May 15, Charlie discusses his new understanding of Dr. Nemur and Dr. Strauss. He reaches the conclusion, "No one I've ever known is what he appears to be on the surface." (a) Explain how this statement applies to the two scientists. (b) Also explain, "Dr. Strauss told me I was giving Dr. Nemur an inferiority complex."

5. Throughout this section you are given clues to Charlie's increasing intelligence. Look back and list one clue for each of the following diary entries: April 18, April 20, April 21, April 22, April 25, April 30, May 15, May 18.

Part III

May 20 I would not have noticed the new dishwasher, a boy of about sixteen, at the corner diner where I take my evening meals if not for the incident of the broken dishes.

They crashed to the floor, shattering and sending bits of white china under the tables. The boy stood there, dazed and frightened, holding the empty tray in his hand. The whistles and catcalls from the customers (the cries of "hey, there go the profits!" . . . "*Mazel-tov!*" . . . and "well, *he* didn't work here very long . . ." which invariably seems to follow the breaking of glass or dishware in a public restaurant) all seemed to confuse him.

● invariably (in VER ee uh blee) **always; unchangingly**

When the owner came to see what the excitement was about, the boy cowered as if he expected to be struck and threw up his arms as if to ward off the blow.

"All right! All right, you dope," shouted the owner, "don't just stand there! Get the broom and sweep that mess up. A broom . . . a broom, you idiot! It's in the kitchen. Sweep up all the pieces."

The boy saw that he was not going to be punished. His frightened expression disappeared and he smiled and hummed as he came back with the broom to sweep the floor. A few of the rowdier customers kept up the remarks, amusing themselves at his expense.

"Here, sonny, over here there's a nice piece behind you . . ."

"C'mon, do it again . . ."

"He's not so dumb. It's easier to break 'em than to wash 'em . . ."

As his vacant eyes moved across the crowd of amused onlookers, he slowly mirrored their smiles and finally broke into an uncertain grin at the joke which he obviously did not understand.

I felt sick inside as I looked at his dull, vacuous smile, the wide, bright eyes of a child, uncertain but eager to please. They were laughing at him because he was mentally retarded.

And I had been laughing at him too.

Suddenly, I was furious at myself and all those who were smirking at him. I jumped up and shouted, "Shut up! Leave him alone! It's not his fault he can't understand! He can't help what he is! But for God's sake . . . he's still a human being!"

The room grew silent. I cursed myself for losing control and creating a scene. I tried not to look at the boy as I paid my check and walked out without touching my food. I felt ashamed for both of us.

How strange it is that people of honest feelings and sensibility, who would not take advantage of a man born without arms or legs or eyes—how such people think nothing of abusing a man born with low intelligence. It infuriated me to think that not too long ago I, like this boy, had foolishly played the clown.

And I had almost forgotten.

I'd hidden the picture of the old Charlie Gordon from myself because now that I was intelligent it was something that had to be pushed out of my mind. But today in looking at that boy, for the first time I saw what I had been. *I was just like him!*

Only a short time ago, I learned that people laughed at me. Now I can see that unknowingly I joined with them in laughing at myself. That hurts most of all.

I have often reread my progress reports and seen the illiteracy,

---

- cower   (KOW ur)   **shrink from in fear**
- vacuous   (VAK yoo us)   **empty; stupid**

the childish naïveté, the mind of low intelligence peering from a dark room, through the keyhole, at the dazzling light outside. I see that even in my dullness I knew that I was inferior, and that other people had something I lacked—something denied me. In my mental blindness, I thought that it was somehow connected with the ability to read and write, and I was sure that if I could get those skills I would automatically have intelligence too.

Even a feeble-minded man wants to be like other men.

A child may not know how to feed itself, or what to eat, yet it knows of hunger.

This then is what I was like, I never knew. Even with my gift of intellectual awareness, I never really knew.

This day was good for me. Seeing the past more clearly, I have decided to use my knowledge and skills to work in the field of increasing human intelligence levels. Who is better equipped for this work? Who else has lived in both worlds? These are my people. Let me use my gift to do something for them.

Tomorrow, I will discuss with Dr. Strauss the manner in which I can work in this area. I may be able to help him work out the problems of widespread use of the technique which was used on me. I have several good ideas of my own.

There is so much that might be done with this technique. If I could be made into a genius, what about thousands of others like myself? What fantastic levels might be achieved by using this technique on normal people? On *geniuses?*

There are so many doors to open. I am impatient to begin.

PROGRESS REPORT 13

May 23 It happened today. Algernon bit me. I visited the lab to see him as I do occasionally, and when I took him out of his cage, he snapped at my hand. I put him back and watched him for a while. He was unusually disturbed and vicious.

May 24 Burt, who is in charge of the experimental animals, tells me that Algernon is changing. He is less co-operative, he refuses to run the maze any more; general motivation has decreased. And he hasn't been eating. Everyone is upset about what this may mean.

May 25 They've been feeding Algernon, who now refuses to work the shifting-lock problem. Everyone identifies me with Algernon. In a way we're both the first of our kind. They're all pretending that Algernon's behavior is not necessarily significant for me. But it's hard to hide the fact that some of the other animals who were used in this experiment are showing strange behavior.

 • naïveté (nah eev TAY) **natural simplicity**

Dr. Strauss and Dr. Nemur have asked me not to come to the lab any more. I know what they're thinking but I can't accept it. I am going ahead with my plans to carry their research forward. With all due respect to both of these fine scientists, I am well aware of their limitations. If there is an answer, I'll have to find it out for myself. Suddenly, time has become very important to me.

May 29   I have been given a lab of my own and permission to go ahead with the research. I'm on to something. Working day and night. I've had a cot moved into the lab. Most of my writing time is spent on the notes which I keep in a separate folder, but from time to time I feel it necessary to put down my moods and my thoughts out of sheer habit.

I find the *calculus of intelligence* to be a fascinating study. Here is the place for the application of all the knowledge I have acquired. In a sense it's the problem I've been concerned with all my life.

May 31   Dr. Strauss thinks I'm working too hard. Dr. Nemur says I'm trying to cram a lifetime of research and thought into a few weeks. I know I should rest, but I'm driven on by something inside that won't let me stop. I've got to find the reason for the sharp regression in Algernon. I've got to know *if* and *when* it will happen to me.

June 4
Letter to Dr. Strauss (*copy*)

Dear Dr. Strauss:

Under separate cover I am sending you a copy of my report entitled, "The Algernon-Gordon Effect: A Study of Structure and Function of Increased Intelligence," which I would like to have you read and have published.

As you see, my experiments are completed. I have included in my report all of my formulae, as well as mathematical analysis in the appendix. Of course, these should be verified.

Because of its importance to both you and Dr. Nemur (and need I say to myself, too?) I have checked and rechecked my results a dozen times in the hope of finding an error. I am sorry to say the results must stand. Yet for the sake of science, I am grateful for the little bit that I here add to the knowledge of the function of the human mind and of the laws governing the artificial increase of human intelligence.

I recall your once saying to me that an experimental *failure* or the *disproving* of a theory was as important to the advancement of learning as a success would be. I know now that this is true. I am

---

• regression (ri GRESH un) **a trend toward a lower state**

sorry, however, that my own contribution to the field must rest upon the ashes of the work of two men I regard so highly.

Yours truly,
Charles Gordon

encl.: rept.

June 5 I must not become emotional. The facts and the results of my experiments are clear, and the more sensational aspects of my own rapid climb cannot obscure the fact that the tripling of intelligence by the surgical technique developed by Drs. Strauss and Nemur must be viewed as having little or no practical applicability (at the present time) to the increase of human intelligence.

As I review the records and data on Algernon, I see that although he is still in his physical infancy, he has regressed mentally. Motor activity is impaired; there is a general reduction of glandular activity; there is an accelerated loss of co-ordination.

There are also strong indications of progressive amnesia.

As will be seen by my report, these and other physical and mental deterioration syndromes can be predicted with statistically significant results by the application of my formula.

The surgical stimulus to which we were both subjected has resulted in an intensification and acceleration of all mental processes. The unforeseen development, which I have taken the liberty of calling the *Algernon-Gordon Effect,* is the logical extension of the entire intelligence speed-up. The hypothesis here proven may be described simply in the following terms: Artificially increased intelligence deteriorates at a rate of time directly proportional to the quantity of the increase.

I feel that this, in itself, is an important discovery.

As long as I am able to write, I will continue to record my thoughts in these progress reports. It is one of my few pleasures. However, by all indications, my own mental deterioration will be very rapid.

I have already begun to notice signs of emotional instability and forgetfulness, the first symptoms of the burnout.

June 10 Deterioration progressing. I have become absent-minded. Algernon died two days ago. Dissection shows my predictions were right. His brain had decreased in weight and there was a general

---

- obscure (ob SKYOOR) **conceal**
- progressive (pruh GRES iv) **increasing in severity**
- deterioration (di TIR ee uh RAY shun) syndromes
  (SIN drohmz) patterns of symptoms growing worse

smoothing out of cerebral convolutions as well as a deepening and broadening of brain fissures.

I guess the same thing is or will soon be happening to me. Now that it's definite, I don't want it to happen.

I put Algernon's body in a cheese box and buried him in the back yard. I cried.

June 15 Dr. Strauss came to see me again. I wouldn't open the door and I told him to go away. I want to be left to myself. I have become touchy and irritable. I feel the darkness closing in. It's hard to throw off thoughts of suicide. I keep telling myself how important this introspective journal will be.

It's a strange sensation to pick up a book that you've read and enjoyed just a few months ago and discover that you don't remember it. I remembered how great I thought John Milton was, but when I picked up *Paradise Lost* I couldn't understand it at all. I got so angry I threw the book across the room.

I've got to try to hold on to some of it. Some of the things I've learned. Oh, God, please don't take it all away.

June 19 Sometimes, at night, I go out for a walk. Last night I couldn't remember where I lived. A policeman took me home. I have the strange feeling that this has all happened to me before—a long time ago. I keep telling myself I'm the only person in the world who can describe what's happening to me.

- cerebral (suh REE brul) convolutions (KON vuh LOO shuns) **ridges on the surface of the brain**
- fissure (FISH ur) **narrow opening or crack**
- introspective (in troh SPEK tiv) **self-examining**

June 21 Why can't I remember? I've got to fight. I lie in bed for days and I don't know who or where I am. Then it all comes back to me in a flash. Fugues of amnesia. Symptoms of senility—second child-hood. I can watch them coming on. It's so cruelly logical. I learned so much and so fast. Now my mind is deteriorating rapidly. I won't let it happen. I'll fight it. I can't help thinking of the boy in the restau-rant, the blank expression, the silly smile, the people laughing at him. No—please—not that again . . .

June 22 I'm forgetting things that I learned recently. It seems to be following the classic pattern—the last things learned are the first things forgotten. Or is that the pattern? I'd better look it up again. . . .

I reread my paper on the *Algernon-Gordon Effect* and I get the strange feeling that it was written by someone else. There are parts I don't even understand.

Motor activity impaired. I keep tripping over things, and it be-comes increasingly difficult to type.

June 23 I've given up using the typewriter completely. My coordina-tion is bad. I feel that I'm moving slower and slower. Had a terrible shock today. I picked up a copy of an article I used in my research, Krueger's *Uber psychische Ganzheit* to see if it would help me un-derstand what I had done. First I thought there was something wrong with my eyes. Then I realized I could no longer read German. I tested myself in other languages. All gone.

June 30 A week since I dare to write again. It's slipping away like sand through my fingers. Most of the books I have are too hard for me now. I get angry with them because I know that I read and under-stood them just a few weeks ago.

I keep telling myself I must keep writing these reports so that somebody will know what is happening to me. But it gets harder to form the words and remember spellings. I have to look up even simple words in the dictionary now and it makes me impatient with myself.

Dr. Strauss comes around almost every day, but I told him I wouldn't see or speak to anybody. He feels guilty. They all do. But I don't blame anyone. I knew what might happen. But how it hurts.

July 7 I don't know where the week went. Todays Sunday I know because I can see through my window people going to church. I think I stayed in bed all week but I remember Mrs. Flynn bringing food to me a few times. I keep saying over and over Ive got to do

---

● fugue (FYOOG) **loss of memory**

287

something but then I forget or maybe its just easier not to do what I say Im going to do.

I think of my mother and father a lot these days. I found a picture of them with me taken at a beach. My father has a big ball under his arm and my mother is holding me by the hand. I dont remember them the way they are in the picture. All I remember is my father drunk most of the time and arguing with mom about money.

He never shaved much and he used to scratch my face when he hugged me. My mother said he died but Cousin Miltie said he heard his mom and dad say that my father ran away with another woman. When I asked my mother she slapped my face and said my father was dead. I dont think I ever found out which was true but I don't care much. (He said he was going to take me to see cows on a farm once but he never did. He never kept his promises . . .)

July 10 My landlady Mrs Flynn is very worried about me. She says the way I lay around all day and dont do anthing I remind her of her son before she threw him out of the house. She said she doesn't like loafers. If Im sick its one thing, but if Im a loafer thats another thing and she wont have it. I told her I think Im sick.

I try to read a little bit every day, mostly stories, but sometimes I have to read the same thing over and over again because I dont know what it means. And its hard to write. I know I should look up all the words in the dictionary but its so hard and Im so tired all the time.

Then I got the idea that I would only use the easy words instead of the long hard ones. That saves time. I put flowers on Algernons grave about once a week. Mrs Flynn thinks Im crazy to put flowers on a mouses grave but I told her that Algernon was special.

July 14 Its sunday again. I dont have anything to do to keep me busy now because my television set is broke and I dont have any money to get it fixed. (I think I lost this months check from the lab. I dont remember)

I get awful headaches and asperin doesnt help me much. Mrs Flynn knows Im really sick and she feels very sorry for me. Shes a wonderful woman whenever someone is sick.

July 22 Mrs Flynn called a strange doctor to see me. She was afraid I was going to die. I told the doctor I wasnt too sick and that I only forget sometimes. He asked me did I have any friends or relatives and I said no I dont have any. I told him I had a friend called Algernon once but he was a mouse and we used to run races together. He looked at me kind of funny like he thought I was crazy.

He smiled when I told him I used to be a genius. He talked to me like I was a baby and he winked at Mrs Flynn. I got mad and chased him out because he was making fun of me the way they all used to.

July 24   I have no more money and Mrs Flynn says I got to go to work somewhere and pay the rent because I havent paid for over two months. I dont know any work but the job I used to have at Don- negans Plastic Box Company. I dont want to go back there because they all knew me when I was smart and maybe theyll laugh at me. But I don't know what else to do to get money.

July 25   I was looking at some of my old progress reports and its very funny but I cant read what I wrote. I can make out some of the words but they dont make sense.

Miss Kinnian came to the door but I said go away I dont want to see you. She cried and I cried too but I wouldnt let her in because I didn't want her to laugh at me. I told her I didn't like her any more. I told her I didnt want to be smart any more. Thats not true. I still love her and I still want to be smart but I had to say that so shed go away. She gave Mrs Flynn money to pay the rent. I dont want that. I got to get a job.

Please . . . please let me not forget how to read and write . . .

July 27 Mr Donnegan was very nice when I came back and asked him for my old job of janitor. First he was very suspicious but I told him what happened to me then he looked very sad and put his hand on my shoulder and said Charlie Gordon you got guts.

Everybody looked at me when I came downstairs and started working in the toilet sweeping it out like I used to. I told myself Charlie if they make fun of you dont get sore because you remember their not so smart as you once thot they were. And besides they were once your friends and if they laughed at you that doesnt mean any-thing because they liked you too.

One of the new men who came to work there after I went away made a nasty crack he said hey Charlie I hear your a very smart fella a real quiz kid. Say something intelligent. I felt bad but Joe Carp came over and grabbed him by the shirt and said leave him alone you lousy cracker or Ill break your neck. I didn't expect Joe to take my part so I guess hes really my friend.

Later Frank Reilly came over and said Charlie if anybody bothers you or trys to take advantage you call me or Joe and we will set em straight. I said thanks Frank and I got choked up so I had to turn around and go into the supply room so he wouldn't see me cry. Its good to have friends.

July 28 I did a dumb thing today I forgot I wasnt in Miss Kinnians class at the adult center any more like I use to be. I went in and sat down in my old seat in the back of the room and she looked at me funny and she said Charles. I dint remember she ever called me that before only Charlie so I said hello Miss Kinnian Im redy for my lesin today only I lost my reader that we was using. She startid to cry and run out of the room and everybody looked at me and I saw they wasnt the same pepul who used to be in my class.

Then all of a suddin I rememberd some things about the operashun and me getting smart and I said holy smoke I reely pulled a Charlie Gordon that time. I went away before she come back to the room.

Thats why Im going away from New York for good. I dont want do to nothing like that agen. I dont want Miss Kinnian to feel sorry for me. Evry body feels sorry at the factery and I dont want that eather so Im going someplace where nobody knows that Charlie Gordon was once a genus and now he cant even reed a book or rite good.

Im taking a cuple of books along and even if I cant reed them Ill practise hard and maybe I wont forget every thing I lerned. If I try reel hard maybe Ill be a littel bit smarter then I was before the operashun. I got my rabits foot and my luky penny and maybe they will help me.

If you ever reed this Miss Kinnian dont be sorry for me Im glad I got a second chanse to be smart becaus I lerned a lot of things that I never even new were in this world and Im grateful that I saw it all for a littel bit. I dont know why Im dumb agen or what I did wrong maybe its becaus I dint try hard enuff. But if I try and practis very hard maybe Ill get a littl smarter and know what all the words are. I remember a littel bit how nice I had a feeling with the blue book that has the torn cover when I red it. Thats why Im gonna keep trying to get smart so I can have that feeling agen. Its a good feeling to know things and be smart. I wish I had it rite now if I did I would sit down and reed all the time. Anyway I bet Im the first dumb person in the world who ever found out somthing importent for sience. I remember I did somthing but I dont remember what. So I gess its like I did it for all the dumb pepul like me.

Good-by Miss Kinnian and Dr Strauss and evreybody. And P.S. please tell Dr Nemur not to be such a grouch when pepul laff at him and he would have more frends. Its easy to make frends if you let pepul laff at you. Im going to have lots of frends where I go.

P.P.S. Please if you get a chanse put some flowrs on Algernons grave in the bak yard . . .

ALL THINGS CONSIDERED _____

1. Charlie is very upset when the new dishwasher at the corner diner breaks some dishes. Charlie feels this way because he (a) dislikes it when customers laugh at a mentally-retarded person. (b) realizes that he had been laughing at the dishwasher. (c) suddenly recognizes that he had been just like the dishwasher. (d) all of the above.

2. After noticing the changes in Algernon, Charlie begins working hard to discover (a) a cure for Algernon. (b) when Algernon will die. (c) if and when the regression will happen to him.

3. Charlie's hypothesis, or idea to test, "Artificially increased intelligence deteriorates at a rate of time directly proportional to the quantity of the increase," means that (a) Charlie will rapidly become dumb again because he learned so fast. (b) it will take more time for Charlie to go back to the way he was originally than it took for him to get smart. (b) there is no connection between what happened to Algernon and what will happen to Charlie.

4. The doctor that Mrs. Flynn, Charlie's landlady, gets to examine Charlie, thinks that Charlie (a) has a bad case of pneumonia. (b) is only pretending to be sick. (c) is stupid and somewhat crazy.

5. At the very end of the story, Charlie plans to (a) go back to work at the factory. (b) marry Miss Kinnian. (c) move from New York to someplace where no one knows him.

6. The time period covered in the story is a little over (a) four weeks. (b) four months. (c) four years.

7. Drs. Strauss and Nemur decide to use Charlie in their experiment because (a) they are looking for someone who has an I.Q. of exactly 68—and Charlie fits this requirement. (b) Charlie is highly motivated to learn. (c) Charlie's parents are dead so no one will sue them if the experiment is a failure.

8. Charlie is asked to take a Rorschach Test twice. The second time he takes it he (a) gives the same answers he gave the first time. (b) laughs because it is so easy for him. (c) realizes how feebleminded he had once been.

9. Charlie learns that his best friends at the factory, Joe Carp and Frank Reilly, really like having him around because (a) he pays for the drinks when they go out. (b) they enjoy making fun of him. (c) Charlie laughs at their jokes.

10. Dr. Strauss and Dr. Nemur argue a lot over (a) who will get most of the credit for the experiment. (b) who is responsible for doing the tests on Charlie. (c) whether or not it is correct to perform the experiment.

THINKING IT THROUGH

1. What are the signs that Charlie, like Algernon, is losing his intelligence? (See diary entries for June 10, 15, 19, 22, 23, and July 7.)

2. When Charlie goes back to Miss Kinnian's class (near the end of the story) and discovers that there are new people there, he says, "holy smoke I reely pulled a Charlie Gordon that time." The phrase "pulled a Charlie Gordon" comes up several times in the story. (a) Where does the phrase originate? (b) What does it mean?

3. Joe Carp and Frank Reilly, Charlie's co-workers at Donnegan's factory, change during the story. (a) What were they like at the beginning of the story? (b) In what way have they changed by the end of the story? (c) Can you think of a reason for the change?

4. The person who changes most in the story is, of course, Charlie Gordon; yet, though his intelligence changes markedly, certain personality traits stay the same. What words would you use to describe Charlie? What interests him? Do you think you would like him? Why, or why not?

5. (a) What is the result of Charlie's scientific experiments? (b) How does this result involve *irony of situation* (see page XX)?

6. Looking back at his past life, the highly intelligent Charlie realizes that he had once inferred that because smart people could read and write, improving his reading and writing would make him smart, too, What is wrong with this inference?

7. In your opinion, why is the story called "Flowers for Algernon"? Think about what makes Charlie add the "P.P.S." at the very end.

8. Suppose you were given the opportunity to have your intelligence tripled by surgical means. Would you go through with the operation? Give good reasons for your answer.

UNIT REVIEW

I. Match the items in Column A with their definitions in Column B.

A	**B**
1. figurative language	**a)** character defect that leads to one's downfall
2. cliché	**b)** language that does not really mean what it seems to say
3. tragic flaw	
4. denotation	**c)** the dictionary meaning of a word
5. connotation	**d)** a common and overused figurative expression
6. hypothesis	**e)** a possible explanation for something
	f) what a word suggests or brings to mind

II. The ability to find and ask the right questions is usually more important than the ability to answer them. That is, if you want to judge or evaluate something, forming the right questions is the place to start.

1. Choose a selection in this unit that you remember well. (a) First, as a warm-up, write a fair question that has a short answer. (b) Next, write a question that would require some thought and insight before it could be answered. (This question should be more difficult. A person who has just skimmed through the selection might have some trouble answering this question. In fact, that's the best reason to ask it.)

2. Choose another selection and write two questions as in the preceding exercise.

Example: "Heaven and Hell"

(a) In just a word or two, what was wrong with the people the angel found in hell?

(b) In their lives before death, which group of people probably considered themselves happier? Explain your answer.

SPEAKING UP

Giving a News Broadcast

This exercise asks you to prepare and read a three-part "news broadcast" based on a selection in the unit. To prepare for this assignment, tune in your favorite radio station and really listen to it. (1) Pay special attention to the news: (a) How is a straight news item reported? (b) How is a human interest item—a short story focused on a particular person, place, or event—reported? (2) How do the commercials sound? Jot down notes on all three items.

The day of the assignment, get together with two or three classmates; take your notes with you. In your small group, do the following:

1. Choose one of the prose selections from Unit IV that you enjoyed and think might work well for the assignment.
2. Read through the selection together, aloud, if possible, by taking turns. As one student reads, the others should be listening for, and taking notes on, anything that might be turned into (a) a good straight news item, (b) a human interest item, and (c) a suitable commercial.
3. When the reading is finished, compile your notes. First, write all suggestions for a straight news story. Do the same for the human interest story. Think of an original commercial that would work well in your broadcast. For example, a savings bank commercial might be an ironic twist to include if you select "The Pot of Gold."
4. From the notes you have made, choose and develop one news story, one human interest story, and one commercial. You may wish to do these written assignments together as a group, or each group member could select a task.
5. Practice your news broadcast. If you have access to a cassette player, tape your performance, play it back, and make any necessary changes.
6. When you are well prepared, give your broadcast before the class. Ask your classmates for comments—both pro and con—about your performance. Their comments should help you make your next broadcast more effective.

WRITING A CRITIQUE

Prewriting

1. Look through the selections in Unit IV. Choose the one that you like best. Use this selection to write a **critique**—a review in which you evaluate the merits of a literary selection.

2. Take out a sheet of paper, preferably unlined. Fold it in half, crosswise. At the top, write *Pros.* Below the fold, write *Cons.*

3. Reread the story. Keep the following points in mind. They may have influenced your choice of ''best'' story:
   a. *Plot:* Was the conflict so interesting that you wanted to see how it would be resolved?
   b. *Character:* Were the characters true-to-life? Did you find your-self identifying with a certain character? What did you learn about human nature through one or more of the characters?
   c. *Language:* Did the writer create pictures in your mind as you read? Was the writer adept at describing the setting and creating a mood? Did the writer use interesting figurative language?
   d. *Theme:* What did you learn from the selection? Did the writer's ideas influence your thinking in any way?

4. As the read, cluster those things that you liked on the top half of your paper. Cluster the things that you disliked on the bottom half.

5. Look at your clustering and decide which of the items made the strongest impression on you. Probably *plot* was one. Choose two more concepts to focus on in your paper.

Writing

The purpose of this assignment is to try to persuade others to your point of view. Therefore you will want to explain *why* you think the way you do about your chosen selection. Be sure to give examples from the selection to support your arguments.

1. *Paragraph 1:* Begin by writing a brief summary of the selection (about three sentences), then go on to describe what you liked about the plot. If there is something you dislike, you can write about that, too. (Turn back to page 209 and review the list of useful transitions for contrast.)

2. *Paragraph 2:* In this paragraph, write about a second major point that made you enjoy the selection. To begin the paragraph, pro-

vide a transition from paragraph 1. (Example: In addition to creating a memorable plot, I thought the writer did an excellent job of _____ .

3. *Paragraph 3:* Now write about your last major point, using the suggestions for writing paragraphs 1 and 2.

4. *Conclusion:* Write a brief concluding paragraph in which you restate your main points. Be sure to restate your points strongly, for this is your last chance to persuade your audience to believe what you believe.

Revising

1. *Editing groups:* Form a small group with two other students. Go through the following process with each group member.
   a. One person reads a critique aloud.
   b. The other group members listen for and give feedback to that person. If you are a listener, ask yourself the following questions as a guide.

   - What main points did the person like about the story?
   - Did the person give at least one *specific* reason for each point? Did the person mention something specific from the story to show why it is a worthwhile story?
   - Were the arguments presented in a convincing way?
   - Would the paper be more effective if the points were put in a different order? If so, how might they be reordered?
   - Was each point clear? If not, what do I, as a reader, need to know?

   c. The person reading the critique should take notes while receiving feedback.

2. After each group member has read a critique and listened to the others for constructive criticism, revise your critique. Rewrite the paper, keeping the feedback in mind. Then make a clean copy of the final draft.

UNIT · 5

MENTAL MAGIC

The man said,
after inventing poetry,
"WOW!"
and did a full somersault.
—William J. Harris

Is the poem sense or nonsense? Probably a little of each. Of course, it doesn't really make sense to talk about a person "inventing poetry." Neither can you believe that the "inventor" celebrated the event by doing a tumble head over heels. On the other hand, the idea behind the poem makes a good deal of sense. It's vital to realize that the human mind has great creative abilities. Figuratively, the mind can take jumps and leaps and do single and double somersaults. The mind can travel down dark, dangerous roads and meet itself coming back. In short, the mind can make sense out of nonsense.

Did you ever think of *imagining* as an important thinking skill? If not, imagine just that to be true as you read the selections that follow. Two of the readings, "The Fall of the House of Usher" and "The Raven," are celebrated classics of fantasy. Anchor your feet firmly in the clouds and get started now.

> This story leaps into the future and somersaults to a surprise ending. Luckily, you'll never have to take a test like the purely imaginary one described in

EXAMINATION DAY

by Henry Slesar

The Jordans never spoke of the exam, not until their son Dickie was 12 years old. It was on his birthday that Mrs. Jordan first mentioned the subject in his presence, and the anxious manner of her speech caused her husband to answer sharply.

"Forget about it," he said. "He'll do all right."

They were at the breakfast table, and the boy looked up from his plate curiously. He was an alert-eyed youngster, with flat blond hair and a quick, nervous manner. He didn't understand what the sudden tension was about, but he did know that today was his birthday, and he wanted harmony above all. Somewhere in the little apartment, there were wrapped, beribboned packages waiting to be opened, and in the tiny wall kitchen, something warm and sweet was being prepared in the automatic stove. He wanted the day to be happy, and the moistness of his mother's eyes, the scowl on his father's face, spoiled the mood of fluttering expectation with which he had greeted the morning.

"What exam?" he asked.

His mother looked at the tablecloth. "It's just a sort of Government intelligence test they give children at the age of twelve. You'll be getting it next week. It's nothing to worry about."

"You mean a test like in school?"

"Something like that," his father said, getting up from the table. "Go read your comic books, Dickie."

The boy rose and wandered toward that part of the living room which had been "his" corner since infancy. He fingered the topmost comic of the stack, but seemed uninterested in the colorful squares of fast-paced action. He wandered toward the window and peered gloomily at the veil of mist that shrouded the glass.

"Why did it have to rain *today?*" he said. "Why couldn't it rain tomorrow?"

His father, now slumped into an armchair with the Government newspaper, rattled the sheets in vexation. "Because it just did, that's all. Rain makes the grass grow."

"Why, Dad?"

"Because it does, that's all."

Dickie puckered his brow. "What makes it green, though? The grass."

"Nobody knows," his father snapped, then immediately regretted his abruptness.

- ● beribboned (bi RIB und) **tied and decorated with ribbons**
- ● shroud (SHROWD) **cover; conceal**
- ● vexation (vek SAY shun) **irritation; annoyance**

Later in the day, it was birthday time again. His mother beamed as she handed over the gaily colored packages, and even his father managed a grin and a rumple of the hair. He kissed his mother and shook hands gravely with his father. Then the birthday cake was brought forth, and the ceremonies concluded.

An hour later, seated by the window, he watched the sun force its way between the clouds.

"Dad," he said, "how far away is the sun?"

"Five thousand miles," his father said.

Dick sat at the breakfast table and again saw moisture in his mother's eyes. He didn't connect her tears with the exam until his father suddenly brought the subject to light again.

"Well, Dickie," he said with a manly frown, "you've got an appointment today."

"I know, Dad. I hope——"

"Now, it's nothing to worry about. Thousands of children take this test every day. The Government wants to know how smart you are, Dickie. That's all there is to it."

"I get good marks in school," he said hesitantly.

"This is different. This is a—special kind of test. They give you this stuff to drink, you see, and then you go into a room where there's a sort of machine——"

"What stuff to drink?" Dickie said.

"It's nothing. It tastes like peppermint. It's just to make sure you answer the questions truthfully. Not that the Government thinks you won't tell the truth, but this stuff makes *sure*."

HAAS.

● **gravely** (GRAYV lee) **very seriously**

Dickie's face showed puzzlement, and a touch of fright. He looked at his mother, and she composed her face into a misty smile.

"Everything will be all right," she said.

"Of course it will," his father agreed. "You're a good boy, Dickie; you'll make out fine. Then we'll come home and celebrate. All right?"

"Yes, sir," Dickie said.

They entered the Government Educational Building 15 minutes before the appointed hour. They crossed the marble floors of the great pillared lobby, passed beneath an archway and entered

an automatic elevator that brought them to the fourth floor.

There was a young man wearing an insignialess tunic, seated at a polished desk in front of Room 404. He held a clipboard in his hand and he checked the list down to the *J*s and permitted the Jordans to enter.

The room was as cold and official as a courtroom, with long benches flanking metal tables. There were several fathers and sons already there, and a thin-lipped woman with cropped black hair was passing out sheets of paper.

Mr. Jordan filled out the form and returned it to the clerk. Then he told Dickie. "It won't be long now. When they call your name, you just go through the doorway at that end of the room." He indicated the portal with his finger.

A concealed loudspeaker crackled and called off the first name. Dickie saw a boy leave his father's side reluctantly and walk slowly toward the door.

At five minutes of 11, they called the name of Jordan.

"Good luck, son," his father said without looking at him. "I'll call for you when the test is over."

Dickie walked to the door and turned the knob. The room inside was dim, and he could barely make out the features of the gray-tuniced attendant who greeted him.

"Sit down," the man said softly. He indicated a high stool beside his desk. "Your name's Richard Jordan?"

"Yes, sir."

"Your classification number is 600-115. Drink this, Richard."

He lifted a plastic cup from the desk

- **compose** (kum POHZ) make calm; put in peaceful order
- tunic (TOO nik) jacket or coat that is part of a uniform
- **flanking** (FLANK ing) set on both sides (flanks) of

and handed it to the boy. The liquid inside had the consistency of buttermilk, tasted only vaguely of the promised peppermint. Dickie downed it and handed the man the empty cup.

He sat in silence, feeling drowsy, while the man wrote busily on a sheet of paper. Then the attendant looked at his watch and rose to stand only inches from Dickie's face. He unclipped a penlike object from the pocket of his tunic and flashed a tiny light into the boy's eyes.

"All right," he said. "Come with me, Richard."

He led Dickie to the end of the room, where a single wooden armchair faced a multidialed computing machine. There was a microphone on the left arm of the chair, and when the boy sat down he found its pin-point head conveniently at his mouth.

"Now, just relax, Richard. You'll be asked some questions, and you think them over carefully. Then give your answers into the microphone. The machine will take care of the rest."

"Yes, sir."

"I'll leave you alone now. Whenever you want to start, just say 'ready' into the microphone."

"Yes, sir."

The man squeezed his shoulder and left.

Dickie said, "Ready."

Lights appeared on the machine, and a mechanism whirred. A voice said:

"Complete this sequence. One, four, seven, ten. . . ."

● consistency (kun SIS tun see) **degree of thickness or firmness**

Mr. and Mrs. Jordan both were in the living room not speaking, not even speculating.

It was almost four o'clock when the telephone rang. The woman tried to reach it first, but her husband was quicker.

"Mr. Jordan?"

The voice was clipped, a brisk, official voice.

"Yes, speaking."

"This is the Government Educational Service. Your son, Richard M. Jordan, Classification 600-115, has completed the Government examination. We regret to inform you that his intelligence quotient has exceeded the Government regulation, according to Rule 84, Section 5, of the New Code."

Across the room, the woman cried out, knowing nothing except the emotion she read on her husband's face.

"You may specify by telephone," the voice droned on, "whether you wish his body interred by the Government, or would you prefer a private burial place? The fee for Government burial is ten dollars."

- (intelligence) quotient (KWOH shunt) **score on an intelligence test ("IQ")**
- inter (in TUR) **bury**

ALL THINGS CONSIDERED

1. Throughout the story, Mr. and Mrs. Jordan try hard to (a) prepare Dickie to do well on the test. (b) stay calm. (c) be truthful.
2. "Thousands of children take this test every day. The Government wants to know how smart you are, Dickie. That's all there is to it." Of these three sentences, the one that is untrue is the (a) first. (b) second. (c) third.
3. Dickie is given something to drink before the test because (a) he complains of thirst. (b) all the children are given the same treat. (c) "the Government" wants to be sure he tells the truth.
4. The Government Educational Service calls to tell the Jordans that Dickie is (a) too smart. (b) average. (c) below average in intelligence.
5. As a result of Dickie's test scores, he will (a) go to a special school for remedial help. (b) receive advanced training in math and science. (c) be killed.

THINKING IT THROUGH

1. Explain how each of the following helps to foreshadow the surprise ending of the story: (a) the father's speech, "Go read your comic books, Dickie" (b) the father's answers to Dickie's questions about rain, grass, and the sun (c) the mother's tears (d) the drink given Dickie before the test
2. In your opinion, just what is "the Government" in the story trying to do? That is, what might "the Government" fear if people like Dickie live to adulthood?
3. What differences do you see between our time and the imagined future in "Examination Day"? For example, in the story the parents are willing to accept "the Government" without a fight.

Literary Skills: Review

If you wish to review the meaning of any term in *italics* in this exercise, refer to the Glossary of Terms.

1. (a) What two or three *plot problems* or *conflicts* keep the reader curious throughout most of the story? (b) Where in the story are these problems resolved?

2. In your opinion, do the four parts (or scenes) of the story follow the principle of *rising action?* Explain.

3. In some short stories, a *resolution* follows the *climax.* Is this true of "Examination Day"?

4. (a) Is the story told from a *first-person* or *third-person point of view?* (b) In your opinion, why didn't the author choose to tell the story entirely from Dickie's point of view?

5. In the first part of the story, the mother and father unwillingly ruin "the mood of fluttering expectation with which he [Dickie] had greeted the morning." (a) What word in this quotation is the best example of *figurative language?* (b) Is this example a *simile* or a *metaphor?*

6. The *subject* of the story can best be said to be (a) governments of the future. (b) intelligence testing. (c) honesty in the family. Explain why one of the answers is better than the other two.

7. Think about "Examination Day" in terms of its *theme.* The meaning of the story seems to be a kind of warning. What do you think the author is warning people about?

Composition

1. Like many other stories, "Examination Day" is a fantasy about the future. What do you think the nation and the world will really be like in 200 years? Write a paragraph explaining at least three differences between that time and the present.

2. Now put your own "mental magic" to work. Choose either (a) or (b) below for a private "brainstorming" session of your own. Your answers don't have to be "logical" or "practical" or even "possible." *Speed* is the key word. When you have at least five answers (try for ten), copy them over neatly.
   (a) How many uses can you think of for an aluminum pie plate?
   (b) In how many ways is an egg carton like a school bus?

▶ Short poems that express a poet's feelings and thoughts can be called **lyric poetry.**

Some people think that a *lyric poem* is simply a beautiful expression of a beautiful subject. This is not true—a lyric poem can be about anything—from lovely flowers to an ugly garbage can. It is not the subject matter that makes a good poem, but how the poet treats the subject matter. A poet's magic can make you see the old and familiar in new and exciting ways.

In performing their mental magic, poets often use *figurative language* (see page 217). Familiar words are put to new uses, and unexpected comparisons flash in the reader's mind. For instance, you can "read" the first poem that follows—or you can "unfold" it.

Note: As you read this section, refer to the Glossary of Terms if you cannot recall the meaning of any terms in *italics.*

UNFOLDING BUD

by Naoshi Koriyama

One is amazed
By a water-lily bud
Unfolding
With each passing day,
Taking on a richer color
And new dimensions.

One is not amazed,
At a first glance,
By a poem,
Which is as tight-closed
As a tiny bud.

Yet one is surprised
To see the poem
Gradually unfolding,
Revealing its rich inner self,
As one reads it
Again
And over again.

WAYS OF KNOWING

1. The last stanza suggests that a reader sees different meanings in a poem on rereading it. Reread the poem. Tell whether or not you gained a deeper understanding or appreciation of the poem by reading it twice.
2. The poem develops a comparison between two things. (a) What are these two things? (b) What are at least two similarities between the things?
3. The poem contains an example of the special kind of comparison called a *simile.* What is the one simile in the poem?
4. (a) Why can the word "unfolding" in the last stanza be called a metaphor? (b) Since "the poem" is not really "unfolding," what is the poet's intended meaning here?

GLIMPSE OF NIGHT

by Frank Marshall Davis

Peddling
From door to door
Night sells
Black bags of peppermint stars
Heaping cones of vanilla moon
Until
His wares are gone
Then shuffles homeward
Jingling the gray coins
Of daybreak.

WAYS OF KNOWING

1. The whole poem is a *metaphor.* To what is the night being compared?
2. (a) How is the word *vanilla* used? (b) What picture do you imagine as you read the last two lines?
3. Why is the poem an excellent example of *personification?*
4. What good example of *onomatopoeia* is found near the end of the poem?

DAWN

by Paul Laurence Dunbar

An angel, robed in spotless white,
Bent down and kissed the sleeping Night.
Night woke to blush; the sprite was gone.
Men saw the blush and called it Dawn.

WAY OF KNOWING

1. "Dawn" is another good example of personification. (a) How is night personified in the poem? (b) What action is used to personify dawn?

2. What comparisons can be made between "Dawn" and "Glimpse of Night"?

3. *Men* usually means "more than one man." In this poem, it has a broader meaning. What does it mean?

● sprite (SPRYT) **unreal and playful creature; elfish spirit or person**

309

DEPOSIT HERE

by Jesús Papoleto Meléndez

garbage cans/   sitting on lonely sidewalks
casting long shadows over broken pavement/
     broken pavement
     where on rain-filled days
     stray houseflies drown

garbage cans/   sitting on lonely sidewalks
filled to the brim with used dreams

people/   run   ning
toofast to keep up with themselves/
passing garbage cans
& as doing so   depositing their used dreams

children/   passing
as slow as life moves itself
     stopping/searching
     & finding dreams in those garbage cans/
     taking them home   & playing with them.

WAYS OF KNOWING

1. Jésus Papoleto Meléndez is known for his "street poetry" about New York City. Do you think his observations and descriptions are accurate? Explain.
2. Why might the poet have written "run   ning" and "toofast"?
3. Read the poem again until you come to the first metaphor. (a) What is this metaphor? (b) What is its real meaning?
4. (a) In what way do garbage cans contain used dreams? (b) Give an example of something you may have thrown out that could be called a "used dream."
5. (a) What value do children find in the used dreams discarded by other people? (b) How might a child use the object you mentioned in your answer to question 4b?
6. The last group of lines contains a simile. What is it?

THE HUMAN HAND

by Eva-Lis Wuorio

▶ Eva-Lis Wuorio is a Canadian master of fantasy. Although she uses England as the setting of many of her stories, the true setting is a fantasy land within her imagination. This selection is from her thrilling book *Escape If You Can*.

I had a dream that the dog came down the stairs from the upstairs apartment, carrying a human hand.

From the wrist down.

The dream was so gruesomely bizarre that I woke up and lay there trembling. From the street lamp outside, light, shivering with gusty rain, was reflected on the ceiling. I lay there and thought of my neighbor upstairs.

I hadn't seen her for some days. Come to think of it, I hadn't seen her milk bottles in the hall either. Without conscious thought I'd presumed she had gone away.

But had she?

We don't visit. We don't even speak. I tried once but got told off so rudely that I never tried again.

I'd said, "Does it ever stop raining in England?"

She said, "If you don't like it, why do you stay?"

The second time she spoke to me she said, "Your dog has dirtied my hall. I'm an artist and I can't have these things happening. Now I won't be able to work all day." Spoke I said. Screamed I mean.

I went up to her hall—that was the one and only time—and cleaned up the mess. It was too small for my big dog to have done. Her cat probably had made it. But I didn't say anything. I never said anything again. We lived in the same building, that was all.

This was a city. This was the world today.

And now I had this dream.

I got up and wandered about the apartment, listening hopefully for some sounds from upstairs. If I went and she wasn't there, I was in the wrong. If I didn't go there and she was in need of aid, I was in the wrong. Whatever I did, I would be in the wrong.

You can't win. In a city. In the world today.

I tried to remember how many days since I'd last seen her. I couldn't remember. Had I seen the cat? I thought I had but I couldn't be sure. It always used the trellis on the garden side of the house to

---

- bizarre (bi ZAR) **odd; strange**
- **trellis** (TREL is) **frame for growing vine**

311

enter and exit, unless it came in with her by the front door, strutting fiercely by my dog.

This is a detached narrow house with just one entrance to the street. It had never really been turned into apartments, and while the upstairs and downstairs are self-contained, there's just the one door. So we use the same hall. I have the small garden because I'm downstairs.

Outside of a sort of coffin-making banging that she indulges in I never even know if she's in or out. Sometimes coffin-shaped boxes are taken out, though of course I can't swear she makes coffins. She might sculpt for all I know.

And now there was this hand. In my dream.

Try to feature it. The night. And the quiet house, and this dream.

I'd been out a lot in the past week. I hadn't even heard her making coffins. I tried to think of friends of hers, but outside of seeing her speaking interminably to the handsome milkman, and a few shadowy characters I'd never seen but sometimes heard enter, I didn't know of anyone. I couldn't just say to the milkman, "Have you seen Mrs. What's-her-name lately? I dreamed my dog brought down her hand last night." Now, could I?

I poured myself a glass of milk, lovely and cold from the refrigerator, and sat at the kitchen table. Then I thought to look at the dog. It was dreaming, jerking and growling, not in its basket but on the couch. I woke it and it gave me a resentful grunt. Lights on at three A.M., it seemed to say. And snored again.

All right, fine, I thought, human beings are horrible. They live right on top of one another, and they don't care for one another even as much as animals do. Her cat and my dog at least pass the time of day. Human beings don't give a hand—did I say hand?—give a hand to one another.

That hand was really getting me down.

I don't know if she's dead or alive, I told myself. All right, so I have my stereo on too loud. I like my music good and loud. And she bangs on the floor. Which of us is wrong? After all, she makes the coffins all day long.

Once when I didn't have enough room in my garbage can for all my junk I put some into her half-full one. She threw it all out on my front lawn. So when I have friends in and they make noise I don't shush them. What do I care, I thought.

But I felt pretty bad now.

The dream had been vivid and disgusting. I walked the rainy

- self-contained (self kun TAYND) **complete as a unit**
- **feature** (FEE chur) **imagine; picture something in the mind**
- interminably (in TUR muh nuh blee) **forever; without end**

garden until dawn, hoping that lights would come on upstairs. Hoping she'd start making coffins as she often does at the most unearthly hours.

It was light already when sleep finally beckoned me. But before I went back to bed I wrote a note and left it on the hall table. If it hadn't gone by milkman time, I decided, I'd go and see what was happening upstairs.

"Shall I ask the milkman to leave you a pint?" I wrote. "I notice he hasn't for a few days."

I slept heavily and dreamlessly. It was much after my usual time that I awakened. Immediately I remembered. I made for the hall.

There was no note there. Not mine, not from her.

But there was a parcel. It was barely wrapped, but it looked like a bone. I guess it was because my dog reached up and grabbed it.

I watched him gallumphing with it in the garden.

I sighed in relief; she had made a friendly overture at last. The house, around me, seemed to heave a sigh too.

In the garden the dog had worried the parcel open. He tossed the bone in the air.

It was a human hand.

- gallumphing (ga LUMPF ing) **playing happily**
- overture (OH vur chur) **opening gesture or act**

ALL THINGS CONSIDERED ⎯⎯⎯⎯⎯⎯⎯⎯⎯⎯⎯⎯⎯⎯⎯⎯

1. The narrator believes that her upstairs neighbor might have gone away because (a) no mail is delivered. (b) they often talked of traveling. (c) she hasn't seen any milk bottles recently.

2. As the story progresses, the narrator (a) cares less and less about her neighbor. (b) tries to make her neighbor angry. (c) becomes truly concerned about her neighbor.

3. The narrator comments sadly on (a) the difficulty of getting along with people in a modern city. (b) the ugliness of modern art. (c) her neighbor's taste in music.

4. The note written by the narrator (a) is taken by the milkman. (b) is removed by the neighbor. (c) disappears mysteriously.

5. At the end of the story, the (a) mystery is explained. (b) narrator laughs at her frightening dream. (c) dream seems to come true.

THINKING IT THROUGH ⎯⎯⎯⎯⎯⎯⎯⎯⎯⎯⎯⎯⎯⎯⎯⎯

1. In your judgment, why is it important to the story that the narrator and her neighbor have never been on good terms with each other?

2. The narrator and her dog both have dreams. Do you think the author suggests what kind of dream the dog is having? If so, what kind?

3. (a) How did you react to the end of the story? (b) If you were the author, would you have ended it in the same way or in a different way? Explain your answer.

Answers to Bonus Questions found on page 62:

1. one hour
2. one hour
3. yes, and a fifth of July, and a sixth of July, etc.
4. one a year
5. She is still alive.
6. the match
7. all of them
8. white
9. half way
10. In God We Trust
11. nine, six
12. a nickel and a half dollar
13. nine
14. 70
15. They weren't playing each other.
16. two
17. This answer is too obvious to list!
18. none
19. She is her sister.
20. He would be dead.

Literary Skills: Review

If you wish to review the meaning of any term in *italics* in this exercise, refer to the Glossary of Terms.

1. Which character in "The Human Hand" can correctly be called the *narrator?*

2. (a) In your opinion, is the narrator a man or a woman? (b) Did you base your answer on a *fact* or an *inference?* Explain.

3. (a) Which two of the four kinds of *conflict* are the most important in the story? (b) In your opinion, which one is the most important? Explain your answer.

4. (a) Is the story told in straight *chronological order?* (b) If not, give one example of a short *flashback.*

5. Although the upstairs neighbor never actually appears, she is characterized in some detail. Give an example for at least three of the four methods of *characterization:*
   (a) Direct statements by the author.
   (b) Speeches and thoughts of the character.
   (c) Actions of the character.
   (d) Reactions of other characters to the character.

6. "Human beings don't give a hand—did I say hand?—give a hand to one another." (a) Is the writer's comment in mid-sentence about an accidental use of a *simile* or of a *metaphor?* (b) In your opinion, can it be called a *cliché?* Explain.

7. "So when I have friends in and they make noise I don't shush them." What word in this sentence is a good example of *onomatopoeia?*

8. "It was light already when sleep finally beckoned me." Explain how *personification* is involved in this sentence.

Composition

1. You probably noticed that the author uses sentence fragments, or incomplete sentences, from time to time. For instance, the second sentence is a fragment: *From the wrist down.* Writers of fiction sometimes use fragments on purpose. Like short sentences and paragraphs, sentence fragments speed up the pace of the story and make for easy reading.

   Skim the story for the four fragments listed. Then rewrite each one as a complete sentence to convey the full meaning.

   In a city.
   In a dream.
   And snored again.
   Not mine, not for her.

2. Write an original story that begins with the first five words of "The Human Hand." ("I had a dream that. . . .") Try to interest your reader as much as Eva-Lis Wuorio does in her beginning sentences. Try to conclude your story with a surprise ending.

Edgar Allan Poe (1809-1849)

The Edgar Allan Poe cottage in the Bronx, New York

One day in the fall of 1849, a small, black-haired man fell to the street near a tavern in Baltimore, Maryland. No one seemed to know who he was. Taken to a hospital, he never recovered his senses. He died four days later, and was buried without ceremony. Twenty-six years later a tombstone was erected, but even then the service attracted little notice and was poorly attended. Even today, what he wanted to be his chief claim to fame—a long prose-poem on the origin and end of the universe, called *Eureka,*—is hard to find in libraries. Thus the fall of Edgar Allan Poe seems complete.

Today most of Poe's writings are ignored and unknown, but his *best* stories and poems refuse to be forgotten. The weird, tormented characters in his works mirror the author's own weirdly tormented life. Orphaned at two, he was reared by foster parents. Although he was a genius, he left both the University of Virginia and West Point in disgrace. Poe had a strong need for the support of older women, but he married a 13-year-old cousin. Although he had talent to spare as an editor and writer, he drifted from job to job. His unstable, romantic nature and an occasional drinking problem kept him in poverty. It's not surprising that many of Poe's best stories end in death and destruction. The brooding and imaginative young narrator of "The Raven" is, in certain ways, Edgar Allan Poe himself.

Oral Interpretation

Oral interpretation means reading aloud with expression. Plays lend themselves to oral interpretation, as do poems. In fact, some poems seem written mainly to be read aloud. "The Raven," a famous narrative poem by Edgar Allan Poe, is an excellent example.

For Poe, nothing was more important than the sounds in a poem. After "The Raven" had become famous, Poe wrote an article that explained, step by step, how the poem had been written. One of the first things Poe had done was to search for a word that could be repeated many times as the key to the poem. That word, he said, had to have a beautiful sound as well as a sorrowful meaning. The word "nevermore," he claimed, "was the very first which presented itself."

According to Poe, the whole poem—the central character, the plot, and even the raven itself—sprang from his decision to use the word "nevermore." He liked the soft, rolling sound of the *r*'s in the word and the mournful quality of the long *o*. He crowded his poem with hundreds of other sound, rhythm, and sense combinations. For instance, in the very first stanza, when someone knocks lightly at the door, Poe wrote "tapping . . . rapping, rapping . . . tapping." The sound, rhythm, and sense are one and the same.

Poe himself enjoyed reading "The Raven" to eager audiences. Practice reading the poem aloud until you can deliver the most difficult lines with ease. Follow this procedure:

1. Since the poem is not a simple one, first master the vocabulary and the meaning stanza by stanza. Read the poem through silently. Use the aids provided to check the definitions of words and to check your understanding of the poem.

2. Next, read the poem aloud softly. After reading each stanza a few times, you'll find that the rhythm is very regular. However, avoid a sing-song effect. Let the meaning of the words govern your stress and speed. For instance, the first part of line 3, "While I nodded, nearly napping," should be read slowly. The second half of that line, "suddenly there came a tapping," should be read quicker to show the narrator's awakened vigor.

3. Let the dialogue sound like spoken words—especially "nevermore."

4. Remember that if you seem to sound silly and ridiculous, it's more your fault than Poe's. The poem is still read aloud by famous actors as a demonstration of talent. It *can* be done!

from THE RAVEN

by Edgar Allan Poe

▶ Poe summarized his most famous poem in this way: "A raven, having learned by rote the single word "nevermore," and having escaped from its owner, is driven at midnight, through a storm, to seek admission at the chamber window of a student, occupied half in pouring over a volume, half in dreaming of a dead love." Poe went on to state that the speaker, once he learns the raven's single word, deliberately asks questions that will add to his "self-torture" and increase "the luxury of sorrow."

1. What is the speaker doing as the poem opens? 2. How does he explain the tapping at the door?

Once upon a midnight dreary, while I pondered, weak and
    weary,
Over many a quaint and curious volume of forgotten lore,—
While I nodded, nearly napping, suddenly there came a
    tapping,
As of someone gently rapping, rapping at my chamber door.
5   "'Tis some visitor," I muttered, "tapping at my chamber door:
    Only this and nothing more."

3. *Why* has the speaker tried to interest himself in books? 4. Who was Lenore, and what had happened to her?

Ah, distinctly I remember it was in the bleak December,
And each separate dying ember wrought its ghost upon the
    floor.
Eagerly I wished the morrow;—vainly I had sought to borrow
10 From my books surcease of sorrow—sorrow for the lost
    Lenore,
For the rare and radiant maiden whom the angels name
    Lenore:
      Nameless here for evermore.

- rote (ROHT) **memory without understanding of meaning**
- **ponder** (PON dur) **think deeply; consider thoughtfully**
- **lore** (LOHR) **old knowledge; wisdom**
- bleak (BLEEK) **cheerless; unhappy**
- **ember** (EM bur) **glowing coal**
- wrought (RAWT) **produced; made**
- morrow (MOR oh) **next day**
- surcease (sur SEES) **ending; final point**

And the silken sad uncertain rustling of each purple curtain
Thrilled me—filled with fantastic terrors never felt before;
15 So that now, to still the beating of my heart, I stood repeating,
"'Tis some visitor entreating entrance at my chamber door:
Some late visitor entreating entrance at my chamber door:
    This it is and nothing more."

5. (a) What (consonant) sound is repeated four times in line 13? (b) What does this sound represent? 6. What are the speaker's feelings at this point?

Presently my soul grew stronger; hesitating then no longer,
20 "Sir," said I, "or Madam, truly your forgiveness I implore;
But the fact is I was napping, and so gently you came rapping,
And so faintly you came tapping, tapping at my chamber door,
That I scarce was sure I heard you"—here I opened wide the
    door:—
    Darkness there and nothing more.

7. What two lines use **internal rhyme** (rhyme within a line)? Look again at each previous stanza. Figure out the pattern of each stanza.

25 Deep into that darkness peering, long I stood there wondering,
    fearing,
Doubting, dreaming dreams no mortals ever dared to dream
    before;
But the silence was unbroken, and the stillness gave no token,
And the only word there spoken was the whispered word,
    "Lenore!"
This I whispered, and an echo murmured back the word,
    "Lenore!"
30   Merely this and nothing more.

8. Exclude the two lines with internal rhyme. What is the **end rhyme?** That is, with what sounds do *all* the lines in the poem end? 9. Why might the speaker whisper the word "Lenore" into the dark night?

Open here I flung the shutter, when, with many a flirt and
    flutter,
In there stepped a stately Raven of the saintly days of yore.
Not the least obeisance made he; not a minute stopped or
    stayed he;

- entreating (en TREET ing) **begging for**
- implore (im PLOR) **request urgently; beg for**
- **stately** (STAYT lee) **dignified**
- yore (YOHR) **olden times**
- obeisance (oh BAY suns) **gesture of respect; bow**

Pallas (line 35): Pallas Athena (PAL us uh THEE nuh), the Greek goddess of wisdom.

10. What is odd about the raven's behavior?

But, with mien of lord or lady, perched above my chamber
    door,
35 Perched upon a bust of Pallas just above my chamber door:
    Perched and sat, and nothing more.

Plutonian (line 42; ploo TOH nee un): pertaining to Pluto, the god of the underworld. The suggestion is that the raven may have crossed the water separating the lower region from earth.

Then this ebony bird beguiling my sad fancy into smiling
By the grave and stern decorum of the countenance it wore,—
"Though thy crest be shorn and shaven, thou," I said, "art
    sure no craven,
40 Ghastly grim and ancient Raven wandering from the Nightly
    shore:
Tell me what thy lordly name is on the Night's Plutonian
    shore!"
    Quoth the Raven, "Nevermore."

A raven, like a parrot, can be taught to "speak" certain words.

11. What meaning is given to the word "nevermore" in this and the preceding stanza?

Much I marvelled this ungainly fowl to hear discourse so
    plainly,
Though its answer little meaning—little relevancy bore;
45 For we cannot help agreeing that no living human being
Ever yet was blessed with seeing bird above his chamber door,
Bird or beast upon the sculptured bust above his chamber door,
    With such name as "Nevermore."

But the Raven, sitting lonely on the placid bust, spoke only
50 That one word, as if his soul in that one word he did outpour.
Nothing further then he uttered, not a feather then he
    fluttered,

- mien (MEEN) **manner; appearance**
- **bust** (BUST) **statue of head**
- beguiling (bi GYL ing) **deceiving; tricking**
- decorum (di KOHR um) **dignity; proper behavior**
- countenance (KOUN tuh nuns) **expression of face**
- craven (KRAY vun) **cowardly**
- ungainly (un GAYN lee) **awkward; ugly**
- discourse (DIS kohrs) **conversation; talk**
- relevancy (REL uh vun see) **direct relation to a subject**
- placid (PLA sid) **very calm**

Till I scarcely more than muttered,—"Other friends have
    flown before;
On the morrow *he* will leave me, as my Hopes have flown
    before."
        Then the bird said, "Nevermore."

12. What is the meaning of *he* (line 53)? 13. What is the meaning of *nevermore* in this stanza?

55 This I sat engaged in guessing, but no syllable expressing
To the fowl whose fiery eyes now burned into my bosom's
    core;
This and more I sat divining, with my head at ease reclining
On the cushion's velvet lining that the lamp-light gloated o'er,
But whose velvet violet lining with the lamp-light gloating o'er
60   *She* shall press, ah, nevermore!

14. Poe claimed that, at least up to this point, "everything is within the limits of the accountable—of the real." Do you agree?

"Prophet!" said I, "thing of evil! prophet still, if bird or devil!
By that Heaven that bends above us, by that God we both
    adore,
Tell this soul with sorrow laden if, within the distant Aidenn,
It shall clasp a sainted maiden whom the angels name Lenore:
65 Clasp a rare and radiant maiden whom the angels name
    Lenore!"
        Quoth the Raven, "Nevermore."

Aidenn (line 63; must rhyme with "laden"): Eden, or any imaginary perfect place.
15. What is the meaning of *nevermore* in this stanza?

"Be that word our sign of parting, bird or fiend!" I shrieked,
    upstarting:
"Get thee back into the tempest and the Night's Plutonian
    shore!
Leave no black plume as a token of that lie thy soul hath spoken!
70 Leave my loneliness unbroken! quit the bust above my door!
Take thy beak from out my heart, and take thy form from off my door!"
        Quoth the Raven, "Nevermore."

16. What "lie" is referred to in line 69? 17. What is the meaning of the metaphor (see page 162) in line 71?

- divining (di VYN ing) **understanding; discovering**
- gloated (GLOHT ed) **beamed; shone over (archaic)**
- upstarting (up START ing) **springing up**

18. The poem has now left the limits . . . of the real and moved into fantasy. Exactly what seems impossible in the last stanza? 19. What is referred to in the final use of *nevermore?*

And the Raven, never flitting, still is sitting, still is sitting,
On the pallid bust of Pallas just above my chamber door;
75 And his eyes have all the seeming of a demon's that is
      dreaming,
And the lamp-light o'er him streaming throws his shadow on
      the floor;
And my soul from out that shadow that lies floating on the
      floor
        Shall be lifted—nevermore!

ALL THINGS CONSIDERED

1. According to Poe, the speaker in the poem is (a) a student. (b) insane. (c) the author himself.

2. According to Poe, the raven (a) understands everything that happens. (b) has been sent by Lenore. (c) is a mindless bird.

3. The speaker seems determined to (a) forget his lost love, Lenore. (b) torture himself with his sorrow. (c) gain the raven's understanding and help.

4. At the end, the raven (a) attacks the speaker. (b) leaves. (c) continues to sit on the statue.

5. The poem is certainly *not* famous for its (a) skillful rhymes. (b) rhythm. (c) realistic quality.

• pallid (PAL id) **pale**

THINKING IT THROUGH

1. Trace the feelings of the speaker throughout the poem. Where is he sad? terrified? surprised? amused? curious? angry? heartbroken? List at least one line (by number) as an example of each feeling.

2. The two lines in each stanza with *internal rhyme* have already been pointed out. With what else does the last word in line 3 of each stanza rhyme? Consider one stanza at a time. For example, in the first stanza, where else is there a word that rhymes with *napping* and *tapping?*

3. From the time the poem first appeared to the present, many readers have had mixed feelings about "The Raven." On one hand, the poem is admired for its brilliant originality and skillful rhymes. On the other hand, some think the whole thing is somewhat ridiculous. Do you agree with this evaluation in whole or in part? Explain.

4. The following cartoon is funny, but it also makes a serious suggestion about the poem. In your opinion, what is this suggestion?

323

Reading and Analyzing: Review

If you wish to review the meaning of any term in *italics* in this exercise, refer to the Glossary of Terms.

1. Turn back to the beginning of the poem (page 318). What *image* in the first stanza appeals to the reader's sense of hearing?

2. What sharp visual image does Poe use in the first part of the second stanza?

3. The third stanza appeals to the *imagery* of feeling. What bodily sensation does the speaker experience?

4. Poe wrote that by the end of the poem the reader should see the raven as a *symbol.* What do you think the raven symbolizes?

5. Now consider your own feelings as you read "The Raven." In just a word or two, what is the mood of the poem?

6. Think about Poe's use of *contrast* throughout the poem, particularly in the last stanza. The word "pallid" (line 74) suggests a contrast in color. What other contrasts are there between the raven and the bust of Pallas?

7. Reread the short profile of Poe on page 316. Then write at least two *hypotheses* that might explain why Poe wrote "The Raven."

8. Try to explain why the poem can be called a rather complicated study in *irony.* These questions will help guide your thinking: (a) Does what the speaker says always reveal what he really believes about the situation? (b) Does the last stanza turn out as the speaker (and perhaps the reader) expected?

Composition

1. Write a paragraph beginning with this topic sentence: *"The Raven" by Edgar Allan Poe is one of the most imaginative poems ever written.* Add at least four sentences that explain that topic sentence. Make your sentences detailed and exact.

2. Poe's genius is revealed in his ability to write stanza after stanza using the same complicated pattern of rhythm and rhyme. Prove this to yourself by trying to write just one stanza that could be inserted into the poem. If you don't succeed, at least describe the process you used and the progress you were able to make.

VOCABULARY AND SKILL REVIEW

Before completing the exercises that follow, you may wish to review the **bold-faced** words on pages 301 to 320.

I. On a separate sheet of paper, mark each item *true* or *false.* If it is *false,* explain in your own words just what is wrong.

1. A *trellis* is the climax of a tennis match.

2. A judge giving someone a sentence would probably speak *gravely.*

3. In some school auditoriums, there are two flags *flanking* the stage.

4. When you feel like crying, it's hard to *compose* your face.

5. Most adults can *feature* the president's face in their minds.

6. A *bust* of the president might have him seated on a horse.

7. Any president would certainly want to create a *stately* image in the public mind.

8. Thoughtful people often *ponder* important decisions carefully.

9. An *ember* constantly increases in both size and weight.

10. Poe's term *forgotten lore* means "forgotten foolishness."

II. Think of three sentences that apply to the cartoon below. The sentences must include three of these terms: (1) *third person;* (2) *inference;* (3) *characterization;* (4) *image;* (5) *contrast.*

"Its hideously deformed lips twisted upward into a sinister sneer, the monster raised one menacing claw-like upper limb and advanced toward Znnrgythh."

THE FALL OF THE HOUSE OF USHER

by Edgar Allan Poe
Screenplay Adaptation by Robert Potter

▶ You are about to read a television play based on a story that demonstrates the mental magic of Edgar Allan Poe. The original story is a famous one. In fact, the long first sentence (the narrator's first speech) has been called the best beginning of any story ever written.

CHARACTERS

Roderick Usher: *A haunted man who looks much older than his middle years. He has a sensitive, pale face; large, liquid eyes; and long, unkempt hair that floats rather than falls around his face. It is the face of an artist. His speech and manner must suggest a nervous person trying very hard to appear calm.*

Lady Madeline: *Usher's sister, near death. She is, nonetheless, a beauti-ful woman, and she bears a resemblance to her brother.*

Narrator: *A thoughtful, well-meaning man of about 45.*

Valet: *A very old family servant.*

Doctor: *A powerful, unfriendly person.*

TIME: About 1800.

SETTING: The land of Poe's imagination. Nothing shown on the TV screen ties the story to any specific location.

- unkempt (un KEMPT) **not combed; wild and messy**
- **valet** (VAL it) **male personal servant; manservant**

ACT I

FADE IN: *A finely drawn, almost photographically clear painting that you will see again: the House of Usher. The building is a decaying, moss-covered stone mansion that rises like a cliff from the edge of a murky tarn. Weird growth hangs from the eves. The windows are vacant and eyelike. A narrow crack zigzags from the top of one turret to the ground. In front of the mansion are a few dried-up bushes and the trunks of dead trees. The whole gloomy scene is reflected in the still waters of a tarn. You do not see the frame of the painting, and at this point there is no reason to think it is not a photo of the real thing. Title and credits over.*

DISSOLVE TO: *Two or three long shots of the* Narrator's *journey, as described below.*

Narrator (*voice over*): During the whole of a dull, dark, and soundless day in the autumn of the year, when the clouds hung oppressively low in the heavens, I had been passing alone, on horseback, through a singularly dreary tract of country, and at length found myself, as the shades of evening drew on, within view of the melancholy House of Usher.

DISSOLVE TO: *Picture of mansion.*

DISSOLVE TO: *The* Narrator *using the*

heavy knocker on an old oak door. The camera follows him throughout. Everything in the mansion—and it is crowded with objects collected over many generations—is old, covered with dust, and in disrepair.

Narrator (*calling*): Hello! Hello! (*The Valet, a lamp in hand, opens the creaking door.*) Ah! A sign of life amid the gloom. I have a letter here from Roderick Usher. I am——

- **murky** (MUR kee) **dark and gloomy**
- tarn (TARN) **pond; pool**
- **turret** (TUR it) **small tower**
- oppressively (uh PRES iv lee) **distressingly; intensely**
- singularly (SING yuh lur lee) **unusually; remarkably**
- **melancholy** (MEL un kol ee) **gloomy; sorrowful**
- **disrepair** (dis ri PAIR) **unrepaired state**

Valet: Come in. You are expected.

Narrator: Expected?

Valet: Few people come here any more. My master knew *you* would come.

Narrator: Roderick Usher is—? Then he is still alive?

Valet: Yes, alive—in a way. (*They start down a dim corridor.*)

Narrator: Usher's letter spoke of an illness. It seemed written in a shaking hand.

Valet: It would be. You knew Roderick Usher when he was sent away to school?

Narrator: Yes, many years ago. He was hardly the sort of person one could forget easily. Just what *is* wrong with him? (*The* Valet *stays silent for several steps.*) Can you tell me nothing?

Valet: The truth is—no one knows, exactly. (*He stops, looking the* Narrator *directly in the face.*) I've worked in this mansion for 70 years, and my father before me. And only this much do I know: My master's malady is, you might say, more mental than physical. It runs in the family. When the Ushers are young, we get art. We get music. We get beauty and charity. Then something happens.

Narrator: How so?

Valet: I should call it—and my master's case is worse than his father's—an oppressive acuteness of the senses. On some days, he can eat only the most bland and tasteless of foods. He can stand only the softest of fabrics next to his skin. The odor of all flowers drives him mad. (*They start up a staircase.*) There are only certain sounds—and these from stringed instruments—that do not fill him with horror.

Doctor (*entering from above, roughly*): Who have we here?

Valet: A friend. An old school friend.

Doctor (*rudely*): Ha!

Narrator: You come from Roderick Usher?

Doctor: Roderick Usher is beyond the skills of my profession. Excuse me. (*He shoulders his way past and out.*)

Narrator: But——

Valet: Save your breath.

DISSOLVE TO: Usher's room, huge and untidy. It is filled with musical instruments, books, and paintings. An easel stands between two doors at the rear corners. Usher is lying on a couch, propped up by many pillows. He wears a tattered robe and his eyes are closed.

SOUND: Knock.

Usher: Yes, yes. (*He jumps up, pulling himself together.*) Enter, please enter. (*They do.*) Oh! Old fellow! So good of you to come. (*He nods at the* Valet, *who exits.*)

Narrator (*shaking hands warmly*): Roderick, it's been many years.

Usher: Too many. We haven't met since school. But you remain—you are—my best and indeed my only personal friend. That's why I sent for you.

Narrator (*awkwardly*): That's what friends are for. (*They sit down.*)

Usher: Would you have recognized me?

Narrator: Perhaps. The same high forehead, the same quick manner, the same——

- malady (MAL uh dee) **illness; complaint**
- **acuteness** (uh KYOOT nes) **sharpness; sensitivity**
- bland (BLAND) **mild; soft**

Usher: Weak chin. The sign of all the Ushers. (*He forces a laugh in an effort to appear calm and jovial.*) The weak chin that means a lack of moral energy. How long can you stay?

Narrator: I don't know. Several weeks, perhaps. How can I help?

Usher: Just *be* here. That's all I want, just the cheerfulness of your society.

Narrator: Your letter spoke of illness.

Usher (*rising*): Oh, that. Just a mere malady of the nerves. It will soon pass away. You see, what's bad is not really the disease itself—it's *thinking* about the disease. (*He's pacing nervously now.*) The truth is, if something should happen to me, if I should die, it would be the end of the House of Usher. (*He tries to chuckle.*) Yes, that's what they call us, those peasants out there beyond the walls. Both the family and this building: "the House of Usher." There have been Ushers in this house since the middle ages.

Narrator: And now——

Usher (*stopping*): And now, when I go, the House of Usher is no more. I have no living relatives, however distant. I never married, and I have no children.

Narrator (*rising suddenly*): Why look! There on the wall: the House of Usher!

PAN TO: The same picture seen previously, but this time framed and on the wall of Usher's room.

Usher: Yes, I painted it myself, many years ago.

Narrator: It looks almost real! (*He examines the painting closely.*) I remember, not an hour ago, stopping my horse on that bank out there and looking down at this very picture. (*He shudders.*)

Usher (*meaningfully, after a pause*): You felt it then?

Narrator: Felt? Felt what?

Usher: Then why did you stop your horse?

Narrator: Well, I must admit that the first sight of the House of Usher rather unnerved me.

Usher: *Unnerved!* The very word! Then think of *me.* There are certain superstitions, certain thoughts about this house. Do you believe—do you believe that there's something about these gray walls and turrets, and the dim tarn into which they look down, that can, over the years, influence the *spirit* of a man?

Narrator (*doing his best with an argument he doesn't wholly believe*): Nonsense. Look, (*points to parts of picture*) these are trees. Trees are trees. Water is only water. Stones are just stones. There's absolutely no way that natural objects can hold a power over any human being.

Usher: But these stones are *not* just stones. (*He points.*) You see, each one, each individual stone, is in crumbling condition. I tell you, at times I can *hear* the stones decaying! Each was quarried hundreds of years ago, and has been exposed to the air for too many centuries. Yet even in my lifetime, not one of them has fallen into the tarn. Is that not remarkable?

Narrator: Why so?

Usher: I mean, just what kind of force holds this old building together?

Narrator: But there *has* been damage.

There is this crack, from top to bottom. (*He points.*)

Usher: The crack, yes! The crack—it's what I fear. (*He sits down and buries face in hands.*) I shall crack, too, in this atmosphere of gloom. I shall perish. I *must* perish. I dread the events of the future, not in themselves, but in their results. I shudder at the thought that any, even the most trivial, incident will cause me to abandon life and reason altogether. I struggle with the grim phantom, Fear.

Narrator (*placing hand on* Usher's *shoulder*): My friend.

Usher (*after a pause, sitting up and clearing his throat*): I owe you an apology for all that talk about my fears.

Narrator: Everything will be all right, I promise you. You yourself said, just moments ago, that all this will soon pass away.

Usher: "Will soon pass away," yes!

Narrator: We will talk together, and walk, and tell old stories, and read, and sing——

Usher: And forget about stones having power over people! (*He does his best to laugh in triumph.*) And always be honest with one another. (*seriously*) I must admit, I lied to you. Much of my peculiar gloom can be traced to a more natural origin. I said I have no living relative. But there lives, within this house, my tenderly beloved sister, the Lady Madeline. She's been my sole companion for these long years, my last and only relative on earth.

Narrator: Is she not well?

Usher: It's been a severe and long-

• **unnerve** (un NURV) disturb greatly; take courage away

continued illness. What it is, her physicians cannot discover. The disease is a general weakness, a slow wasting away of the person, and temporary spells of a somewhat cataleptic character.

Narrator (*not knowing the word*): Cataleptic?

Usher: Catalepsy. It's a kind of sleep. Her muscles grow rigid.

PAN TO: Far end of room. The strangely beautiful Lady Madeline, dressed in a long white robe, enters through one of the doors. Her pale and sad face is without expression, even when she notices the guest and stops.

Usher (*continuing without a pause*): Her eyes glaze over. She loses all contact with her environment. For years she has struggled, but only today has she spent most of the time in bed. (*He shudders.*) I fear her death, not only because of her loss as a person, but also because it will leave me the last of the ancient race of Ushers. Oh! (*He sees* Madeline *for the first time, as does the* Narrator. *Both remain silent as she slowly walks backward and sideways to the other door and exits.*)

Narrator: That was the Lady Madeline?

Usher: That was the Lady Madeline. She has surrendered, I think, to the dim destroyer. I fear the lady, at least while living, shall be seen by you no more.

FADE OUT.

- cataleptic (kat uh LEP tic) **having to do with a sleep-like illness**
- catalepsy (KAT uh lep see) **illness involving rigid muscles and loss of contact with environment**

ACT II

FADE IN: Usher's room, late evening. *The* Narrator, *on his knees, is examining some paintings stacked against the wall.* Usher, *now fully dressed and seated in a straight chair, is improvising a haunting melody on a guitar.*

Narrator (*voice over*): For the next several days, the name of the Lady Madeline was unmentioned by either Roderick Usher or myself. During this period I did everything I could think of to lessen the melancholy of my friend. We painted and read together, or I listened, as if in a dream, as he improvised wild melodies on his speaking guitar. Yet the longer I stayed, the more sure I became that there was no way to cheer a mind from which such darkness poured forth.

Usher (*putting guitar aside as the* Narrator *reaches a certain painting*): That one is the best painting of the lot.

Narrator (*standing up with painting*): What is it?

Usher: "What is it?" A meaningless question. I no longer paint *things.* How could I stand to paint the very things that hold such a power over me?

CLOSE UP: Painting in the Narrator's *hands. It shows a long vault or tunnel with low walls. The entire painting is done in shades of white. There are no doors, and the walls are smooth, without interruption. Something suggests that the area pictured is deep within the earth. Although no light is shown, a flood of intense rays brightens the whole in a ghastly splendor.*

Usher (*continuing*): No, in recent years I paint only myself. I mean, I paint my own mind. I paint ideas.

Narrator: Yes. The utter simplicity is amazing. If anyone ever painted an idea, that person is Roderick Usher.

PAN TO: Usher's *face, then camera moves back.*

Usher: Put the painting down. I must tell you. The Lady Madeline is no more.

Narrator: *Dead?*

Usher: This morning.

Narrator: I'm sorry. What can I—what are the arrangements?

- **improvising** (IM pruh vyz ing) **making up on the spot**
- utter (UT er) **complete; total**

Usher (*very businesslike*): The arrangements? There are none. None are needed, for my sister's only companion was myself. She has been placed in a coffin, but there will be no burial, at least for two weeks.

Narrator: Why not?

Usher: The doctors. You see, her disease has baffled the physicians for years. If they were notified of her death, they would demand an autopsy. And the thought of that! (*He shudders.*) It would be like someone slicing into my own flesh! But if I refuse to give the body to them, they will stop at nothing. I have no doubt that they would dig it up. The family burial ground is some distance away, and cannot be watched.

Narrator: Still, it is strange——

Usher: I have decided, and I am firm.

Narrator (*thoughtfully*): Yes, I remember meeting one of the physicians. But do you think—in your condition—that your thoughts should so dwell upon a corpse? You must get rid of it—out of this house and out of your mind!

Usher: There is a vault, deep under this building—under your very room, in fact. In feudal days, it was a dungeon. More recently, it held powder and arms. There we must take her.

Narrator: No!

Usher: There is no other way.

DISSOLVE TO: Some time later, Usher *and the* Narrator *are carrying the coffin toward the heavy iron door of the vault. Two lanterns on the coffin provide the only light. The six or eight screws that hold the lid on the coffin are in place but not screwed down.*

Usher: Here we are. (*They set the coffin down on two convenient boxes. Usher takes an ancient key from his pocket and opens the massive iron door, which grates loudly on its hinges. He returns to the coffin.*) Ready.

Narrator (*as they enter*): What an oppressive place!

PAN AROUND: The copper walls of the vault. Then camera back as the coffin is set on two stands in the center. The Narrator starts to leave.

Usher: No, wait. (*He slides the coffin lid down so that he can see his sister's face. Tears roll down his cheeks.*)

Narrator (*looking down*): A smile is terrible in death.

Usher: Yes. I've read all I can on catalepsy. When death finally comes, it can even bring a faint blush.

Narrator: I never realized . . . how much you two look alike.

Usher (*simply*): We were twins. Throughout her life, we shared a kind of intelligence, as though our minds were one. (*He puts the lid back in place.*)

CLOSE UP: Usher's hands screwing down the lid.

FADE OUT.

ACT III

FADE IN: The Narrator's face as he lies in bed with open eyes and clenched jaw. He is obviously having trouble with sleep. We see the top of a long-sleeved nightgown. During the following the camera moves back to reveal the whole bed.
SOUND: A storm brewing outside. The wind and thunder are heard irregularly throughout the scene.

Narrator (*voice over*): Seven or eight days after we placed the Lady Madeline in the dungeon, I began to worry about my *own* mind. Like Usher's, it refused to rest. And Usher had changed completely. His music, his art, his books—all were forgotten. He roamed from room to room with hurried but purposeless steps. Either that, or he would sit quite still for hours, as though gazing at nothing,

or listening for imaginary sounds. His face, if possible, had grown even more pale, but the light in his eyes had utterly gone out.

DISSOLVE TO: The picture of the House of Usher seen earlier, but now without the frame; the objects within the picture begin to move. Low clouds seem to press on the turrets. An eerie and mysterious light plays on the scene. A bolt of lightning strikes nearby.
DISSOLVE TO: Narrator's room, as before.

Narrator (*throwing back covers in irritation, then burning fingers as he attempts to light a bedside lamp*): Ouch! (*He succeeds with the lamp, then reaches for his clothing on a nearby chair.*)

● eerie (EER ee) **weird; fearful**

DISSOLVE TO: The life-like picture, with movement as before.
DISSOLVE TO: Narrator's room, as he finishes throwing on his clothes.
SOUND: During an interval in the storm, a low, indistinct, straining and scraping noise.

Narrator: What was that? (*He picks up a book, looks at the title, slams it down in disgust, and then begins pacing to and fro.*)

SOUND: A harsh rapping on the door.

Usher (*as he enters in nightdress, looking more wild than ever*): You have not seen it? You have not seen it? Well, you shall! (*He slides a drapery aside and throws open a window. The force of the wind sways the heavy curtains and strikes both men in the face. The irregular light from outside pulsates on their faces.*) Look! Look at that light!

Narrator: You must not—you shall not—look at this! (*He forces Usher from the window to a seat.*)

Usher: What *is* that light? Where does it come from?

Narrator (*trying for calm*): During a storm, such electrical phenomena are not uncommon, are they?

Usher: But we saw no lightning just then—only the light itself!

Narrator (*closing window*): Then it could be caused by some gas from the stale, swampy waters of the tarn. Who knows? There are many . . .

Usher (*starting to rise*): Let me . . .

Narrator (*forcing Usher back down*): No!

Usher: What do we do then—just sit here?

Narrator (*in desperation; he will try anything*): Here—here is one of our favorite books. (*Picks up book.*) *The Mad Tryst* by Sir Launcelot Canning. (*He sits down next to Usher and begins to read.*) "This is the story of Ethelred, a knight famous the world over for his bravery in the face of any danger. In the days of Arthur, it came to pass upon the land that . . .

DISSOLVE TO: The same scene, some time later. The storm seems to have stopped. The Narrator reads with only pretended interest. Usher sits in a kind of paralyzed terror.

Narrator (*pausing in his reading*): Oh, yes. Here comes the part where Ethelred forces his way into the house of the hermit. "And Ethelred, who was by nature of a mighty heart, and being denied entrance by the hermit, and feeling the rain on his shoulders, and fearing the rising of the tempest, uplifted his face and made quick work of the planks of the door, cracking and ripping and tearing all apart, so that the noise resounded throughout the forest."

SOUND: A far-off cracking and ripping noise like the one just described.

Narrator (*trying to ignore the sound*): "But the good champion Ethelred, finding no sight of the hermit, was amazed to see instead a large dragon of scaly body and fiery tongue. And

- **pulsate** (PUL sayt) beat; throb
- **phenomena** (fi NOM uh nuh) events; happenings
- tryst (TRIST) appointment; meeting

Ethelred uplifted his mace, and struck upon the head of the dragon, which fell before him with a shriek so horrid, harsh, and piercing that Ethelred had to close his ears with his hands.

SOUND: *A screaming, grating noise.*

Usher (*softly through trembling lips*): Oh! Oh! Oh! (*The reason for the murmur is uncertain; his chin is on his chest and he seems not to have heard the sound. By now he has inched his chair around so that both men sit facing the door.*)

Narrator: "And now the champion, having escaped the terrible fury of the dragon, sighted the object of his quest, the silver shield, on the wall, and approaching the shield, was surprised to find that it waited not for his full coming, but fell down upon the floor, with a great and mighty ringing sound."

SOUND: *The hollow clang of metal.*

Narrator (*leaping up*): Did you . . . ? (*He stops to examine* Usher, *who sits in frozen fear. At the touch of the* Narrator's *hand,* Usher *shudders violently. Then a sickly smile hovers on his lips.*)

Usher (*starting softly and rising to an uncontrolled pitch*): Not hear it? Yes, I heard it, and *have* heard it. Many minutes, many hours, many days, have I heard it. Yet I dared not—oh, pity me—I dared not—I *dared* not speak! *We have put her living into the tomb!* Oh, too acute—too acute are my senses. I *now* tell you that I heard her first feeble movements in the hollow coffin. And tonight—Ethelred—the breaking of the hermit's door, the death cry of the dragon, and the clang of the shield! Say, rather, the breaking of her coffin, the grating of the iron hinges of the door, and her struggle within the copper archway of the vault! Will she not be here soon? Is she not hurrying to punish me for my haste? Do I not hear a footstep on the stair, the horrible beating of her heart? MADMAN! (*He springs to his feet and shrieks as though he were giving up his soul.*) MADMAN! I TELL YOU THAT SHE NOW STANDS OUTSIDE THAT DOOR!

PAN TO: *The door of the room, which opens slowly. There stands the* Lady Madeline, *wavering unsteadily. There is blood on her white robe, and her beautiful, pale mask of a face shows signs of a struggle. Trembling, she reels her way into the room. The camera moves back and* Usher *enters the picture. He stops a yard from her. With a low moan, she falls heavily upon him. In her violent and now final death agonies, she bears him to the floor a corpse, and a victim to the terrors he has anticipated. Now the* Narrator *enters the frame. He looks with horror at the bodies as the whole room starts to shake. The camera follows him as he dashes out the door and into the darkness of a long corridor.*

DISSOLVE TO: *The picture of the house, again with movement within the scene. Although the storm has stopped, the same strange light still plays on the walls. You see what the* Narrator's *voice describes in the following.*

● mace (MAYS) **metal-headed club**

Narrator (*voice over*): From that chamber, and from that mansion, I fled aghast. The odd light still gleamed here and there as I crossed the old causeway. Suddenly there shot along the path a wild beam, and I turned to see where it could have come from, for the vast house and its shadows were alone behind me. The radiance was that of the full, setting, and blood-red moon. It now shone brightly through that once-small crack, that fissure that extended from the roof of the building, in a zigzag direction, to the base. While I gazed, the fissure rapidly widened, and the entire moon burst at once upon my sight. My brain reeled as I saw the mighty walls collapse and fall—there was a long, terrible shouting sound like the voice of a thousand waters—and the deep and dark tarn at my feet closed sullenly and silently over the fragments of the House of Usher.

FADE OUT.

- **aghast** (uh GAST) terrified; frightened
- causeway (KAWZ way) **raised road across watery area**
- fissure (FISH ur) **crack**

ALL THINGS CONSIDERED _____

1. The narrator goes to the House of Usher because (a) he calls on Roderick Usher often. (b) Usher has sent for him. (c) he wants to meet Madeline.

2. The narrator soon learns that Usher's illness is (a) mostly physical. (b) mostly mental. (c) called catalepsy.

3. Usher seems to believe that (a) his servants are out to kill him. (b) he has strange powers over natural objects. (c) natural objects can influence his spirit.

4. Usher tells the narrator that his sister's body (a) must be buried immediately. (b) will not decay. (c) will be taken to an underground vault.

5. The story ends with (a) the narrator fleeing and both Usher and Madeline dead. (b) Usher dead but Madeline still alive. (c) a quotation from *The Mad Tryst*.

THINKING IT THROUGH _____

1. The first sentence of Poe's story (the Narrator's first speech) has attracted a lot of attention. How does the sentence *itself* support what it says?

2. The reader is told early that Usher's senses are very sharp. Why is this fact important when the play draws to a close?

3. Many readers have wondered why Usher's painting (page 332) is described as it is. Give one possible connection between the picture and the rest of the plot.

4. (a) What reason does Usher give for his plans concerning his sister's body? (b) Does this reason make sense to you? Explain.

5. Usher's appearance changes greatly between Act II and Act III. What causes this change?

6. Some readers infer that Usher somehow knows the truth about his sister before he hears the noises. Upon what details might this inference be based?

7. Local people call both the building and the family "the House of Usher." (a) All things considered, what are the similarities between the mansion and the family? (b) Does the title apply to both house and family? Explain.

8. Although the story seems supernatural, Poe is careful to provide natural explanations for most of the events. What are the explanations for (a) Madeline's "death" and (b) the destruction of the mansion?

Critical Thinking: Review

If you wish to review the meaning of any term in *italics* in this exercise, refer to the Glossary of Terms.

1. Think critically about how the story illustrates the human imagination at work. The notion of *mental maps* and *territories* will help. (a) Is any real territory involved? That is, did a real House of Usher—or Roderick Usher—ever exist? (b) Is it accurate to say that the whole story is a series of Poe's mental maps? Explain your opinion.

2. How does Poe try to get his audience to accept his "territory" as if it were real? Comment on (a) his use of a *first person*—rather than a *third person*—narrator, and (b) his detailed description of the setting.

3. Early in the story, Roderick Usher makes an *analogy* between himself and the House of Usher. (a) What is this analogy? (b) Is it false, or does it turn out to be true?

4. Throughout the story, Poe depends upon his audience to make good *inferences* from the setting. (a) What might a reader infer from the crack that zigzags down the front of the mansion? (b) What can be inferred about Roderick Usher from the description of his room (page 328)? (c) How do the storm and the mysterious light heighten the climax? (d) With the last sentence, Poe makes the setting *disappear!* What might be a good reader's feelings and inferences at this point?

Composition

1. Choose a room in your school in which the teacher or the students have done something interesting or unusual to the setting. Describe the interesting features and explain what a complete stranger could infer about the "designers" from the room.

2. Literary classics like "The Fall of the House of Usher" should not only interest their readers but also teach them something about living their own lives. Think about the informative, practical value of Poe's story. Explain what is suggested in the story as good and as bad for human beings—including yourself.

Edna St. Vincent Millay (1892-1950)

Millay and her husband enjoying a leisurely cruise

Like Kate Chopin (see page 105), Edna St. Vincent Millay was a literary rebel, a writer who wanted to tell the truth about life and love from a woman's point of view. Kate Chopin was born "ahead of her time" and faced rejection and final defeat. However, in the "roaring 20s," Edna St. Vincent Millay won fast fame as a symbol of life, love, and a newfound freedom. She would start a poem:

What lips my lips have kissed, and
    where, and why,
I have forgotten . . .

In the 1920s, this was scandalous, but for many people delightfully so. Curiosity seekers flocked to her poetry readings across the country. There they found a small, very attractive young woman with golden red hair, a sensitive voice, and a dignified manner. They also found that Millay's reputation as a symbol of bright, adventurous youth was only part of the picture. Most of her best poems did not concern love at all, and she often spoke of sorrow, hardship, and loss. It is upon this wider reputation that her continuing fame rests.

Hardship and loss were hardly strangers to the young poet. Her early life on the coast of Maine had been generally happy but far from easy. Her parents were divorced when she was a young girl, and for years her mother supported the family on what she could earn as a nurse. Although Millay was an active, prize-winning student in high school, there was no money for college. Accepting this loss as a fact of life, she continued to work at her poetry. A long poem called "Renascence," written when she was 19, brought her early fame. Then came college, success, years of travel, and a good marriage. Much of her later work reveals an inner anguish caused by what she saw as human injustice and stupidity. Her last sorrow was that even a perfect poem can do little to remake an imperfect world.

THE COLLECTOR'S MILLAY

poems by Edna St. Vincent Millay

▶ Millay's poetry sizzles with a high-voltage originality. Here is a collection of eight of her poems. These lyric poems form a kind of sequence. Try to discover how the poems are related to each other. Also, remember that Millay was probably the most popular poet of her time. After reading the poems several times, try to explain this popularity.

Note: If you have trouble with any of the terms in *italics*, refer to the Glossary of Terms.

THE PHILOSOPHER

And what are you that, wanting you,
   I should be kept awake
As many nights as there are days
   With weeping for your sake?

And what are you that, missing you,
   As many days as crawl
I should be listening to the wind
   And looking at the wall?

I know a man that's a braver man
   And twenty men as kind,
And what are you, that you should be
   The one man in my mind?

Yet women's ways are witless ways,
   As any sage will tell,—
And what am I, that I should love
   So wisely and so well?

WAYS OF KNOWING

1. The most original *stanza* is, of course, the last. Explain the meaning of this stanza. Is the speaker "witless," "wise," or both at the same time?
2. The poem is not rich in *figurative language,* but there is a good example in the second stanza. What is it?

• sage (SAYJ) **very wise person; philosopher**

RECUERDO

We were very tired, we were very merry—
We had gone back and forth all night on the ferry.
It was bare and bright, and smelled like a stable—
But we looked into a fire, we leaned across a table,
We lay on a hill-top underneath the moon;
And the whistles kept blowing, and the dawn came soon.

We were very tired, we were very merry—
We had gone back and forth all night on the ferry.
And you ate an apple, and I ate a pear,
From a dozen of each we had bought somewhere;
And the sky went wan, and the wind came cold,
And the sun rose dripping, a bucketful of gold.

We were very tired, we were very merry—
We had gone back and forth all night on the ferry.
We hailed, "Good morrow, mother!" to a shawl-covered head,
And bought a morning paper, which neither of us read;
And she wept, "God bless you!" for the apples and pears,
And we gave her all our money but our subway fares.

- recuerdo (ri KWER doh) **Spanish for memory *or* souvenir**
- wan (WAHN) **very pale**

WAYS OF KNOWING

1. (a) Who seems to be the speaker in the poem? (b) What other person seems to be included in the "we"? (c) What details in the poem led you to make *inferences* to answer the preceding questions?

2. Notice how the stanzas are linked together. (a) Omitting the first two lines, what in the first stanza is mentioned in the second? (b) What in the second is mentioned in the third?

3. The poem has what might be called a "happy rhythm" that supports the *mood.* Explain.

4. Which statement does the poem best support? (a) A good poem must be a difficult poem. (b) When you're in love, the whole world looks lovely. (c) Lack of sleep makes people foolish and giddy.

5. *Contrast* "Recuerdo" with "The Philosopher" in at least two ways.

6. The last four words of line three are probably NOT a *simile.* Can you explain why?

7. (a) Which line in the second stanza contains two *metaphors?* (b) In your opinion, why are these metaphors particularly well chosen?

FIRST FIG

My candle burns at both ends;
    It will not last the night;
But ah, my foes, and oh, my friends—
    It gives a lovely light!

● fig (FIG) *either* a worthless little bit *or short for* figurative

SECOND FIG

Safe upon the solid rock the ugly houses stand:
Come and see my shining palace built upon the sand!

MIDNIGHT OIL

Cut if you will, with Sleep's dull knife,
    Each day to half its length, my friend, —
The years that Time takes off my life,
    He'll take from off the other end!

WAYS OF KNOWING

1. "First Fig" and "Midnight Oil" contain *allusions* to familiar *clichés*. What are these familiar expressions?
2. The three poems are unusual in that they consist almost entirely of *figurative language*. *Paraphrase* the meaning of each poem in a clear, original sentence.
3. All three poems support a general philosophy of life: *Live the most wonderful life you can, right now!* In your opinion, what is good—and what is bad—about this advice?
4. *Application of knowledge.* Relate this fact to one of the poems: In her late fifties, Millay died of a heart attack after working nearly all night.
5. Which poem contains an excellent example of *personification?* Explain the comparison involved.

SONNET XXXI

Oh, oh, you will be sorry for that word!
Give back my book and take my kiss instead.
Was it my enemy or my friend I heard,
"What a big book for such a little head!"
5 Come, I will show you now my newest hat,
And you may watch me purse my mouth and prink!
Oh, I shall love you still, and all of that.
I never again shall tell you what I think.
I shall be sweet and crafty, soft and sly;
10 You will not catch me reading any more:
I shall be called a wife to pattern by;
And some day when you knock and push the door,
Some sane day, not too bright and not too stormy,
I shall be gone, and you may whistle for me.

WAYS OF KNOWING

1. (a) Who is the speaker in the poem? (b) Who is being spoken to?
2. (a) What had the speaker been doing a few minutes earlier? (b) Then what happened? (c) How has this changed the relationship of the two people involved?
3. What is the speaker's *prediction* about the future?
4. Since the entire poem is a little speech, it offers you an opportunity for good *oral interpretation.* Practice reading the poem aloud until it sounds exactly right. Pay particular attention to the *irony* in line 7.

GROWN-UP

Was it for this I uttered prayers,
And sobbed and cursed and kicked the stairs,
That now, domestic as a plate,
I should retire at half-past eight?

- purse (PURS) **wrinkle up; pucker**
- prink (PRINK) **fuss over one's dress**
- domestic (duh MES tik) **of the household**

345

TRAVEL

The railroad track is miles away,
    And the day is loud with voices speaking,
Yet there isn't a train goes by all day
    But I hear its whistle shrieking.

All night there isn't a train goes by,
    Though the night is still for sleep and dreaming,
But I see its cinders red on the sky,
    And hear its engine steaming.

My heart is warm with the friends I make,
    And better friends I'll not be knowing;
Yet there isn't a train I wouldn't take,
    No matter where it's going.

WAYS OF KNOWING

1. Write a short *précis* of "Travel," using as few of the poet's words as possible.
2. How can "Travel" be related to the poem entitled, "Sonnet XXXI"?
3. "Grown-up" *contrasts* two ages of the speaker. In your opinion, what are these two ages? Be as specific as you can.
4. With which one of the poems preceding it does "Grown-up" best *contrast?* Explain.
5. The two poems contain only one example of truly original *figurative language.* (a) What is it? (b) Is it a *simile* or a *metaphor?*
6. The introduction to the poems asked you to think about the reasons for Millay's popularity. Finish this exercise by finding at least three reasons. Be able to support your reasons by referring to the poems.

Willa Cather (1873-1947)

The Cather family's home in Red Cloud, Nebraska

Prize-winning writer Willa Cather was born in Virginia but moved with her family to the plains of Nebraska when she was nine. There she grew up as a tomboy, fishing and canoeing with her brothers. During the early years, she spent much of her time outdoors since there was no school for her to attend. One of her favorite childhood activities was chloroforming and dissecting small animals. She fully intended to become a doctor when she grew up.

A few years later, however, her plans changed. At the University of Nebraska, her professors were highly impressed with her writing. An essay she wrote as a first-year student was published in a newspaper. The effect on her was hypnotic: she decided to become a writer rather than a doctor. She found that she was an excellent student of literature and languages. However, if she didn't like a subject, she tended to cut up and act the clown. She almost failed to graduate.

Her low grades in math were always a source of trouble.

After college, Willa Cather taught high-school English for a time. She also continued to practice her writing skills and soon had some of her stories published. She went on to edit *McClure's,* a famous magazine of the day, leaving to devote her full time to writing.

You might be amused by one strongly held belief of Willa Cather's: she felt a book was ruined if a student were *made* to read it! She often said she didn't want her books assigned to students as part of the grind. For many years she refused to allow her stories to be reprinted for classroom use. Fortunately for you, this is no longer the case—or you might never had had the opportunity to meet Anton Rosicky. Rarely in literature—or in life—do we have a chance to get to know a person as warm, as kind, as wonderful as is Neighbor Rosicky.

NEIGHBOR ROSICKY

by Willa Cather

▶ One of the things Willa Cather loved about growing up in Nebraska was getting to know the immigrants—Swedes, Bohemians, Russians, Germans—who were planting the land on the Great Plains. She knew many immigrants personally—their histories and their hopes, their determination and their dreams. She admired the mental magic that transformed a land of sod houses, dry fields, and backbreaking work into a land of opportunity for them. One such immigrant was John Pavelka, the Bohemian on whom she based her tender story, "Neighbor Rosicky." When you read the story, you'll see why she admired his vision and his ability to see beyond the territory toward the fulfillment of a dream.

I

When Doctor Burleigh told Neighbor Rosicky he had a bad heart, Rosicky protested.

"So? No, I guess my heart was always pretty good. I got a little asthma, maybe. Just a awful short breath when I was pitchin' hay last summer, dat's all."

"Well now, Rosicky, if you know more about it than I do, what did you come to me for? It's your heart that makes you short of breath, I tell you. You're sixty-five years old, and you've always worked hard, and your heart's tired. You've got to be careful from now on, and you can't do heavy work any more. You've got five boys at home to do it for you."

The old farmer looked up at the doctor with a gleam of amusement in his queer triangular-shaped eyes. His eyes were large and lively, but the lids were caught up in the middle in a curious way, so that they formed a triangle. He did not look like a sick man. His brown face was creased but not wrinkled, he had a ruddy color in his smooth-shaven cheeks and in his lips, under his long brown mustache. His hair was thin and ragged around his ears, but very little gray. His forehead, naturally high and crossed by deep parallel lines, now ran all the way up to his pointed crown. Rosicky's face had the habit of looking interested—suggested a contented disposition and a reflective quality that was gay rather than grave. This gave him

---

● ruddy (RUH dee) **healthy red color**

a certain detachment, the easy manner of an onlooker and observer.

"Well, I guess you ain't got no pills fur a bad heart, Doctor Ed. I guess the only thing is fur me to git me a new one."

Doctor Burleigh swung round in his desk chair and frowned at the old farmer. "I think if I were you I'd take a little care of the old one, Rosicky."

Rosicky shrugged. "Maybe I don't know how. I expect you mean fur me not to drink my coffee no more."

"I wouldn't, in your place. But you'll do as you choose about that. I've never yet been able to separate a Bohemian from his coffee or pipe. I've quit trying. But the sure thing is you've got to cut out farm work. You can feed the stock and do chores about the barn, but you can't do anything in the fields that makes you short of breath."

"How about shelling corn?"

"Of course not!"

Rosicky considered with puckered brows.

"I can't make my heart go no longer'n it wants to, can I, Doctor Ed?"

"I think it's good for five or six years yet, maybe more, if you'll take the strain off it. Sit around the house and help Mary. If I had a good wife like yours, I'd want to stay around the house."

His patient chuckled. "It ain't no place fur a man. I don't like no old man hanging round the kitchen too much. An' my wife, she's a awful hard worker her own self."

"That's it; you can help her a little. My Lord, Rosicky, you are one of the few men I know who has a family he can get some comfort out of; happy dispositions, never quarrel among themselves, and they treat you right. I want to see you live a few years and enjoy them."

"Oh, they're good kids, all right," Rosicky assented.

The doctor wrote him a prescription and asked him how his oldest son, Rudolph, who had married in the spring, was getting on. Rudolph had struck out for himself, on rented land. "And how's Polly? I was afraid Mary mightn't like an American daughter-in-law, but it seems to be working out all right."

"Yes, she's a fine girl. Dat widder woman bring her daughters up very nice. Polly got lots of spunk, an' she got some style, too. Da's nice, for young folks to have some style." Rosicky inclined his head gallantly. His voice and his twinkly smile were an affectionate compliment to his daughter-in-law.

"It looks like a storm, and you'd better be getting home before it comes. In town in the car?" Doctor Burleigh rose.

- Bohemian (boh HEE mee un) **native** of Bohemia (in Czechoslovakia)
- assent (uh SENT) **agree**
- **spunk** (SPUNK) **courage**

"No, I'm in de wagon. When you got five boys, you ain't got much chance to ride round in de Ford. I ain't much for cars, noway."

"Well, it's a good road out to your place; but I don't want you bumping around in a wagon much. And never again on a hay-rake, remember!"

Rosicky placed the doctor's fee delicately behind the desk telephone, looking the other way, as if this were an absent-minded gesture. He put on his plush cap and his corduroy jacket with a sheepskin collar, and went out.

The doctor picked up his stethoscope and frowned at it as if he were seriously annoyed with the instrument. He wished it had been telling tales about some other man's heart, some old man who didn't look the doctor in the eye so knowingly, or hold out such a warm brown hand when he said good-by. Doctor Burleigh had been a poor boy in the country before he went away to medical school; he had known Rosicky almost ever since he could remember, and he had a deep affection for Mrs. Rosicky.

Only last winter he had had such a good breakfast at Rosicky's, and that when he needed it. He had been out all night on a long, hard confinement case at Tom Marshall's—a big rich farm where there was plenty of stock and plenty of feed and a great deal of expensive farm machinery of the newest model, and no comfort whatever. The woman had too many children and too much work, and she was no manager. When the baby was born at last, and handed over to the assisting neighbor woman, and the mother was properly attended to, Burleigh refused any breakfast in that slovenly house, and drove his buggy—the snow was too deep for a car—

- **stethoscope** (STETH uh SKOHP) **instrument used to hear a heartbeat**
- confinement (kon FYN ment) **period of childbirth**
- slovenly (SLUV un lee) **untidy**

eight miles to Anton Rosicky's place. He didn't know another farm-house where a man could get such a warm welcome, and such good strong coffee with rich cream. No wonder the old chap didn't want to give up his coffee!

He had driven in just when the boys had come back from the barn and were washing up for breakfast. The long table, covered with a bright oilcloth, was set out with dishes waiting for them, and the warm kitchen was full of the smell of coffee and hot biscuit and sausage. Five big handsome boys, running from twenty to twelve, all with what Burleigh called natural good manners—they hadn't a bit of the painful self-consciousness he himself had to struggle with when he was a lad. One ran to put his horse away, another helped him off with his fur coat and hung it up, and Josephine, the young-est child and only daughter, quickly set another place under her mother's direction.

With Mary, to feed creatures was the natural expression of affec-tion—her chickens, the calves, her big hungry boys. It was a rare pleasure to feed a young man whom she seldom saw and of whom she was as proud as if he belonged to her. Some country house-keepers would have stopped to spread a white cloth over the oil-cloth, to change the thick cups and plates for their best china, and the wooden-handled knives for plated ones. But not Mary.

"You must take us as you find us, Doctor Ed. I'd be glad to put out my good things for you if you was expected, but I'm glad to get you any way at all."

He knew she was glad—she threw back her head and spoke out as if she were announcing him to the whole prairie. Rosicky hadn't said anything at all; he merely smiled his twinkling smile, put some more coal on the fire, and went into his own room to pour the doctor a little drink in a medicine glass. When they were all seated, he watched his wife's face from his end of the table and spoke to her in Czech. Then, with the instinct of politeness which seldom failed him, he turned to the doctor and said slyly, "I was just tellin' her not to ask you no questions about Mrs. Marshall till you eat some breakfast. My wife, she's terrible fur to ask questions."

The boys laughed, and so did Mary. She watched the Doctor devour her biscuit and sausage, too much excited to eat anything herself. She drank her coffee and sat taking in everything about her visitor. She had known him when he was a poor country boy, and was boastfully proud of his success, always saying, "What do people go to Omaha for, to see a doctor, when we got the best one in the state right here?" If Mary liked people at all, she felt physical plea-sure in the sight of them, personal exultation in any good fortune that came to them. Burleigh didn't know many women like that, but he knew she was like that.

• Czech (CHEK) **language of Czechoslovakia**

When his hunger was satisfied, he did, of course, have to tell them about Mrs. Marshall, and he noticed what a friendly interest the boys took in the matter.

Rudolph, the oldest one (he was still living at home then), said, "The last time I was over there, she was lifting them big heavy milk cans, and I knew she oughtn't to be doing it."

"Yes, Rudolph told me about that when he come home, and I said it wasn't right," Mary put in warmly. "It was all right for me to do them things up to the last, for I was terrible strong, but that woman's weakly. And do you think she'll be able to nurse it, Ed?" She sometimes forgot to give him the title she was so proud of. "And to think of your being up all night and then not able to get a decent breakfast! I don't know what's the matter with such people."

"Why, Mother," said one of the boys, "if Doctor Ed had got breakfast there, we wouldn't have him here. So you ought to be glad."

"He knows I'm glad to have him, John, any time. But I'm sorry for that poor woman, how bad she'll feel the doctor had to go away in the cold without his breakfast."

"I wish I'd been in practice when these were getting born." The doctor looked down the row of close-clipped heads. "I missed some good breakfasts by not being."

The boys began to laugh at their mother because she flushed so red, but she stood her ground and threw up her head. "I don't care, you wouldn't have got away from this house without breakfast. No doctor ever did. I'd have had something ready fixed that Anton could warm up for you."

The boys laughed harder than ever, and exclaimed at her: "I'll bet you would!" "She would, that!"

"Father, did you get breakfast for the doctor when we were born?"

"Yes, and he used to bring me my breakfast, too, mighty nice. I was always awful hungry!" Mary admitted with a guilty laugh.

While the boys were getting the doctor's horse, he went to the window to examine the house plants. "What do you do to your geraniums to keep them blooming all winter, Mary? I never pass this house that from the road I don't see your windows full of flowers."

She snapped off a dark red one, and a ruffled new green leaf, and put them in his buttonhole. "There, that looks better. You look too solemn for a young man, Ed. Why don't you git married? I'm worried about you. Settin' at breakfast, I looked at you real hard, and I seen you've got some gray hairs already."

"Oh, yes! They're coming. Maybe they'd come faster if I married."

"Don't talk so. You'll ruin your health eating at the hotel. I could send your wife a nice loaf of nut bread, if you only had one. I don't like to see a young man getting gray. I'll tell you something, Ed; you make some strong black tea and keep it handy in a bowl, and every morning just brush it into your hair, an' it'll keep the gray from showin' much. That's the way I do!"

Sometimes the Doctor heard the gossipers in the drugstore wondering why Rosicky didn't get on faster. He was industrious, and so were his boys, but they were rather free and easy, weren't pushers, and they didn't always show good judgment. They were comfortable, they were out of debt, but they didn't get much ahead. Maybe, Doctor Burleigh reflected, people as generous and warmhearted and affectionate as the Rosickys never got ahead much; maybe you couldn't enjoy your life and put it into the bank, too.

II

When Rosicky left Doctor Burleigh's office he went into the farm-implement store to light his pipe and put on his glasses and read over the list Mary had given him. Then he went into the general-merchandise place next door and stood about until the pretty girl with the plucked eyebrows, who always waited on him, was free. Those eyebrows, two thin India-ink strokes, amused him, because he remembered how they used to be. Rosicky always prolonged his shopping by a little joking; the girl knew the old fellow admired her, and she liked to chaff with him.

"Seems to me about every other week you buy ticking, Mr. Rosicky, and always the best quality," she remarked as she measured off the heavy bolt with red stripes.

"You see, my wife is always makin' goose-fedder pillows, an' de thin stuff don't hold in dem little down fedders."

"You must have lots of pillows at your house."

"Sure. She makes quilts of dem, too. We sleeps easy. Now she's makin' a fedder quilt for my son's wife. You know Polly, that married my Rudolph. How much my bill, Miss Pearl?"

"Eight eighty-five."

"Chust make it nine, and put in some candy for de women."

"As usual. I never did see a man buy so much candy for his wife. First thing you know, she'll be getting too fat."

"I'd like dat. I ain't much fur all dem slim women like what de style is now."

"That's one for me, I suppose, Mr. Bohunk!" Pearl sniffed and elevated her India-ink strokes.

When Rosicky went out to his wagon, it was beginning to snow— the first snow of the season, and he was glad to see it. He rattled out

- chaff (CHAF) **light, good-natured talk; gentle teasing**
- ticking (TIK ing) **mattress cover cloth**
- bohunk (BOH hunk) **(slang) an immigrant from eastern Europe**

of town and along the highway through a wonderfully rich stretch of country, the finest farms in the country. He admired this High Prairie, as it was called, and always liked to drive through it. His own place lay in a rougher territory, where there was some clay in the soil and it was not so productive. When he bought his land, he hadn't the money to buy on High Prairie; so he told his boys, when they grumbled, that if their land hadn't some clay in it, they wouldn't own it at all. All the same, he enjoyed looking at these fine farms, as he enjoyed looking at a prize bull.

After he had gone eight miles, he came to the graveyard, which lay just at the edge of his own hay land. There he stopped his horses and sat still on his wagon seat, looking about at the snowfall. Over yonder on the hill he could see his own house, crouching low, with the clump of orchard behind and the windmill before, and all down the gentle hill slope the rows of pale gold cornstalks stood out against the white field. The snow was falling over the cornfield and the pasture and the hay land, steadily, with very little wind—a nice dry snow. The graveyard had only a light wire fence about it and was all overgrown with long red grass. The fine snow, settling into this red grass and upon the few little evergreens and the headstones, looked very pretty.

It was a nice graveyard, Rosicky reflected, sort of snug and homelike, not cramped or mournful—a big sweep all round it. A man could lie down in the long grass and see the complete arch of the sky over him, hear the wagons go by; in summer the mowing machine rattled right up to the wire fence. And it was so near home. Over there across the cornstalks his own roof and windmill looked so good to him that he promised himself to mind the doctor and take care of himself. He was awful fond of his place, he admitted. He wasn't anxious to leave it. And it was a comfort to think that he would never have to go farther than the edge of his own hayfield. The snow, falling over his barnyard and the graveyard, seemed to draw things together like. And they were all old neighbors in the graveyard, most of them friends; there was nothing to feel awkward or embarrassed about. Embarrassment was the most disagreeable feeling Rosicky knew. He didn't often have it—only with certain people whom he didn't understand at all.

Well, it was a nice snowstorm; a fine sight to see the snow falling so quietly and graciously over so much open country. On his cap and shoulders, on the horses' backs and manes, light, delicate, mysterious it fell; and with it a dry cool fragrance was released into the air. It meant rest for vegetation and men and beasts, for the ground itself; a season of long nights for sleep, leisurely breakfasts, peace by the fire. This and much more went through Rosicky's mind, but he merely told himself that winter was coming, clucked to his horses, and drove on.

When he reached home, John, the youngest boy, ran out to put away his team for him, and he met Mary coming up from the outside cellar with her apron full of carrots. They went into the house together. On the table, covered with oilcloth figured with clusters of blue grapes, a place was set, and he smelled hot coffeecake of some kind. Anton never lunched in town; he thought that extravagant, and anyhow he didn't like the food. So Mary always had something ready for him when he got home.

After he was settled in his chair, stirring his coffee in a big cup, Mary took out of the oven a pan of kolache stuffed with apricots, examined them anxiously to see whether they had got too dry, put them beside his plate, and then sat down opposite him.

Rosicky asked her in Czech if she wasn't going to have any coffee.

She replied in English, as being somehow the right language for transacting business, "Now what did Doctor Ed say, Anton? You tell me just what."

"He said I was to tell you some compliments, but I forgot 'em." Rosicky's eyes twinkled.

"About you, I mean. What did he say about your asthma?"

"He says I ain't got no asthma." Rosicky took one of the little rolls in his broad brown fingers. The thickened nail of his right thumb told the story of his past.

"Well, what is the matter? And don't try to put me off."

"He don't say nothing much, only I'm a little older, and my heart ain't so good like it used to be."

Mary started and brushed her hair back from her temples with both hands as if she were a little out of her mind. From the way she glared, she might have been in a rage with him.

"He says there's something the matter with your heart? Doctor Ed says so?"

"Now don't yell at me like I was a hog in the garden, Mary. You know I always did like to hear a woman talk soft. He didn't say anything de matter wid my heart, only it ain't so young like it used to be, an' he tell me not to pitch hay or run de corn sheller."

Mary wanted to jump up, but she sat still. She admired the way he never under any circumstances raised his voice or spoke roughly. He was city-bred, and she was country-bred; she often said she wanted her boys to have their papa's nice ways.

"You never have no pain there, do you? It's your breathing and your stomach that's been wrong. I wouldn't believe nobody but Doctor Ed about it. I guess I'll go see him myself. Didn't he give you no advice?"

- kolache (KOH lawch) **a filled bun**
- transacting (trans AK ting) **attending to**

"Chust to take it easy like, an' stay round de house dis winter. I guess you got some carpenter work for me to do. I kin make some new shelves for you, and I want dis long time to build a closet in de boys' room and make dem two little fellers keep dere clo'es hung up."

Rosicky drank his coffee from time to time, while he considered. His mustache was of the soft long variety and came down over his mouth like the teeth of a buggy rake over a bundle of hay. Each time he put down his cup, he ran his blue handkerchief over his lips. When he took a drink of water, he managed very neatly with the back of his hand.

Mary sat watching him intently, trying to find any change in his face. It is hard to see anyone who has become like your own body to you. Yes, his hair had got thin, and his high forehead had deep lines running from left to right. But his neck, always clean shaved except in the busiest seasons, was not loose or baggy. It was burned a dark reddish-brown, and there were deep creases in it, but it looked firm and full of blood. His cheeks had a good color. On either side of his mouth there was a halfmoon down the length of his cheek, not wrinkles, but two lines that had come there from his habitual expression. He was shorter and broader than when she married him; his back had grown broad and curved, a good deal like the shell of an old turtle, and his arms and legs were short.

He was fifteen years older than Mary, but she had hardly ever thought about it before. He was her man, and the kind of man she liked. She was rough, and he was gentle—city-bred, as she always said. They had been shipmates on a rough voyage, and had stood by each other in trying times. Life had gone well with them because, at bottom, they had the same ideas about life. They agreed, without discussion, as to what was most important and what was secondary. They didn't often exchange opinions, even in Czech—it was as if they had thought the same thought together. A good deal had to be sacrificed and thrown overboard in a hard life like theirs, and they had never disagreed as to the things that could go. It had been a hard life, and a soft life, too. There wasn't anything brutal in the short, broad-backed man with the three-cornered eyes and the forehead that went on to the top of his skull. He was a city man, a gentle man, and though he had married a rough farm girl, he had never touched her without gentleness.

They had been at one accord not to hurry through life, not to be always skimping and saving. They saw their neighbors buy more

---

- buggy rake (BUG ee RAYK) **long horse-drawn rake**
- **intently** (in TENT lee) **with close attention**
- **habitual** (huh BICH uh wul) **regular**

land and feed more stock than they did, without discontent. Once when the creamery agent came to the Rosickys to persuade them to sell him their cream, he told them how much money the Fasslers, their nearest neighbors, had made on their cream last year.

"Yes," said Mary, "and look at them Fassler children! Pale, pinched little things, they look like skimmed milk. I'd rather put some color into my children's faces than put money into the bank."

The agent shrugged and turned to Anton.

"I guess we'll do like she says," said Rosicky.

CHECKPOINT

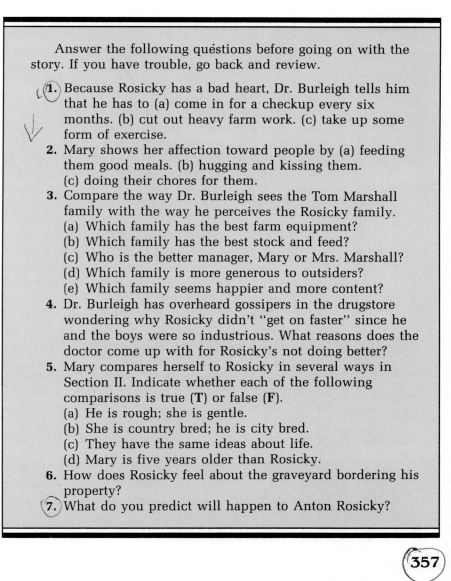

Answer the following questions before going on with the story. If you have trouble, go back and review.

1. Because Rosicky has a bad heart, Dr. Burleigh tells him that he has to (a) come in for a checkup every six months. (b) cut out heavy farm work. (c) take up some form of exercise.

2. Mary shows her affection toward people by (a) feeding them good meals. (b) hugging and kissing them. (c) doing their chores for them.

3. Compare the way Dr. Burleigh sees the Tom Marshall family with the way he perceives the Rosicky family.
   (a) Which family has the best farm equipment?
   (b) Which family has the best stock and feed?
   (c) Who is the better manager, Mary or Mrs. Marshall?
   (d) Which family is more generous to outsiders?
   (e) Which family seems happier and more content?

4. Dr. Burleigh has overheard gossipers in the drugstore wondering why Rosicky didn't "get on faster" since he and the boys were so industrious. What reasons does the doctor come up with for Rosicky's not doing better?

5. Mary compares herself to Rosicky in several ways in Section II. Indicate whether each of the following comparisons is true (**T**) or false (**F**).
   (a) He is rough; she is gentle.
   (b) She is country bred; he is city bred.
   (c) They have the same ideas about life.
   (d) Mary is five years older than Rosicky.

6. How does Rosicky feel about the graveyard bordering his property?

7. What do you predict will happen to Anton Rosicky?

III

Mary very soon got into town to see Doctor Ed, and then she had a talk with her boys and set a guard over Rosicky. Even John, the youngest, had his father on his mind. If Rosicky went to throw hay down from the loft, one of the boys ran up the ladder and took the fork from him. He sometimes complained that though he was getting to be an old man, he wasn't an old woman yet.

That winter he stayed in the house in the afternoons and carpentered, or sat in the chair between the window full of plants and the wooden bench where the two pails of drinking water stood. This spot was called "Father's corner," though it was not a corner at all. He had a shelf there, where he kept his Bohemian papers and his pipes and tobacco, and his shears and needles and thread and tailor's thimble. Having been a tailor in his youth, he couldn't bear to see a woman patching at his clothes, or at the boys'. He liked tailoring, and always patched all the overalls and jackets and work shirts. Occasionally he made over a pair of pants one of the older boys had outgrown, for the little fellow.

While he sewed, he let his mind run back over his life. He had a good deal to remember, really; life in three countries. The only part of his youth he didn't like to remember was the two years he had spent in London, in Cheapside, working for a German tailor who was wretchedly poor. Those days, when he was nearly always hungry, when his clothes were dropping off him for dirt, and the sound of a strange language kept him in continual bewilderment, had left a sore spot in his mind that wouldn't bear touching.

He was twenty when he landed at Castle Garden in New York, and he had a protector who got him work in a tailor shop in Vesey Street, down near the Washington Market. He looked upon that part of his life as very happy. He became a good workman, he was industrious, and his wages were increased from time to time. He minded his own business and envied nobody's good fortune. He went to night school and learned to read English. He often did overtime work and was well paid for it, but somehow he never saved anything. He couldn't refuse a loan to a friend, and he was self-indulgent. He liked a good dinner, and a little went for beer, a little for tobacco; a good deal went to the girls. He often stood through an opera on Saturday nights; he could get standing room for a dollar. Those were the great days of opera in New York, and it gave a fellow something to think about for the rest of the week. Rosicky had a quick ear, and a childish love of all the stage splendor; the scenery, the costumes, the ballet. He usually went with a chum, and after the performance they had beer and maybe some oysters somewhere. It was a fine life;

- self-indulgent (SELF in DUL junt) **inclined to obey one's desires and passions**

358

for the first five years or so it satisfied him completely. He was never hungry or cold or dirty, and everything amused him: a fire, a dog-fight, a parade, a storm, a ferry ride. He thought New York the finest, richest, friendliest city in the world.

Moreover, he had what he called a happy home life. Very near the tailor shop was a small furniture factory, where an old Austrian, Loeffler, employed a few skilled men and made unusual furniture, most of it to order, for the rich German housewives uptown. The top floor of Loeffler's five-story factory was a loft, where he kept his choice lumber and stored the odd pieces of furniture left on his hands. One of the young workmen he employed was a Czech, and he and Rosicky became fast friends. They persuaded Loeffler to let them have a sleeping room in one corner of the loft. They bought good beds and bedding and had their pick of the furniture kept up there. The loft was low-pitched, but light and airy, full of windows, and good-smelling by reason of the fine lumber put up there to season. Old Loeffler used to go down to the docks and buy wood from South America and the East from the sea captains. The young men were as foolish about their house as a bridal pair. Zichec, the young cabinetmaker, devised every sort of convenience, and Rosicky kept their clothes in order. At night and on Sundays, when the quiver of machinery underneath was still, it was the quietest place in the world, and on summer nights all the sea winds blew in. Zichec often practiced on his flute in the evening. They were both fond of music and went to the opera together. Rosicky thought he wanted to live like that forever.

But as the years passed, all alike, he began to get a little restless. When spring came round, he would begin to feel fretted, and he got to drinking. He was likely to drink too much of a Saturday night. On Sunday he was languid and heavy, getting over his spree. On Monday he plunged into work again. So he never had time to figure out what ailed him, though he knew something did. When the grass turned green in Park Place, and the lilac hedge at the back of Trinity churchyard put out its blossoms, he was tormented by a longing to run away. That was why he drank too much; to get a temporary illusion of freedom and wide horizons.

Rosicky, the old Rosicky, could remember as if it were yesterday the day when the young Rosicky found out what was the matter with him. It was on a Fourth of July afternoon, and he was sitting in Park Place in the sun. The lower part of New York was empty. Wall Street, Liberty Street, Broadway, all empty. So much stone and asphalt with nothing going on, so many empty windows. The emptiness was intense, like the stillness in a great factory when the machinery stops and the belts and bands cease running. It was too great a change, it took all the strength out of one. Those blank buildings, without the

---

• languid (LAN gwid) **without energy**

stream of life pouring through them, were like empty jails. It struck young Rosicky that this was the trouble with big cities; they built you in from the earth itself, cemented you away from any contact with the ground. You lived in an unnatural world, like the fish in an aquarium, who were probably much more comfortable than they ever were in the sea.

On that very day be began to think seriously about the articles he had read in the Bohemian papers, describing prosperous Czech farming communities in the West. He believed he would like to go out there as a farm hand; it was hardly possible that he could ever have land of his own. His people had always been workmen; his father and grandfather had worked in shops. His mother's parents had lived in the country, but they rented their farm and had a hard time to get along. Nobody in his family had ever owned any land— that belonged to a different station of life altogether. Anton's mother died when he was little, and he was sent into the country to her parents. He stayed with them until he was twelve, and formed those ties with the earth and the farm animals and growing things which are never made at all unless they are made early. After his grandfather died, he went back to live with his father and stepmother, but she was very hard on him, and his father helped him to get passage to London.

After that Fourth of July day in Park Place, the desire to return to the country never left him. To work on another man's farm would be all he asked; to see the sun rise and set and to plant things and watch them grow. He was a very simple man. He was like a tree that has not many roots, but one taproot that goes down deep. He subscribed for a Bohemian paper printed in Chicago, then for one printed in Omaha. His mind got farther and farther west. He began to save a little money to buy his liberty. When he was thirty-five, there was a great meeting in New York of Bohemian athletic societies, and Rosicky left the tailor shop and went home with the Omaha delegates to try his fortune in another part of the world.

IV

Perhaps the fact that his own youth was well over before he began to have a family was one reason why Rosicky was so fond of his boys. He had almost a grandfather's indulgence for them. He had never had to worry about any of them—except, just now, a little about Rudolph.

On Saturday night the boys always piled into the Ford, took little Josephine, and went to town to the moving-picture show. One Saturday morning they were talking at the breakfast table about starting early that evening, so that they would have an hour or so to see the

---

- **taproot** (TAP root) **main root**
- indulgence (in DUL juns) **tolerance**

Christmas things in the stores before the show began. Rosicky looked down the table.

"I hope you boys ain't disappointed, but I want you to let me have de car tonight. Maybe some of you can go in with de neighbors."

Their faces fell. They worked hard all week, and they were still like children. A new jackknife or a box of candy pleased the older ones as much as the little fellow.

"If you and Mother are going to town," Frank said, "maybe you could take a couple of us along with you, anyway."

"No, I want to take de car down to Rudolph's, and let him an' Polly go in to de show. She don't git into town enough, an' I'm afraid she's gettin' lonesome, an' he can't afford no car yet."

That settled it. The boys were a good deal dashed. Their father took another piece of apple cake and went on: "Maybe next Saturday night de two little fellers can go along wid dem."

"Oh, is Rudolph going to have the car every Saturday night?"

Rosicky did not reply at once; then he began to speak seriously: "Listen, boys; Polly ain't lookin' so good. I don't like to see nobody lookin' sad. It comes hard fur a town girl to be a farmer's wife. I don't want no trouble to start in Rudolph's family. When it starts, it ain't so easy to stop. An American girl don't git used to our ways all at once. I like to tell Polly she and Rudolph can have the car every Saturday night till after New Year's, if it's all right with you boys."

"Sure it's all right, Papa," Mary cut in.

"And it's good you thought about that. Town girls is used to more than country girls. I lay awake nights, scared she'll make Rudolph discontented with the farm."

The boys put as good a face on it as they could. They surely looked forward to their Saturday nights in town. That evening Rosicky drove the car the half mile down to Rudolph's new, bare little house.

Polly was in a short sleeved gingham dress, clearing away the supper dishes. She was a trim, slim little thing, with blue eyes and shingled yellow hair, and her eyebrows were reduced to a mere brush stroke like Miss Pearl's.

"Good evening, Mr. Rosicky. Rudolph's at the barn, I guess." She never called him father, or Mary mother. She was sensitive about having married a foreigner. She never in the world would have done it if Rudolph hadn't been such a handsome, persuasive fellow and such a gallant lover. He had graduated in her class in the high school in town, and their friendship began in the ninth grade.

Rosicky went in, though he wasn't exactly asked. "My boys ain't goin' to town tonight, an' I brought de car over fur you two to go in to de picture show."

● dashed (DASHT) **depressed; saddened**

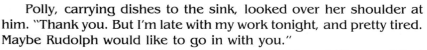

Polly, carrying dishes to the sink, looked over her shoulder at him. "Thank you. But I'm late with my work tonight, and pretty tired. Maybe Rudolph would like to go in with you."

"Oh, I don't go to de shows! I'm too old-fashioned. You won't feel so tired after you ride in de air a ways. It's a nice clear night, an' it ain't cold. You go an' fix yourself up, Polly, an' I'll wash de dishes an' leave everything nice fur you."

Polly blushed and tossed her bob. "I couldn't let you do that, Mr. Rosicky. I wouldn't think of it."

Rosicky said nothing. He found a bib apron on a nail behind the kitchen door. He slipped it over his head and then took Polly by her two elbows and pushed her gently toward the door of her own room. "I washed up de kitchen many times for my wife, when de babies was sick or somethin'. You go an' make yourself look nice. I like you to look prettier'n any of dem town girls when you go in. De young folks must have some fun, an' I'm goin' to look out fur you, Polly."

That kind, reassuring grip on her elbows, the old man's funny bright eyes, made Polly want to drop her head on his shoulder for a second. She restrained herself, but she lingered in his grasp at the door of her room, murmuring tearfully: "You always lived in the city when you were young, didn't you? Don't you ever get lonesome out here?"

As she turned round to him, her hand fell naturally into his, and he stood holding it and smiling into her face with his peculiar, knowing, indulgent smile without a shadow of reproach in it. "Dem big cities is all right fur de rich but dey is terrible hard fur de poor."

"I don't know. Sometimes I think I'd like to take a chance. You lived in New York, didn't you?"

"An' London, Da's bigger still. I learned my trade dere. Here's Rudolph comin', you better hurry."

"Will you tell me about London some time?"

"Maybe. Only I ain't no talker, Polly. Run an' dress yourself up."

The bedroom door closed behind her, and Rudolph came in from the outside, looking anxious. He had seen the car and was sorry any of his family should come just then. Supper hadn't been a very pleasant occasion. Halting in the doorway, he saw his father in a kitchen apron, carrying dishes to the sink. He flushed crimson and something flashed in his eye. Rosicky held up a warning finger.

"I brought de car over fur you an' Polly to go to de picture show, an' I made her let me finish here so you won't be late. You go put on a clean shirt, quick!"

"But don't the boys want the car, Father?"

- **restrain** (ri STRAYN) hold back
- indulgent (in DUL junt) **tolerant**
- reproach (ri PROHCH) blame

"No, tonight dey don't." Rosicky fumbled under his apron and found his pants pocket. He took out a silver dollar and said in a hurried whisper: "You go an' buy dat girl some ice cream an' candy tonight, like you was courtin'. She's awful good friends wid me."

Rudolph was very short of cash, but he took the money as if it hurt him. There had been a crop failure all over the county. He had more than once been sorry he'd married this year.

In a few minutes the young people came out, looking clean and a little stiff. Rosicky hurried them off, and then he took his own time with the dishes. He scoured the pots and pans and put away the milk and swept the kitchen. He put some coal in the stove and shut off the draughts, so the place would be warm for them when they got home late at night. Then he sat down and had a pipe and listened to the clock tick.

Generally speaking, marrying an American girl was certainly a risk. A Czech should marry a Czech. It was lucky that Polly was the daughter of a poor widow woman; Rudolph was proud, and if she had a prosperous family to throw up at him, they could never make it go. Polly was one of four sisters, and they all worked; one was bookkeeper in the bank, one taught music, and Polly and her younger sister had been clerks, like Miss Pearl. All four of them were musical, had pretty voices, and sang in the Methodist choir, which the eldest sister directed.

Polly missed the sociability of a store position. She missed the choir, and the company of her sisters. She didn't dislike housework, but she disliked so much of it. Rosicky was a little anxious about this pair. He was afraid Polly would grow so discontented that Rudy would quit the farm and take a factory job in Omaha. He had worked for a winter up there, two years ago, to get money to marry on. He had done very well, and they would always take him back at the stockyards. But to Rosicky that meant the end of everything for his son. To be a landless man was to be a wage earner, a slave all your life; to have nothing; to be nothing.

Rosicky thought he would come over and do a little carpentering for Polly after the New Year. He guessed she needed jollying. Rudolph was a serious sort of chap, serious in love and serious about his work.

Rosicky shook out his pipe and walked home across the fields. Ahead of him the lamplight shone from his kitchen windows. Suppose he were still in a tailor shop on Vesey Street, with a bunch of pale, narrow-chested sons working on machines, all coming home tired and sullen to eat supper in a kitchen that was a parlor also; with another crowded, angry family quarreling just across the dumb-waiter shaft, and squeaking pulleys at the windows where dirty

---

• dumbwaiter (DUM WAYT ur) **small service elevator**

washings hung on dirty lines above a court full of old brooms and mops and ash cans . . .

He stopped by the windmill to look up at the frosty winter stars and drew a long breath before he went inside. That kitchen with the shining windows was dear to him; but the sleeping fields and bright stars and the noble darkness were dearer still.

CHECKPOINT

Answer the following questions before going on with the story. If you have trouble, go back and review.

1. List three or more things that gave Rosicky pleasure in New York.
2. Which of the following show why Rosicky loved his loft-home in New York City?
   (a) It smelled of fine lumber put up there to season.
   (b) It had a panoramic view of the city.
   (c) It was light and airy, and full of windows.
   (d) It had wall-to-wall carpeting and an all-electric kitchen.
   (e) His roommate played the flute.
   (f) It was only two blocks from Mary's home.
3. What does Rosicky hope to experience in his life as a farmer?
4. Put the following events from this section of the story in chronological order. That is, which event actually took place first, which second, and so on?
   (a) Rosicky moves to Nebraska to try his fortune.
   (b) Rosicky spends two years in London working for a German tailor.
   (c) Rosicky marries Mary.
   (d) Rosicky lives with his grandparents.
   (e) Rosicky lives in a loft above a small furniture factory in New York.
5. Rosicky is obviously concerned about Polly and Rudolph's marriage—he even lends them the family car every Saturday night so they can go to town. What do you think will happen in Rudolph and Polly's marriage? Will Polly be content to stay on the farm with her husband?
6. What do you think will happen to Rosicky?

V

On the day before Christmas the weather set in very cold; no snow, but a bitter, biting wind that whistled and sang over the flat land and lashed one's face like fine wires. There was baking going on in the Rosicky kitchen all day, and Rosicky sat inside, making over a coat that Albert had outgrown into an overcoat for John. Mary had a big red geranium in bloom for Christmas, and a row of Jerusalem cherry trees, full of berries. It was the first year she had ever grown these; Doctor Ed brought her the seeds from Omaha when he went to some medical convention. They reminded Rosicky of plants he had seen in England; and all afternoon, as he stitched, he sat thinking about those two years in London, which his mind usually shrank from even after all this while.

He was a lad of eighteen when he dropped down into London, with no money and no connections except the address of a cousin who was supposed to be working at a confectioner's. When he went to the pastry shop, however, he found that the cousin had gone to America. Anton tramped the streets for several days, sleeping in doorways and on the Embankment, until he was in utter despair. He knew no English, and the sound of the strange language all about him confused him. By chance he met a poor German tailor who had learned his trade in Vienna, and could speak a little Czech. This tailor, Lifschnitz, kept a repair shop in a Cheapside basement, underneath a cobbler. He didn't much need an apprentice, but he was sorry for the boy and took him in for no wages but his keep and what he could pick up. The pickings were supposed to be coppers given you when you took work home to a customer. But most of the customers called for their clothes themselves, and the coppers that came Anton's way were very few. He had, however, a place to sleep. The tailor's family lived upstairs in three rooms; a kitchen, a bedroom, where Lifshnitz and his wife and five children slept, and a living room. Two corners of this living room were curtained off for lodgers; in one Rosicky slept on an old horsehair sofa, with a feather quilt to wrap himself in. The other corner was rented to a wretched, dirty boy, who was studying the violin. He actually practiced there. Rosicky was dirty, too. There was no way to be anything else. Mrs. Lifshnitz got the water she cooked and washed with from a pump in a brick court, four flights down. There were bugs in the place, and multitudes of fleas, though the poor woman did the best she could. Rosicky knew she often went empty to give another potato or a spoonful of dripping to the two hungry, sad-eyed boys who lodged with her. He used to think he would never get out of there, never get

---

- Embankment (im BANK ment) **bank of Thames River, London**
- dripping (DRIP ing) **fatty juice**

a clean shirt to his back again. What would he do, he wondered, when his clothes actually dropped to pieces and the worn cloth wouldn't hold patches any longer?

It was still early when the old farmer put aside his sewing and his recollections. The sky had been a dark gray all day, with not a gleam of sun, and the light failed at four o'clock. He went to shave and change his shirt while the turkey was roasting. Rudolph and Polly were coming over for supper.

After supper they sat round in the kitchen, and the younger boys were saying how sorry they were it hadn't snowed. Everybody was sorry. They wanted a deep snow that would lie long and keep the wheat warm, and leave the ground soaked when it melted.

"Yes, sir!" Rudolph broke out fiercely; "If we have another dry year like last year, there's going to be hard times in this country."

Rosicky filled his pipe. "You boys don't know what hard times is. You don't owe nobody, you got plenty to eat an' keep warm, an' plenty water to keep clean. When you got them, you can't have it very hard."

Rudolph frowned, opened and shut his big right hand, and dropped it clenched upon his knee. "I've got to have a good deal more than that, Father, or I'll quit this farming gamble. I can always make good wages railroading, or at the packing house, and be sure of my money."

"Maybe so," his father answered dryly.

Mary, who had just come in from the pantry and was wiping her hands on the roller towel, thought Rudy and his father were getting too serious. She brought her darning basket and sat down in the middle of the group.

"I ain't much afraid of hard times, Rudy," she said heartily. "We've had a plenty, but we've always come through. Your father wouldn't never take nothing very hard, not even hard times. I got a mind to tell you a story on him. Maybe you boys can't hardly remember the year we had that terrible hot wind, that burned everything up on the Fourth of July? All the corn an' the gardens. An' that was in the days when we didn't have alfalfa yet—I guess it wasn't invented.

"Well, that very day your father was out cultivatin' corn, and I was here in the kitchen makin' plum preserves. We had bushels of plums that year. I noticed it was terrible hot, but it's always hot in the kitchen when you're preservin', an' I was too busy with my plums to mind. Anton come in from the field about three o'clock, an' I asked him what was the matter.

"'Nothin',' he says, 'but it's pretty hot, an' I think I won't work no more today.' He stood round for a few minutes, an' then he says: 'Ain't you near through? I want you should git up a nice supper for us tonight. It's Fourth of July.'

"I told him to git along, that I was right in the middle of pre-servin', but the plums would taste good on hot biscuit. 'I'm goin' to have fried chicken, too,' he says, and he went off an' killed a couple. You three oldest boys was little fellers, playin' around outside, real hot an' sweaty, an' your father took you to the horse tank down by the windmill an' took off your clothes an' put you in. Them two box elder trees was little then, but they made shade over the tank. Then he took off all his own clothes, an' got in with you. While he was playin' in the water with you, the Methodist preacher drove into our place to say how all the neighbors was goin' to meet at the school-house that night, to pray for rain. He drove right to the windmill, of course, and there was your father and you three with no clothes on. I was in the kitchen door, an' I had to laugh, for the preacher acted like he ain't never seen a naked man before. He surely was embar-rassed, an' your father couldn't git to his clothes; they was all hangin' up on the windmill to let the sweat dry out of 'em. So he laid in the tank where he was, an' put one of you boys on top of him to cover him up a little, an' talked to the preacher.

"When you got through playin' in the water, he put clean clothes on you and a clean shirt on himself, an' by that time I'd begun to get supper. He says: 'It's too hot in here to eat comfortable. Let's have a picnic in the orchard. We'll eat our supper behind the mulberry hedge, under them linden trees.'

"So he carried our supper down, an' a bottle of my wild grape wine, an' everything tasted good, I can tell you. The wind got cooler as the sun was goin' down, and it turned out pleasant, only I noticed how the leaves was curled up on the linden trees. That made me think, an' I asked your father if that hot wind all day hadn't been terrible hard on the gardens an' the corn.

"'Corn,' he says, 'there ain't no corn.'

"'What you talkin' about?' I said. 'Ain't we got forty acres?'

"'We ain't got an ear,' he says, 'nor nobody else ain't got none. All the corn in this country was cooked by three o'clock today, like you'd roasted it in an oven.'

"'You mean you won't get no crop at all?' I asked him. I couldn't believe it, after he'd worked so hard.

"'No crop this year," he says. 'That's why we're havin' a picnic. We might as well enjoy what we got.'

"An' that's how your father behaved, when all the neighbors was so discouraged they couldn't look you in the face. An' we enjoyed ourselves that year, poor as we was, an' our neighbors wasn't a bit better off for bein' miserable. Some of 'em grieved till they got poor digestions and couldn't relish what they did have."

The younger boys said they thought their father had the best of it. But Rudolph was thinking that, all the same, the neighbors had managed to get ahead more, in the fifteen years since that time. There must be something wrong about his father's way of doing things. He wished he knew what was going on in the back of Polly's mind. He knew she liked his father, but he knew, too, that she was afraid of something. When his mother sent over coffee-cake or prune tarts or a loaf of fresh bread, Polly seemed to regard them with a certain suspicion. When she observed to him that his brothers had nice manners, her tone implied that it was remarkable they should have. With his mother she was stiff and on her guard. Mary's hearty frankness and gusts of good humor irritated her. Polly was afraid of being unusual or conspicuous in any way, of being "ordinary," as she said!

When Mary had finished her story, Rosicky laid aside his pipe.

"You boys like me to tell you about some of dem hard times I been through in London?" Warmly encouraged, he sat rubbing his forehead along the deep creases. It was bothersome to tell a long story in English (he nearly always talked to the boys in Czech), but he wanted Polly to hear this one.

"Well, you know about dat tailor shop I worked in in London? I had one Christmas dere I ain't never forgot. Times was awful bad before Christmas; de boss ain't got much work, an' have it awful hard to pay his rent. It ain't so much fun, bein' poor in a big city like London, I'll say! All de windows is full of good t'ings to eat an' all de pushcarts in de streets is full, an' you smell 'em all de time, an' you ain't got no money—not a darn bit. I didn't mind de cold so much, though I didn't have no overcoat, chust a short jacket I'd outgrowed so it wouldn't meet on me, an' my hands was chapped raw. But I always had a good appetite, like you all know, an' de sight of dem pork pies in the windows was awful fur me!

"Day before Christmas was terrible foggy dat year, an' dat fog gits into your bones and makes you all damp like. Mrs. Lifschnitz didn't give us nothin' but a little bread an' drippin' for supper, because she was savin' to try for to give us a good dinner on Christmas Day. After supper de boss say I can go an' enjoy myself, so I went into de streets to listen to de Christmas singers. Dey sing old songs an' make very nice music, an' I run round after dem a good ways, till I got awful hungry. I t'ink maybe if I go home, I can sleep till morning an' forgit my belly.

"I went into my corner real quiet, and roll up in my fedder quilt. But I ain't got my head down till I smell somet'ing good. Seem like it git stronger an' stronger, an' I can't git to sleep noway. I can't understand dat smell. Dere was a gas light in a hall across de court, dat always shine in at my window a little. I got up and look around. I got a little wooden box in my corner fur a stool, 'cause I ain't got no chair. I picks up dat box, and under it dere is a roast goose on a platter! I can't believe my eyes. I carry it to de window where de light comes in, an' touch it and smell it to find out, an' den I taste it to be sure. I say, I will eat chust one little bite of dat goose, so I can go to sleep, and tomorrow I won't eat none at all. But I tell you, boys, when I stop, one half of dat goose was gone!"

The narrator bowed his head, and the boys shouted. But little Josephine slipped behind his chair and kissed him on the neck beneath his ear.

"Poor little Papa, I don't want him to be hungry!"

"Da's long ago, child. I ain't never been hungry since I had your mudder to cook fur me."

"Go on and tell us the rest, please," said Polly.

"Well, when I come to realize what I done, of course, I felt terrible. I felt better in de stomach, but very bad in de heart. I set on my bed wid dat platter on my knees, an' it all come to me; how hard dat poor woman save to buy dat goose, and how she get some neighbor to cook it dat got more fire, an' how she put it in my corner to keep it away from dem hungry children. Dey was a old carpet hung up to shut my corner off, an' de children wasn't allowed to go in dere. An' I know she put it in my corner because she trust me more'n she did de

violin boy. I can't stand it to face her after I spoil de Christmas. So I put on my shoes and go out into de city. I tell myself I better throw myself in de river; but I guess I ain't dat kind of a boy.

"It was after twelve o'clock, an' terrible cold, an' I start out to walk about London all night. I walked along de river while, but dey was lots of drunks all along; men, and women too. I chust move along to keep away from de police. I git onto de Strand, an' den over to New Oxford Street, where dere was a big German restaurant on de ground floor, wid big windows all fixed up fine, an' I could see de people havin' parties inside. While I was lookin' in, two men and two ladies come out, laughin' an' talkin' and feelin' happy about all dey been eatin' an' drinkin', and dey was speakin' Czech—not like de Austrians, but like de homefolks talk it.

"I guess I went crazy, an' I done what I ain't never done before nor since. I went right up to dem gay people an' begun to beg dem: 'Fellow countrymen, for God's sake give me money enough to buy a goose!'

"Dye laugh, of course, but de ladies speak awful kind to me, an' dey take me back into de restaurant and give me hot coffee and cakes, an' make me tell all about how I happened to come to London, an' what I was doin' dere. Dey take my name and where I work down on paper, an' both of dem ladies give me ten shillings.

"De big market at Covent Garden ain't very far away, an' by dat time it was open. I go dere an' buy a big goose an' some pork pies, an' potatoes and onions, an' cakes an' oranges fur de children—all I could carry! When I git home, everybody is still asleep. I pile all I bought on de kitchen table, an' go in an' lay down on my bed, an' I ain't waken up till I hear dat woman scream when she come out into her kitchen. My goodness, but she was surprise! She laugh an' cry at de same time, an' hug me and waken all de children. She ain't stop fur no breakfast; she git de Christmas dinner ready dat mornin', and we all sit down an' eat all we can hold. I ain't never seen dat violin boy have all he can hold before.

"Two three days after dat, de two men come to hunt me up, an' dey ask my boss, and he give me a good report an' tell dem I was a steady boy all right. One of dem Bohemians was very smart an' run a Bohemian newspaper in New York, an' de odder was a rich man, in de importing business, an' dey been traveling togedder. Dey told me how t'ings was easier in New York, an' offered to pay my passage when dey was goin' home soon on a boat. My boss say to me: 'You go. You ain't got no chance here, an' I like to see you git ahead, fur you always been a good boy to my woman, and fur dat fine Christmas dinner you give us all.' An' da's how I got to New York."

That night when Rudolph and Polly, arm in arm, were running home across the fields with the bitter wind at their backs, his heart leaped for joy when she said she thought they might have his family come over for supper on New Year's Eve. "Let's get up a nice supper, and not let your mother help at all; make her be company for once."

"That would be lovely of you, Polly," he said humbly. He was a very simple, modest boy, and he, too, felt vaguely that Polly and her sisters were more experienced and worldly than his people.

VI

The winter turned out badly for farmers. It was bitterly cold, and after the first light snows before Christmas there was no snow at all—and no rain. March was as bitter as February. On those days when the wind fairly punished the country, Rosicky sat by his window. In the fall he and the boys had put in a big wheat planting, and now the seed had frozen in the ground. All that land would have to be plowed up and planted over again, planted in corn. It had happened before, but he was younger then, and he never worried about what had to be. He was sure of himself and of Mary; he knew they could bear what they had to bear, that they would always pull through. But he was not so sure of the young ones, and he felt troubled because Rudolph and Polly were having such a hard start.

Sitting beside his flowering window while the panes rattled and the wind blew in under the door, Rosicky gave himself to reflection as he had not done since those Sundays in the loft of the furniture factory in New York, long ago. Then he was trying to find what he wanted in life for himself; now he was trying to find what he wanted for his boys, and why it was he so hungered to feel sure they would be here, working this very land, after he was gone.

They would have to work hard on the farm, and probably they would never do much more than make a living. But if he could think of them as staying here on the land, he wouldn't have to fear any great unkindness for them. Hardships, certainly; it was a hardship to have the wheat freeze in the ground when seed was so high; and to have to sell your stock because you had no feed. But there would be other years when everything came along right, and you caught up. And what you had was your own. You didn't have to choose between bosses and strikers, and go wrong either way. You didn't have to do with dishonest and cruel people. They were the only things in his experience he had found terrifying and horrible; the look in the eyes of a dishonest and crafty man, of a scheming and rapacious woman.

In the country, if you had a mean neighbor, you could keep off his land and make him keep off yours. But in the city, all the foulness and misery and brutality of your neighbors was part of your life. The worst things he had come upon in his journey through the world

---

- **reflection** (ri FLEK shun) **serious thought**
- rapacious (ruh PAY shus) **greedy**

were human—depraved and poisonous specimens of man. To this day he could recall certain terrible faces in the London streets. There were mean people everywhere, to be sure, even in their own country town here. But they weren't tempered, hardened, sharpened, like the treacherous people in cities who live by grinding or cheating or poisoning their fellow men. He had helped to bury two of his fellow workmen in the tailoring trade, and he was distrustful of the organized industries that see one out of the world in big cities. Here, if you were sick, you had Doctor Ed to look after you; and if you died, fat Mr. Haycock, the kindest man in the world, buried you.

It seemed to Rosicky that for good, honest boys like his, the worst they could do on the farm was better than the best they would be likely to do in the city. If he'd had a mean boy, now, one who was crooked and sharp and tried to put anything over on his brothers, then town would be the place for him. But he had so such boy. As for Rudolph, the discontented one, he would give the shirt off his back to anyone who touched his heart. What Rosicky really hoped for his boys was that they could get through the world without ever knowing much about the cruelty of human beings. "Their mother and me ain't prepared them for that," he sometimes said to himself.

These thoughts brought him back to a grateful consideration of his own case. What an escape he had had, to be sure! He, too, in his time, had had to take money for repair work from the hand of a hungry child who let it go so wistfully; because it was money due his boss. And now, in all these years, he had never had to take a cent from anyone in bitter need—never had to look at the face of the woman become like a wolf's from struggle and famine. When he thought of these things, Rosicky would put on his cap and jacket and slip down to the barn and give his work horses a little extra oats, letting them eat it out of his hand in their slobbery fashion. It was his way of expressing what he felt, and made him chuckle with pleasure.

The spring came warm, with blue skies—but dry, dry as a bone. The boys began plowing up the wheat fields to plant them over in corn. Rosicky would stand at the fence corner and watch them, and the earth was so dry it blew up on clouds of brown dust that hid the horses and the sulky plow and the driver. It was a bad outlook.

The big alfalfa field that lay between the home place and Rudolph's came up green, but Rosicky was worried because during that open windy winter a great many Russian thistle plants had blown in there and lodged. He kept asking the boys to rake them out; he was afraid their seed would root and "take the alfalfa." Rudolph said that was nonsense. The boys were working so hard planting corn, their

---

- depraved (di PRAYVD) **evil**
- tempered (TEM purd) **hardened (as metal)**
- **wistfully** (WIST ful ee) **longingly**

father felt he couldn't insist about the thistles, but he set great store by that big alfalfa field. It was a feed you could depend on—and there was some deeper reason, vague, but strong. The peculiar green of the clover woke early memories in old Rosicky, went back to something in his childhood in the old world. When he was a little boy, he had played in fields of that strong blue-green color.

One morning, when Rudolph had gone to town in the car, leaving a work team idle in his barn, Rosicky went over to his son's place, put the horses to the buggy rake, and set about quietly raking up those thistles. He behaved with guilty caution, and rather enjoyed stealing a march on Doctor Ed, who was just then taking his first vacation in seven years of practice and was attending a clinic in Chicago. Rosicky got the thistles raked up, but did not stop to burn them. That would take some time, and his breath was pretty short, so he thought he had better get the horses back to the barn.

He got them into the barn and to their stalls, but the pain had come on so sharp in his chest that he didn't try to take the harness off. He started for the house, bending lower with every step. The cramp in his chest was shutting him up like a jackknife. When he reached the windmill, he swayed and caught at the ladder. He saw Polly coming down the hill, running with the swiftness of a slim greyhound. In a flash she had her shoulder under his armpit.

"Lean on me, Father, hard! Don't be afraid. We can get to the house all right."

Somehow they did, though Rosicky became blind with pain; he could keep on his legs, but he couldn't steer his course. The next thing he was conscious of was lying on Polly's bed, and Polly bending over him wringing out bath towels in hot water and putting them on his chest. She stopped only to throw coal into the stove, and she kept the teakettle and the black pot going. She put these hot applications on him for nearly an hour, she told him afterward, and all that time he was drawn up stiff and blue, with the sweat pouring off him.

As the pain gradually loosed its grip, the stiffness went out of his jaws, the black circles around his eyes disappeared, and a little of his natural color came back. When his daughter-in-law buttoned his shirt over his chest at last, he sighed.

"Da's fine, de way I feel now, Polly. It was a awful bad spell, an' I was so sorry it all come on you like it did."

Polly was flushed and excited. "Is the pain really gone? Can I leave you long enough to telephone over to your place?"

Rosicky's eyelids fluttered. "Don't telephone, Polly. It ain't no use to scare my wife. It's nice and quiet here, an' if I ain't too much trouble to you, just let me lay still till I feel like myself. I ain't got no pain now. It's nice here."

Polly bent over him and wiped the moisture from his face. "Oh, I'm so glad it's over!" she broke out impulsively. "It just broke my heart to see you suffer so, Father."

Rosicky motioned her to sit down on the chair where the teakettle had been, and looked up at her with that lively affectionate gleam in his eyes. "You was awful good to me, I won't never forget dat. I hate it to be sick on you like dis. Down at de barn I say to myself, dat young girl ain't had much experience in sickness, I don't want to scare her, an' maybe she's got a baby comin' or somet'ing."

Polly took his hand. He was looking at her so intently and affectionately and confidingly; his eyes seemed to caress her face, to regard it with pleasure. She frowned with her funny streaks of eyebrows, and then smiled back at him.

"I guess maybe there is something of that kind going to happen. But I haven't told anyone yet, not my mother or Rudolph. You'll be the first to know."

His hand pressed hers. She noticed that it was warm again. The twinkle in his yellow-brown eyes seemed to come nearer.

"I like mighty well to see dat little child, Polly," was all he said. Then he closed his eyes and lay half smiling. But Polly sat still, think-

----

- **impulsively** (im PUL siv lee) **with sudden desire**
- confidingly (kun FYD ing lee) **trustingly**

ing hard. She had a sudden feeling that nobody in the world, not her mother, not Rudolph, or anyone, really loved her as much as old Rosicky did. It perplexed her. She sat frowning and trying to puzzle it out. It was as if Rosicky had a special gift for loving people, something that was like an ear for music or an eye for color. It was quiet, unobtrusive; it was merely there. You saw it in his eyes—perhaps that was why they were merry. You felt it in his hands, too. After he dropped off to sleep, she sat holding his warm, broad, flexible brown hand. She had never seen another in the least like it. She wondered if it wasn't a kind of gypsy hand, it was so alive and quick and light in its communications—very strange in a farmer. Nearly all the farmers she knew had huge lumps of fists, like mauls, or they were knotty and bony and uncomfortable looking, with stiff fingers. But Rosicky's was like quicksilver, flexible, muscular, about the color of a pale cigar, with deep, deep creases across the palm. It wasn't nervous, it wasn't a stupid lump; it was a warm, brown, human hand, with some cleverness in it, a great deal of generosity, and something else which Polly could only call "gypsylike"—something nimble and lively and sure, in the way that animals are.

Polly remembered that hour long afterward; it had been like an awakening to her. It seemed to her that she had never learned so much about life from anything as from old Rosicky's hand. It

- **perplexed** (pur PLEKST) **puzzled**
- unobtrusive (un ob TROO siv) **hard to notice**
- maul (MAWL) **heavy hammer**
- quicksilver (QUIK sil vur) **mercury**

brought her to herself; it communicated some direct and untranslatable message.

When she heard Rudolph coming in the car, she ran out to meet him.

"Oh, Rudy, your father's been awful sick! He raked up those thistles he's been worrying about, and afterward he could hardly get to the house. He suffered so I was afraid he was going to die."

Rudolph jumped to the ground. "Where is he now?"

"On the bed. He's asleep. I was terribly scared, because, you know, I'm so fond of your father." She slipped her arm through his and they went into the house. That afternoon they took Rosicky home and put him to bed, though he protested that he was quite well again.

The next morning he got up and dressed and sat down to breakfast with his family. He told Mary that his coffee tasted better than usual to him, and he warned the boys not to bear any tales to Doctor Ed when he got home. After breakfast he sat down by his window to do some patching and asked Mary to thread several needles for him before she went to feed her chickens—her eyes were better than his, and her hands steadier. He lit his pipe and took up John's overalls. Mary had been watching him anxiously all morning, and as she went out of the door with her bucket of scraps, she saw that he was smiling. He was thinking, indeed, about Polly, and how he might never have known what a tender heart she had if he hadn't got sick over there. Girls nowadays didn't wear their heart on their sleeve. But now he knew Polly would make a fine woman after the foolishness wore off. Either a woman had that sweetness at her heart or she hadn't. You couldn't always tell by the look of them; but if they had that, everything came out right in the end.

After he had taken a few stitches, the cramp began in his chest, like yesterday. He put his pipe cautiously down on the window sill and bent over to ease the pull. No use—he had better try to get to his bed if he could. He rose and groped his way across the familiar floor, which was rising and falling like the deck of a ship. At the door he fell. When Mary came in, she found him lying there, and the moment she touched him she knew that he was gone.

Doctor Ed was away when Rosicky died, and for the first few weeks after he got home he was hard-driven. Every day he said to himself that he must get out to see that family that had lost their father. One soft, warm moonlight night in early summer he started for the farm. His mind was on other things, and not until his road ran by the graveyard did he realize that Rosicky wasn't over there on the hill where the red lamplight shown, but here, in the moonlight. He stopped his car, shut off the engine, and sat there for awhile.

A sudden hush had fallen on his soul. Everything here seemed strangely moving and significant, though signifying what, he did not know. Close by the wire fence stood Rosicky's mowing machine, where one of the boys had been cutting hay that afternoon; his own work horses had been going up and down there. The new-cut hay perfumed all the night air. The moonlight silvered the long, billowy grass that grew over the graves and hid the fence; the few little evergreens stood out black in it, like shadows in a pool. The sky was very blue and soft, the stars rather faint because the moon was full.

For the first time it struck Doctor Ed that this was really a beautiful graveyard. He thought of city cemeteries; acres of shrubbery and heavy stone, so arranged and lonely and unlike anything in the living world. Cities of the dead, indeed; cities of the forgotten, of the "put away." But this was open and free, this litle square of long grass which the wind forever stirred. Nothing but the sky overhead, and the many-colored fields running on until they met that sky. The horses worked here in summer; the neighbors passed on their way to town; and over yonder, in the cornfield, Rosicky's own cattle would be eating fodder as winter came on. Nothing could be more undeathlike than this place; nothing could be more right for a man who had helped to do the work of great cities and had always longed for the open country and had got to it at last. Rosicky's life seemed to him complete and beautiful.

- billowy (BIL oh wee) **surging with waves**
- fodder (FAHD ur) **cattle food**

ALL THINGS CONSIDERED _____

1. Rosicky's farm (a) is the best in the county. (b) has clay in the soil and is not so productive. (c) will be divided up among the Rosicky children when Anton Rosicky dies.

2. In his earlier years, Rosicky had been a (a) tailor. (b) cobbler. (c) carpenter.

3. Rosicky decides to try farming because (a) his family had always been farmers and he felt he'd be good at it. (b) he lived with his grandparents on a farm as a child and formed ties with the earth and farm animals. (c) he can't seem to make a living as a craftsman.

4. Before she married Rudolph, Polly was (a) dating a doctor. (b) the wealthiest young woman in town. (c) a clerk in a store.

5. Mary's story about the ultra-hot Fourth of July shows that (a) Mary resented Rosicky's poor farming techniques. (b) Rosicky always tried to make the best of things. (c) during a crop failure, even Rosicky could get depressed.

6. Rosicky gets the money to pay for the lavish Christmas feast in London by (a) working overtime for a month. (b) begging from some Czechs. (c) stealing from the violin boy.

7. Rosicky gets to New York through (a) some Bohemians offering to pay his passage. (b) stowing away on a cargo ship. (c) working for five years and saving for his fare.

8. Rosicky's raking the thistles from the alfalfa field at Rudolph's leads to (a) Rudolph's telling him to stay away from the farm. (b) a better yield of alfalfa and more money for Rudolph and Polly. (c) his having a heart attack.

9. Rosicky guesses correctly that Polly (a) is going to have a baby. (b) plans to leave Rudolph. (c) dislikes him.

10. Polly thinks that Rosicky has (a) a lot of money hidden away. (b) many annoying habits. (c) a special gift for loving people.

THINKING IT THROUGH _____

1. Why do you think Rosicky wants Polly to hear his story about his hard times in London?

2. What reasons does Rosicky give for preferring country life to city life?

3. "Neighbor Rosicky" tells about two marriages, one that is successful (Rosicky and Mary's) and one that is not so successful (Rudolph and Polly's). Compare the two marriages. Why, do you think, are Rudolph and Polly having problems while Rosicky and Mary are not?

4. Cather could have chosen to tell the story without the flashbacks (see page 124). How do the flashbacks help the reader understand Rosicky's character near the end of his life?

5. At the end of the story, Doctor Ed visits the graveyard in which Rosicky is buried. Rather than being unhappy about his friend's death, he thinks that "nothing could be more right" for Rosicky than to be buried in this graveyard. Explain Dr. Ed's reasons for this thought.

6. After reading the story, you should feel that you know Anton Rosicky well. He represents the type of person Willa Cather knew well and admired highly. (a) In your opinion, what three adjectives (for example, a *kind* person) best sum up Rosicky's character? (b) What details in the story best illustrate each of the three adjectives you selected?

Critical Thinking: Review

If you wish to review the meaning of any term in *italics* in this exercise, refer to the Glossary of Terms.

1. You know that in the real world, every *effect* usually has several *causes,* and every cause has several effects. Thinking in terms of ONE cause leading to ONE effect can often lead you astray.

   A complex story like "Neighbor Rosicky" illustrates the complex relationships between causes and effects. Answer these questions with care.

   (a) ". . . Dr. Burleigh told Neighbor Rosicky he had a bad heart. . . ." What effects does this news have in the story? Think about the effects on different characters, including the doctor himself.

   (b) Consider as a cause the Fourth-of-July heat wave that ruins the corn. Compare the different effects the disaster has on Rosicky and on his neighbors.

   (c) How many causes can you name for Rosicky's move from New York City to the Midwest?

   (d) Consider the effect that the story as a whole has on some readers. These readers finish the story with tears in their eyes, feeling both wiser and more joyful about what it means to be a human being. This may or may not be true of you. However, what causes can you find in the story that might produce this effect in some readers?

2. Consider the title in terms of *denotation* and *connotation.* Why is "*Neighbor* Rosicky" better than a title like "*Farmer* Rosicky" or "*Old* Rosicky"?

3. Willa Cather often points out the differences between actual *territories* and the *mental maps* people have of them. Go back and reread the physical description of the cemetery in the early part of Section II. How does Rosicky's mental map of this territory differ from one a casual passer-by might have?

Composition

1. On your paper, write three *facts* from the story about any of the characters. Then write three opinions based on the facts.

2. One of the most moving parts of the story is Polly's reflection on Rosicky's hand in Section VI. Some people believe that the hands reveal much about a person's life and character. Try to duplicate Willa Cather's little essay on a hand. Consider the hand of someone you know well (even yourself). Connect your description with the person's actual life and character.

VOCABULARY AND SKILL REVIEW

Before completing the exercises that follow, you may wish to review the **bold-faced** words on pages 326 to 375.

I. On a separate sheet of paper, write the term on each line that means the same, or nearly the same, as the word in *italics*.

1. *spunk:* cleaning liquid, doubt, courage, cheerfulness
2. *melancholy:* rotten, gloomy, expensive, thoughtful
3. *valet:* purse, mountain goat, opera singer, manservant
4. *wistfully:* longingly, gracefully, angrily, without hope
5. *pulsate:* digest, estimate, throw away, beat
6. *perplexed:* overjoyed, exhausted, puzzled, thoroughly tested
7. *aghast:* exhausted, terrified, proud, broken down
8. *habitual:* regular, proud, excellent, dangerous to health
9. *restrain:* replace, redo, recover, hold back
10. *turret:* kitchen tool, couch, small tower, spicy fruit

II. Write the *italicized* word that best fills the blank in each sentence.

disrepair	acuteness
unnerve	impulsively
stethoscope	phenomena
reflection	taproot
intently	murky

1. The teacher asked us to listen _____ at all times.
2. What _____ usually make up a thunderstorm?
3. We couldn't see far into the _____ water of the canal.
4. That old school is in a sad state of _____ .
5. The _____ of a dandelion can be 18 inches long.
6. "Stop that thief!" I shouted _____ .
7. Dr. Ruiz took a _____ from her black bag.
8. Gerry tried to _____ me with nasty whispers.
9. The word _____ compares serious thought to examination in a mirror.
10. Drunk drivers lack _____ and often have accidents.

III. Mark each statement about the cartoon below **T** (true) or **F** (false). Be prepared to state clearly the reasons for your choices.

1. The cartoon carefully illustrates a *territory* that thousands of people have actually seen.

2. It is probably the cartoonist's *opinion* that there is a kind of greatness in the common people of the world.

3. Here, the cartoonist is having fun with the *stereotyped mental maps* most people have of a "statue."

4. The word *FREDS* is used mainly for its *denotation,* not for its *connotation.*

5. It is a reasonable *inference* to think that the cartoonist has several close friends named Fred.

DIG INTO THE WORLD

by Alan Alda

▶ Can you put mental magic to work in your own life? Of course you can—and this selection can help you get started. It's a speech that the popular actor Alan Alda delivered at his daughter's college graduation. Dig into it!

The best things said come last. People will talk for hours saying nothing much and then linger at the door with words that come with a rush from the heart.

We are all gathered at a doorway today. We linger there with our hand on the knob chattering away like Polonius to Laertes.* Now remember, *Neither a borrower nor a lender be . . .* and don't forget, *This above all: To thine own self be true . . .*

But the very best things said often

---

*Polonius (puh LOH nee us) and **Laertes**—(lay AYR teez) father and son in William Shakespeare's *Hamlet.*

slip out completely unheralded, preceded by, "Oh, by the way." In real life, when Polonius had finished giving all that fatherly advice to his son—who probably wasn't paying much attention anyway—he must have said, "Oh, by the way, if you get into any trouble, don't forget you can always call me at the office."

As we stand in the doorway today, these are my parting words to my daughter. There are so many things I want to tell you, Eve.

The first thing is: don't be scared. You're being flung into a world that's running about as smoothly as a car with square wheels. It's okay to be uncertain. You're an adult in a time when the leaders of the world are behaving like children. Where the central image of the day is a terrorist one: humane concerns inhumanely expressed. And the only response to this is impotent fury. If you weren't a little uncertain, I'd be nervous for you.

Adulthood has come upon you and you're not all that sure you're ready for it. I think that sometimes I'm not ready for adulthood either—yours *or* mine.

The day before yesterday you were a baby. I was afraid to hold you because you seemed so fragile. Yesterday, all I could feel was helplessness when you broke your nine-year-old arm. Only this morning you were a teen-ager. As I get older, the only thing that speeds up is time. But if time is a thief, time also leaves something in exchange: experi-

ence. And with experience, at least in your own work you will be sure.

Love your work. If you always put your heart into everything you do, you really can't lose. Whether you wind up making a lot of money or not, you will have had a wonderful time, and no one will ever be able to take that away from you.

I want to squeeze things great and small into this lingering good-by. I want to tell you to keep laughing. You gurgle when you laugh. Be sure to gurgle three times a day for your own well-being. And if you can get other people to join you in your laughter, you may help keep this shaky boat afloat. When people are laughing, they're generally not killing one another.

I have this helpless urge to pass on maxims to you, things that will see you through. But even the Golden Rule doesn't seem adequate to pass on to a daughter. There should be something added to it. Here's my Golden Rule for a tarnished age: Be fair with others, but then keep after them until they're fair with you.

It's a complex world. I hope you'll learn to make distinctions. A peach is not its fuzz, a toad is not its warts, a person is not his or her crankiness. If we can make distinctions, we can be tolerant, and we can get to the heart of our problems instead of wrestling endlessly with their gross exteriors.

Once you make a habit of making

- unheralded (un HER uld ed) **unannounced; not prepared for**
- humane (hyoo MAYN) **caring; kind**
- impotent (IM puh tunt) **powerless; feeble**
- maxim (MAK sim) **saying; rule of conduct**
- tarnished (TAR nisht) **stained; disgraced**
- gross (GROHS) **general; not detailed**

distinctions, you'll begin challenging your own assumptions. Your assumptions are your windows on the world. Scrub them off every once in a while, or the light won't come in. If you challenge your own, you won't be so quick to accept the unchallenged assumptions of others. You'll be a lot less likely to be caught up in bias or prejudice, or be influenced by people who ask you to hand over your brains, your soul, or money because they have everything all figured out for you.

Be as smart as you can, but remember that it's always better to be wise than to be smart. And don't be upset that it takes a long, long time to find wisdom. Like a rare virus, wisdom tends to break out at unexpected times, and it's mostly people with compassion and understanding who are susceptible to it.

The door is inching a little closer toward the latch and I still haven't said it. Let me dig a little deeper. Life is absurd and meaningless—unless *you* bring meaning to it, unless *you* make something of it. It is up to us to create our own existence.

No matter how loving or loved we are, it eventually occurs to most of us that deep down inside, we're all alone. When the moment comes for you to wrestle with that cold loneliness, which is every person's private monster, I want you to face the damn thing. I want you to see it for what it is and win.

When I was in college, 25 years ago, the philosophy of existentialism was very popular. We all talked about nothingness; but we moved into a world of effort and endeavor. Now no one much talks about nothingness; but the world itself is filled with it.

Whenever that sense of absurdity hits you, I want you to be ready. It will have a hard time getting hold of you if you're already in motion. You can use the skills of your profession and other skills you have learned here, dig into the world and push it into better shape.

For one thing, you can try to clean the air and water. Or you can try to make the justice system work, too. You can bring the day a little closer when the rich and privileged have to live by the same standards as the poor and the outcast.

You can try to put an end to organized crime—that happy family whose main objective is to convince us they don't exist while they destroy a generation with drugs and suck the life from our economy.

You can try to find out why people of every country and religion have at one time or another found it so easy to make other people suffer. (If you really want to grapple with absurdity, try understanding how people can be capable of both nurture and torture; can worry and fret over a little girl caught in a mineshaft, yet destroy a village and everyone in it with hardly the blink of an eye.) You can try to stop the next war now, *before* it starts, to keep old men from sending children away to die.

And while you're doing all of that,

- bias (BY us) **one-sided viewpoint**
- compassion (kum PASH un) **sympathy; mercy**
- susceptible (suh SEP tuh bul) **easily affected by**
- existentialism (eg zis TEN shuh liz um) **the belief that humans exist as their own makers in a purposeless universe**
- grapple (GRAP ul) **wrestle; lay hold of**
- nurture (NUR chur) **loving care and training**

remember that every right you have as a woman was won for you by women fighting hard. There are little girls being born right now who won't even have the same rights you do unless you act to maintain and extend the range of equality. The nourishing stew of civilized life doesn't keep bubbling on its own. Put something back in the pot for the people in line behind you.

There's plenty to keep you busy for the rest of your life. I can't promise this will ever completely reduce that sense of absurdity, but it may get it down to a manageable level. It will allow you once in a while to bask in the feeling that, all in all, things do seem to be moving forward.

I can see your brow knitting in that way that I love. That crinkle between your eyebrows that signals your doubt and your skepticism. Why—on a day of such excitement and hope—should I be talking of absurdity and nothingness? Because I want you to focus that hope and level that excitement into coherent rays that will strike like a laser at the targets of our discontent.

I want you to be potent; to do good when you can, and to hold your wit and your intelligence like a shield against other people's wantonness. And above all, to laugh and enjoy yourself in a life of your own choosing and in a world of your own making. I want you to be strong and aggressive and tough and resilient and full of feeling. I want you to be everything that's you, deep at the center of your being.

I want you to have chutzpah. Nothing important was ever accomplished without chutzpah. Columbus had chutzpah. The signers of the Declaration of Independence had chutzpah. Laugh at yourself, but don't ever aim your doubt at yourself. Be bold. When you embark for strange places, don't leave any of yourself safely on shore. Have the nerve to go into unexplored territory.

Be brave enough to live life creatively. The creative is the place where no one else has ever been. You have to leave the city of your comfort and go into the wilderness of your intuition. You can't get there by bus, only by hard work and risk and by not quite knowing what you're doing. What you'll discover will be wonderful. What you'll discover will be yourself.

Well, those are my parting words as today's door closes softly between us. So long, be happy. . . .

Oh, by the way, I love you.

- bask (BASK) **warm or sun oneself**
- skepticism (SKEP ti siz um) **doubt; disbelief**
- coherent (koh HEER unt) **understandable; logical**
- laser (LAY zur) **concentrated beam of light**
- potent (POHT unt) **able to act; powerful**
- wantonness (WAHN tun nes) **visciousness; recklessness**
- resilient (ri ZIL yunt) **able to bounce back and recover**
- chutzpah (KHOOT spuh) **real nerve; daring courage**

ALL THINGS CONSIDERED

1. Alan Alda does *not* tell the graduates to (a) love their work. (b) take everything seriously. (c) have courage.

2. Alda's advice to live life creatively (a) will lead to a life of comfort. (b) probably brought a laugh from his audience. (c) is illustrated in the speech itself.

3. The speech makes it clear that Alda (a) is an actor. (b) has thought about the meaning of life. (c) has only one child.

4. A metaphor used five times in the speech is (a) "Golden Rule." (b) "chutzpah." (c) "door" or "doorway."

5. The title refers to (a) adding meaning to one's life by trying to improve the world. (b) spending one's life studying the world. (c) getting back to nature, away from so-called civilized society.

THINKING IT THROUGH

1. Read the first sentence of the speech, then read the last. What can you infer about the relationship between them?

2. Different members of the graduating class probably took different parts of the speech to heart. Suppose you had been in the audience. What piece of advice do you think is most important for you to remember in your life? Explain.

3. Alda's graduation address pulls together several of the critical thinking strands in this anthology. Find at least one part of the speech that you can relate to the following:

Unit I: Getting the Picture. Where does Alda say you should try to see things as they *are,* not as others see them or as you assume them to be?

Unit II: Discovering Differences. Where are you told about the importance of recognizing distinctions?

Unit III: Changes. Where does Alda speak of the passage of time, the past, or the future?

Unit IV: Some Matters of Judgment. Where does Alda speak of wisdom or making good decisions?

Unit V: Mental Magic. Where is creativity recognized as a key to life?

UNIT REVIEW

I. Match the terms in Column A with their definitions in Column B.

A	B
1. effect	**a)** something known to be true that can be checked
2. fact	
3. opinion	**b)** a comparison made with a special word such as *like* or *as*
4. simile	
5. metaphor	**c)** the result of a cause or causes
6. onomatopoeia	**d)** the use of words that sound like what they mean
7. personification	
8. symbol	**e)** what a person thinks or believes about something
9. theme	
10. imagery	**f)** a poetic comparison made directly by substituting one word for another
	g) language that appeals to the reader's senses
	h) giving human qualities to nonhuman subjects
	i) something that stands for something else
	j) underlying meaning or message of a piece of literature

II. In one way or another, the selections in this unit are all examples of the creative imagination at work. The authors used figurative language or tried to brainstorm their way into fantasy. Did the authors succeed? That depends partly on their skill as writers. It also depends on your skill as a reader.

Literature is a two-way process. All a writer can do is put words on paper. The words remain dead until your own mental magic brings them to life. *All creative literature demands creative reading.*

Review your creative reactions to the selections in this way. Think about each of the possible reactions listed on page 389, which any reader may experience. How many of them can you connect with a selection in this unit? Choose five of the reactions and use them to express your feelings. Be sure to refer to specific parts from the selections.

pity
confusion
disgust
amazement
relief
boredom
curiosity
disappointment (with an author)
disappointment (with an event)
sense of identity with a character

Example: *disbelief*

I experienced a sense of disbelief when I read the end of "The Raven" by Edgar Allan Poe. The poet asks the reader to believe that a raven arrives at the student's room at just the right time and speaks the one word it knows at just the right moments. Then when Poe says that the raven "still is sitting" on the statue at the end, who could believe it? How long must it have taken the speaker to write such a long, complicated poem? That poor bird would have shut up and keeled over. Poe got it wrong. It would have been the *raven* "on the floor"—forevermore.

(Your explanations do not have to be as long as this one, but be sure to state reasons for your reactions.)

SPEAKING UP

Roleplaying for an Interview

To prepare yourself for this assignment, try to recall two different kinds of TV interviews. In one type of interview, the interviewer is pleasant, humorous, and uses pre-planned questions to help the interviewee show off. In another type of interview, on the other hand, the interviewer seems hostile and may even try to embarrass the person being interviewed.

Pair up with another student. One of you will be the interviewer; the other will be the person being interviewed. Glance over the selections in Unit V. Look for either an author or a character who would be a good candidate to interview. To help you decide on which type of interview to conduct, here are a few examples of how each interview might develop:

1. (from "Examination Day")
    Hostile Interviewer: Mr. Jordan, you claim that the government actually *killed* your son? Yet you—and thousands like you—sit by and let such things happen. Why? Didn't you care about your son?
2. (from "The Fall of the House of Usher")
    Pleasant Interviewer: Edgar, we're certainly glad you could be on the show tonight. Perhaps you'd like to start by telling the viewers how you happened to write your remarkable story "The Fall of the House of Usher." What gave you the idea for this gruesome story?

    If you choose to do the sweet and supportive kind of interview, the "guest" might walk on from behind a curtain (read classroom door). For the other type of interview, the interviewer would probably first have to corner the person who's about to be embarrassed.

    To develop the interview, the two students working together should prepare an informal script. (This will not be collected, but a successful interviewer plans questions in advance. The "guest" also needs to have a clear idea of how to answer.) If you can bring in your sense of humor, do! These interviews can be great fun for both the "stars" and for the audience.

WRITING FOR TELEVISION

Prewriting

In Unit V you read a short story by Poe that had been turned into a television play. Now *you* will be turning a short story—"Examination Day"—into a television play. (If this is a class assignment, your teacher may want you to write only one act or scene of the whole play. Follow instructions.)

Before starting to write, answer these questions.

1. What might you include in your description of the Jordan home to clue the television audience that this story takes place in the future? You'll need to describe the *breakfast room* and the *living room;* don't forget to describe *Dickie's corner.*

2. Some description is already given of the *Government Education Building.* Do you want to add anything to the description of the lobby? Does it seem gray, drab—or brilliant with lights? How will you describe the room where Dickie takes his test?

3. The story doesn't state what Dickie gets for his birthday. What do you think would be suitable gifts? Remember that none of the gifts should force Dickie to think—so electronic games, chess sets, books, and puzzles are out.

Writing

As you set up your play, be sure to refer back to "The Fall of the House of Usher" (page 326) as often as necessary. It will prove a useful guide.

1. First, list the characters, with a description of each. Don't forget the "young man wearing an insignialess tunic" and the "gray-tunicked attendant" who gives Dickie the test.

2. *Time:* In what year (or century) will your play take place?

3. *Setting:* Indicate the setting (kind of city and perhaps country) briefly. Then skip a line and write "ACT I."

4. *Fade in:* Using your answer to question #1 in Prewriting, describe what the camera will show the audience.

5. Begin the scene with Dickie's father saying, "Forget about it." Be sure to set up the dialogue in drama form as shown in the example below.
   Mr. Jordan: Forget about it.

6. When Dickie wanders over to his corner, write *Dissolve to* and put in your description of this place.

7. You may alter the time sequence of the story. For example, after Dickie's father answers the question about what makes grass green, the story states, "Later in the day. . . ." You could have Dickie's mother bring in the presents without having a time delay.

8. Look at the first series of three dots (. . .) in the story. These indicate a scene change. You'll need a *Dissolve to.*

9. At the second series of three dots, conclude Act I. Write *Fade out.* Skip a line and center the words "ACT II."

10. *Fade in* on your description of the Government Education Building.

11. Note that in this scene there are other 12-year-old boys waiting with their fathers. You may want to have the *voice on the loud-speaker* call off several names before Dickie's.

12. When Dickie's name is called and he leaves, *Dissolve to* the test room. Describe the actions of the two characters.

13. At the last series of dots you'll again have a *Dissolve to.* Find a way to indicate the time. Complete writing this last scene, using the dialogue as printed in the story.

Revising

1. Refer often to "The Fall of the House of Usher" to see if you have followed the rules for television scripts. For instance, did you use *italics* (*underlining*) in your script properly? Italics are used for scene description and for indicating *how* a character speaks (*nervously, with excitement,* etc.).

2. Finally, read through your screenplay and try to visualize (see) each scene. If at any point you cannot visualize the scene, add sufficient detail to make it clear.

Glossary of Terms

This glossary defines terms that you have studied. The page references shown with the terms indicate where the terms are first defined and discussed. Turn to those pages if you need to review the lessons.

Alliteration p. 156 *Alliteration* is the repetition of consonant sounds, usually at the beginning of words, for poetic effect.

Allusion p. 48 An *allusion* in a story is a reference to some other work of literature or to some person, place, or event in history. For example, in "The Turn of the Tide" an allusion is made to Oscar Wilde's book *The Picture of Dorian Grey.*

Analogy p. 21 An *analogy* is a statement that two things, or two pairs, are alike in some way.

Application of Knowledge p. 238 The thinking process whereby knowledge gained in one area is applied to another is called *application of knowledge.* For example, ideas in a work of literature can often be applied to the reader's life.

Autobiography p. 103 An *autobiography* is a personally written account of one's life.

Blank Verse p. 223 *Blank verse* is unrhymed poetry with five strong vocal stresses per line.

Cause and Effect p. 222 A *cause* is an event or idea that leads to a certain result, which is called an *effect.*

Cause/Effect Fallacy *(After the fact, therefore because of the fact)* p. 21 There is a tendency to believe that if Event A occurs before Event B, then A must have caused B. This is the cause/effect fallacy—one of the fallacies of logic.

Character Clues p. 76 The clues the author gives readers through a character's actions and speeches are called *character clues.* A character may be **dynamic** or **static.** A *dynamic character* changes in some way as the story progresses. The change may be shown through the character's thoughts, words, or actions. A *static character* remains the same throughout the story.

Characterization p. 88 *Characterization* refers to the methods that writers use to develop each character in a story. There are four main methods of characterization:

A. Direct statements made by the writer
B. Speeches and thoughts of the character
C. Actions of the character
D. Reactions of other characters to the character

Chronological Order p. 124 Most stories that you read take place in *chronological order,* the order that events take place in real life. When stories are written in chronological order, the reader expects the plot to be a continual sequence of beginning, middle, and end.

Cliché p. 217 An overworked figurative expression is called a *cliché.*

Climax p. 33 The *climax,* or most exciting part of the story, comes at or near the end. It acts as a turning point in the story. It is at this point that the final major conflict is resolved.

Comparison and Contrast p. 95 A *comparison* shows how two (or more) things, ideas, or feelings are alike. A *contrast,* on the other hand, shows how they are different. (Note: The word *comparison* is sometimes used to establish both similarities and dissimilarities.)

Conflict p. 111 All plots depend on *conflict* and rising action. A conflict develops when two opposite forces meet. There are four main kinds of conflict:

A. Conflict between people
B. Conflict within a single person
C. Conflict between people and things
D. Conflict between people and nature

Connotation p. 249 Many words have two kinds of meanings. A word's *connotation* is everything that the word suggests or brings to the mind of the reader (or listener). (See also *Denotation.*)

Denotation p. 249 Many words have two kinds of meanings. The *denotation* of a word is its dictionary meaning. (See also *Connotation.*)

Emotional Appeal p. 21 An *emotional appeal* is an argument based not on reasoning but on personal feelings. It is one of the fallacies of logic.

Fact p. 14 A *fact* is something known to be true. Most facts can be checked and proved by examining something in the world around you. Fact language is territory language.

Fallacy p. 21 An error in reasoning is called a *fallacy.* For example, it is a fallacy to assume that if Item A is more expensive than Item B, it is also better than Item B.

False Analogy p. 21 An analogy is a statement about the similarity or relationship between things or people. However, there is a tendency to infer that because two things or people are alike in some ways, they are alike in other ways. When this happens, a *false analogy* results—a fallacy of logic.

Fiction p. 51 Stories and novels that are made up by a writer are called *fiction.*

Figurative Language p. 217 *Figurative language* is language that does not really mean what it seems to say. Both poetry and prose are often rich in figurative language. *Simile* and *metaphor* are the two most common forms of figurative language. (See also *Literal Language.*)

Flashback p. 124 In a *flashback,* the author interrupts the natural time sequence of a story to relate an episode or scene that occurred prior to the opening situation. In this way, the author can make the reader aware of some background information important to the story's action, characterization, and/or theme.

Foreshadowing p. 203 *Foreshadowing* is a technique used by authors to help the reader make reasonable predictions. The author does this by casting certain shadows of possibility before an event happens. (See also *Making Predictions.*)

Hasty Generalization p. 21 A *hasty generalization* is a sweeping statement made on the basis of too few examples. It is one of the fallacies of logic.

Hypothesis/Hypotheses p. 258 A *hypothesis* is a possible answer to some question, or a possible explanation for something. Frequently, there are several possible answers or explanations. These are called *hypotheses.*

Imagery p. 154 In everyday language, the word *image* refers to something that can be seen or imagined as being seen.

In literary use, however, image and imagery have wider meanings. An author or a poet may use words or phrases to create an *image,* or vivid sensory impression for the reader. *Imagery* refers not only to what the reader can see but also to what the reader can hear, smell, taste, and feel. Imagery allows readers to experience what is being described by the writer.

Inference p. 4 An *inference* is a guess based on the available evidence.

Internal Rhyme p. 319 *Internal rhyme* is rhyme within a line of poetry. An example from "The Raven" is as follows:

> Once upon a midnight *dreary,* while
> I pondered, weak and *weary,* . . .

Irony p. 58 *Irony* is the use of words to say something quite different from what is actually meant or appears true. **Irony of situation** occurs when there is a striking difference between what a character expects to happen and what actually does happen. **Dramatic irony** goes further than irony of situation by involving the reader's understanding. Dramatic irony occurs when a reader knows something important that a character doesn't know.

Logic p. 21 *Logic* is clear reasoning. For instance, it is logical to say that if A is bigger than B, and if B is bigger than C, then A is bigger than C.

Lyric Poem p. 307 A short poem that expresses a poet's feelings and thoughts is called a *lyric poem.* A lyric poem can be about anything. It is not the subject matter, but how the poet treats the subject matter that allows you to see the old and familiar in new and exciting ways.

Mental Maps p. 5 *Mental maps* include people's impressions and thoughts about the world around them, other people, and themselves. Such maps, of course, can be either accurate or inaccurate. (See also *Territories.*)

Metaphor p. 162 A *metaphor* is a figure of speech in which one person or thing is compared to something else, usually by suggesting the one *is* the other. Sometimes a metaphor creates a picture by saying, in a figurative way, that a person or thing *is doing* something.

Mood and Tone p. 49 The *mood* of a piece of literature is the feeling it gives the reader. For instance, some stories create a mood of fear, or even terror. A suspenseful mood makes the reader desperate to know what happens next. The word *tone* refers to the attitude a writer seems to have toward the subject matter. It involves the general atmosphere or quality that the writer is conveying to the reader. For example, a writer may pretend to be critical about a subject, but really not have a critical attitude about the subject at all.

Narrative Poem p. 57 A *narrative poem* tells a story. It has a rather regular pattern of rhyme and rhythm. "The Pardoner's Tale" is an example of a narrative poem.

Narrator p. 32 The *narrator* is the person who tells the story. Sometimes the narrator is involved as a character in the story.

Nonfiction p. 51 *Nonfiction* is a writing about events that actually happened in real life.

Onomatopoeia p. 57 The use of a word that imitates a natural sound is called *onomatopoeia.* The word *buzz* is a good example.

Opinion p. 14 An *opinion* is what you think or believe about something. Opinions exist in your mind, and may or may not be based on facts. Opinions are part of your mental maps. (See also *Fact.*)

Oral Interpretation p. 166 *Oral interpretation* means reading aloud with expression. Most poems and plays require good oral interpretation for total understanding and enjoyment by the audience.

Paraphrase p. 238 To *paraphrase* means to rewrite something—a speech, for example—by using mostly your own words.

Personification p. 164 *Personification* is a figure of speech in which something non-human is given human qualities and abilities. A fielder's glove that "eats" baseballs is an example.

Plot p. 33 The *plot* of a story concerns not only what happens but also the way things happen—the way different scenes relate to each other so that the reader is satisfied when the story is concluded. A well-written plot has a careful sequence of events and actions that progress through *conflict* and *rising action* to a climax. A *resolution* or a *surprise ending* may follow the climax.

Point of View p. 139 The *point of view* is the position from which a story is told. The two most common points of view are the *first person* and the *third person.*

In the *first-person point of view,* the narrator is a character in the story. Everything that happens in the story must be presented as observed and interpreted by this character. In some stories told in the first person, the narrator is the main character. In others, the narrator is not the main character but another character who always happens to be around when the important action takes place.

In the *third-person point of view,* the narrator, or storyteller, is not a character in the story. Sometimes the narrator presents the feelings and thoughts of a single character. This is called *third-person limited point of view.* At other times, the narrator skips around and enters the mind of one character and then another at will. The reader learns what each character thinks and feels. This is called *third-person omniscient.*

Précis p. 160 A *précis* is a very short summary of a literary selection, such as a poem or a story.

Predictions p. 203 Making *predictions,* or judgments about future events, is a skill that adds enjoyment to any reading experience. To help the reader make reasonable predictions, authors often use a technique called foreshadowing. (See also *Foreshadowing.*)

Resolution p. 33 Sometimes, a short *resolution* follows the climax of a story. A resolution solves any unanswered minor questions and gives the story a "rounded out" feeling.

Rising Action p. 33 A writer creates excitement, or *rising action,* by making each plot problem or conflict more interesting than the one before it.

Satire p. 23 A *satire* is a work of literature that pokes fun at some form of literature, at some idea, or at some human weakness. Most satires have a serious purpose: to improve the reader's thinking on a certain subject.

Setting p. 4 The *setting* of a story includes the place, the time, and certain natural events, such as the weather.

Simile p. 39 A *simile* is a figurative comparison between two things that is made with a special comparing word (usually *like* or *as*). "Clumsy as an ox" is a common example.

Stanza p. 79 A *stanza* is a division of a poem. Very often a new stanza signifies a change in ideas. At other times, the tone of the poem changes with a new stanza.

Stereotype p. 94 A *stereotype* is a general mental picture that a certain word creates. A stereotype usually is an unfair representation. The mental picture results in a distorted judgment of a certain group of people.

Subject and Theme p. 110 The *subject* of a piece of literature is simply what it is about. The word *theme* refers to a larger idea than the word subject. A theme is an underlying meaning within a piece of literature.

Subplot p. 202 Many longer literary selections contain a *subplot,* or a minor plot related in some way to the main plot. (See also *Plot.*)

Surprise Ending p. 33 A story may end quickly after the climax with a short, single sentence—a "punch line." A quick, unexpected ending is called a *surprise ending.*

Symbol and Symbolic Action p. 104 A *symbol* is something that stands for something else. In literature, a person, a place, an object, an action, or even an idea can take on special symbolic meaning. *Symbolic action* is important in literature, too. In "Love Is a Fallacy" Petey sees the raccoon coat as a symbol of a current fashion. His wearing the raccoon coat is a symbolic action. He wants to show others that he is a stylish dresser.

Territories p. 5 In the vocabulary of critical thinking, the *territories* include what the world really is and what the human beings are really like. Of course, people can only interpret their mental maps of the territories. (See also *Mental Maps.*)

Tragic Flaw p. 237 A *tragic flaw* is a personality defect that forces a character to act in ways that lead that person to a downfall. Most tragic flaws involve an excess of some quality—for example, too much ambition, pride, or suspicion.

Index of Authors and Titles

Page numbers in **bold-faced** type indicate profiles (short biographies).

ACKNOWLEDGMENTS

We thank the following authors, agents, and publishers for their permission to reprint copyrighted material:

ALAN ALDA—for "Dig Into the World" by Alan Alda. Copyright © 1982, Alan Alda. All rights reserved. Reprinted by permission from the *Reader's Digest* and Connecticut College.

ATHENEUM—for "Grandmother, Rocking" from *Rainbow Writing* by Eve Merriam. Copyright © 1976 by Eve Merriam. Published by Atheneum. Reprinted by permission of the author.

BARLENMIR HOUSE, PUBLISHERS—for "Deposit Here" by Jesús Papoleto Meléndez, from *Street Poetry and Other Poems.* Copyright © 1972.

BRANDT & BRANDT LITERARY AGENTS, INC.—for "A Kind of Murder" by Hugh Pentecost. First published in *Ellery Queen Mystery Magazine,* copyright © 1962 by Hugh Pentec Pentecost. Reprinted by permission of Brandt & Brandt Literary Agents, Inc.

CARTOON FEATURES SYNDICATE—for the drawing by H. Martin. Reprinted by permission of Cartoon Features Syndicate.

CHRISTIAN SCIENCE MONITOR—for "Unfolding Bud" by Naoshi Koriyama. Reprinted by permission from *The Christian Science Monitor.* Copyright © 1957. The Christian Science Publishing Society. All rights reserved.

EUGENIA COLLIER—for "Sweet Potato Pie" by Eugenia Collier. Reprinted by permission of Eugenia Collier and Howard University.

DELACORTE PRESS/SEYMOUR LAWRENCE—for "Long Walk to Forever" excerpted from the book *Welcome to the Monkey House* by Kurt Vonnegut Jr. Copyright © 1960 by Kurt Vonnegut Jr. Originally published in *The Ladies' Home Journal.* Reprinted by permission of Delacorte Press/Seymour Lawrence.

DOUBLEDAY & COMPANY, INC.—for "Marriage Is a Private Affair" from *Girls at War and Other Stories* by Chinua Achebe. Copyright © 1972, 1973 by Chinua Achebe. Reprinted by permission of Doubleday & Company, Inc. and Harold Ober Associates.

E. P. DUTTON, INC.—for "Red" from *A Precocious Autobiography* by Yevgeny Yevtushenko, translated by Andrew R. Mac Andrew. English translation copyright © 1963 by E. P. Dutton.—for "Shame" from *Nigger: An Autobiography* by Dick Gregory with Robert Lipsyte. Copyright © 1964 by Dick Gregory Enterprises, Inc. Reprinted by permission of the publisher, E. P. Dutton, a division of New American Library.

Mari Evans—for "The Sudden Sight" from *Where Is All The Music?,* published by P. B. Breman Heritage Series. Copyright © 1968.

HARPER & ROW, PUBLISHERS, INC.—for eight poems by Edna St. Vincent Millay from *Collected Poems,* Harper & Row. Copyright © 1921, 1922, 1924, 1948, 1950, 1951 by Edna St. Vincent Millay and Norma Millay Ellis.—for "Metaphors" from *Collected Poems by Sylvia Plath,* edited by Ted Hughes. Copyright © 1960 by Ted Hughes.

HARCOURT, BRACE JOVANOVICH, INC.—for "New Face" from *Revolutionary Petunias & Other Poems,* copyright © 1973 by Alice Walker, Reprinted by permission of Harcourt Brace Jovanovich, Inc.

HOLT, RINEHART AND WINSTON, PUBLISHERS—for "When I Was One-and-Twenty" from "A Shropshire Lad"—authorized edition—from *The Collected Poems* of A. E. Housman. Copyright © 1939, 1940, 1965 by Holt, Rinehart and Winston. Copyright © 1967, 1968 by Robert E. Symons. Reprinted by permission of Holt, Rinehart and Winston, Publishers.

OLWYN HUGHES LITERARY AGENCY—for "Metaphors" by Sylvia Plath. Olwyn Hughes Literary Agency.

INTERNATIONAL PUBLISHERS CO., INC.—for "Battle Won Is Lost" by Phil George from *Voices from Wah' Kon-Tah: Contemporary Poetry of Native Americans.*

ITHACA HOUSE—for "An Historic Moment" by William J. Harris. "An Historic Moment" is reprinted with permission from *In My Own Dark Way* by William J. Harris. (Ithaca House, 1977).

DANIEL KEYES/THE MAGAZINE OF FANTASY AND SCIENCE FICTION—for "Flowers for Algernon." Copyright © 1959 by Mercury Press, Inc. Reprinted by permission of the author. Copyright © 1979 by Mercury Press, Inc. Reprinted from *The Magazine of Fantasy and Science Fiction.*

BERTHA KLAUSNER INTERNATIONAL LITERARY AGENCY, INC.—for "The Richer, the Poorer" by Dorothy West. Permission granted by Bertha Klausner International Literary Agency, Inc.

LITTLE, BROWN AND COMPANY—for "Dreams of the Animals" by Margaret Atwood from *Procedures for the Underground.* Copyright © 1970 by Oxford University Press. By permission of Little, Brown and Company in association with Atlantic Monthly Press and Oxford University Press Canada.—for "April" from *Chapters: My Growth As a Writer"* by Lois Duncan. Copyright © 1982 by Lois Duncan.

MC INTOSH AND OTIS, INC.—for "Too Soon a Woman" by Dorothy M. Johnson. Copyright © 1953 by Dorothy M. Johnson. Copyright © renewed 1981 by Dorothy M. Johnson. Reprinted by permission of Mc Intosh and Otis, Inc.

MAGAZINE OF FANTASY AND SCIENCE FICTION—for the drawing by Joseph Dawes. Copyright © 1984 by Mercury Press, Inc. Reprinted from *The Magazine of Fantasy and Science Fiction.*

HAROLD MATSON COMPANY, INC.—for "Love Is a Fallacy" by Max Shulman. Publish notice that the story is an adaptation. Copyright © 1951. Copyright © renewed 1979 by Max Shulman.—for "The Turn of the Tide" by C. E. Forester. Copyright © 1934. Copyright renewed 1962 by C. S. Forester. Reprinted by permission of Harold Matson Company, Inc.

TONI MENDEX, INC.—for "Deeper Meanings #36." Reprinted by permission of Toni Mendez, Inc., from *Whack Your Porcupine.*

THE NEW YORKER—for two New Yorker drawings. "Don't worry. . . ." Drawing by Garrett Price; Copyright © 1958. The New Yorker Magazine, Inc.—for The Raven drawing by Charles Addams; Copyright © 1983. The New Yorker Magazine, Inc.

NOTES PLUS—for the section "Think Logically, Write Logically" from the November 1984 issue (submitted by John W. Davis). Reprinted by permission of the National Council of Teachers of English.

RAINES & RAINES—for "Examination Day" by Henry Slesar. Originally appeared in Playboy Magazine; Copyright © 1958 by Playboy Magazine. Reprinted by permission of the author and his agent, Raines & Raines.

RANDOM HOUSE, INC./ALFRED A. KNOPF, INC.—for "Neighbor Rosicky." Copyright © 1932 by Willa Cather and renewed

1960 by the Executors of the Estate of Willa Cather. Reprinted from *Obscure Destinies,* by Willa Cather, by permission of Alfred A. Knopf, Inc.—for "Pot of Gold," pages 314–317. Adapted by permission of Alfred A. Knopf, Inc. from *The Golden Land: An Anthology of Latin American Folklore in Literature,* edited and translated by Harriet de Onis. Copyright © 1948 and renewed 1976 by Harriet de Onis.—for "The 1st" from *Good Times,* by Lucille Clifton. Copyright © 1969 by Lucille Clifton. Reprinted by permission of Random House, Inc.—for "The Clockmaker and the Timekeeper," text only and "Heaven and Hell" text only. From *Tales From Old China* by Isabelle Chang. Reprinted by permission of Random House, Inc.

SATURDAY REVIEW—for "Cemetery Path" by Leonard Q. Rose. Copyright © 1972, *Saturday Review of Literature,* Nov. 29, 1941. Reprinted by permission.

THE SOCIETY OF AUTHORS—for "When I Was One-and-Twenty" by A. E. Housman. The Society of Authors as the literary representative of the Estate of A. E. Housman, and Jonathan Cape Ltd., publishers of A. E. Housman's *Collected Poems.*

UNIVERSAL PRESS SYNDICATE—for a Doonesbury drawing. Copyright © 1971, G. B. Trudeau. Reprinted with permission of Universal Press Syndicate. All rights reserved.

UNIVERSITY OF CALIFORNIA PRESS—for "The Sparrow" by Ivan Turgenev, in *A Harvest of Russian Children's Literature,* Miriam Morton: editor and translator. Copyright © 1967 Miriam Morton. Used by permission of the University of California Press.

UNIVERSITY OF PITTSBURGH—for "Black Hair" by Gary Soto. Reprinted from *Black Hair* by Gary Soto by permission of the University of Pittsburgh Press. Copyright © 1985 by Gary Soto.

VIKING PENGUIN, INC.—for "The Human Hand" by Eva-Lis Wuorio from *Escape If You Can* by Eva-Lis Wuorio. Copyright © 1977 by Eva-Lis Wuorio. Reprinted by permission of Viking Penguin, Inc.

GAHAN WILSON—for permission to use "The Manuscript of Dr. Arness" by Gahan Wilson.

Every effort has been made to locate Frank Marshall Davis to obtain permission to reprint his poem "Glimpse of Night"; Dudley Randall to obtain permission to reprint his poem "The Ballad of Birmingham"; Martha Scheiner to obtain permission to reprint her poem "The Bog Turtle"; A. Avechenko to obtain permission to reprint his story "A Point of View." If either the authors or heirs are located subsequent to publication, they are hereby entitled to due compensation.

The following selections are in the public domain. Some have been slightly adapted for the modern reader by Globe Book Company: Robert Burns, "To a Mouse"; Geoffrey Chaucer, "The Pardoner's Tale"; Kate Chopin, "The Story of an Hour"; Guy de Maupassant, "The False Gems"; Paul Laurence Dunbar, "Dawn"; Oliver Goldsmith, "She Stoops to Conquer"; O. Henry, "While the Auto Waits"; Henry Wadsworth Longfellow, " A Psalm of Life"; Edgar Allan Poe, "The Raven" and "The Fall of the House of Usher"; William Shakespeare, "Macbeth"; Percy Bysshe Shelley, "Ozymandias"; William Wordsworth, "Daffodils."

Photo Acknowledgments

Trans World Airways, Inc.: xi; Leo de Wys, Inc.: xii; Culver Pictures: 52 (left); The Bettmann Archive: 52 (right); Leo de Wys, Inc.: 66; UPI/Bettmann Archive: 98; Missouri Historical Society: 105 (left); Culver Pictures, Inc.: 105 (right); Frederic Lewis: 132; The Bettmann Archive: 165 (left); Culver Pictures: 165 (right); Frederic Lewis: 210; Folger Shakespeare Library: 223 (left); Culver Pictures, Inc.: 223 (right); Comstock Inc.: 298; Frederic Lewis: 309; Library of Congress: 316 (left); The Bettmann Archive: 316 (right); Culver Pictures: 340 (left & right); Brown Brothers: 349 (left); Gail Folda: 349 (right). **Cover:** Missouri Historical Society (Kate Chopin); Brown Brothers (Robert Burns); Library of Congress (Henry Wadsworth Longfellow); Culver Pictures, Inc. (Edna St. Vincent Millay, Geoffrey Chaucer); Wide World (Alice Walker); Brown Brothers (Percy Bysshe Shelley); Culver Pictures (Guy de Maupassant); Folger Shakespeare Library (William Shakespeare).

Illustrators

Bill Angressano: 89, 90, 92, 326, 327, 329, 331, 332–333, 337; Virginia Arnold: 215, 241; Ted Burwell: 54, 56, 352, 354, 356, 357, 360, 364, 369, 372, 375, 377, 379; Peter Catalanato: 212, 220; Anna Divito: 77; Alan Eitzen: 17, 19; Julie Evans: 264, 270, 277, 283, 286, 289, 291; Jeff Fischer: 3, 322; Joseph Forté: 229, 233; Gordon Haas: 301, 302, 303, 304; Eileen McKeating: 6, 10, 12, 50, 107, 108; Kathy Krantz: 155, 159; Charles Molina: 81, 83, 86; Keith Murray: 251, 252–253, 256; Joanne Pappas: 113, 115, 117, 119, 122, 383; Don Schlegel: 68, 70, 72–73, 136; Clare Seiffert: 141, 143, 145, 149, 150, 152; Gerald Smith: 25, 27, 31, 168–169, 170, 171, 173, 178, 182, 185, 192, 196, 199, 200, 343, 344; Cindy Spencer: 40, 44, 46, 100–101, 245, 247, 342; Kimanne Uhler: 313.

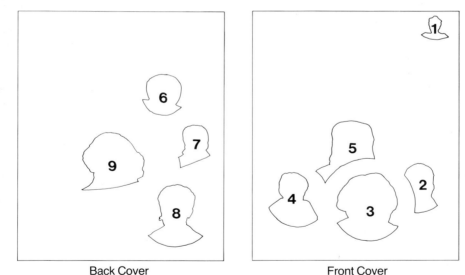

Back Cover   Front Cover

Authors on the Cover:

1. Kate Chopin   6. Alice Walker
2. Robert Burns   7. Percy Bysshe Shelley
3. Henry Wadsworth Longfellow 8. Guy de Maupassant
4. Edna St. Vincent Millay   9. William Shakespeare
5. Geoffrey Chaucer